THE CAMBRIDGE COMPANION TO
SIMONE DE BEAUVOIR

Each volume of this series of companions to major philosophers contains specially commissioned chapters by an international team of scholars, together with a substantial bibliography, and will serve as a reference work for students and nonspecialists. One aim of the series is to dispel the intimidation such readers often feel when faced with the work of a difficult and challenging thinker.

Simone de Beauvoir was a philosopher and writer of notable range and influence whose work is central to feminist theory, French existentialism, and contemporary moral and social philosophy. The chapters in this volume examine all the major aspects of her thought, including her views on issues such as the role of biology, sexuality and sexual difference, and evil; the influence on her work of Heidegger, Sartre, Merleau-Ponty, Husserl, and others; and the philosophical significance of her memoirs and fiction.

New readers and nonspecialists will find this the most convenient and accessible guide to Beauvoir currently available. Advanced students and specialists will find a conspectus of recent developments in the interpretation of Beauvoir.

CLAUDIA CARD is Emma Goldman Professor at the Department of Philosophy, University of Wisconsin, Madison.

The Cambridge Companion to

SIMONE DE BEAUVOIR

Edited by Claudia Card
University of Wisconsin

CAMBRIDGE
UNIVERSITY PRESS

PUBLISHED BY THE PRESS SYNDICATE OF THE UNIVERSITY OF CAMBRIDGE
The Pitt Building, Trumpington Street, Cambridge CB2 1RP,
United Kingdom

CAMBRIDGE UNIVERSITY PRESS
The Edinburgh Building, Cambridge, CB2 2RU, UK
40 West 20th Street, New York, NY 10011-4211, USA
477 Williamstown Road, Port Melbourne, VIC 3207, Australia
Ruiz de Alarcón 13, 28014 Madrid, Spain
Dock House, The Waterfront, Cape Town 8001, South Africa

http://www.cambridge.org

First published 2003

Printed in the United Kingdom at the University Press, Cambridge

Typeface Trump Medieval 10/13 pt   *System* LaTeX 2$_\varepsilon$ [TB]

A catalogue record for this book is available from the British Library

Library of Congress Cataloguing in Publication data

The Cambridge companion to Simone de Beauvoir / edited by
Claudia Card.
        p.   cm. – (Cambridge companions to philosophy)
Includes bibliographical references and index.
ISBN 0 521 79096 4 (hardback) – ISBN 0 521 79026 3 (paperback)
1. Beauvoir, Simone de, 1908–1986. I. Card, Claudia. II. Series.
B2430.B344C36   2002
194 – dc21   2002067378

ISBN 0 521 79096 4 hardback
ISBN 0 521 79429 3 paperback

In memory of Elaine Marks

CONTENTS

x   Contents

TABLE

CONTRIBUTORS

BARBARA S. ANDREW, Assistant Professor of Philosophy at the University of Oregon, is the author of "The Psychology of Tyranny: Wollstonecraft and Woolf on the Gendered Dimension of War," *Hypatia*, 9, 2 (1994) as well as articles on Simone de Beauvoir and feminist ethics. She is at work on a book on love and freedom in feminist ethics.

DEBRA B. BERGOFFEN, Professor of Philosophy and Cultural Studies and Director of Women's Studies at George Mason University, is the author of *The Philosophy of Simone de Beauvoir* (1997) and essays attentive to epistemological, ethical, political, and feminist issues raised by the work of Nietzsche, Lacan, Irigaray, and Beauvoir.

SUSAN J. BRISON, Associate Professor of Philosophy at Dartmouth College, is the author of *Aftermath: Violence and the Remaking of a Self* (2001) and *Speech, Harm, and Conflicts of Rights* (2002). She is the coeditor of *Contemporary Perspectives on Constitutional Interpretation* (1993).

JUDITH BUTLER, Maxine Elliot Professor of Rhetoric and Comparative Literature at the University of California at Berkeley, has published in continental, feminist, social, and political philosophy, literary theory, and psychoanalysis and sexuality studies. She is the author of *Gender Trouble* (1990) and, most recently, *Antigone's Claims: Kinship Between Life and Death* (2000).

CLAUDIA CARD, Emma Goldman Professor of Philosophy at the University of Wisconsin, is the author of *The Atrocity Paradigm: A*

Theory of Evil (2002), *The Unnatural Lottery* (1996), and *Lesbian Choices* (1995). She is the editor of *On Feminist Ethics and Politics* (1999), *Adventures in Lesbian Philosophy* (1994), and *Feminist Ethics* (1991).

PENELOPE DEUTSCHER, Senior Lecturer in Philosophy at the Australian National University, is the author of *Yielding Gender* (1997), coeditor of *Enigmas: Essays on Sarah Kofman* (1999), and guest editor of *Hypatia*, 15, 4 (2000), *Special Issue on Contemporary French Women Philosophers*. She is completing a manuscript on the later work of Luce Irigaray.

MIRANDA FRICKER, Lecturer in Philosophy at Birkbeck College, University of London, is coeditor of *The Cambridge Companion to Feminism in Philosophy* (2000) and author of articles in epistemology, ethics, and social philosophy. She is completing a manuscript, *Epistemic Injustice: Power and the Ethics of Knowing*, which explores a first-order ethics of epistemic practices.

MOIRA GATENS, Professor of Philosophy, University of Sydney, is the author of *Feminism and Philosophy* (1991) and *Imaginary Bodies* (1996) and coauthor of *Collective Imaginings: Spinoza, Past and Present* (1999). She is the editor of *Feminist Ethics* (1998) and coeditor of the *Oxford Companion to Australian Feminism* (1998) and *Gender and Institutions* (1998).

EVA GOTHLIN, Associate Professor of the History of Ideas and Science at the University of Göteborg, Sweden, is the author of *Sex and Existence: Simone de Beauvoir's "The Second Sex"* (1996; Swedish edition, 1991; French edition, 2001) and essays in Swedish, Norwegian, French, and English on Beauvoir, Sartre, Hegel, and gender.

SARA HEINÄMAA, Docent of Theoretical Philosophy at the University of Helsinki and Professor of Humanist Women's Studies at the Center for Feminist Studies, University of Oslo, is the author of two monographs on the phenomenology of the body (1996, 2000) and articles on Husserl, Merleau-Ponty, Beauvoir, and Irigaray. She is completing a monograph on the phenomenology of the body, comparing Beauvoir's discussion with Husserl's and Merleau-Ponty's.

SUSAN JAMES, Professor of Philosophy at Birkbeck College, University of London, is the author of *Passion and Action: The Emotions in Seventeenth-Century Philosophy* (1997) and "Feminism and the Imaginary" in *Visible Women: Feminist Legal Theory and Political Philosophy*, ed. Susan James and Stephanie Palmer (2000).

MONIKA LANGER, Associate Professor of Philosophy at the University of Victoria, has also taught at Toronto, Yale, Alberta, and Dalhousie. She is the author of several articles and *Merleau-Ponty's Phenomenology of Perception: A Guide and Commentary* (1988, 1989). She is currently writing a book on Nietzsche's *The Gay Science*.

ROBIN MAY SCHOTT, Associate Research Professor of Philosophy at the University of Copenhagen, is the author of *Cognition and Eros* (1988/1993), editor of *Feminist Interpretations of Immanuel Kant* (1997), and coeditor of *Reproduction, Gender and Technology* (1995). She is currently working on the problem of evil in relation to war rape.

MARGARET A. SIMONS, Professor of Philosophy at Southern Illinois University, Edwardsville, is the author of *Beauvoir and "The Second Sex"* (1999), editor of *Feminist Interpretations of Simone de Beauvoir* (1995) and a special issue of *Hypatia* on Beauvoir's philosophy (1999), and coeditor of *Hypatia Reborn* (1990). She is coediting a six-volume series of Beauvoir's texts in English translation.

MARY SIRRIDGE, Professor of Philosophy at Louisiana State University, is the author of "The Moral of the Story: Exemplification and the Literary Work," *Philosophical Studies*, 38 (1980) and other articles on philosophical aesthetics, the philosophy of literature, and dance aesthetics, as well as on St. Augustine, medieval syntax and semantics, and ancient and medieval philosophy of the mind.

ACKNOWLEDGMENTS

This Companion is dedicated, in honor and gratitude, to the memory of Elaine Marks (1930–2001), who is world-renowned for her work on Beauvoir, French feminism, and women's studies. Elaine Marks was a cherished teacher, friend, and mentor to generations of Beauvoir students at the University of Wisconsin. She wrote the first book on Beauvoir in English and edited the first English-language anthology (in book form) of essays on Beauvoir. I sought and received her guidance at the outset of this project. Sadly, she died a few months before its completion.

The advice and suggestions of Beauvoir scholars on three continents (many of whom are also authors of chapters in this book) went into the creation of this Companion. I especially thank Robin Schott and Margaret A. Simons for counsel in the early stages. Eva Gothlin's sketch of Beauvoir's childhood, education, and early maturity in her book *Sex and Existence* was very helpful for constructing those parts of the chronology. Consistent support came from my editor Hilary Gaskin. Ann Cothran, Sonia Kruks, Nancy Bauer, and Lester Embree responded promptly and helpfully to queries. Contributors helped frequently with bibliographic matters, especially Susan Brison, Penelope Deutscher, Eva Gothlin, Sara Heinämaa, and Monika Langer. Andrea Veltman, my assistant, provided invaluable help with editing. The introductory chapter benefited immeasurably from her suggestions as well as from suggestions by my colleague Ivan Soll. Finally, I owe a debt of gratitude to past and present Beauvoir scholars who are not directly represented in this volume, especially to Beauvoir's biographers and the editors of other volumes on Beauvoir, for much that was useful in constructing the chronology of Beauvoir's life, devising a system of abbreviations, creating the bibliography, and writing the introductory chapter.

CHRONOLOGY

1908	Born 9 January in Paris to Françoise Brasseur de Beauvoir and Georges Bertrand de Beauvoir; christened Simone Lucie Ernestine Marie Bertrand de Beauvoir.
1910	Birth of sister, Hélène ("Poupette").
1913–25	Educated at Institut Adeline Désire (Cours Désire), where she meets Zaza (Elizabeth Mabille), who becomes her best friend; awarded Baccalaureat in 1924–25; studies mathematics at Institut Catholique, Paris, in 1925.
1927–28	Degree in literature, Latin, Greek, and philosophy at Institut Sante-Marie, Neuilly.
1928–29	Attends philosophy courses at the Sorbonne and attends lectures at the Ecole Normale Supérieure, where she meets Maurice Merleau-Ponty, Claude Lévi-Strauss, and Jean-Paul Sartre, who becomes a lifelong intellectual companion.
1929	Awarded Agrégée de Philosophie; death of Zaza.
1931–33	Teaching post at Lycée Montgrand, Marseille.
1933–37	Teaching post at Lycée Jeanne d'Arc, Rouen.
1934–35	Reads Husserl in German.
1938–43	Teaching posts at Lycée Molière at Passy and Lycée Camille-Sée, Paris.
1939	She and Sartre begin serious study of Heidegger; World War Two declared; Sartre drafted.
1940	Reads Richard Wright, *Native Son*, on recommendation by Sylvia Beach; Sartre captured by invading Germans and sent to POW camp.

1941   Father dies; Sartre released from POW camp;
        Resistance group "Socialisme et Liberté" (Socialism
        and Freedom) founded with Sartre and Merleau-Ponty;
        crosses border with Sartre into Vichy zone hoping to
        make contact with Resistance but fails; meets André
        Gide and André Malraux.

1943   First novel, *L'Invitée* (Paris: Gallimard); translated as
        She Came to Stay by Y. Moyse and R. Senhouse
        (London: Secker & Warburg and Lindsay Drummond,
        1949; Cleveland, OH: World Publishing, 1954).

1944   First published essay in moral philosophy, *Pyrrhus et
        Cinéas* (Paris: Gallimard).

1945   Lectures in Portugal and writes articles for *Combat*
        criticizing Portuguese and Spanish dictatorships;
        founds independent leftist journal *Les Temps
        modernes* with Sartre, Merleau-Ponty, Albert Ollivier,
        Jean Paulhan, Raymond Aron, and Michele Leiris;
        publishes play *Les Bouches inutiles* (Paris: Gallimard);
        translated as *Who Shall Die?* by C. Francis and
        F. Gontier (Florissant, MO: River Press, 1983),
        "La Phénoménologie de la perception de Maurice
        Merleau-Ponty," *Les Temps modernes*, 1: 1153–63 and
        second novel *Le Sang des autres* (Paris: Gallimard),
        translated as *The Blood of Others* by Y. Moyse and R.
        Senhouse (London: Secker & Warburg and Lindsay
        Drummond, 1948; New York: Knopf, 1948).

1946   Meets Richard Wright when he visits Paris; lectures in
        Switzerland, Italy, and Holland with Sartre; third
        novel, *Tous les hommes sont mortels* (Paris:
        Gallimard), translated as *All Men are Mortal* by
        L. Friedman (Cleveland, OH: World Publishing, 1955).

1947   Lecture tour of the US under the auspices of the
        Ministry of Culture of the French government; meets
        Nelson Algren and begins a relationship and a
        correspondance that continues until 1964; publishes
        Pour une morale de l'ambiguïté (Paris: Gallimard),
        translated as *The Ethics of Ambiguity* by B. Frechtman
        (New York: Philosophical Library, 1948).

1948   Publishes *L'Amérique au jour le jour* (Paris: Editions Paul Marihien), translated as *America Day by Day* by Patrick Dudley (pseud.) (London: Duckworth, 1952; New York: Grove, 1953) and by Carel Cosman (Berkeley: University of California Press, 1999); she and Sartre become founding members of the anti-Stalinist leftist group Rassemblement Démocratique et Révolutionnaire (RDF).

1949   Publishes *Le Deuxième sexe*, vols. I and II (Paris: Gallimard), translated as *The Second Sex* by H. M. Parshley (London: Jonathan Cape, 1953; New York: Knopf, 1952, Vintage 1989, Bantam, 1989).

1951   Publishes "Faut-il brûler Sade?" in *Les Temps modernes* 74 (Dec. 1951): 1002–33, 75 (Jan. 1952): 1197–230, translated by Annette Michelson as *Must We Burn de Sade?* (London: Peter Neville, 1953; New York: Grove, 1955); reprinted in *The Marquis de Sade: The 120 Days of Sodom, and Other Writings*, translated by Austryn Weinhaus and Richard Seaver (New York: Grove, 1966); meets Claude Lanzmann and begins relationship that continues for several years.

1954   Fourth novel, *Les Mandarins* (Paris: Gallimard), translated as *The Mandarins* by L. Friedman (Cleveland, OH: World Publishing, 1956; London: Collins, 1957), dedicated to Nelson Algren; awarded Prix Goncourt.

1955   Publishes *Privilèges* ("Faut-il brûler Sade?," "La Pensée de droite aujourd'hui," "Merleau-Ponty ou le pseudo-sartrisme") (Paris: Gallimard); visits Moscow and China with Sartre.

1957   Publishes *La Longue marche: essai sur la Chine* (Paris: Gallimard), translated by Austryn Wainhouse as *The Long March* (Cleveland, OH: World Publishing, 1958) about her visit to China.

1958   First of four volumes of memoirs, *Mémoires d'une jeune fille rangée* (Paris: Gallimard), translated as *Memoirs of a Dutiful Daughter* by J. Kirkup (London: André Deutsch and Weidenfeld & Nicolson, 1959; Cleveland, OH: World Publishing, 1959).

1959   Publishes "Brigitte Bardot and the Lolita Syndrome," a
        specially commissioned article for *Esquire* magazine
        (August), translated by Bernard Frechtman (London:
        André Deutsch and Weidenfeld & Nicolson, 1960;
        New York: Arno, 1972).

1960   Death of friend, Albert Camus; second volume of
        memoirs, *La Force de l'âge* (Paris: Gallimard),
        translated as *The Prime of Life* by P. Green (Cleveland,
        OH: World Publishing, 1962; London: André Deutsch
        and Weidenfeld & Nicolson, 1965); meets Sylvie Le
        Bon, an 18-year-old philosophy student at Rennes, who
        becomes her companion for the rest of SdB's life; visit
        to Cuba with Sartre, spends three days with Castro.

1961   Marches with Lanzmann and Sartre for peace in
        Algeria.

1962   Preface (listed as coauthor with Gisèle Halimi) to
        Djamila Boupacha (Paris: Gallimard), translated as
        *Djamila Boupacha: The Story of the Torture of a
        Young Algerian Girl which Shocked Liberal French
        Opinion* by P. Green (London: Weidenfeld & Nicolson,
        1962; New York: Macmillan, 1962).

1963   Third volume of memoirs, *La Force des choses* (Paris:
        Gallimard), translated as *Force of Circumstance* by
        R. Howard (London: André Deutsch and Weidenfeld &
        Nicolson, 1965; New York: Putnam, 1965); her mother
        dies in November.

1964   Preface to *La Bâtarde* by Violette Leduc (Paris:
        Gallimard), translated as *La Bâtarde: An
        Autobiography* by Derek Coltman (Manchester:
        C. Nicholls & Co., 1965; New York: Farrar, Straus &
        Giroux, 1965), and *Une Mort très douce* (Paris:
        Gallimard), translated as *A Very Easy Death* by
        P. O'Brian (André Deutsch and Weidenfeld &
        Nicolson, 1966; New York: Putnam, 1966), reflecting
        on her mother's dying.

1966   Fifth novel, *Les Belles images* (Paris: Gallimard),
        translated by Patrick O'Brian as *Les Belles Images*
        (London: Collins, 1968; New York: Putnam, 1968), and
        preface to *Tréblinka* by Jean-François Steiner (Paris:

Arthème Fayard); translated by Helen Weaver (New
York: Simon & Schuster, 1967).

1967   First collection of stories, *La Femme rompue* (Paris:
        Gallimard), translated as *The Woman Destroyed* by
        Patrick O'Brian (London: Collins, 1969; New York:
        Putnam, 1969); attends International Russell Tribunal
        on Vietnam with Sartre.

1968   Joins in student street demonstrations.

1970   Publishes *La Vieillesse* (Paris: Gallimard), translated
        by Patrick O'Brian as *Old Age* (London: André
        Deutsch, 1972) and as *The Coming of Age* (New York:
        Putnam, 1972); marches for abortion and
        contraception rights for women.

1971   On being asked by the Mouvement de la Libération des
        Femmes (MLF), includes her signature in "The
        Manifesto of 343," a list of 343 women declaring that
        they had all had an abortion (illegal in France),
        published in *Le Nouvel observateur*, although her
        sister Hélène, also a signatory, said in 1987 that
        neither of them actually had an abortion; Simone had
        allowed them to be performed in her apartment and
        had sometimes paid for them.

1972   Fourth volume of memoirs, *Tout compte fait* (Paris:
        Gallimard), translated as *All Said and Done* by Patrick
        O'Brian (London: André Deutsch and Weidenfeld &
        Nicolson, 1972; New York: Putnam, 1974); becomes
        president of the society, Choisir, to promote
        knowledge and availability of contraception.

1974   Becomes president of the Ligue du Droit des Femmes
        (League of Women's Rights), to end discrimination
        against women in speech and in documents.

1975   Accepts the Jerusalem Prize, awarded to writers who
        have promoted the concept of individual liberty
        (winners include Bertrand Russell, Jorge Luis Borges,
        and Ionesco).

1976   Preface to *Crimes Against Women: Proceedings of the
        International Tribunal*, edited by D. H. Russell and
        N. Van de Ven (Milbrae, CA: Les Femmes).

1979   Second collection of stories, *Quand prime le spirituel*
        (Paris: Gallimard), translated as *When Things of the
        Spirit Come First: Five Early Tales* by Patrick O'Brian
        (London: André Deutsch, 1982; New York: Pantheon,
        1982); publication of *Les Ecrits de Simone de Beauvoir*,
        ed. C. Francis and F. Gontier (Paris: Gallimard), which
        includes "Brigitte Bardot et le syndrome de Lolita,"
        translated from English; founds journal *Questions
        feministes* with Christine Delphy and Monique Wittig.

1980   Legally adopts Sylvie Le Bon after Sartre's death on
        15 April in Paris.

1981   Publishes *La Cérémonie des adieux, suivi de
        entretiens avec Jean-Paul Sartre, Âout-/Septembre
        1974* (Paris: Gallimard), translated by Patrick O'Brian
        as *Adieux: A Farewell to Sartre* (London: André
        Deutsch, 1984; New York: Pantheon, 1984); death of
        Nelson Algren on 9 May.

1985   Preface to *Shoah* by Claude Lanzmann, translated as
        *Shoah: An Oral History of the Holocaust: The
        Complete Text of the Film*, subtitles of the film in
        English by A. Whitelaw and W. Byron (New York:
        Pantheon, 1985).

1986   Dies on 14 April in Paris of "pulmonary edema,"
        following a respiratory illness; 5,000 people attend the
        funeral; buried next to Sartre.

1990   Publication of *Lettres à Sartre*, vol. I, *1930–1939*;
        vol. II, *1940–1963*. Edited by Sylvie Le Bon de Beauvoir
        (Paris: Gallimard), edited and translated as *Letters to
        Sartre* by Q. Hoare (New York: Little, Brown, 1992);
        Journal de guerre, Septembre 1939–Janvier 1941,
        edited by Sylvie Le Bon de Beauvoir (Paris: Gallimard).

1997   Publication of *Lettres à Nelson Algren: un amour
        transatlantique: 1947–1964*, compiled, annotated, and
        translated from English and annotated by Sylvie Le
        Bon de Beauvoir (Paris: Gallimard), translated by
        Sylvie Le Bon de Beauvoir as *Transatlantic Love Affair:
        Letters to Nelson Algren* (New York: New Press,
        distributed by Norton, 1998).

ABBREVIATIONS

The bibliography at the end of this volume gives full particulars of the works cited below. Where the bibliography gives more than one edition or publisher, or where a chapter cites an edition or publisher other than those listed in the bibliography, the chapter's endnotes give particulars for the editions it cites.

AD	*America Day by Day*
AM	*All Men are Mortal*
AS	*All Said and Done*
BI	*Les Belles images*
BI (tr.)	*Les Belles Images* (the English translation)
BN	*Being and Nothingness: An Essay on Phenomenological Ontology* (Sartre)
BO	*The Blood of Others*
BT	*Being and Time* (Heidegger)
DB	*Djamila Boupacha: The Story of the Torture of a Young Algerian Girl which Shocked Liberal French Opinion*
DS I	*Le Deuxiéme sexe, I, Les Faits et les mythes*
DS II	*Le Deuxiéme sexe, II, L'Expérience vécue*
EA	*The Ethics of Ambiguity*
EN	*L'Etre et le néant: Essai d'ontologie phénomènologique* (Sartre)
FA	*La Force de l'âge*
FB	*"Faut-il brûler Sade?"*
FC	*Force of Circumstance*
FCh	*La Force des choses*
FR	*La Femme rompue*

Ideas I	*Ideas Pertaining to a Pure Phenomenology and to a Phemonenological Philosophy, First Book: General Introduction to a Pure Phenomenology* (Husserl)
Ideas II	*Ideas Pertaining to a Pure Phenomenology and to Phenomenological Philosophy, Second Book: Studies in the Phenomenology of Constitution* (Husserl)
Ideen II	*Ideen zu einer reinen Phänomenologie under phänomenologischen Philosophie, Zweites Buch: Phäenomenologische Undersuchung zur Konstitution* (Husserl)
LI	*L'Invitée*
LM	*"Littérature et métaphysique"*
M	*Les Mandarins*
M (tr.)	*The Mandarins*
MBS	*Must We Burn Sade?*
MD	*Memoirs of a Dutiful Daughter*
MJF	*Mémoires d'une jeune fille rangée*
MP	"Merleau-Ponty et pseudo-sartrisme"
MPPS	"Merleau-Ponty and Pseudo-Sartreanism"
OA	*Old Age* (British title; US title: *The Coming of Age*)
PC	*Pyrrhus et Cinéas*
PL	*The Prime of Life*
PMA	*Pour une morale de l'ambiguïté*
PP	*Phénomenologie de la perception* (Merleau-Ponty)
PP (tr.)	*The Phenomenology of Perception* (Merleau-Ponty)
PPMP	"La phénoménologie de la perception de Merleau-Ponty" (Beauvoir)
QPL	"Simone de Beauvoir" in *Que peut la littérature?* (ed. Yves Buin)
QPS	*Quand prime le spirituel*
SCS	*She Came to Stay*
SNS	*Sense and Non-Sense* (Merleau-Ponty)
SS	*The Second Sex*
SZ	*Sein und Zeit* (Heidegger)
TC	*Tout compte fait*
V	*La Vieillesse*
VED	*A Very Easy Death*
WD	*The Woman Destroyed*
WT	*When Things of the Spirit Come First*

Introduction: Beauvoir and the ambiguity of "ambiguity" in ethics

BACKGROUNDS AND BASICS

During the 1950s, an era when feminism was at a particularly low ebb, American college students encountered translations of Simone de Beauvoir's *The Second Sex* and *The Ethics of Ambiguity* in courses on French existentialism.[1] The popularity of these courses was due in no small part to the French existentialists' addition of sexuality to the philosophical agenda. Jean-Paul Sartre's *Being and Nothingness* was the centerpiece, and Beauvoir's *The Ethics of Ambiguity* was introduced to show how, contrary to Sartre's early view, existentialism might indeed provide a ground for ethics. *The Second Sex*, however, was presented as though it simply applied Sartre's philosophy to women's situations, a view later to be challenged by feminist scholarship, as many chapters in this Companion show in detail. Yet readers were astonished even then by perspectives *The Second Sex* offered on female sexuality. Raising ethical and political issues, Beauvoir's *The Second Sex* nicely complemented Alfred Kinsey's "scandalous" but coldly scientific report on sexual behavior in the human female, which appeared in the same year as the paperback edition of the English translation of Beauvoir's treatise on women.[2]

Beauvoir's most widely read philosophical works are still *The Second Sex* and *The Ethics of Ambiguity*. But her later work as well is philosophically deep and often original. It offers mature perspectives on such topics as torture and old age in addition to new perspectives on her earlier work. Beauvoir's total output (still being translated into English) is prodigious. The chronology and bibliography in this Companion show how highly varied in form her published writings are, ranging from letters, diaries, memoirs, and novels to prefaces, book reviews, philosophical essays and treatises. The scope of her philosophical interests is impressive. Many of her topics are standard in the philosophical repertoire: ethics, politics, evil, relationships between selves (articulated as relationships between self and Other). Others were not conventional among philosophers when she took them up, some unconventional for women writers in most fields: psychoanalysis, biology, sexuality, gender, women, lesbians, prostitution, marriage, love.

Equally popular with philosophers and nonphilosophers are Beauvoir's stories and novels, especially *She Came to Stay* (explored by Margaret Simons in chapter 5 and Mary Sirridge in chapter 6) and *The Mandarins*, which won the prestigious Goncourt Prize in 1954. Her short memoir, *A Very Easy Death*, reflecting on the death of her mother, and the longer treatise, *Old Age* (interpreted by Penelope Deutscher in chapter 14 and known as *The Coming of Age* in the American edition), belong in anyone's list of classics on aging and dying. The four volumes chronicling her life and intellectual development, *Memoirs of a Dutiful Daughter*, *The Prime of Life*, *The Force of Circumstance*, and *All Said and Done*, revisit many of her earlier ideas and together construct what Miranda Fricker in chapter 10 calls a "life-story." Less well known are Beauvoir's travel diaries from her visits to the United States for four months in 1947 (*America Day by Day*) and to China in 1955 (*The Long March*). The *America* diary includes wonderful descriptions of life in Beauvoir's favorite city, New York, as well as detailed and painful observations of racial segregation in the South (noted by Robin Schott in chapter 11). Also noteworthy are Beauvoir's prefaces (cited by Schott as well) to such works as Gisèle Halimi's *Djamila Boupacha: The Story of the Torture of a Young Algerian Girl Which Shocked Liberal French Opinion*, Claude Lanzmann's filmscript *Shoah*, and Jean-François Steiner's *Treblinka*. And there is more, much more, including letters, book reviews, and such essays as "Must We Burn Sade?" (analyzed by Judith Butler in chapter 8) and "Brigitte Bardot and the Lolita Syndrome." This Companion covers the full span of Beauvoir's work, not just *The Second Sex* and *The Ethics of Ambiguity*.

Nevertheless, ethics forms a persistent core of Beauvoir's philosophical concerns. Hence it is appropriate to make it the eventual focus of this introduction. It was Beauvoir's view, in fact, that *only* existentialism could provide the basis for ethics. Yet her conception

of ethics would have puzzled most British and American philosophers of that era, trained as they were in traditions of analytic philosophy. For although she rejected the search for universal principles
to distinguish right from wrong, and she took emotion seriously,
she was no "emotivist" in the sense of the logical positivists of the
Vienna Circle.[3] Logical positivists held that the meaning of a propo-
sition is given by its method of verification. Finding no method of
verification for moral principles, they concluded that such principles
and judgments based on them were literally meaningless, "pseudo-
propositions." Moral pseudo-propositions, they insisted, had only
"emotive meaning," not "literal meaning." Yet with a noncogni-
tive understanding of emotions, positivists were at a loss to clarify,
beyond crude notions of approval and disapproval, what moral emotions meant. Beauvoir, in contrast, is articulate about the meanings
of moral philosophies, traditions, sentiments, and choices. Today her
agent-centered, relational, and situational approach to ethics finds
natural homes not only in continental European philosophy, but
also in fairly analytical character ethics, feminist ethics, and conversations about moral luck. Her concerns lie with the complexities
of situations, their impact on how we develop character, and with
liberation from oppression, taking responsibility for ourselves, and
negotiating human relationships.

Beauvoir's major contributions to philosophical thought, to ethics
in particular, lie in her development and employment of the concepts
of ambiguity, freedom, the Other, embodiment, disclosure, temporality, and situation. These concepts have roots in the traditions of
French and German phenomenology. English-speaking readers of the
1950s tended to lack the training and philosophical background to
read Beauvoir in the context of German phenomenology, or even contemporary French philosophy (with the exception of Sartre's *Being
and Nothingness*), not to mention earlier French philosophy other
than Descartes'. Divisions between Anglo-American and continental European philosophies are less severe today than then. Still, training in post-Kantian continental European philosophy remains a continuing weakness in the philosophical education offered by many
American universities. Hence, this volume offers several chapters on
how to read Beauvoir in relation to post-Kantian German and post-
Cartesian French traditions of philosophical thought, introducing
readers to important features of some of those traditions at the same
time.

Many groupings of chapters in this Companion are natural for study purposes. The next section highlights continuities and overlaps not always evident from chapter titles, as a prelude to reflecting, in the concluding section, on an ambiguity of "ambiguity" in Beauvoir's ethics.

OVERVIEW OF CHAPTERS

The opening chapter by Barbara Andrew introduces Beauvoir as an existential phenomenologist and explains what that means. Andrew sketches Beauvoir's education and early intellectual development and then places her mature writings in the context of four areas of contemporary philosophy where her ideas remain influential today: social philosophy, existentialism, phenomenology, and feminist theory. Andrew also takes up similarities and differences between Beauvoir's work and that of her lifelong companion, Jean-Paul Sartre (1905–80). The themes of Beauvoir's relationship with Sartre and his work recur in other chapters as well (chapters 2, 4, 10, and 14, by Eva Gothlin, Monika Langer, Miranda Fricker, and Penelope Deutscher, for example). Andrew organizes most of her discussion around Beauvoir's ideas of freedom, ambiguity, and situation, concepts also further explored in other chapters.

Taking the phenomenological strand as central, chapter 2 by Eva Gothlin and chapter 3 by Sara Heinämaa present key elements of Beauvoir's thought as having developed in the context of the German phenomenology of Edmund Husserl (1859–1976) and Martin Heidegger (1889–1976), whom Beauvoir and Sartre began reading in the late 1930s. Chapter 3 by Heinämaa and chapter 4 by Monika Langer take up in detail the influence of Beauvoir's engagement with the philosophy of her friend, Maurice Merleau-Ponty (1908–61).

In chapter 2, on reading Beauvoir in relation to Heidegger's *Being and Time*, Eva Gothlin finds that Beauvoir's phenomenology differs from Sartre's (at least, in *Being and Nothingness*) in being closer to Heidegger's break with the classic Cartesian dualism of mind and body. She notes that the Heideggerian concept of disclosure occurs in Beauvoir's writings more often than the Sartrean concepts of in-itself (the being of things) and for-itself (conscious existence). Gothlin's discussion is organized around the concepts of disclosure, corporeality, "Being-with," and authenticity. These concepts enable her to clarify differences between Beauvoir's philosophy and Sartre's and also to clarify Beauvoir's own emphases or uses of these concepts as distinct from Heidegger's. She notes, for example, that for both Beauvoir and Heidegger, *Mitsein* (Being-with) is real, contrary to Sartre's denial in *Being and Nothingness* of intersubjective reality, but that, unlike Heidegger, Beauvoir emphasizes the possibility of conflict as well as harmony in *Mitsein*.

In chapter 3 Sara Heinämaa agrees with Gothlin in situating Beauvoir's work in relation to the phenomenological tradition. But she builds a case for going further back in that tradition to the work of Husserl in order to appreciate Beauvoir's concept of embodiment. Beauvoir's discussions of female embodiment have been widely misunderstood by readers who take her negative portrayals of the female body as though they represented her own final view rather than a social construction of which she was profoundly critical. Heinämaa argues that Beauvoir's notion of embodiment is a critical elaboration of Merleau-Ponty's description of the living body and that through Merleau-Ponty, Beauvoir was influenced by Husserl's work in *Thing and Space, Ideas volume II*, and the *Crisis of European Sciences and Transcendental Phenomenology*.

Monika Langer, who has authored a book on Merleau-Ponty,[4] argues in chapter 4 that Beauvoir's concept of ambiguity is much closer to that of Merleau-Ponty than to Sartre's. It is Merleau-Ponty's phenomenology, not Sartre's, she finds, that provides the basis for Beauvoir's ethics of ambiguity. "Ambiguity," Langer reminds us, "comes from the Latin *ambiguitas*, meaning doubt, uncertainty, or paradox," and "the adjective *ambiguus* means ambiguous, obscure, dark, wavering, changeable, doubtful, uncertain, disputed, unreliable, and untrustworthy." The negative approach conveyed in such adjectives draws on Descartes' project of achieving certainty through clarity and distinctness. For Beauvoir and Merleau-Ponty, however, Langer finds that ambiguity is neither equivocation nor dualism nor ambivalence. (An interesting discussion of the relationships between ambiguity and ambivalence in Beauvoir's work on evil is found, however, in chapter 11 by Robin Schott, discussed below.) Rather, Beauvoir's concept of ambiguity involves irreducible indeterminacy and "multiple, inseparable significations and aspects." Exploring many uses of ambiguity by Beauvoir and Merleau-Ponty, Langer considers how, in different ways, the thought of each illuminates or supplements that of the other. We should celebrate Beauvoir, she concludes, not just Merleau-Ponty, as a philosopher of ambiguity.

Precisely because she was educated in France from early childhood, Beauvoir may not always be conscious of earlier French philosophy's influences on her own. Yet in correspondance and diaries she mentions several philosophers she has read. Chapter 5 by Margaret Simons and chapter 7 by Susan James explore continuities and possible influences of Henri Bergson (1859–1941) and Nicolas Malebranche (1638–1715) in relation to Beauvoir's thought. Together with chapter 8 by Judith Butler on Beauvoir's long essay on the Marquis de Sade (1749–1814), who is not often appreciated as a philosopher, these chapters provide for Beauvoir's philosophy a context in French philosophy earlier than that of Sartre and Merleau-Ponty.

Margaret Simons made a powerful case in her book on Beauvoir for an African American influence on Beauvoir's views regarding oppression, especially through Richard Wright and his work.[5] In chapter 5 of this Companion she presents and develops the new hypothesis that Bergson was a significant early influence on Beauvoir's methodology. Examining Beauvoir's early diaries, she discovers that the young Beauvoir read and was excited by the work of Bergson. In his early books, *Time and Free Will*, *Matter and Memory*, and *Creative Evolution*, Simons finds sources of at least three aspects of Beauvoir's methodology. They are, first, the use of novels as a vehicle for doing philosophy; second, an interest in exposing distortions of reality in perception and thought; and third, the turn to immediate experience. Although Beauvoir and Bergson were both interested in the problem of self in relation to the Other, Simons finds diary evidence that Beauvoir began to focus on this topic prior to Bergson's published work on it and concludes that we cannot infer an influence there. But in *Time and Free Will* Bergson celebrated the idea of doing philosophy in writing novels, an idea that Beauvoir – unlike Bergson – then carried out. Chapter 5 by Simons and chapter 6 by Mary Sirridge examine how Beauvoir did that in her first novel, *She Came to Stay*.

In chapter 6 Mary Sirridge also discusses some of Beauvoir's other fictional works. Pursuing the question of what literature can contribute to our understanding that mere factual information cannot, Sirridge argues that literature, perhaps especially the novel, acquaints us intimately with other points of view by allowing us to enter imaginatively into the situations of others, albeit without losing the awareness that we are not those others and that their situations are not our own. She considers how well Beauvoir succeeds in that endeavor in *She Came to Stay* and reaches a different, more positive evaluation from that reached by Beauvoir herself when she reflected in her memoirs on the writing of that novel.

In chapter 7 Susan James examines Beauvoir's treatment of women's apparently voluntary participation in and maintenance of their own oppression, a sensitive phenomenon for feminists that is known as the problem of women's complicity. James, who has written a book on emotions in seventeenth-century philosophy,[6] looks at Beauvoir's treatment of this problem in relation to the thought of Malebranche, whose philosophical writings no doubt formed part of Beauvoir's education. Beauvoir appears to offer more than one answer to the question of why men have been so very successful in dominating women. An interesting and, to many, disturbing part of her answer is that women have been complicit in their own domination by embracing patriarchal marriage. Without discussing marriage specifically, James argues that Beauvoir seems at times to appreciate that it is too reductive to understand women's complicity in their own domination in relationships with men simply in terms of choices women make in bad faith. She finds Malebranche's account of the interpersonal structure of hierarchical social relations closer to, and a better explanation of, Beauvoir's own account of women's subordination than the Hegelian master–slave account to which Beauvoir actually appeals. James finds Beauvoir, in tune with Malebranche, conceiving of complicity "as a condition of an embodied self whose abilities, and therefore options, have been formed by its social circumstances," a view that goes beyond Hegel's interpretation of the relations between master and slave.

Feminists are often embarrassed and puzzled by Beauvoir's respectful and substantial attention to the writings of the notorious Marquis de Sade, whose unashamed eroticism in inflicting pain on women has given us the concept of sadism. Beauvoir's surprisingly sympathetic "Must We Burn Sade?" neither condemns him nor protests the pornography of sadism. In chapter 8 Judith Butler briefly reviews the career of Sade (who was in prison at the Bastille during the French Revolution where, Butler reports, "he is said to have helped incite the crowd on the street from his prison window") and then develops the idea that Beauvoir's essay attempts to understand Sade's aim in his writings and in his life as making sexuality into an ethic. It was not an ethic Beauvoir could endorse, nor did she find Sade entirely successful in his own project. Yet she thought we could learn from understanding what he made, or tried to make, of his situation.

As these chapters and others show, Beauvoir scholarship has broken free of the model of viewing Beauvoir's philosophical work as an appendix to Sartre's (a view she often encouraged). Today Beauvoir is studied as an important philosopher in her own right, despite her disclaimers. One of the most prolific and influential female thinkers of the twentieth century, she is widely acknowledged as in many ways the leading philosophical grandparent of women's studies and contemporary feminist theory. Although she did not explicitly and publicly identify herself as a feminist or with a women's movement until later, her sympathies definitely moved in that direction in *The Second Sex*, which is sprinkled throughout with criticisms of "antifeminists." Beauvoir's critics sometimes read that book's concluding section, "Toward Liberation" (Vers la libération), as encouraging simply liberation from sexual mores, and point out that such freedom is arguably more advantageous for men than for women. The impression of a focus on sexual liberation may stem from Beauvoir's extraordinarily frank, unromantic discussions of female sexuality in earlier chapters – unusual (to say the least) for an intellectual woman writing in the 1940s. Yet in the work as a whole, freedom from restrictions on female sexuality is only part of a larger vision of women liberated from oppressive social constructions of femininity. The liberation that Beauvoir appears to find most fundamental in this work is economic.

Beauvoir's relationship to feminism, a recurrent theme in many chapters of this volume, is explored in detail by Susan Brison in chapter 9, which consists of Brison's 1976 interview in Rome with Beauvoir on that topic (translated and published here for the first time), followed by Brison's essay reflecting twenty-five years later on that interview. Brison explores Beauvoir's connections with French feminist activism and theory and her positions in relation to controversies in French feminism, including controversies about *The Second Sex*. Feminists in the 1970s often criticized Beauvoir as valorizing "masculine" values and disparaging "feminine"ones. At the Second Sex conference in New York City in 1979, Audre Lorde quoted Beauvoir favorably as having said: "It is in the knowledge of the genuine conditions of our lives that we must draw our strength to live and our reasons for acting." But Lorde is remembered more for having argued at that conference that "the master's tools will never dismantle the master's house."[7] Brison's interview makes it clear that Beauvoir's position was complex regarding the values women should espouse. We can and should, she thought, use some of what Lorde might later have called "the master's tools," but we should not be prevented from changing them while we use them. Beauvoir also clarifies her position on the role of sexuality in women's lives. She observes that although of course women should have sexual pleasure, if sex becomes more important for women than for men, that is not because of biology but because women are deprived of so much else. Brison finds a model in the ways that Beauvoir's life integrated concrete political action with feminist theory.

Although Beauvoir gradually came to identify herself as a feminist, she consistently refused the label, philosopher (although she taught philosophy), on the grounds that she did not offer a systematic comprehensive theory or worldview. Rather, she explored interconnected philosophical issues, and she did so not only in essays, prefaces, and treatises but in novels and travel diaries – not then, nor even now, standard formats for academic philosophy. If unsystematic, Beauvoir's approach to issues is nevertheless reliably philosophical, focused on meanings and values, and her ideas evolve and mature over time. This Companion frequently cites her diaries as well as her novels and memoirs in tracking the development of her philosophical thought.

In chapter 10 Miranda Fricker presents Beauvoir's memoirs as "a project of intrapersonal alignment, both psychological and ethical." The memoirs became a way for Beauvoir to establish lines of solidarity with her past selves, to align the mature author with the younger women with whom she shared a single life, and to restore unity to what she at one point described as the "scattered, broken" object that was her life. Fricker explores Beauvoir's techniques for doing this, showing how the memoirs took shape as a life-story. A highlight is Fricker's feminist reading of Beauvoir's recounting (in *Memoirs of a Dutiful Daughter*) of her youthful encounter with Sartre at the Medici Fountain in the Luxembourg Garden, where Sartre rapidly

convinced her of the worthlessness of her thoughts favoring a pluralist ethics. Reflecting on the pathos of the older Beauvoir's account
of this incident (in which Beauvoir remains convinced of Sartre's
intellectual superiority), Fricker's reading presents this event as a
likely significant influence on Beauvoir's decision to own the identity simply of a writer and not that of a philosopher. Ironically, it is
largely thanks to Beauvoir's pioneering work as a feminist, Fricker
notes, that today's reader finds this passage in the memoir so very
poignant. In *The Prime of Life*, however, Fricker also finds an independent philosophical reason why Beauvoir rejected the identity of
philosopher: philosophical systematizations of the world seemed to
Beauvoir to be incapable of making adequate room for ambiguity,
whereas more literary forms could do that better, and Beauvoir remained convinced of the fundamental, irreducible ambiguity of the
world.

   In her memoirs Beauvoir integrates discussions of her philosophical development with reflections on her relationships with such
well-known figures as Sartre, Nelson Algren, and Claude Lanzmann.
She also discusses her relationships with women but does not write
about their erotic elements. Yet her chapter on the lesbian in *The
Second Sex* is probably the first published sympathetic and respectful philosophical treatment of that subject in modern times. In an era
when "coming out" as a lesbian was for middle-class women nearly
unthinkable and could cost one one's job, Beauvoir boldly wrote
about such relationships from the points of view of insiders.[8] The
contrast is stark between the then prevailing psychiatric and criminal law views of "homosexuality" as sick or immoral (if not both)
and Beauvoir's account of the lesbian as making rational choices in
relation to a situation.

   Beauvoir's memoirs also track the development of her political consciousness and her involvement in resisting major evils.
In chapter 11 Robin Schott explores different levels of analysis of
the concept of evil to which the idea of ambiguity provides a key,
thus continuing the discussion of Beauvoir on ambiguity begun in
chapters 1 and 4 by Andrew and Langer. The levels of analysis Schott
explores are first, an ontological level, fundamental structures of
human existence that include facticity and the risk of evil; second,
a social and political level, where we find the evils of oppression, injustice, and misery; and third, a cultural symbolic level, linking evil

with the feminine. Schott concludes that extreme situations, such as genocide, which prompt use of the term "absolute evil," reveal limits to Beauvoir's concept of ambiguity, because they show limitations of the agent perspective in ethics. She suspects that Beauvoir senses this, as her treatment of evil through the discourse of agent ambiguities is supplemented in *The Second Sex* with discourses of historical dynamics and symbolic representations.

In-depth looks at Beauvoir's thoughts on sex/gender are found in chapter 12, in Debra Bergoffen's "recounting" of the sexual difference in Beauvoir's thought, and in chapter 13, in Moira Gatens' "second look" at Beauvoir and biology. Readers may wonder whether Beauvoir's critique of the social constructions of masculinity and femininity should move us toward one or the other of the following two ideas. One idea is that, as Bergoffen puts it, "any sexed body can become whatever gender it chooses." This view seems to imply that gender is a wholly arbitrary and contingent construction. An alternative idea is that sexual difference is fundamental to human existence. On this view, the different materialities of human bodies really do constitute us as sexually distinct, even if the particular sex/gender differences mandated by patriarchy are untenable and should be abandoned. Bergoffen asks whether a woman's experience of herself as sexed is "a product of a patriarchal mystification" or "an existential certainty that requires certification." Observing that *The Second Sex* seems to speak, on this issue, in two voices, she builds a case for the second position. Drawing on less frequently cited passages in that work and on Beauvoir's idea of an ethic of ambiguity, she argues that in supporting women's equality, Beauvoir was also supporting women's sexual difference.

Chapter 13, by Moira Gatens, agrees that Beauvoir supports the idea of women's sexual difference. Like Bergoffen, Gatens challenges the assumption, widespread in early women's studies scholarship, that Beauvoir meant to articulate a dichotomy between sex and gender, putting sex on the side of nature and gender on the side of culture. But Gatens also challenges the assumption that Beauvoir regarded "woman" as a gender concept, like "feminine." The idea is not simply that postmodernist readers are hasty in concluding that "woman," for Beauvoir, is socially constructed all the way down. Biology, in Gatens' reading of Beauvoir, does play a role in the construction of women, although not a determining role. If "woman" is not a gender concept, then what is it? No simple answer will do. Gatens argues that Beauvoir's conception of the relations among the concepts of "female," "feminine," and "woman" were more complex than a reductive dichotomy of sex versus gender allows. It is possible, for example, for some people to identify themselves as female but neither as feminine nor as women, and it is possible for some to identify themselves as neither female nor feminine but as women nonetheless. It should not be surprising, then, that so much scholarship has grown up around the most famous sentence in *The Second Sex*: "One is not born, but rather becomes, a woman" (*SS* 267).

Like many philosophers, Beauvoir writes about death. But, as Penelope Deutscher notes in her chapter on Beauvoir's book *Old Age*, Beauvoir is one of the first since antiquity to give sustained attention to the topic of old age independently of a focus on death and to appreciate old age as presenting existential problems not reducible to those of the finality of death. Deutscher contrasts Beauvoir's positive view, in her sixties, of a life with novelties appearing against a background of repetition with her earlier view in *The Second Sex*, which found lives of repetition stagnant and boring. Beauvoir's later writings, which depict physical and satisfying lives for older women, supply a counternarrative to the negative depictions of the earlier work. Deutscher finds that reflecting on the social marginalization of the aged led Beauvoir to appreciate how social inequality "produces a body experienced as limiting." But she also sees Beauvoir's mature thoughts on aging leading to the conclusion that even ontological freedom (Sartre's "radical freedom"), not just practical freedom to engage in activities like climbing mountains, is limited as one's future becomes shorter.

AMBIGUITIES IN ETHICS

Collectively, the chapters in this book call attention to paradoxes and ambivalences in Beauvoir's appreciation of "the second sex" and in her thinking about ethics. Certain of these may be due, as critics suggest, to a reluctance to disagree openly with the positions of Sartre or Hegel. Certainly, her understanding of situatedness suggests a more complex conception of human responsibility than is presupposed in Sartre's notion of radical freedom. This understanding helps to make sense of aspects of her work that may astonish some readers.

For example, it seems paradoxical that she treats the life and work of Sade so very sympathetically, despite his appalling treatment of women, and that her own portraits of women in *The Second Sex* are often so very unflattering, despite her evident commitment to promoting an understanding of women's situations and development. In both cases, Beauvoir goes against the grain of likely expectations in a female – or, at any rate, feminist – readership. Perhaps that fact also had a bearing on her early reluctance to identify herself as feminist. Unsettling as these approaches are, however, Beauvoir remains acutely sensitive to how situations, including our bodies, shape character development. Her attitudes in each case reflect an appreciation of moral luck, how forces beyond our control shape us without determining us, presenting us with different possibilities and different challenges. Instead of dismissing sex-based stereotypes as hasty generalizations, *The Second Sex* interprets stereotypical differences between women's and men's characters as emerging from systematic situational differences. Appreciating this underlying theme goes a long way to soften the impact of Beauvoir's sometimes unrelentingly negative depictions of women, especially women at maturity.

Yet, if Beauvoir is no romantic about female existence, she is no determinist, certainly no fatalist, either. Although individuals are often powerless to alter significantly the social dimensions of their situations, effective collective resistance to oppressive practices is sometimes possible.

An important part of Beauvoir's own situation as a philosopher and writer is the Nazi Occupation of France from 1940 to 1944, which changed her life and the lives of her friends. As Miranda Fricker (chapter 10) and Robin Schott (chapter 11) point out, World War Two, the Occupation, and the French Resistance – not just the academic traditions of French and German philosophy – form the critical setting in which Beauvoir began to think seriously about ethics and politics. Concerns for friends (some lost) in the Resistance triggered a growing political awareness. Beauvoir's responses began her many lifelong political involvements and concerns.

Schott notes in chapter 11 that Beauvoir departs from her own reliance on the concept of ambiguity in ethics when it comes to real evils, such as the death camps, slavery, or the torture in Algeria of Djamila Boupacha. Such things, even in Beauvoir's view, were absolutely intolerable. Calling them "ambiguous" seems to dilute their seriousness. Yet there are also pockets of ethical ambiguity even in the midst of horrendous evils. There may be no serious ambiguity regarding whether a deed, such as the torture of Djamila Boupacha, or an institution, such as slavery, is evil. It may be clear that the deed or the institution embodies culpable wrongdoing that produces intolerable harm or makes the lives or deaths of victims indecent.[9] But there can be serious ambiguity, in some of the senses that Langer discusses in chapter 4, regarding the responsibility of some individuals who are implicated in the perpetration of such evils and regarding the failures of many to resist or even to aid its victims. Such ambiguities arise from a multitude of inseparable facets of one's situation, together with an absence of any conventional way to put them together coherently, perhaps even an impossibility of putting them together so as to yield a coherent and unproblematic conclusion regarding an agent's responsibility.

In both Anglo-American philosophy and ordinary life, ambiguity is not generally treated as either inevitable or desirable. "Ambiguous" is, on the contrary, often a term of criticism or derogation. The analytic tradition in philosophy tends to view ambiguity as a flaw, which, because it interferes with clarity (and thus with vision, to continue the Cartesian metaphor for knowledge), should be eliminated wherever possible. From that point of view, the very idea of an ethic of ambiguity is apt to seem an abdication of responsibility, rather than a way of taking responsibility seriously. Ambiguity can, of course, be used to dodge responsibility, as in the Nazi's deliberate use of language games, which George Orwell later called "doublethink," to mask evils of the Holocaust.[10] But there are cases in which justice requires acknowledging that agency is genuinely problematic. The flight from responsibility can consist in a failure to acknowledge ambiguities that are avoidable only at the price of unacceptable reductions.

Beauvoir wished to avoid, as unacceptable, both the reduction of consciousness to material bodies and the reduction of the material world to objects of consciousness. The central ambiguity of her concern is that of a being who is, on one hand, conscious, a choosing subject, an agent, and on the other hand (at the same time), an object of perception (both others' perceptions and one's own), at the mercy of forces beyond its control. This description inevitably sounds more

Cartesian than it should; the idea is not that of a subject *in* or even *related to* an object but, rather, a "subject" (consciousness) who *is* at the same time an "object," an incarnated subject, embodied consciousness, a chooser who is also and at the same time at the mercy of what lies beyond its control. As situated beings, all humans share this fundamental ambiguity of being at once subject and object. Beauvoir's attitude toward this condition is not to regard it or the tension it produces as undesirable, a flaw to be eliminated if possible. For Beauvoir, ideally we embrace and live our ambiguity. This belief lies at the heart of her humanism. Failure to acknowledge and appreciate either facet of human ambiguity produces failures of ethical responsibility and of compassion.

Yet there are further ethical ambiguities made possible by this one but not universally shared, not pervasive of the human condition, and not examples of Orwellian "doublethink." Being forced to act under extraordinary pressure and to face unthinkable choices produces special ambiguities in moral agency. The complicity of agents who suffer oppression embodies ambiguities that go beyond those of ordinary human agency. Appreciating such agency calls for different responses from those appropriate to agents who act under more favorable conditions. Such appreciation suggests ways to develop the ethics of ambiguity beyond the point at which Beauvoir left it. The ethics of ambiguity might be extended to address ambiguities of oppressed agency in addition to ambiguities that are universal to the human condition. At times Beauvoir's discussions of women's situations point toward such a development. Yet she continually returns to the fundamental ambiguity of being human instead of acknowledging unambiguously that ambiguity is not the same for the oppressed as for the privileged.

In extreme situations we find writ large some differences between oppressed and ordinary ambiguity in human agency. Consider, for example, the extremes of what Holocaust survivor Primo Levi called "the gray zone," a "zone of ambiguity," an area of complicity among prisoners in the Nazi death camps and ghettos. The elements that distinguish Levi's gray zone from ordinary zones of human activity lead us to note an ambiguity in the very concept of ambiguity in Beauvoir's foundational work in this area. For some elements of the ambiguity of oppressed agency may also be found, to a degree, in women who become complicit in their own oppression.

In 1986, the year Beauvoir died, Levi published (in Italian) *The Drowned and the Saved*, reflecting after four decades on his experience of Auschwitz and questions of ethics raised for him by that experience.[11] "The Gray Zone" (Levi, *Drowned and Saved*, pp. 39–69) explores "the fundamental theme of human ambiguity fatally provoked by oppression" (ibid., pp. 60–01). That chapter is a rumination on prisoners who prolonged their existence by providing services to their captors, ranging from clerical and supervisory work to assisting in medical atrocities and ushering the condemned into gas chambers. Were these prisoner-functionaries traitors? Helpless victims? Both? Neither? Something else? In Levi's words, they were "gray, ambiguous persons, ready to compromise" (ibid., p. 49). Captives not just of circumstances but of other agents, their very subjectivity, their capacity for choice, became an instrument for others' evil projects. At once decision-making agents and the tools of others, they were neither *mere* instruments nor *simply agents*, although they did choose among options they assessed as better or worse.

In the camps some prisoners became *kapos* (captains) or were members of the *Sonderkommando* (special squad), charged with cremation detail. In ghettos some became police or served on ghetto councils, the *Judenräte*. The prisoners were simultaneously targets of evil deeds and implicated in the perpetration on other prisoners of the very evils that threatened to engulf themselves. Their complicity was not obviously the product of Sartrean bad faith. Nor was it a response to conventional social hierarchies of the sort that James discusses in chapter 7 in her reflections on Beauvoir's views of women's complicity.

Although Levi regards gray-zone prisoners as bearing "a quota of guilt," he thinks no one should judge them, not even other survivors. Yet, is it not a judgment, one may wonder, to regard them as bearing "a quota of guilt"? A judgment, perhaps. Not necessarily a condemnation. Levi's attitude suggests an ambivalence to which some ambiguities may give rise, perhaps owing to inadequacies in our concepts, but perhaps owing more basically to complexities of reality.

Appreciating the ambiguities of the gray zone may lead us to temper judgments of responsibility for evil. Consider, for example, judgments suggested in Hannah Arendt's book on the trial of Adolph Eichmann. Her "report on the banality of evil" provoked criticism not only for its portrayal of Eichmann's character as banal but even more for its criticism of Jewish leaders, which many found harsh. She wrote of the Jewish councils, the *Judenräte*, who compiled lists of prisoners for deportation and maintained discipline within ghettos, "To a Jew this role of the Jewish leaders in the destruction of their own people is undoubtedly the darkest chapter of the whole dark story," and she quoted another writer, approvingly, as having observed that "there can be no doubt that, without the cooperation of the victims, it would hardly have been possible for a few thousand people ... to liquidate many hundreds of thousands of other people."[12] Such judgments came across to many survivors as inappropriately unambiguous, lacking in nuance.

Zygmunt Bauman, in his reflections on modernity and the Holocaust, writes of how highly rational the choices of ghetto council members in fact were, how the Holocaust ushered in a new era in the perpetration of evil by enlisting the large-scale cooperation of rationality itself.[13] Isaiah Trunk records elaborate reasonings that went into unimaginably difficult decisions taken by the *Judenräte*.[14] If Trunk is right in his conclusions, it is not clear that fewer people would have been murdered without the *Judenräte*. It is possible that, on the contrary, more people would have been murdered. They might have died more rapidly and more violently if the Reich had used more overtly and physically coercive (less "rational") methods. And yet, the *Judenräte* relieved National Socialists of much organizational and hands-on labor that led to the slaughters. The *Judenräte* prevented a level of chaos and physical confrontation that might have made the slaughters psychologically, if not also physically, more costly for perpetrators. Even if Arendt was wrong on how many would have been killed, she put her finger on an ethically sensitive issue.

Levi, like Beauvoir, focused on human ambiguity, but not as a universal. He might have learned from Beauvoir to see continuities between gray zones and other areas of human activity. And Beauvoir might have learned from Levi's later reflections to delineate ethical ambiguities that are not universal and to be clearer about those differences in writing about oppression. Levi wrote, in a passage that Beauvoir could sympathize with, that readers and writers of the history of the camps have an unrealistic tendency, "indeed the need, to separate evil from good, to be able to take sides" and that "the young above all demand clarity, a sharp cut; their experience of the world being meager, they do not like ambiguity" (Levi, *Drowned and Saved*, p. 37). And yet his protest is specific to extreme situations: "The network of human relationships inside the *Lager* [camp] was not simple: it could not be reduced to the two blocs of victims and persecutors" (ibid.). He refused good and evil as an absolute dichotomy *within* the camp setting, however unambiguous an evil the very existence of the camps, and insisted that "gray" areas within that setting "confuse our need to judge" (ibid., p. 42). These ambiguities are not simply those of a being who is both a subject (agent) and an object (of perception) – as true of captors as of their prisoners. Rather, ambiguity in the prisoners' status infects their agency, the subject facet of their fundamental ambiguity as situated beings. Gray-zone ambiguity can leave us ambivalent about blaming and excusing. It can make us want to turn away and refuse, with Levi, the idea of judging such "choices" at all. Yet, for the prisoners, turning away or refusing to evaluate was not always or obviously their best option, when it was an option.

It seems likely that Beauvoir read at least the exerpt from the French translation of Levi's first volume of memoirs that appeared in 1961 in *Les Temps modernes*, the journal she helped to found and edit, although I do not know whether Levi, a chemist, ever read Beauvoir.[15] She also knew the work of Claude Lanzmann, with whom she had a relationship, and she wrote the preface to his filmscript *Shoah*, which was published in 1985, a year before she died.[16] We know she gave serious thought to the predicaments of friends who were members of the Resistance and who faced decisions Levi might have found "gray." She appears to have realized earlier than Sartre that situations limit our freedom to act and that they do so differently, that the limits for some people are far more severe than those for others and that the limits for all people at certain ages (as Deutscher argues in chapter 14 on *Old Age*) are more severe than in "the prime of life." This same realization should lead us to find some situations more ambiguous than others and ambiguous in different ways.

What differentiates the ambiguity of the gray zone from the fundamental ambiguity that all humans share? When does human ambiguity become ambiguity regarding the responsibility for evil? Answers to these questions emerge when we contrast the situations of the *Judenräte* with those of Nazi leaders. Choices confronting the

Judenräte were unusually difficult because council members were lied to, kept ignorant of vital facts for so long, and threatened, overtly and covertly. Council members shared a fundamental human ambiguity as situated beings like everyone else. But, in addition, they were the captives of other human beings, many of whom were not likewise captives of yet others. Ambiguities specific to their situation arose from manipulations of their agency by oppressors.

Gray zones are not universal, although they share continuities with other zones of activity and shade imperceptibly into the more normal. This is part of what makes them gray. And yet, difficult as it can be to know what is right in any situation that contains elements exceeding one's control (true of all situations), it is far more difficult when information is deliberately withheld and when one is lied to and threatened. The difference is not *just* one of degree (although it is surely that). There is a moral difference. If choices of the oppressed are often morally ambiguous – neither clearly right nor clearly wrong – some choices of oppressors are unambiguously wrong. Levi's gray zones are artifacts, created by wrongdoing. The universal ambiguity of embodied agents is not the product of human choice. Human beings are subject to it universally without having chosen it.

In contrast to the *Judenräte*, some Nazi leaders knew the facts and held power as a result of having volunteered their services to the Reich. Reinhardt Heydrich, for example, presided over the Wannsee conference in January 1941, where the Final Solution was openly discussed, and Eichmann was its secretary. Their choices were not clouded by the lies and secrets clouding the conduct of the *Judenräte*. Nazi leaders were, of course, at once subjects of action, with projects of their own, and objects of perception, embedded in a situation that, like all situations, inevitably limited their choices. Yet the limits on their choices were more generous. Heydrich, Eichmann, and others were not compelled to turn their victims into instruments of their own destruction. The Final Solution was deliberately masked with ambiguous language (including the term "Final Solution"). But the evil in the intentions of many who shaped that project was not ambiguous.

In *The Second Sex* and *The Ethics of Ambiguity* Beauvoir comes close, a few times, to discussing women's complicity in ways that might suggest to contemporary readers Levi's responses in discussing the gray zone. In *The Ethics of Ambiguity* she wrote, "The oppressor would not be so strong if he did not have accomplices among the oppressed themselves" (*EA* 98). But then, disappointingly, the "accomplice" she goes on to cite is a youth whose ignorance she finds nonculpable: "When a young 16-year-old Nazi died crying, 'heil Hitler!' he was not guilty, and it was not he whom we hated but his masters" (*EA* 98). In *The Second Sex*, however, she considers adult women who, in the twentieth century, really did have possibilities for economic independence but who instead became complicit in their own (and other women's) oppression by embracing marriage as a career in forms that presuppose, facilitate, and support male dominance. Many women, she notes, enjoy being in the role of the Other and acquiesce in the use of their subjectivity to support their own domination. "It must be admitted," she writes in her conclusion to *The Second Sex*, "that males find in woman more complicity than the oppressor usually finds in the oppressed" (*SS* 721). In this case, however, she maintains that "the wrongs done by one [sex] do not make the other innocent," which suggests a contrast with the 16-year-old Nazi youth, who remains blameless. Apparently, women, unlike the Nazi youth, are not free of culpability. But she also finds, regarding the complicitous woman, that although "she does wrong in yielding to the temptation," "man is in no position to blame her, since he has led her into the temptation" (*SS* 721). Being at fault is one thing. But deserving someone's blame is another.

Being led into temptation is also ethically different from being forcibly kept in ignorance. Nonculpable ignorance exonerates. Temptation does not, or not completely. Beauvoir does not consider explicitly whether women (such as herself) who do not embrace marriage are in any position to blame other women who do. Women who reject marriage are not generally guilty of tempting others to accept it and do not generally profit from the very institution they reject. In that regard, their position is ethically cleaner than that of married men who, in response to complaints by female partners, may be tempted to blame them for complicity in their own oppression. The wrongs of women that Beauvoir goes on to discuss, however, are not wrongs that women do to other women (or even to themselves) but wrongs they do to men.

On wrongs done by women, Beauvoir seems at first to take something like Levi's position when he refused to blame prisoners who became *kapos*. She writes, "It is useless to apportion blame and excuses: justice can never be done in the midst of injustice" (*SS* 723). Yet she seems to apply this judgment as much to men as to women and as much to those who hold relatively advantaged positions under systems of oppression as to those who suffer most under them. For she goes on to say that "a colonial administrator has no possibility of acting rightly toward the natives, nor a general toward his soldiers; the only solution is to be neither colonist nor military chief" (*SS* 723). She compares this situation with that of men and women trapped in an evil marriage system. "The evil originates," she writes, "not in the perversity of individuals – and bad faith first appears when each blames the other – it originates rather in a situation against which all individual action is powerless" (*SS* 724).

Yet such oppressive situations are the products of many human choices. If individual action is powerless, collective action, she recognizes, is not. It is individuals who sometimes choose to act (or not) in concert with others. The ambiguity of choices facing women who fail to join with others to resist oppression might well produce in women who do resist an ambivalence regarding blame that bears some kinship to Levi's response to prisoners in the gray zone. Beauvoir's focus, however, is not on blame but on enhancing the agency of both women and men.

Beauvoir's centering of the concept of ambiguity in ethics changes the traditional focus in moral philosophy from right versus wrong and blame versus excuse to a focus instead on enhancing agency in a world where agency is always limited, never perfect. Centering ambiguity also tempers the analytical demand for clarity and definition. Its danger is, of course, the risk of tolerating what we should reject. (Will a sympathetic treatment of Sade encourage others to emulate his cruelty to women?) Its advantages, however, include generosity in attempting to comprehend the struggles of others, as well as a certain realism and optimism. Beauvoir is realistic in recognizing that our lives are replete with fuzzy edges and that many of our ethical concepts are more suggestive than definitive. But she is also optimistic in her vision of reshaping situations so as to enhance free human agency.

NOTES

1   *Pour une morale de l'ambiguïté* (Paris: Gallimard, 1947), trans. Bernard
    Frechtman (New York: Philosophical Library, 1948). *Le Deuxième sexe*
    (Paris: Gallimard, 1949), I, *Les Faits et les mythes*, and II, *L'Expérience*
    vécue was translated by H. M. Parshley as *The Second Sex* (New York:
    Knopf, 1952) and followed by a Bantam paperback edition in 1953 (and
    many others since). Both works have been in print continuously to date.
    The edition of *The Second Sex* cited in this introduction is that of
    the Modern Library (New York, 1968), based on the Knopf edition of
    1952.
2   Institute for Sex Research, *Sexual Behavior in the Human Female*, Staff
    of the Institute for Sex Research, Indiana University: Alfred C. Kinsey
    (and others), (Philadelphia: Saunders, 1953).
3   For a sketch of the logical positivists' emotive theory of ethics, see A.
    J. Ayer, *Language, Truth, and Logic* (London: Victor Gollancz, 1938),
    pp. 149–70.
4   Monika M. Langer, *Merleau-Ponty's Phenomenology of Perception: A*
    Guide and Commentary (Gainesville, FL: Florida State University Press,
    1989).
5   Margaret A. Simons, *Beauvoir and the Second Sex: Feminism, Race,*
    and the Origins of Existentialism (Lanham, MD: Rowman & Littlefield,
    1999), pp. 167–84.
6   Susan James, *Passion and Action: The Emotions in Seventeenth-*
    Century Philosophy (Oxford: Oxford University Press, 1997).
7   Audre Lorde, *Sister Outsider: Essays and Speeches* (Freedom, CA: Cross-
    ing Press, 1984), pp. 110–12. Lorde does not cite a source for the remark
    she attributes to Beauvoir.
8   See Simons, *Beauvoir and the Second Sex*, pp. 115–43 for discussion of
    Beauvoir's same-sex relationships with some students and what those
    relationships cost her.
9   For the theory that evils are reasonably foreseeable intolerable harms
    produced by culpable wrongdoing, see Claudia Card, *The Atrocity*
    Paradigm: A Theory of Evil (Oxford: Oxford University Press, 2002).
10 George Orwell, *Nineteen Eighty-Four* (New York: Harcourt, Brace,
    Jovanovich, 1984).
11 Primo Levi, *The Drowned and the Saved*, trans. Raymond Rosenthal
    (New York: Vintage, 1989). For extended discussion of gray zones and
    their implications for the concept of evil, see the final chapter of Card,
    Atrocity Paradigm.
12 Hannah Arendt, *Eichmann in Jerusalem: A Report on the Banality of*
    Evil, revised and enlarged edn (Harmondsworth: Penguin, 1977), p. 117.

13 Zygmunt Bauman, *Modernity and the Holocaust* (Ithaca, NY: Cornell University Press, 1989), pp. 117–50.

14 Isaiah Trunk, *Judenräte: The Jewish Councils in Eastern Europe under Nazi Occupation* (Lincoln, NE: University of Nebraska Press, 1972).

15 Levi's two volumes of memoirs are *Survival in Auschwitz: The Nazi Assault on Humanity*, trans. Stuart Woolf (New York: Collier, 1961) (*Si questo è un uomo*, Torino: Einaudi, 1963; *If This is a Man*, trans. Stuart Woolf, New York: Orion, 1959) and *The Reawakening* (*La tregua*): *A Liberated Prisoner's Long March Home Through East Europe*, trans. Stuart Woolf (Boston: Little, Brown, 1965) (originally, Torino: Einaudi, 1963). Paul Steinberg says in *Speak You Also: A Survivor's Reckoning*, trans. Linda Coverdale with Bill Ford (New York: Picador, 2000), p. 129 that he skimmed Levi's account in *Les Temps modernes* "somewhere around 1950." I found only the exerpt 11 years later, "J'étais un homme" by Primo Levi in #181 (May 1961), 1533–69.

16 Claude Lanzmann, *Shoah: An Oral History of the Holocaust*, the complete text of the film, English subtitles by A. Whitelaw and W. Byron (New York: Pantheon, 1985).

1 Beauvoir's place in philosophical thought

Simone de Beauvoir was an existential phenomenologist who was centrally concerned with problems of oppression and embodiment. Her philosophy, novels, and autobiography remain popular, especially *The Second Sex*, which continues to influence feminist thought. Beauvoir lived her life as an intellectual. She considered her life's work to be social commentary. Her tools for social analysis were philosophical.

Beauvoir was born in Paris in 1908 and died there in 1986. She went to school with Simone Weil, Maurice Merleau-Ponty, Claude Levi-Strauss, and Jean-Paul Sartre. She and Sartre became lovers and companions, and although their relationship was not exclusive, it continued throughout most of their lives. Beauvoir had many friendships and love affairs with women and men. Some are revealed in her autobiography, others in posthumously published letters. Beauvoir traveled widely and wrote about her experiences and views in fiction, plays, journalistic articles, autobiography, and philosophy.

Beauvoir's philosophical training began early. She went to a Catholic girls' school, which, like many schools in France at the time, included a great deal of philosophical reading, especially Aquinas and other writers thought to be significant to religious and moral life. In addition to medieval philosophers, Beauvoir read medieval mystics, Immanuel Kant, René Descartes, and Jean-Jacques Rousseau, and was generally well versed in the history of philosophy by the time she went to the Sorbonne. Taking a degree at the Sorbonne was acceptable to her parents only because she had no dowry, which made them believe her unlikely to marry and that she would therefore have to work to support herself. She obtained teaching certificates in literature, philosophy, Latin, Greek, and mathematics and wrote her thesis on Gottfried Wilhelm Leibniz. In 1929 she was the youngest student ever to pass the degree exam in philosophy.

Beauvoir's philosophical training is evident in all her writing. In this chapter I consider Beauvoir's place in philosophical thought in relation to existentialism, phenomenology, social philosophy, and feminist theory. Obviously, no single chapter could do justice to all of these themes. And so I organize my discussion around the development of three ideas central to understanding Beauvoir's philosophical thought – her notions of freedom, ambiguity, and situation – in order to show the complexity of a fourth idea, her notion of human subjectivity as embodied will. I focus on *The Ethics of Ambiguity* and *The Second Sex*, two extended philosophical treatises.[1]

The first section defines existentialism through Beauvoir's discussion of its major themes, such as freedom and bad faith. In the second I explain Beauvoir's use of phenomenology and her development of the notion of situation. The third section examines similarities and differences in the work of Beauvoir and Sartre. I further analyze Beauvoir's notion of freedom in the fourth section, on her social philosophy, especially her arguments for the necessity of universal liberation. In the fifth section I consider Beauvoir's influence on feminist thought.

BEAUVOIR AND EXISTENTIALISM

Existentialism is a branch of philosophy best known from French writers during the 1940s and 1950s, especially Beauvoir, Sartre, and Albert Camus. Existentialism is mostly concerned with ideas of choice, meaning, and the limits of existence. In general, existentialists think human existence has no predetermined meaning. It is up to each of us to use our freedom to choose our actions and interactions in the world. Each individual carries the burden of finding, revealing, and making meaning in the world.

Existentialism's roots are found in the work of Fyodor Dostoevsky, Søren Kierkegaard, Friedrich Nietzsche, and Martin Heidegger. Existentialists are often rebelling against G. W. F. Hegel and Kant. But they are rebelling in very close dialogue and critique. A hallmark of existentialism is the authors' preoccupation with death, anxiety, and fear. In contrast to novelists who focus on escape from reality, existential literature tries to express the always tenuous and questioning aspect of human consciousness, the human tendency to ask: why? A second hallmark is the focus on freedom, especially the burden of responsibility that taking up one's freedom entails. The focus on anxiety correlates with the focus on individual choice and freedom, because choosing freedom means constantly and repeatedly taking up the burden of one's own responsibility, and this constant burden creates anxiety, fear, and dread. As Beauvoir points out in *The Ethics of Ambiguity*, most of us feel great anxiety in adolescence, the moment when we are first faced with freedom or with choosing for ourselves. It is also the moment at which we begin to realize that parents and authority figures are fallible. "But whatever the joy of this liberation may be, it is not without great confusion that the adolescent finds himself cast into a world which is no longer ready-made" (*EA* 39). Beauvoir, like Nietzsche, focuses on joy as well as anxiety. Also reminiscent of Nietzsche, she rejoices in the shedding of old values and the dynamic creation of choosing value.[2]

Existentialism is sometimes accused of being nihilistic. If there is no predetermined meaning, say critics, the world is meaningless. Beauvoir counters these claims in *The Ethics of Ambiguity*. She argues that value and meaning are ambiguous. It is a very different thing to argue that the meaning and value that exist in the world are ambiguous than it is to argue that there are no meanings or values. Ambiguity refers to the idea that meaning is not predetermined; however, there are meanings and values, but it is up to each of us to discover, create, or reveal them.

Beauvoir explicitly rejects nihilism, the view that nothing matters. Instead, she ascribes enormous responsibility to the individual. According to Beauvoir, each person "bears the responsibility for the world which is not the work of a strange power, but of himself, where his defeats are inscribed and his victories as well" (*EA* 16). It is the individual's responsibility to create meaning through her choices. Thus, individuals are free to make meaning, but they are also free to fail to make meaning. Freedom carries with it an enormous burden. Individuals are responsible for the ethical consequences of their actions – their successes and their failures. Failure to take up one's freedom results in failure to create and reveal meaning. Thus, the world becomes more bleak if one rejects or ignores one's responsibilities.

For Beauvoir, human freedom has meaning because of what we do with it. The value that we find in the world we find through our actions, our choices, and our investments in other people. Life has meaning, but it is up to us to find, discover, or reveal that meaning. Some value in the world must be revealed, other value must be created. Sometimes value must be revealed and created simultaneously.

Although it is not commonly stated this way, the existential crisis of how to act on and be responsible for one's own freedom brings into view the need for connection to others. Beauvoir's work, more than that of other existentialists, characteristically emphasizes the need for relationship.[3] For Beauvoir, others are both obstacles to freedom and liberators. They attempt to block freedom by predetermining the world, and they liberate freedom by recognizing the meaning that one makes. The existential crisis is most often thought of as the realization that each individual must act for herself, make her own decisions, and bear responsibility for her own decisions and actions – alone, without the help of parents or the pregiven meaning of religious or social mores. This creates enormous anxiety, often paralysis. Suddenly, one no longer knows what to do but must decide. For Beauvoir, this crisis also involves the problem of the Other. One is alone in choosing. But one chooses amongst actions that involve others who may hinder or facilitate one's freedom. Crisis occurs because others do not seem to realize or notice that life has no predetermined meaning, or they fail to take up the meaning one makes. Those others can take one over by force. Parents are tyrannical. Lovers can be hardhearted. The crisis of being alone occurs, in part, in failing to make genuine connections with others.

Another significant theme of existentialist literature is self-deception or bad faith. Bad faith is believing in something about yourself or the world even in the face of blatant counterevidence. The existentialist idea of bad faith is meant to replace the psychoanalytic idea of unconscious motivation. Individuals act in bad faith when they refuse to face their freedom or try to hide it from themselves, especially by refusing to see that one has to choose values for oneself. One can also be in bad faith by refusing to acknowledge others' freedom. Beauvoir's fictional characters wrestle with the self-deception of bad faith. They turn away from what they know must be true. Françoise in *She Came to Stay* convinces herself that murder is permissible, rather than face her own failures. For Beauvoir, the persistent seduction of bad faith must be constantly refused. Taking up this struggle against self-deception is part of what is necessary in taking responsibility for one's own freedom.

Another example of bad faith is given in *The Second Sex*. Women's failure to take responsibility for their freedom is seen both as women's bad faith and as the trap of patriarchal society. In patriarchal society women are led to believe that they are happier rejecting their freedom than they would be taking responsibility for it. In fact, patriarchal femininity is defined by refusing responsibility – or, as Beauvoir puts it, by choosing to be Other, to be inessential. Beauvoir adds to this the phenomenological idea of woman's "situation." Women are so situated in patriarchal society that choosing against themselves may seem to be the only way to choose. But, once one becomes aware of the possibility of liberation, one must act. Otherwise one is in bad faith. The idea of situation counters ideas of human nature or essence. What structures lived experience is the social, political, and historical situation one finds oneself in. The gendered, sexed body is part of a person's situation, given that bodies are treated and regulated differently in various cultures and eras.

In addition to concerns about freedom and bad faith, another characteristic of existentialism is the rejection of given systems. Since existentialists reject given systems of value, they often pose the question of whether system-building is the best way to explore questions of human existence. Beauvoir rejected the idea of building a system to explain the world or human consciousness and instead used existentialism and phenomenology as analytical tools for understanding the human situation. Like Sartre and Camus, she used fiction and plays as well as philosophical treatises to explore philosophical thought. *She Came to Stay* (her first novel) is a fictional account of some of the philosophical questions found in Sartre's *Being and Nothingness*. Beauvoir won the Prix Goncourt, the highest literary prize in France, for her novel *The Mandarins*, which asks whether ethical action is possible. Much of her philosophical thought can be found in her novels.

Beauvoir's philosophical thought is not only existentialist, but it takes existentialism as its foundation. Existentialism considers people to be actors rather than knowers. Initially, this may seem contradictory to the philosophical pursuit. Philosophers understand themselves as seekers of knowledge. Philosophy, however, is traditionally defined as the love of wisdom. The existentialist philosopher chooses, acts, desires, feels anxious, and knows that meaning must be made. For Beauvoir, philosophers should not be as interested in acquiring knowledge as they are in engaging with it. She pushes herself and her readers to experience love, or engagement, with the world and human reality, rather than to abstractly possess wisdom.

BEAUVOIR AND PHENOMENOLOGY

Phenomenology is centrally concerned with engagement with the world, or between the world and the self. Phenomenologists often discuss "lived experience." Phenomenology is a philosophy of embodiment that views all knowledge as situtated. Recent feminist scholars Sara Heinämaa, Karen Vintges, Sonia Kruks, Eva Gothlin, and Kristana Arp understand Beauvoir's work to be phenomenological as well as existential.

Edmund Husserl is generally regarded as the first phenomenologist. Heidegger, Sartre, and Merleau-Ponty are also foundational to understanding phenomenology. Beauvoir could be added to this list. Some philosophers think of phenomenology as a method of analysis, whereas others identify it as a collection of ideas about analyzing human interaction with and human understanding of the relation of self and world.

Beauvoir was well versed in phenomenology. She reviewed Merleau-Ponty's *Phenomenology of Perception* in *Les Temps modernes* in 1945. In her memoir, *The Prime of Life*, she discusses reading Husserl and Heidegger.[4] *The Ethics of Ambiguity* is first and foremost an existential ethic. However, Beauvoir's ethics also incorporates phenomenology. Heinämaa finds evidence of Husserl's influence in *The Ethics of Ambiguity* and argues that Beauvoir presents a phenomenological ethic in which the ethical agent strives to reveal her relationships with others and the world. Part of the task of the ethical agent is to be cognizant of the "modes of reality" and the way in which reality is being represented.[5] Gothlin argues that *The Ethics of Ambiguity* employs a phenomenological method by starting with the idea of the significance of the individual consciousness and from there developing a critique of the socialist idea that the end (such as a socialist utopia) can justify the means (such as a socialist dictatorship).[6] Vintges calls Beauvoir's ethics "an art of living," a phrase Beauvoir used in the novel *The Mandarins* to describe her ethical view.[7] In *The Mandarins* the experience of joy is bodily. The main character, Anne, experiences a bodily celebration of her connection to the world. That the moment of ethical connection is, in part, physical, is significant to understanding Beauvoir as developing a phenomenological ethic. The bodily connection signifies Anne's experience of ethics as a lived connection to the world, an ethical understanding of human reality.

For phenomenologists, "the world" usually denotes a combination of the natural world and human relationships. A key aspect of phenomenology is the interaction between self and world, and *The Second Sex* may be best understood as a work of phenomenology in which Beauvoir examines the interaction between the gendered self and the gendered world. *The Second Sex* looks at how social ideas of femininity shape women's experiences of self. One of the most significant aspects of *The Second Sex* is its encyclopedic indexing of women's lived experience: biology, psychology, the experience of living in a female body and developing and living with a feminine mind-set. Many contemporary women's first reaction to reading it is that they do not experience themselves in the way Beauvoir describes. But this is to miss the point. Most of *The Second Sex* is a phenomenological, descriptive analysis. Beauvoir is not claiming that there is one way that we who are women experience ourselves, our bodies or our minds. Instead, she describes, and argues against taking as prescriptive, literary representations of femininity, biological sciences' accounts of femininity, psychoanalytic theories about femininity, and so on. It is easy, initially, to confuse her work as participating in negative stereotypes of femininity, rather than in cataloging them and analyzing their effect. Although Beauvoir's descriptions of women's bodies may seem negative, Arp argues that she is describing women's experience of bodily alienation in understanding their social bodies, that is, the body as known through the experience of a sexist world.[8]

Part of the misunderstanding among American readers correlates with H. M. Parshley's translation of *The Second Sex*, which disregards Beauvoir's use of philosophical terminology. For example, the French title of the second volume is *L'Expérience vécue*, or lived experience, which recalls Merleau-Ponty's phenomenological account of the lived body. Parshley translates this title as *Woman's Life Today*. He also translates "la réalité humaine" as "human nature" or "the real nature of man" rather than as the Heideggerian idea of human reality. Beauvoir particularly regretted this flaw, as she argued that there is no such thing as human nature.[9]

Beauvoir's most famous statement from *The Second Sex* shows the influence of phenomenology: "One is not born, but rather becomes, a woman" (*SS* 267). Beauvoir's suggestion is that being female does not make one a woman. Instead one becomes a woman through interactions with the world, through lived experience. One's lived experience may make one experience femininity as "real" in the sense that there are actual expectations about women's behavior that one may internalize and therefore experience as part of one's own understanding of the world. Femininity can be understood as an aspect of human reality but not as natural or innate. Beauvoir is clear about this interaction between self and world, between bodily experience and one's understanding of it. She wrote in the *Prime of Life* that her thesis in *The Second Sex* was that "femininity is neither a natural nor an innate entity, but rather a condition brought about by society, on the basis of certain physiological characteristics" (*PL* 291). Yet, she also held on to the belief in freedom associated with existentialists. "I attached small importance to the actual conditions of my life: nothing, I believed, could impede my will" (*PL* 291).

BEAUVOIR'S WORK AND SARTRE'S: THE DIFFICULTY OF SEEING BOTH EQUALITY AND DIFFERENCE

The relationship between Beauvoir's philosophical work and Sartre's has been the subject of much recent scholarship. Beauvoir and Sartre represented their own relationship with each other as a philosophical partnership. But Beauvoir also gave Sartre center stage as a philosopher. There is no question that Sartre's work was highly influential on Beauvoir's thought. But there is much debate regarding how influential her work was on his thought and how much her work differed from his. While Beauvoir was alive many philosophers understood her work as purely derivative of Sartre's. Some philosophers continue to hold this view, and Beauvoir is often excluded from textbooks on existentialism and phenomenology. She is interpreted as applying Sartre's philosophy to women's situation or to other particular issues, but not as contributing original work (as if such analyses were not original work!). Current Beauvoir scholarship, on the other hand, argues that Beauvoir's philosophical work differs significantly from Sartre's, that she changed her idea of freedom from the radical freedom of Sartre's *Being and Nothingness* early in her work, at least by *The Ethics of Ambiguity*, and that her version of existentialism has more to offer contemporary thinkers than Sartre's. Margaret Simons has shown that many central tenets of existentialism can be found in an undeveloped form in Beauvoir's early diaries, before she had met Sartre, evidence that Beauvoir was thinking along those lines in developing her own thought.[10] Beauvoir was able to develop a social philosophy early on, whereas Sartre was impeded by his notion of radical freedom. Beauvoir's recognition of the significance of situation is evident throughout her work, another idea that Sartre came to more slowly.

Beauvoir repeatedly commented that Sartre was the creator of philosophical systems where she was not, suggesting that she was Sartre's disciple.[11] But what she means by the claim that she is not a philosopher is not to deny categorically the philosophical import of her writing. She insisted that the ideas and philosophical analyses in her books were her own. However, during her career, "philosophy" traditionally designated a systematic, comprehensive theory. What Beauvoir points to is a different understanding of her own work. As an existentialist, admittedly of her own stripe, Beauvoir was not interested in constructing a philosophical system, which might turn into a system of given meaning for others. Instead, she developed what we may think of as a set of tools for philosophical analysis, including her ideas of freedom, ambiguity, situation, the human condition, social ethics, reciprocity, and gendered existence. In our contemporary use of the term, Beauvoir is a philosopher precisely because her work engages in philosophical analysis. Her sets of theories are in line with many contemporary philosophers' understanding of their own methodology. Part of what we learn in studying Beauvoir's work on its own merits is that she came to view systems of thought as too rigid, as not recognizing the shifting nature of knowledge.[12]

Ideas of freedom are central to existential analysis, and it is generally agreed among Beauvoir scholars that Beauvoir's idea of freedom differed significantly from Sartre's. Sartre maintains in *Being and Nothingness* that we are always free to choose, even if that freedom takes the form merely of refusing the situation, perhaps by committing suicide. Kruks, Kate and Edward Fullbrook, and Gothlin have written detailed analyses of Beauvoir's and Sartre's evolving notions of freedom. In fact, both Kruks and the Fullbrooks argue that Beauvoir disagreed with Sartre about freedom before the publication of *Being and Nothingness*.[13] Kruks and Gothlin argue that Beauvoir's idea of freedom is much closer to Merleau-Ponty's and that Beauvoir was influenced by Merleau-Ponty long before Sartre was.[14] The Fullbrooks argue that, contrary to popular belief, it is Beauvoir who inspired Sartre's idea of freedom and not the other way around.

In *The Ethics of Ambiguity* Beauvoir argues that each person needs the other's freedom for her own to be realizable. This is already a huge move away from the radical freedom of *Being and Nothingness*. She also argues that human reality is constituted from both facticity and freedom. One is simultaneously body and mind, whereas Sartre saw the mind or freedom as determining facticity's or the body's influence. Consequently, for Beauvoir, not all situations equally allow the ability to act on or take up one's own freedom. Freedom is situated, subject not only to the whims of embodiment but also to those of historical, social location.

Beauvoir is likewise aware of the effects of social institutions on freedom. The importance of situation in her work – and of social institutions on the historical, cultural, and political understanding of the self as free – begins in *The Ethics of Ambiguity* and is fully developed in *The Second Sex*. Sartre's radical existential freedom assumes that each of us is equally free, regardless of our situation. Attempts to destroy another's freedom are only actions against the person's physical situation. Beauvoir's embodied notion of self allows her to argue that political oppression obstructs freedom because body, mind, and will are all one entity. Contrary to Sartre's idea that two freedoms are always in conflict, Beauvoir emphasizes that individuals have an important alliance and affinity through their mutual recognition of the ambiguity of the human condition and the meaning of their projects. Social institutions that allow for oppression predetermine human political inequality and thus harm our ability to recognize each other's freedom.

However, there is also no question that Beauvoir and Sartre shared many philosophical beliefs and that their mutual influence is enormous. They read each other's work and commented on it before publication. They were continually discussing philosophy and presented themselves as a philosophical pair throughout many years. Regardless of the failures of reciprocity found by contemporary scholars and biographers, Beauvoir's and Sartre's own understandings were ones of mutual intellectual influence and regard.

Beauvoir's contribution to existential and phenomenological philosophy is to make situation and embodiment central to philosophical questions. *The Second Sex* makes it impossible to deny that philosophy must no longer ask the question of human existence, but must instead ask about situated or gendered embodied existence. This is a huge step forward in feminist philosophy, but it is also a huge step forward in philosophy generally. Situated, embodied existence cannot be ignored.

BEAUVOIR AND SOCIAL PHILOSOPHY

Beauvoir's idea of situated, embodied existence develops from existentialism and phenomenology. However, her idea of situation makes social philosophy central to her work. The significance of her work for social philosophy is broad-ranging. During her lifetime, Beauvoir wrote many journalistic articles regarding political events, most of which philosophical scholars have not yet considered. Beauvoir wrote about the Algerian war, women's rights, and a plethora of the political issues of her day. In addition to these topical essays, she develops a social philosophy in her philosophical essays and novels. Her autobiographical work can be understood as being similar to the ethical self-styling that Michel Foucault discusses.[15] *The Second Sex* generated a huge shift in feminist social thought and was inspirational to a great deal of social philosophy more generally. In this section I concentrate on the importance of her central philosophical ideas for social philosophy, especially her argument for the relational nature of freedom and the consequent necessity of universal liberation.

Beauvoir's basic understanding of the human condition is one that puts each of us at the mercy of the other as well as giving us tremendous power over each other. She writes, "This privilege, which he [the human individual] alone possesses, of being a sovereign and unique subject amidst a universe of objects, is what he shares with all his fellow-men. In turn an object for others, he is nothing more than an individual in the collectivity on which he depends" (*EA* 7). Each person is simultaneously sovereign and object; powerful and weak, the perpetrator of deeds and the dependent of the collectivity. While it is tempting to understand the existentialist position as advocating radical freedom, Beauvoir does not allow this. This ambiguity, being simultaneously free and dependent, is the basis of Beauvoir's ethic and the basis of her social thought. Individuals must and always do choose for themselves, but those choices are always situated in a social context. It may be tempting to interpret this ambiguity as replicating Cartesian mind–body dualism; however, what Beauvoir aims at is an embodied subjectivity. There may be moments in her writing where mind–body dualism slips in, but what Beauvoir attempts to accomplish is a phenomenological description of embodied consciousness in which we experience ourselves as willed bodies, passionate bodies, and thoughtful bodies, both at union with and in contradiction to the natural and the social worlds.

In *The Ethics of Ambiguity* Beauvoir argues that all value arises from freedom. But freedom only has meaning when other people exist to recognize it. These two claims lead to a social ethics, in which each person must work not only for her own freedom but for the freedom of every other person. For Beauvoir, we need free others who will recognize the meaning of our projects. Consequently, we must work for universal liberation. One way to understand this is through the notion of reciprocity. Beauvoir has a complex notion of reciprocity that entails understanding both self and other as ambiguous as well as recognizing the importance of others' freedom.

Freedom is inescapable for the individual in the sense that one cannot escape one's own freedom, but also in the sense that one cannot escape from others' freedom. Thus, for Beauvoir, freedom is relational. It requires reciprocal recognition. To deny others' freedom is to live in bad faith, just as denying one's own freedom is living in bad faith. Beauvoir writes: "To will that there be being is also to will that there be men by and for whom the world is endowed with human significations. One can reveal the world only on a basis revealed by other men" (*EA* 71). Simply stated, we need others to recognize our meaning. Those others must be free so that they too can see the world as endowed with human meaning. Beauvoir continues by arguing that "every man needs the freedom of other men and, in a sense, always wants it, even though he may be a tyrant; the only thing he fails to do is to assume honestly the consequences of such a wish. Only the freedom of others keeps each one of us from hardening in the absurdity of facticity" (*EA* 71). We desire each other's freedom because we desire that others recognize the meaning we make and the significance of our projects. It is not enough to make meaning in front of slavish devotees, for their recognition is not valuable because it is not free.

When we deny another's freedom we simply deny what is patently true about that other, namely that the person is free, can make meaning, and that we need that person to recognize the meaning of our own actions. Oppression is "transcendence condemned to fall uselessly back upon itself because it is cut off from its goals" (*EA* 81). Oppression is a failure, in bad faith, to recognize the other's freedom. However, it is also a failure to recognize one's own ambiguity. The oppressor takes her own freedom as paramount, and acting out of hubris, fails to see that she is nothing but an object without the other's recognition. She falls into, or rather, chooses, a staid role that denies the flexibility of her own freedom and trades that flexibility for a violent power. In a sense, the oppressor uses herself as an object of force.

For Beauvoir we are each both subject and object, free and acted upon. Recognizing this ambiguity simultaneously in oneself and in others is another form of reciprocity. While Beauvoir's concerns about oppression in *The Ethics of Ambiguity* point to this, the idea is more fully developed in *The Second Sex*, especially in terms of interpersonal relationships. Beauvoir's novel *All Men are Mortal* also picks up her concerns about ambiguity. The main character, Fosca, reveals that he is immortal, but instead of making him the best human possible, his immortality makes him take an immoral view – immoral because outside of human reality. Fosca adopts a historical view that allows him to justify particular wrongs for broad historical goals. His focus turns to the overall progress of the human race, or progress itself, or the good for all without recognizing the significance of every individual. Such a utilitarian calculus will also lead to oppression, according to Beauvoir, because one is apt to forget whose liberation one is fighting for – the liberation of individuals.[16] Immortality allows Fosca to stand outside human reality. He cannot risk his life for a cause or dedicate himself to loving one person. He will live forever; his life cannot be risked, his beloved will be left. He forgets the significance of others' existence, the importance of each individual's freedom. And so he forgets where value springs from, and he is no longer part of the human world. His own freedom no longer has meaning. As such, he views himself as outside morality. He is surely outside an embodied ethic. He is also outside ambiguity, because the limitations of his bodily existence are no longer meaningful. Thus he cannot participate in making meaning.

Beauvoir's emphasis on the ambiguity of the human condition and the impact of taking up one's freedom led her to argue for radical political change. *The Second Sex* is the most influential analysis of women's situation in the twentieth century. Many fail to see it as a political work, in part because the analysis moves through literature, biology, and psychology. Nonetheless, *The Second Sex* is a political analysis of women's social, historical, and cultural situation. In it Beauvoir rejects liberalism and instead uses a Marxist critique to argue that women, as a class, are so situated that they are less able and less likely than men to act on their freedom. Beauvoir goes beyond Marxism, however, in arguing that women's psychology, education, and desire are so shaped by social influences that they learn to choose against themselves.

Margaret Simons compares *The Second Sex* to Marxist and radical feminism, to Richard Wright's phenomenological work on African-American lived existence, and to Gunnar Myrdal's comprehensive and influential analysis of racism in the United States. For Simons, the arguments for class, caste, and race struggle are similar insofar as they require a historical materialist approach as well as a phenomenology of oppressed consciousness.[17] This position, as well as Beauvoir's unique views of freedom, ambiguity, and reciprocity, made *The Second Sex* one of the most influential books of the twentieth century. In it, Beauvoir further develops her analysis of the political workings of oppression and how the ambiguity of the human condition demands a risky freedom.

BEAUVOIR'S INFLUENCE ON FEMINIST THOUGHT

Beauvoir's influence on feminist thought is remarkable, even paradigmatic.[18] *The Second Sex* influenced all subsequent feminist philosophy. Philosophy is the project of considering what it means to be human and of asking what it means to experience and create a human reality. Beauvoir's work considers what it means to be a gendered human and asks what it means to experience and create a gendered human reality. Beauvoir takes up many of the central problems for feminist philosophy today: equality and difference; developing a postcolonial feminism; ethics for morally corrupt times; embodied consciousness; and a theory of the self that is both free and socially constructed. Beauvoir's work was quite influential to the second-wave feminist movement. Liberal, socialist, and radical feminists as diverse as Kate Millett, Betty Friedan, and Shulamuth Firestone each acknowledge Beauvoir's influence on their own work. Beauvoir's work is referred to by psychoanalytic feminists, such as Juliet Mitchell and Carol Gilligan. Her influence on French feminists, such as Luce Irigaray, Hélène Cixous and Toril Moi is foundational, as is her influence on feminist postmodernists, such as Judith Butler. Beauvoir is the one author with whom most contemporary feminist theorists have some familiarity, regardless of their own theoretical preferences.

While Beauvoir's influence on feminist writers has been profound, it is important to remember that she was influenced by earlier feminists. She had, for example, read all of Virginia Woolf's work,[19] and she refers to a wide variety of women writers in *The Second* Sex, including Madame de Staehl, Mary Wollstonecraft, Christine de Pisan, Emily Dickinson, Isadora Duncan, and Clara Zetkin. Although I focus in this chapter on the impact of *The Second Sex*, Beauvoir's fiction has also been quite influential to feminist theory.

Beauvoir's most famous statement, "One is not born, but rather becomes, a woman," argues that there is nothing natural or inherent about woman or femininity. All of our lived experiences, our psychologies, our understandings of our physical and mental capabilities and gifts – everything that we know and experience about ourselves – is filtered through our situatedness. Beauvoir's famous statement initiated a storm of controversy as well as a plethora of commentary. Whereas many feminists understand Beauvoir to restate the distinction between sex and gender, others, especially postmodernist feminists, understand Beauvoir to confound that distinction. An enormous amount of feminist thought interprets Beauvoir's famous sentence and ponders what it might mean.

How does the statement "One is not born but rather becomes a woman" correspond to Beauvoir's notions of freedom, ambiguity, and situation? I have argued that these three ideas lead to Beauvoir's distinctive analysis of embodied subjectivity. Beauvoir uses women's failure to take up freedom as an example of bad faith. *The Second Sex* is a phenomenological work that catalogs women's situation. Women's situation in patriarchal societies limits freedom. For Beauvoir, the ambiguity of each individual's freedom requires universal liberation. The complexity of Beauvoir's idea of freedom is only now being taken up feminists. In part, this is because her analyses of situation and ambiguity and how they lead to a new idea of freedom are only now being fully understood.

Women's freedom is the most important theme of *The Second Sex*. From the 1980s to early 1990s many feminists understood Beauvoir simply to advocate that women, like men, could be free if they would only take up their freedom. Beauvoir is saying this in part. But it is important to notice that this understanding by itself forgets the ambiguity of the human situation, on which she insisted. We are simultaneously free and completely dependent. For each of us, women and men, social situation moderates our freedom. Women's historical, social, political, legal, psychological, and economic situation renders them less able to take up their freedom than the situations of some men. Recall that Beauvoir sees women's situation in relation to men as similar to African-Americans' situation in relation to white Americans and to the Jews' situation in relation to Christians (and, later, to the Algerians' situation in relation to mainland French). Beauvoir's analysis strives to take political and economic situations into account. To do this requires more than an argument for equality; it requires changing our view of the meanings of equality and freedom.

When Beauvoir was understood to advocate women's freedom and equality in relation to men, without noticing the sophistication with which that claim is moderated by her understanding of situation and the ambiguity of the human condition, then she was understood to advocate a liberal notion of equality in which women would become more like men. This misunderstanding is connected with the popularity of *The Second Sex*, which generated many interpretations and some misunderstandings. Although Beauvoir's work does emphasize freedom, her notion of freedom is not simplistic. As feminist theory grew more complex, thinkers began to interpret Beauvoir's work differently, seeing the importance of situation and ambiguity. Like Beauvoir herself, who wrote that the first thing she had to say about herself is "I am a woman," feminist philosophy had first to negotiate the right of women to speak philosophically on their own behalf. In other words, it is only after feminist philosophy is somewhat successful in making arguments for women's equality and freedom that it has the luxury of understanding and responding to the complexity of Beauvoir's work, especially the complexity of her notion of freedom in terms of situation and ambiguity.

The phenomenological notion of situation tempers Beauvoir's idea of freedom. For Beauvoir, everyone is equally metaphysically capable of freedom. However, women are situated in ways that make it less likely that they can act on their freedom. Women's situation may influence and even impede women's freedom. While Beauvoir holds women culpable for not taking up their freedom and for the choices they make, she argues that some choices are not available. Neither men nor women can be radically free. All human freedom is situated, according to Beauvoir. All humans experience ambiguous subjectivity, and this ambiguity is constitutive of human reality and moral experience.

The idea of situation plays an important role in *The Second Sex*. For example, Beauvoir writes that "it is clear that none of woman's traits manifest an originally perverted essence or will: they reflect a situation" (*SS* 615). Femininity is a situation, for Beauvoir. There is no such thing as femininity itself, an eternal Feminine, a female essence or a feminine will. Contemporary feminist thought discusses femininity as a social, cultural, historical, economic situation, as socialization (or psychological or cultural identity), or even as a performance. Beauvoir's analysis in *The Second Sex* suggests all of these interpretations. In fact, one can understand the strands of feminist theory, liberal and Marxist, psychological, and postmodern and postcolonial feminism, as working through these understandings. Liberal and Marxist feminists take up political analyses of women's socioeconomic and historical situation and how it affects freedom. Psychoanalytic and psychological feminism take up how culture molds women's psyches into femininity and discusses what parts of women's cultural situation need to be deconstructed to allow for women's freedom, as well as what parts can be maintained. Postmodern feminists see gender as a performance. Women's psychic freedom, or lack of it, plays out in and through the body and their self-knowledge of their bodies, completely informing their lived experience. The situation of femininity shapes the things we know about the world, the ways in which we think about ourselves, the ways in which we relate to others and so on.

These ideas of situation reflect one aspect of Beauvoir's idea of ambiguity: that we are both subject and object, body and mind. The second aspect of ambiguity is the idea of reciprocity, that we have to understand this simultaneous empowerment and disempowerment not only about ourselves but about each other, which means that we recognize both the other's freedom and her facticity. This simultaneous ambiguity is what we recognize in sexual activity. When we understand another in this way we can see that other as willed body and take delight in the pleasure brought by both the other's objecthood and subjecthood. Thus Beauvoir explains in writing about heterosexual sexual activity:

The verbs to give and to receive exchange meanings; joy is gratitude, pleasure is affection. Under a concrete and carnal form there is mutual recognition of the ego and of the other in the keenest awareness of the other and of the ego. Some women say that they feel the masculine sex organ in them as a part of their own bodies; some men feel that they are the women they penetrate. These are evidently inexact expressions, for the dimension, the relation of the other still exists; but the fact is that alterity has no longer a hostile implication, and indeed this sense of the union of really separate bodies is what gives its emotional character to the sexual act; and it is the more overwhelming as the two beings, who together in passion deny and assert their boundaries, are similar and yet unlike. [SS 401]

This description does not deny the tension of objectifying the other, but reframes it. Eros entails being drawn to the other, desiring the other, which may seem to make the other into a thing to be desired. Yet, in Beauvoir's description, part of the pleasure of eros is in experiencing the other as embodied will through the denial and assertion of boundaries. Beauvoir calls erotic activity the experience in which humans most poignantly experience their ambiguity. It is in erotic activity that human ambiguity in all its aspects is played out. As embodied consciousness, we reciprocally recognize each other, we act with and on each other, together, we express desire. We desire the other's freedom as much as our own in erotic activity, for the other's freedom is part of assertion and the denial of boundaries. What is erotic about sexual activity is its expression of ambiguity. For this reason, Beauvoir's work emphasizes the importance of sexual activity. It is also for this reason that early receptions of *The Second Sex* described it as calling for sexual liberation and more recent interpreters describe it as philosophy of joy, philosophy as passion, an erotic ethic, and an ethic of liberation.[20]

But Beauvoir does not solely rely on passion and the eroticism of ambiguity. The social and economic conditions of women's liberation are also significant. In order to analyze women's situation, Beauvoir combines traditional political concerns (social and economic systems) with ideas about ambiguity, freedom, and their effects on women's sense of self. Rather than using one system of analysis, she combines phenomenology, existentialism, psychology, historical materialism, and liberal political concerns to come up with a unique and comprehensive view of women's lived reality. She makes a traditional liberal call for rights and equality, develops a political phenomenology, and uses an existential psychology. For Beauvoir, everything must be taken into account.

Beauvoir suggests that what we know about woman could change completely. What contemporary feminists find most provocative about Beauvoir's work is her idea of embodied consciousness and the ethic which develops from it. Would the embodied subject change social thought? What would existential ethics be if it focused on joy and engagement rather than anxiety and alienation? What Beauvoir understood was a connection to the world as ethical engagement. And it is this engagement that contemporary scholars seek to understand and employ in their own work. Of course, this was not always the question that feminist theorists interpreted Beauvoir as posing. As feminist thought evolves, so do our interpretations of Beauvoir. Her work serves as a place from which to ask the questions of feminist philosophy. She began the dialogue in which we are now engaged.

CONCLUSION

Through her writing and theorizing, Beauvoir attempts to engage the world. "Literature is born when something in life goes slightly adrift... the first essential condition is that *reality should no longer be taken for granted*; only then can one both perceive it, and make others do so" (*PL* 290, emphasis original). Existentialist writers are

often viewed as portraying the tragedy of human existence: our isolation from one another, the meaninglessness of our attempts to engage one another and the world, our failure to make meaning and
our insignificance. Beauvoir is an existentialist whose work, faced
with this tragedy, turns toward engagement and sees its possibilities
as well as its dangers and potential failures. Her writing finds joy in
moments of connection with others and the world, while it never
forgets the potential oppression this connection may bring. The ambiguity of the human condition, for Beauvoir, is not a cause of misery.
Instead, although it may produce anxiety and dread, it also produces
a need for connection with others and engagement with the world.
Ambiguity is erotic, for Beauvoir, and it produces the conditions for
joy, engagement, and a celebration of the fecundity of the world.
Ambiguity produces a celebratory excursion, a journey of discovering what it means to be a thinking animal or an embodied will. For
Beauvoir, the world is a place of excess. There is always something
to comment on, to fix, to strive for – in short, always something or
someone to engage with. "Before writing *She Came to Stay* I spent
years fumbling around for a subject. From the moment I began that
book I never stopped writing, . . . Why was it that from this point on
I always had 'something to say'?" Beauvoir goes on to answer her
question: "each book thenceforth impelled me toward its successor,
for the more I saw of the world, the more I realized that it was brim-
ming over with all I could ever hope to experience, understand, and
put into words" (*PL* 478–79).

NOTES

1 *SS* (New York: Vintage, 1989 [1949]); *EA* (Secaucus, NJ: Citadel, 1948
   [1947]). Because this chapter is written for the common reader, I have
   chosen the widely available English translations of these books. I note
   problems with translations of *The Second Sex* later in the chapter.
2 Beauvoir claims several significant differences between her ethic and
   Nietzsche's. See *EA* 72.
3 In fact, Beauvoir's idea of freedom can be understood as relational, an
   idea developed in Barbara Andrew, "Care, Freedom, and Reciprocity in
   the Ethics of Simone de Beauvoir," *Philosophy Today*, 42, 3/4 (fall 1998):
   290–300. Cf. Linda Singer, "Interpretation and Retrieval," in Azizah Y.
   al-Hibri and Margaret A. Simons, ed., *Hypatia Reborn* (Bloomington, IN:

Indiana University Press, 1990), pp. 323-35; Jo-Ann Pilardi, "Philosophy Becomes Autobiography: The Development of the Self in the Writings of Simone de Beauvoir," in Hugh J. Silverman, ed., *Writing the Politics of Difference* (Albany, NY: State University of New York Press, 1991); Sonia Kruks, *Situation and Human Existence* (London: Unwin Hyman, 1990); and Margaret A. Simons, *Beauvoir and* The Second Sex (Lanham, MD: Rowman & Littlefield, 1999).

4 Simone de Beauvoir, *The Prime of Life* (hereafter *PL*), trans. Peter Green (Cleveland, OH: World Publishing, 1962 [1960]), pp. 178 and 373.

5 Sara Heinämaa, "Simone de Beauvoir's Phenomenology of Sexual Difference," *Hypatia*, 14, 4 (1999): 114-32.

6 Eva Gothlin, *Sex and Existence*, trans. Linda Schenck (Middletown, CN: Wesleyan University Press, 1996), p. 153.

7 Karen Vintges, *Philosophy as Passion*, trans. Anne Lavelle (Bloomington, IN: Indiana University Press, 1996 [1992]).

8 Kristana Arp, "Beauvoir's Concept of Bodily Alienation," in Margaret A. Simons, ed., *Feminist Interpretations of Simone de Beauvoir* (University Park, PA: Pennsylvania State University Press, 1995), pp. 161-77.

9 See Simons, *Beauvoir and* The Second Sex, p. 59.

10 ibid., pp. 185-243.

11 See *PL* 178 and Simons, *Beauvoir and* The Second Sex, p. 12.

12 See Vintges, *Philosophy as Passion* for an analysis of Beauvoir's ideas of truth and knowledge.

13 See Kruks, *Situation and Human Existence*, pp. 83-112, and Kate Fullbrook and Edward Fullbrook, "Sartre's Secret Key," in *Feminist Interpretations*.

14 Gothlin, *Sex and Existence* and Eva Gothlin, "Simone de Beauvoir's Notions of Appeal, Desire and Ambiguity and their Relationship to Jean-Paul Sartre's Notions of Appeal and Desire," *Hypatia*, 14, 4 (fall 1999): 83-95.

15 I borrow this suggestion from Vintges, who compares Beauvoir's ethics to that of Foucault, both in Vintges, *Philosophy as Passion* and in her "Simone de Beauvoir: A Feminist Thinker for Our Times," *Hypatia*, 14, 4 (fall 1999): 133-44.

16 Beauvoir also makes this point in *EA*.

17 Simons, *Beauvoir and* The Second Sex.

18 Vintges (*Philosophy as Passion*, p. 140) calls Beauvoir paradigmatic.

19 See *PL* 37 and 46.

20 See Vintges, Fullbrook and Fullbrook, and Bergoffen for these recent descriptions.

2   Reading Simone de Beauvoir
     with Martin Heidegger

In the field of Beauvoir research, one of the least explored philosophical connections is that between Simone de Beauvoir and Martin Heidegger. Although a number of works have been written regarding the Heideggerian influence on Sartre's philosophy, few exist on Beauvoir's appropriation of the same thinker.[1]

This chapter explores ways in which Heidegger can be seen as decisive for Beauvoir's philosophy and why it is important to consider this. Showing philosophical influences and connections is, in my view, important only if it adds to the analysis and understanding of a philosopher. In regard to Heidegger and Beauvoir, I definitely believe this is the case. Reading Beauvoir with Heidegger can deepen our understanding of Beauvoir's view of human beings and their relation to the world and to others. This approach might be called hermeneutical in the Heideggerian sense: it reveals new meanings without assuming that a final comprehension is ever possible.

The intention of this chapter is less to argue for a Heideggerian influence on Beauvoir's philosophy than to situate Beauvoir in relation to the phenomenological tradition. Doing so will show how her phenomenology differs from Sartre's in the way they both relate to Heidegger's philosophy. It could be said that Sartre's philosophy has picked up many Heideggerian themes, such as authenticity and anxiety, although in *Being and Nothingness* he remained essentially inside the Cartesian tradition, as Husserl did. Beauvoir, in contrast, is closer to the main tenet of Heidegger's philosophy in its break with Cartesianism. This is especially evident in her use of the concepts of "disclosure" (*Erschlossenheit*) and "Being-with" (*Mitsein*).

READINGS OF HEIDEGGER, RECEPTIONS OF HEIDEGGER

Before 1930 neither Husserl nor Heidegger was well known in France. During the 1930s interest began to rise. Lectures were held and books published about German phenomenology. The first translations of Heidegger came in 1931 in the periodicals *Bifur* and *Recherches philosophiques*, followed by Henry Corbin's *Qu'est-ce que la métaphysique?* (What is Metaphysics?) in 1938. This selection of texts contained chapters from *Being and Time*. The first reception of Heidegger in France was characterized by its anthropological and existentialist interpretation, which was evident in lectures and texts by Alexandre Koyré, Emmanuel Lévinas, Jean Wahl, and Alexandre Kojève.[2]

Beauvoir and Sartre first learned about phenomenology through their friend Raymond Aron. Aron told Sartre that if he was a phenomenologist, he could take his own life-world as an object for philosophical study. This made Sartre decide to go to Germany.[3] But neither he nor Beauvoir read Heidegger seriously before 1939. Very little is said in Beauvoir's memoirs about her reactions to phenomenology or her reading of Husserl and Heidegger. She tells us, "The novelty and richness of phenomenology filled me with enthusiasm; I felt I had never come so close to the real truth" (*PL* 201; *FA* 208). She says Heidegger's philosophy convinced her about certain things, such as individual responsibility (*PL* 469; *FA* 483).[4] In her published diary for the years 1939 to 1941 she refers to Heidegger's theory of inauthenticity several times while reflecting on everyday events, but she also ponders the choice between Hegel and Heidegger.[5] It is thus reasonable to conclude that she read Heidegger, even if she does not tell us in her memoirs which books. The most important case for a philosophical connection between Beauvoir and Heidegger, however, must be based on a reading of her texts, where we find both explicit and implicit references to Heidegger. This chapter demonstrates that such a connection exists.

There are several possible reasons for Beauvoir's reluctance to admit to an interest in Heidegger's philosophy. Heidegger's political affiliations with Nazism were known even before the war. After the war, the question of those affiliations came into focus. In Germany few wanted to defend Heidegger at the time when his philosophy became more and more influential in France. In leading intellectual journals there was continuous debate regarding the relationship between Heidegger's politics and his philosophy. In *Les Temps Modernes*, the journal edited by Sartre, Beauvoir, and Maurice Merleau-Ponty, there was a whole series of articles. Beauvoir, as well as Sartre, was thus definitely aware of Heidegger's political engagement and the difficult questions it poses for his philosophy.

Another reason for the relative silence concerning Heidegger may be the critique Heidegger directed against Sartre's interpretation of his philosophy in *Brief über den Humanismus* (Letter on Humanism). Part of this text was published in French translation in the journal *Fontaine* in 1947. It inaugurated the second reception of Heidegger in France, which was dominated by a critique of anthropological and existentialist interpretations.[6]

It is evident from the way phenomenology came to influence her work that the possibilities that phenomenology opened up were important also for Beauvoir. Phenomenological descriptions of women's life experiences are frequent in *The Second Sex*. Beauvoir's philosophy belongs to the existential phenomenological tradition, and the significance of Heidegger's development of Husserl's phenomenology is easily recognizable in her works.[7] Not only is her phenomenology interpretative like Heidegger's and Sartre's, rather than mainly descriptive like Husserl's,[8] it also deals with ontological questions, as is evident in her book *The Ethics of Ambiguity*.

DISCLOSURE/*ERSCHLOSSENHEIT*/*DÉVOILEMENT*

In late 1946 and early 1947 Beauvoir published a series of philosophical essays in *Les Temps Modernes*. These were collected in 1947 in the book *Pour une morale de l'ambiguïté* (The Ethics of Ambiguity). This book outlines Beauvoir's conception of human beings and their relation to the world and to each other. Here it is not primarily the Sartrean concepts of in-itself and for-itself that recur, but instead disclosure (*dévoilement*), which, as we will see, has close connections to Heidegger's concept of disclosure (*Erschlossenheit*).

Disclosure is closely related in Heidegger's philosophy to *Dasein*, the concept he uses for human reality. Dasein, which is "Being-in-the-world" (*In-der-Welt-sein*), is said to be "cleared" in such a way that "it *is* itself the clearing" (*BT* 171; *SZ* 133). This means that it is an opening, a clearing of Being, a part of Being for whom other parts of Being can become "accessible." Heidegger summarizes this in the phrase: *"Dasein is its disclosedness"* (*BT* 171; *SZ* 133). Disclosure is thus simultaneously of Dasein as Being-in-the world, that is, of the self, "Being-in," the world, and its "entities." This also means that these entities can remain concealed. Dasein's disclosedness is the condition for anything to appear and for the type of disclosure that characterizes Dasein – "understanding." It is also a condition for "discourse" and language. In Leslie P. Thiele's words, "Heidegger is not suggesting...that human beings must exist for there to be a universe of extant things. But human being is the only place where the Beingness of beings comes to presence, revealing a contextual world of meaning." [9]

Erschlossenheit was not unknown in France in the 1940s. It was introduced in the first volume of Heidegger texts to be translated into French, Corbin's selection, *Qu'est-ce que la métaphysique?* It is mentioned already in the introduction, where Corbin presents some Heideggerian concepts. For Corbin disclosure implies that Dasein is comprehension, interpretation of the world.[10] Jean Beaufret, who was to become one of the most important Heidegger interpreters in France, also treats the concept in his articles on existentialism in 1945. He uses it to demonstrate that Heidegger does not take solipsistic consciousness as his point of departure, but that human being for him is "in-the-world" and related to others.[11]

As I will show, Beauvoir's interpretation of disclosure is in accord with both of these brief characterizations of *Erschlossenheit*, each of which highlights a different aspect. It is also, in many respects, true to Heidegger's development of the concept in *Being and Time*. It might be noted that while Heidegger defines Dasein as disclosure as a clearing in, a clearing of, Being, Corbin, Beaufret, and Beauvoir emphasize the "disclosing," "revealing" aspect. These linguistic differences result in some connotative differences.

Corbin translated Dasein as "human reality" (*réalité humaine*), a translation that recurs in Sartre's and Beauvoir's texts and later was criticized as being too anthropological. In contrast to Heidegger, Beauvoir also explicitly refers to "man" (*homme*) or "the subject," which means that her interpretation is clearly anthropological, as was that of most French philosophers, such as Sartre, Corbin, and Beaufret, at that time. But I maintain that, in spite of this, she retains some of the most important insights that the concept of disclosure conveyed.

In *The Ethics of Ambiguity* Beauvoir outlines her ethics, founding it on a conception of human beings in which disclosure (*dévoilement*) is significant.[12] At the time she wrote *The Ethics of Ambiguity*, Sartre's *Being and Nothingness* had been criticized for its lack of an ethical perspective. In the beginning of the book, she says that those critical of existentialism have argued that existentialist ontology cannot give a foundation for ethics, a critique based on Sartre's characterization of the human being as a "useless passion." Beauvoir sets out to show, by giving her view of existentialist ontology, that this assumption is mistaken. In her elucidation she also clarifies, in a manner she seldom does, differences between her own and Sartre's philosophy.

Beauvoir begins by declaring that, like Sartre, she contends that human being is a "lack of being." It has no specific nature or essence but rather is characterized by transcendence. Beauvoir cites approvingly Sartre's formulation in *Being and Nothingness* that a human being is "a being who *makes himself* a lack of being *in order that there might be* being." Like Sartre, she sees this "lack" as resulting in a "wanting to be" (*vouloir être*), something which in *The Second Sex* becomes a "desire of being/desire to be" (*désire d'être*) (*EA* 11; *PMA* 17). But for Beauvoir, in contrast to Sartre, this "wanting" or "desire" cannot be said to be either useful or useless, since it describes a fact prior to all values. Beauvoir underlines furthermore that human being is not only this "lack" and this "desire," but, more fundamentally, a being that "discloses being" (*dévoile l'être*):

It is not in vain that man nullifies being. Thanks to him, being is disclosed and he desires this disclosure. There is an original type of attachment to being which is not the relationship "wanting to be" but rather "wanting to disclose being." Now, here there is not failure but rather success. This end, which man proposes to himself by making himself lack of being, is, in effect, realized by him. By uprooting himself from the world, man makes himself present to the world and makes the world present to him. [*EA* 12; *PMA* 18]

Through this disclosure human being makes not only itself but the world present, just as Heidegger declares in relation to Dasein as disclosure. This idea can be discerned not only in the quotation above and in other parts of *The Ethics of Ambiguity*, but also in Beauvoir's first philosophical essay, *Pyrrhus et Cinéas* (*PC* 111). The fundamental relation of disclosure is defined, as seen above, not as some sort of "failure" but instead as a "success," not least since thereby the world is given a "human signification": "Every man casts himself into the world by making himself a lack of being; he thereby contributes to reinvesting it with human signification. He discloses it" (*EA* 41; *PMA* 59 f.).

I have already mentioned that Beauvoir as well as Sartre maintains that human being makes itself a lack of being and that it is this negating moment, when human being differentiates and separates itself from being as not being it, that being also appears. This reveals the negating character of consciousness, a Hegelian element in Sartre's and Beauvoir's phenomenology. It is the negation that consciousness performs which makes the world, its things and objects and others, come forth. This movement, Beauvoir contends, is positive in that it discloses being. A human being should therefore not be characterized as a "useless passion," as Sartre says, but more fundamentally as "disclosure." Beauvoir displaces the center of gravity toward a more positive definition of the human being as disclosure, in line with Heidegger, instead of holding a negative definition as lack, in line with Sartre, even though lack and the concomitant "desire of being" continue to be important (especially in Beauvoir's view of inauthenticity). It should also be noted that in *The Ethics of Ambiguity* Beauvoir refers more frequently to disclosure and being than to for-itself and in-itself. When these differences are seen in the larger context of her philosophy, their significance will hopefully become clearer.

SITUATION/THROWNNESS/FACTICITY

Another important aspect of Heidegger's concept of disclosure is "thrownness" (*Geworfenheit*), which means that Dasein "is already in a definite world and alongside a definite range of definite entities within-the-world" (*BT* 264; *SZ* 221); disclosure is always "essentially factical" (*wesenhaft faktische*).[13] For Heidegger, a human being exists in the world before it has knowledge of the world; it does not meet the world as a subject related to the world as object. It exists under specific conditions, in a certain historical situation and culture, and in relation to things it uses for certain purposes. It is there (*Da-sein*). This is Dasein's facticity (*Faktizität*). The human being opens up, discloses a specific there. This further means that its disclosure never can be complete or final. Even if Dasein is characterized by facticity and thrownness, Heidegger also emphasizes its lack of essence in statements like *"The 'essence' of Dasein lies in its existence"* (*BT* 67; *SZ* 42).

All of these concepts appear in Sartre's and Beauvoir's philosophies. Both reject the idea that humans could be defined as having an essence. *The Second Sex* puts it thus: "An existent *is* nothing other than what he does; the possible does not extend beyond the real; essence does not precede existence: in pure subjectivity, the human being *is not anything*."[14] Both see the human being as thrown into the world and characterized by facticity (*facticité*), which is delineated with the concept *situation*.

Beauvoir, as well as Sartre, uses the concept of situation in relation to that of freedom. But as several other commentators have noted, Beauvoir emphasizes earlier than Sartre the limits that one's situation sets for one's freedom.[15] This difference in their philosophies is even more fundamental in my opinion, since I see it as based on their differing views of what freedom and situation are, not only on a difference in their views of the relationship between freedom and situation. As I will show, their interpretations of the Heideggerian concepts differ.

In *Being and Nothingness* Sartre concludes, from his rejection of essentialism, the absolute freedom of human consciousness, even though he also emphasizes that human beings are always situated, that they have a facticity. For Beauvoir as well as for Heidegger, proceeding from the concept of disclosure, the fact that disclosure is always of a specific "there" – in her terminology, "in and of a situation" – leads to a different conclusion. According to Beauvoir, we do not all have a knowledge of our freedom, as Sartre maintains in *Being and Nothingness*. Whether we suppose that human beings always have a prereflective intuition of their freedom, as Sartre says, or that freedom is disclosed in and by a situation, as Beauvoir contends, is an important difference. Her idea of freedom explains why she argues in *The Ethics of Ambiguity* that freedom is not disclosed for a child until a certain age, since autonomy is not given at birth. It also makes understandable why she maintains that if you live in a historical situation where freedom is denied a group of people because their situation of oppression is defined as a natural condition, freedom is not something you are aware of (see, for example,

EA 85). If your situation does not really offer possibilities, you cannot have an intuition of freedom. This conception of freedom, nevertheless, does not exclude the argument that human beings are essentially characterized by their freedom, in the sense that they lack an essence but are defined by their existence, which Beauvoir also maintains, even if this freedom has not yet been disclosed or realized in any substantial way.

In a Heideggerian vein Beauvoir thus emphasizes that we always exist under specific conditions, in a certain historical and cultural situation, something evident from *The Ethics of Ambiguity* to *The Second Sex*. This emphasis can also be related to a Hegelian and Marxist influence in her work.[16] In *The Second Sex* Beauvoir delineates the general situation of women during different historical periods. In these descriptions and analyses she stresses, like Marxists, the role of women in production and the importance of private property. But she also analyzes the role of ideology, of things like laws and customs.

Thus, for Beauvoir, human beings are not free to be anything whatsoever, since they are situated. On the other hand, a human being is not defined in advance as having an essence, for example, feminine or masculine, evil or good. This is the other side of the coin, manifest in Beauvoir's rejection in *The Second Sex* of the idea of a "woman's nature" or "female essence." But one should note here an interesting difference between Sartre and Beauvoir and an interesting resemblance between Heidegger and Beauvoir in the conceptualization of existence, something that also has to do with their view of "possibilities."

Even if human reality according to Heidegger is situated in a world, it is, as an opening, not fixed but a way of being there that is "projection" (*Entwurf*). In Dasein's existence lies that "it has its Being to be" (*BT* 32 f.; *SZ* 12) or "The 'essence' [*Wesen*] of this entity lies in its 'to Be' [*Zu-sein*]" (*BT* 67; *SZ* 42). This thesis, as I will show, recurs in Beauvoir's philosophy.

In *Pyrrhus et Cinéas* Beauvoir cites Heidegger and concludes that a human being is always much more than what it is at any given moment, something she connects to transcendence, to human being as project (*PC* 26). And further on in the text she says, "in one sense, a man is always all that he has to be, since as Heidegger shows, it is his existence that defines his essence" (*PC* 82).[17] In this second observation one should note that she says "that he has to be," which echoes Heidegger's "*Zu-sein*." In *The Second Sex* this idea appears in relation to femininity, for example in the well-known formulation: "One is not born, but rather becomes, a woman" (*SS* 295; *DS* 11 13).[18] Femininity is neither a substance nor an essence, as Beauvoir underlines time and again in this book. It is a "becoming" (*devenir*).

If we return to the quotation above, where Beauvoir discusses the relationship between existence and essence, we can note that Beauvoir maintained in relation to human beings that "the possible does not extend beyond the real." The possible thus always has a relationship to what is "real," to the existing situation. This has implications for her view of women and sexual difference. In another part of *The Second Sex*, where Beauvoir defines woman as "becoming," she further explains this becoming in relationship to possibilities (*possibilités*). She says, "Woman is not a completed reality, but rather a becoming, and it is in her becoming that she should be compared with man; that is to say, her *possibilities* should be defined" (*SS* 66; *DS* 1 72). This idea of possibilities as related to a human being's existence as becoming can also be found in Heidegger's *Being and Time*.

According to Heidegger, Dasein is a structure of possibilities (*Möglichkeiten*), a structure it discloses and retains in different ways: "Dasein is in every case what it can be, and in the way in which it is its possibility" (*BT* 183; *SZ* 143). Herein also lies Dasein's freedom or transcendence, that is, that it transcends the given towards the possible, or that it always is more than it is, which does not mean that it has any possibilities whatsoever, since it is exactly a "thrown possibility."

In the quotation above it can be seen that Beauvoir, like Heidegger, thinks in terms of "possibilities"; a situation is characterized by certain possibilities, which are also part of facticity. With her concept of situation Beauvoir delineates the common overall aspects of women's situations that the productive relations, economic systems, law, and customs define. This also sets general limits to a woman's possibilities in a specific society, like the health, education, and work limits for women in Afghanistan. Women's situations have generally been characterized by lesser possibilities, Beauvoir concludes. This results from the fact that she has been defined as "the Other." Their situation is thus not the same even when a man and a woman have the same job and the same salary. But Beauvoir's concept of situation also takes into account human beings' corporeality. In order to understand the importance of the body in Beauvoir's philosophy, it helps us less to read her with Hegel or Marx than to read her with Heidegger.

CORPOREALITY

Everyone discloses the world, but everyone does so in different ways, according to different projects and different bodies. For Beauvoir, that we are corporeal beings is part of our facticity, but also that we are mortal. Like Heidegger, she sees mortality as one important element in human beings' situation. Were we not mortal, we would no longer be human. The same cannot be said about two-sexed reproduction. Even a society that reproduced itself through parthenogenesis would be human (SS 39; DS 1 40).

The body is an important part of one's situation, and Beauvoir gives it a great deal of space in *The Second Sex*. In her discussion of the body she refers to Heidegger, but also to Sartre and Merleau-Ponty, and she concludes that the body "is not a *thing*, it is a situation" (SS 66; DS 1 72). For Beauvoir, a human being is not a consciousness related as a subject to the body as an object. Rather, one lives one's body as a situation. This way of characterizing one's corporeality becomes more understandable if it is related to Heidegger's conception of human being as a disclosure and facticity.

How the world and oneself are disclosed is thus dependent on one's body and physiological possibilities. Another part of a woman's situation is having a female body. If the body is a situation, it is also part of a larger sociocultural situation. The body must always be interpreted in a human perspective, Beauvoir says, since the human being is, in Merleau-Ponty's words, "a historical idea," not "a natural species" (SS 66; DS 1 72). The body does not constitute a destiny, and it is not in itself an explanation of gender hierarchy, as Beauvoir indicates time and again. The "figure" woman in society is therefore not biologically and psychologically determined. Instead, it is produced by our "civilization," which applies also to women's bodies. The body has different significations in different situations, and it is also individually disclosed and "lived" (*vécue*).

Human being is corporeal; this facticity is the same for both men and women. And yet women's bodies have been seen as more "bodily" than men's have. Women's bodies have been interpreted in ways that limit them, and they have been charged with negative significations. Apart from this, the fact is that women's and men's bodies differ in some ways. According to Beauvoir, there are some biological differences, such as the greater subordination of women to the species (because of women's role in reproduction) and a general difference in muscular strength. This leads her to conclude that woman's "grasp on the world is thus more restricted" (SS 66; DS 1 73). What does she mean by this?

Human beings' relationship to the world is mediated through the body by which it "grasps" and "apprehends" the world. Beauvoir writes, for example, "For, the body being the instrument of our grasp upon the world, the world is bound to seem a very different thing when apprehended in one manner or another" (SS 65; DS 1 70). The idea that one apprehends the world through the body resonates with Marx, Hegel, Heidegger, and Merleau-Ponty. It is thus not only through consciousness but also through the body and instruments that are its extension that the world is disclosed. The world "presents itself" very differently, not only, as Sartre says, depending on the (freely chosen) project, but also according to the body through which it is lived and apprehended. On the other hand, true to her concept of situation, Beauvoir sees these biological differences as dependent on the context; for example, apprehension might not be effected in any significant sense by lesser muscular strength if one lived in a society where strength was rather irrelevant. And the significance of the fact that women, not men, give birth is always dependent on a specific society's gender relations and its organization of human reproduction.

Thus Beauvoir's concept of situation differs from Sartre's in *Being and Nothingness* and not only in the sense that he emphasizes the possibility to freely surpass a situation whereas she emphasizes the limits a situation imposes. The importance of the concepts of disclosure, possibilities, and becoming (with their Heideggerian background) makes her conceptualization of situation and facticity different. Heidegger seldom uses the term "situation." But, as I have tried to show, the signification Beauvoir gives to situation is close to Heidegger's description of Dasein's disclosure, thrownness, and facticity.

Noticing the Heideggerian element in Beauvoir's philosophy can deepen our understanding of Beauvoir's concept of situation and sex.

The male and female body differ, and this fact must be taken into account as something that belongs to our facticity and is part of our possibilities. On the other hand, outside of a specific historical and cultural situation, we can say hardly anything about what these differences imply, what importance they have, for example, in relation to our possibilities. This is in accord with a Heideggerian kind of phenomenology whose logical consequence would be being unable to determine the meaning of sexual difference in itself and absolutely, while at the same time recognizing its existence. And we must also be aware of the fact that the signification of the sexed body is always dependent on how the body as situation is concretely lived and disclosed by the individual, a disclosure that in turn is related to a situation of significations already given.

Thus reading Beauvoir with Heidegger enables us to understand why it is important to take women's bodies and physiological differences into account and at the same time why the meaning of these differences is always dependent on a number of factors. It is thus no coincidence that when Beauvoir describes sexual initiation, for example, she relates a whole spectrum of different ways to live it, ways that are dependent on the general cultural situation and the specific situation of an individual woman, a situation that, in turn, is dependent on her relationship to her parents, previous erotic experiences, and so forth.

Beauvoir can thus be read as having adopted a Heideggerian approach to sexual difference, even though Heidegger himself does not analyze sex. Even Sartre talks about possibilities as characteristic of the for-itself. But he emphasizes freedom, not facticity, and he does not connect it to disclosure in a Heideggerian sense. Nor does he take the sexed body into consideration. Since for Beauvoir disclosure is in and by a situation, we also understand why the sexed body is for her an important part of one's situation in all societies where sexual difference exists, where it is disclosed. Disclosure has to do with signification; signification of bodily differences has to be taken into account.

BEING-WITH (*MITSEIN*)

If disclosure is for Heidegger and Beauvoir something that characterizes human being and its relationship to the world, it also affects one's relationship to others. Heidegger does not take his point of departure in solipsistic consciousness; Dasein is Being-with (*Mitsein*) and has a primordial understanding of this. Dasein is in a world shared with others, a *Mitwelt* that reigns even if one is totally alone, like Robinson Crusoe on his island.

Neither, for Beauvoir, is there any doubt that others exist. In both *The Ethics of Ambiguity* and *The Second Sex* individuality and autonomy are seen as developed and acquired in human life, both individually and historically. In *The Second Sex* she describes, for example, the different phases of separation that a child goes through, beginning in a symbiotic relationship with its mother. Thus, for Beauvoir, human beings are born into a world of others. This is for her, as for Heidegger, part of disclosure. Time and again, in both *The Ethics of Ambiguity* and in *The Second Sex* (where the meaning of being a woman is, as I have shown, dependent on social and cultural codes regarding women and femininity), it is emphasized that the significations that human being discloses are dependent on previous significations.

In *The Ethics of Ambiguity* the term Being-with (*Mitsein*) does not appear, but, as I have tried to show, the sense of that concept can be found there. Another term captures this sense in *The Ethics of Ambiguity*, namely, "interdependence," or that "each one depends upon others" (*EA* 82; *PMA* 115 f.).[19] As Beauvoir often expresses it, we are both separate individuals and dependent on a collectivity we belong to, always already in relation to others. Her view of human relationships is closer to that of Heidegger, Hegel, and Merleau-Ponty than to Sartre's view in *Being and Nothingness*, where Sartre rejects Heidegger's *Mitsein*, which he interprets as denoting an impossible intersubjectivity.[20]

In *The Second Sex* the term *Mitsein* occurs in the sense outlined above, that is, as "Being-with"; the human couple, for example, is said to be "an original *Mitsein*" (*SS* 67; *DS* 1 74). Men and women have always been *Mitsein*, not two distinct and separate groups that have appeared and confronted each other during the course of history, such as the bourgeoisie and the proletariat. Not only is the couple *Mitsein* but also human being in general, and this condition, according to Beauvoir, can be lived in different ways. In one of the places where the couple is defined as "an original *Mitsein*" Beauvoir adds that it is out of this *Mitsein* that "their opposition took form."[21]

Mitsein, then, for Beauvoir does not exclude the possibility of conflict, something even more directly declared in her claim, "These phenomena [conflicts] would be incomprehensible if in fact human reality were exclusively a *Mitsein* based on solidarity and friendliness" (*SS* 17; *DS* I 16 f.).[22] For Beauvoir, humans are *Mitsein*, but this *Mitsein* can be lived either in separation and conflict or in friendship and solidarity. *Mitsein*, for her, then, does not mean that humanity is one and that everyone has the same goals and aspirations, living in some kind of friendly symbiosis. *Mitsein* is not an ethical concept, nor is it connected to authenticity. It expresses simply the fact that human reality is a being-with, even if not a being-one but being-many, which is spelled out in the words: "human reality... is at once *Mitsein* and separation" (*SS* 79; *DS* I 88). In this context *Mitsein* is used to explain the existence of a common language and symbolism at the same time as the occurrence of differences and inventions.

The weight Beauvoir lays on conflict in her interpretation of *Mitsein* is understandable if one takes into consideration that she connects it, in *The Second Sex*, to a Hegelian view of human relationships. Like the French Hegel interpreter Alexandre Kojève, she sees self-consciousness and historical development as arising from a confrontation with the Other. This results in a life-and-death struggle and a division into two groups of people, masters and slaves, a conflict that can be transcended by reciprocal recognition. Human development would not even have resulted had this original conflict not occurred.[23]

Like many others in Paris in the 1940s, Beauvoir considered it possible to combine Heidegger, with his concept of *Mitsein*, and Hegel, with his master–slave dialectic, a reading put forward by Kojève. The concept of *Mitsein* was widely discussed in the 1940s, especially its political and ethical implications, such as whether an authentic *Mitsein* is possible for Heidegger. Alphonse de Waehlens, in an article in *Les Temps Modernes* published in 1947, the same year as Beauvoir's *The Ethics of Ambiguity*, concludes that even if *Mitsein* in *Being and Time* is often related to inauthenticity, it is clear that to Heidegger the possibility of an authentic *Mitsein* exists. Waehlens argues that Heidegger's anthropology is close to that of the young Hegel and of the young Marx, because Heidegger defines authentic *Mitsein* as letting the other realize its freedom. Heidegger, like Hegel, therefore sees the meaning of history as to "make man's recognition of man possible."[24]

In *The Second Sex* a Hegelian/Marxian view of history, which sets the tendency to affirm oneself against the other as fundamental to historical change and individual development, is important. But as previously mentioned, Beauvoir presupposes that human relationships can be characterized either by conflict and oppression or by friendship and solidarity. It is the second form that she sees as most authentic, when human being is in its "truth." In *The Second Sex* this idea is conceptualized in the form of a Hegelian reciprocal recognition: "each individual freely recognizes the other" (*SS* 172; *DS* 1 232). In this combination of authenticity, *Mitsein*, and reciprocal recognition, Beauvoir was not alone during the 1940s, as the reference to Waehlens above shows.

AUTHENTICITY

The ontological fact that we are disclosure and *Mitsein* can be dealt with in different ways for both Heidegger and Beauvoir, and this difference also plays an important role in their view of authenticity, the true way to live as a human being. In relation to Beauvoir I have already treated these questions somewhat. But how are they viewed in Heidegger's philosophy? If one looks at the way authenticity is conceptualized in Heidegger and Beauvoir, it is possible to see both a resemblance and a difference.

For Heidegger, authenticity and inauthenticity are closely related to the fact that Dasein is *Mitsein*. Our being-in-the-world and our being-with-others are, in turn, a precondition for the fact that we can "lose ourselves" in the world and in others. Dasein is even for the most part "lost in its world" since "falling" belongs to Dasein's mode of being. This implies being absorbed by *"das Man"* ("the They" or "the one"),[25] which also means that Dasein "flees" from itself "as an authentic potentiality-for-Being-its-Self" (*BT* 229; *SZ* 184). To Dasein's facticity it thus belongs to live most often inauthentically, in the way *"das Man"* does, to apprehend oneself and the world the way that others do. Dasein then in some sense "forgets" that it is a disclosure, that it is a "project." In its daily life it becomes so filled up by the world that its way of being in the world, which in fact is contingent, appears instead as something given.

Heidegger distinguishes between disclosure as something characteristic of Dasein and true or authentic disclosure. In authentic understanding Dasein discloses its possibilities as being-in-the-world.
It can understand itself not only from "*das Man*" but also in terms of
"its ownmost potentiality-for-Being," the potentiality to be it-self,
to be free, "authentic" (*BT* 232; SZ 188). This understanding is disclosed in the state of anguish, where the possibility of living authentically appears. For Dasein to be in its truth is to *be* the disclosure it
fundamentally is. Heidegger names this authentic disclosure "resoluteness" (*Entschlossenheit*) (*BT*, SZ § 60). It means not following
the crowd but instead deliberately choosing how to live one's life
and realizing one's individuality according to available possibilities,
understanding that existence is groundless.[26]

If we now turn to Beauvoir's view of authenticity, we remember that in *The Ethics of Ambiguity* human being is described not
only as "disclosure" but also as the "lack of being" that resulted in
"desire of being." Disclosure is set in *The Ethics of Ambiguity* as the
foundation for authenticity. In *The Second Sex*, where the analysis
of inauthenticity prevails, lack of being and the concomitant desire
of being and what it can lead to if pursued are more in the fore-
front. Authenticity is connected to seeing oneself (or in Beauvoir's
terminology, affirming oneself) as disclosure and not to pursuing the
desire of being, thus, for a human being to being its disclosure, just
as I showed above that Heidegger emphasizes that Dasein "is in its
truth" when it is the disclosure that it fundamentally is.

Disclosure is related to another aspect of the human being – its
freedom. Beauvoir makes affirming oneself as disclosure synony-
mous with affirming oneself as a free human being: "To wish for
the disclosure of the world and to assert oneself as freedom are
one and the same movement" (*EA* 24; *PMA* 34). To be authentic
for Heidegger was also, as I have shown, to be one's potentiality, to
be free, not to be "lost in the world" and in others. Here we find
a resemblance in Beauvoir, who underscores time and again that
human beings – if possible – should recognize their freedom and take
responsibility for their own lives. In *Being and Time* there is seldom
talk about Dasein's freedom, as in Beauvoir's philosophy. But there
is a resemblance in that authenticity for both is connected to the
affirmation of "groundlessness" and the fact of actively choosing

one's way of life, thus not living one's life passively in the way that "*das Man*" says one should live. Beauvoir emphasizes, for example, that not recognizing one's freedom is apprehending everything as "given" – the world, values, one's circumstances, and life.

Since *Mitsein* is of importance in Beauvoir's philosophy, as it is in Heidegger's, inauthenticity is connected to the risk of getting lost in the negative aspects of "*das Man*" much more in her philosophy than in Sartre's. This is evident, for example, in her critique of the oppression of women in *The Second Sex*. She insists, time and again, that women have seldom had the chance to live according to human potentiality, to be free and authentic. Women have for the most part had to live according to "general opinion" and have had to conform to society's definition of Woman. For women, being the Other has meant being as others want them to be, not being self-defining, individualized subjects. The possibility of disclosing and realizing oneself as a subject has thus often been missing. Women have had to accept ready-made roles, such as mother and housewife. Following "general opinion" has been of extreme importance, since women's virtue has depended on doing so.

The above discussion has also made it clear that in Beauvoir's philosophy, as opposed to Heidegger's, the possibilities that a specific situation opens up for an individual to be free and authentic are the center of interest. One could say that Beauvoir draws Heideggerian conclusions that Heidegger himself does not draw. In Beauvoir's philosophy authenticity is explicitly related to a context of shared meanings and possibilities. The question of the conditions of authenticity is central, a question Heidegger rarely poses. In her answer the Marxist influence on her philosophy is apparent.

Heidegger does not analyze or criticize oppression. But he presupposes that authentic disclosure (resoluteness) also changes one's relation to others. According to Heidegger, "Dasein's resoluteness toward itself is what first makes it possible to let the Others who are with it 'be' in their ownmost potentiality-for-Being, and to co-disclose this potentiality in the solicitude which leaps forth and liberates" (*BT* 344 f.; *SZ* 298). In this quotation authentic disclosure is connected to the possibility of letting others also be their "potentiality-for-Being." Others can also be seen as present-at-hand or ready-to-hand, that is, more in the way entities appear, as something to use[27] – objects, not subjects, as Beauvoir expresses it – which means others are treated as means rather than as ends, something Beauvoir criticizes in *The Ethics of Ambiguity*.

Heidegger's indication of a relation between one's own authenticity and that of others is replaced in Beauvoir by insistence on interdependence. She declares that "To will oneself free is also to will others free" (*EA* 73; *PMA* 102). Neither for Beauvoir nor for Heidegger is freedom necessarily connected to conflict, as it is in Sartre's early philosophy. For Beauvoir, since we are interdependent, the other is not, ontologically speaking, a hindrance to my freedom but a condition for my freedom to be realized. Authenticity for Beauvoir is disclosing the world with and for others (see *EA* 71; *PMA* 100). On the other hand, since she focuses on conflict, in contrast to Heidegger but like Sartre and Hegel, others can very well appear, in the concrete situation, as a hindrance to my freedom. But she does not contend, as Sartre does in *Being and Nothingness*, that they always do.

Mitsein is, as mentioned, not in itself an ethical concept, although its ethical implications have been widely discussed, not only during the 1940s. Some commentators maintain that *Mitsein* can be developed into an ethical concept,[28] while others doubt that, pointing out that *Mitsein* for Heidegger most often seems to be related to inauthenticity, to being lost in "*das Man*." Another way of looking at it, as Hubert Dreyfus does, is to insist that *Mitsein* and "*das Man*" have two interrelated meanings: on the one hand, that we can neither understand anything nor disclose truth outside of a specific historical context, but, on the other hand, that truth is not to be found in general opinion, either. There is thus both something positive in *Mitsein* and "*das Man*," representing the shared world of practices and language, and something negative in that "*das Man*" also represents conformity.[29] On this interpretation, which corresponds to the one developed in this chapter, the fact that human being is *Mitsein* and "*das Man*" can be lived both authentically and inauthentically. I have pointed to this same pattern in Beauvoir's philosophy. An important difference is that unlike Heidegger, Beauvoir focuses on conflict and oppression. Authenticity is thus also related to how the ever-present possibility of conflict is lived.

If we maintain, with Heidegger and Beauvoir, that seeing human being as being-with gives a foundation for ethics, the question of what type of ethics remains unanswered, as does the question of the implications this foundation really has for one's relationships to others. This voyage of reading Beauvoir with Heidegger, limited as it is by the space of this chapter, concludes with these open questions.

NOTES

For valuable comments on this chapter I would especially like to thank Mats Furberg, but also Nancy Bauer, Claudia Card, Ulla Holm, Berit Larsson, and William McBride.

1 Elaine Marks (*Simone de Beauvoir: Encounters with Death*, New Brunswick, NJ: Rutgers University Press, 1973) discusses the influence of Heidegger's view of death on Beauvoir's work. Also, Margaret A. Simons, in her paper, "L'independence de la pensée philosophique de Beauvoir" at the Groupe d'Etudes Sartriennes conference "Sartre en parallele/s," 23–25 June 2000 in Paris, pointed to Heidegger's importance for Beauvoir.

2 See Bernhard Waldenfels, *Phänomenologie in Frankreich* (Frankfurt- on-Main: Suhrkamp, 1983), p. 34 and Tom Rockmore, *Heidegger and French Philosophy* (London and New York: Routledge, 1995), pp. 71–76.

3 *PL* (Harmondsworth: Penguin, 1981) 135 f.; *FA* 141 f.

4 Regarding Sartre's Heidegger-reading, Beauvoir writes that Sartre read Corbin's translation and Heidegger in German and discussed it with her (*PL* 355; *FA* 363). She mentions that she read Husserl in German (*PL* 201; *FA* 208).

5 Simone de Beauvoir, *Journal de guerre, septembre 1939 – janvier 1941* (Paris: Gallimard, 1990), pp. 53, 265, 362.

6 The entire text was published in French in 1953 in the review *Cahiers du sud* (Rockmore, *Heidegger and French Philosophy*, pp. 81–98).

7 Elsewhere I have indicated why Beauvoir's philosophy is best characterized as existential phenomenology. See Eva Gothlin, "Simone de Beauvoir's Existential Phenomenology and Philosophy of History in 'Le Deuxième sexe,'" in Lester Embree and Wendy O'Brien, ed., *The Existential Phenomenology of Simone de Beauvoir* (Dordrecht: Kluwer, 2001).

8 For these distinctions, see *BT* (Oxford: Blackwell, 1995) 59 ff.; *SZ* (Tübingen: Max Hiemayer, 1986) 35 ff.

9 Leslie Paul Thiele, *Timely Meditations: Martin Heidegger and Postmodern Politics* (Princeton, NJ: Princeton University Press, 1995), p. 45. See also Dana R. Villa, *Arendt and Heidegger: The Fate of the Political* (Princeton, NJ: Princeton University Press, 1996), p. 124.

10 Martin Heidegger, *Qu'est-ce que la métaphysique?*, translated by Henry Corbin (Paris: Gallimard, 1938), p. 15. Corbin translates *Erschlossenheit*

as *réalité-révélé* (reality-revealed), while Beauvoir, for the most part, uses *dévoiler* (disclose) or *dévoilement* (disclosure), occasionally *révéler* (reveal).

11 Jean Beaufret, "A propos de l'existentialisme (II): Martin Heidegger," *Confluences*, 3 (April 1945): 310.

12 Disclosure (*dévoilement*) does not have the same importance in Sartre's philosophy. Debra B. Bergoffen has also analyzed this concept ("Out from Under: Beauvoir's Philosophy of the Erotic," in Margaret A. Simons, ed., *Feminist Interpretations of Simone de Beauvoir*, University Park, PA: Pennsylvania State University Press, 1995, pp. 179–92, and *The Philosophy of Simone de Beauvoir: Gendered Phenomenologies, Erotic Generosities*, Albany, NY: State University of New York Press, 1997), but unlike my view, her view is that disclosure is a Husserlian concept.

13 In rendering "*faktische*" as "factical," I follow *BT* translators John Macquarrie and Edward Robinson, who coined the term "factically" for "*faktisch*" in order to keep that concept distinct from "*tatsächlich*" (factual) and "*wirklich*" (actual). *BT* 27, n. 2.

14 *SS* (London: Jonathan Cape, 1997) 287; *DS* 1 388.

15 Margaret A. Simons, "Beauvoir and Sartre: The Philosophical Relationship" in Hélène Vivienne Wenzel, ed., *Simone de Beauvoir: Witness to a Century* (New Haven, CN: Yale University Press, 1986); Sonia Kruks, *Situation and Human Existence: Freedom, Subjectivity and Society* (London: Unwin Hyman, 1990); and Eva Lundgren-Gothlin, *Sex and Existence: Simone de Beauvoir's "The Second Sex"* (London: Athlone, 1996; Hanover, NH: Wesleyan University Press, 1996).

16 See Lundgren-Gothlin, *Sex and Existence*. This reading of Beauvoir with Heidegger supplements that earlier analysis.

17 My translation, as in all cases where there is no reference to an English edition.

18 Judith Butler (*Gender Trouble: Feminism and the Subversion of Identity*, London and New York: Routledge, 1990) analyzes Beauvoir's characterization of femininity as becoming, but in a very different and interesting way. She sees it as a constant creation through repeated performances and does not relate it to Heidegger's philosophy.

19 On the concept of interdependence, see also Kruks, *Situation and Human Existence*.

20 *EN* (Paris: Gallimard, 1970 [1943]) 484 f., 497, 502; *BN* (New York: Philosophical Library, 1956) 413 f., 425, 492; DS 1 19.

21 My translation of "leur opposition s'est dessinée." Cf. *SS* 19.

22 Translation modified; cf. *DS* 1 19. Note that Beauvoir refers to "la réalité humaine," the French translation of "*Dasein*."

23 See Alexandre Kojève, *Introduction to the Reading of Hegel: Lectures on the Phenomenology of Spirit*, assembled by Raymond Queneau, trans. James H. Nichols, Jr. (New York: Basic Books, 1969) and Lundgren-Gothlin, *Sex and Existence*, pp. 56–82.

24 Alphonse de Waehlens, "La philosophie de Heidegger et le nazisme," *Les Temps Modernes*, 22 (July 1947). For another view of *Mitsein* and authenticity from the same time period, see Ferdinand Alquié, "Existentialisme et philosophie chez Heidegger (Fin)," *La Revue Internationale*, 4 April 1946.

25 Hubert L. Dreyfus argues, in *Being-in-the-World: A Commentary on Heidegger's "Being and Time,"* Division I (Cambridge, MA: MIT Press, 1999 [1991]), p. 151 f., that "das Man" should be translated as "the one" instead of "the They" (as Macquarrie and Robinson had translated it in *Being and Time*), since "the They" can give the impression that "das Man" is separate from us.

26 See ibid., p. 26 f.

27 See Thiele, *Timely Meditations*, p. 50.

28 Frederick A. Olafsen, *Heidegger and the Ground of Ethics: A Study of Mitsein* (Cambridge: Cambridge University Press, 1998) does this, proceeding from the fact that *Mitsein* is connected to solicitude (*Fürsorge*) in *BT*.

29 Dreyfus, *Being-in-the-World*, pp. 143, 154 f.

3   The body as instrument and
     as expression

Simone de Beauvoir's *The Second Sex* is well known for its negative descriptions of the female body.[1] Several interpreters claim that
Beauvoir presents the female body as a mere obstacle: being dominated by the cycles of menstruation, pregnancies, and nursing, the
female body severely limits the free choice and self-fulfillment of the
woman. Critics argue further that such a view of the female body is
partial, and worse, biased by a male – Sartrean or Cartesian – point
of view. According to the critics, Beauvoir ends up describing the
female body as a burden (*DS* II 511; *SS* 630) because she accepts
Sartre's voluntarist notion of subjectivity.[2]

This common reading of *The Second Sex* is mistaken. Beauvoir's
negative comments regarding the female body do not disclose her
fundamental concept of feminine embodiment. They constitute only
a provisional step in a more far-reaching argument. Beauvoir's discussion of femaleness can be understood only if its philosophical
starting points are understood and appreciated. The aim of this chapter is to clarify and make explicit these starting points. I argue that
Beauvoir's notion of embodiment is a critical elaboration of the description of the *living body* (*corps vivant, corps vécu*) that she found
in Merleau-Ponty's *Phenomenology of Perception*.[3]

Through Merleau-Ponty, Beauvoir was influenced by Edmund
Husserl, the founder of the phenomenological movement.[4] Thus
her work can be characterized as existentialist-phenomenological.
The traces of phenomenology that we find in *The Second Sex* are
not, however, from Husserl's early publications, which have been
criticized as logicistic and solipsistic. They stem, rather, from manuscripts in which Husserl focused on questions of corporeality and
intersubjectivity.[5]

So my chapter adds a new element to the literature that argues that Beauvoir's work is not a simple application of Sartre's philosophy.[6] But this is not the only result, for my argument also questions the more recent interpretation according to which Beauvoir based her thinking primarily on Martin Heidegger's concepts.[7]

Direct evidence of Beauvoir's engagement with phenomenology can be found in *The Second Sex*.[8] There Beauvoir tells us that the basic concepts of her work – the concepts of embodiment – are taken from the phenomenological tradition of thought. In the introduction she emphasizes several times that her description of sexual difference takes its starting point from the phenomenological understanding of the living body. She states: "In the perspective I am adopting – that of Heidegger, Sartre, and Merleau-Ponty – if the body is not a *thing* [*chose*], it is a situation: it is our grasp upon the world and the outline of our projects" (*DS* I 73; *SS* 66).[9] And again, "It is not the body-object [*corps-objet*] described by the biologist that actually exists, but the living body of the subject [*corps vécu*]" (*DS* I 78; *SS* 69).

Thus, the basis of Beauvoir's discussions of sexual difference is a methodic framework in which the body is described as a subject of perception, not as a bioscientific object. The body understood in this way is not determined by causal relations but is moved by motivational connections. Beauvoir reminds us about this starting point throughout her argumentation, from the introduction to the last pages of the book. At the very end she repeats again: "The body is never the *cause* of subjective experiences, since it is, under its objective shape [*figure*], the subject himself" (*DS* II 586; *SS* 682).

In order to understand Beauvoir's argument it is necessary to study the concept of the body as used by Heidegger, Sartre, and Merleau-Ponty. But if we agree to take such a step, we must go deeper into the phenomenological tradition, for these thinkers base their discussions of embodiment on Husserl's writings.

Husserl first introduced the concept of the living body (*Leib*) in his lectures of 1907 on objectivity and spatiality, *Thing and Space*.[10] Five years later he gave it an extensive explication in the second part of his *Ideas*.[11] This work, together with the first two parts of his *The Crisis of European Sciences and Transcendental Phenomenology*, first published in 1936, is the source of existentialist-phenomenological studies of embodiment and sexuality.

THE LIVING BODY IN THE NATURALISTIC ATTITUDE

The starting point of Husserl's analysis in *Ideas* II is the simple fact that we have two different kinds of experiences of material bodies. We perceive mere physical things (*Körper*), that is, pieces of inert matter (stone or metal, for example), and we experience living bodies: vegetable bodies, animal bodies, and human bodies, other people's bodies as well as our own.

Husserl points out that we can relate to living bodies in two fundamentally different ways. On the one hand, we can take the attitude of the natural scientist and abstract from the bodies we study all meaning, value, and purpose. Thus the bodies' positions and movements appear to us as mere effects of external and internal causes. We can then try to explain and predict their behavior by subsuming them under general laws. In the natural scientific attitude, we no longer experience people or human societies; "instead we experience merely material things"[12] (*Ideen* II 25; *Ideas* II 27).

On the other hand, we can – and do – relate to living bodies as meaningful and purposeful agents, "persons" in Husserl's terminology. In this case, our own activity and interest are not in explaining or predicting the behavior of others but in responding to their movements and gestures.

The first two extensive sections of Husserl's *Ideas* II are dedicated to a description and analysis of the living body as it is conceived in the natural scientific attitude. Nature, understood in this attitude, includes all material or spatiotemporal things. In addition to mere material bodies or physical things, it consists of the "psychic nature" founded on the material. Psychic nature is the object of the psychological sciences but is also presupposed by zoology and all other sciences of animal behavior. When the psyche is studied within the natural scientific attitude, however, it appears "as nothing *per se*," nothing more than a layer or stratum of the material.

The living body is a specific kind of material reality, because it is the meeting point of the physical and the psychical, a turning point (*Umschlagspunkt*) from one to the other. This said, we must make an observation about language: The metaphor of a "meeting point" or "turning point" is illuminating in conveying the idea of connection. It helps us realize that the physical and the psychic are fundamentally different but related. This is crucial in Hussserl's analysis. The metaphor is also problematic, however, in suggesting that the connection between body and soul is spatial in nature. Husserl rejects such an interpretation and emphasizes that we should not try to base our understanding of the body–soul relation on the model of two distinct entities.[13] The soul does not appear as part of the physical body. Nor do we see it beside the body. Nor is it inside or above the body. Instead, it appears as a reality *belonging* (*gehören*) to the body:

> The excess of reality beyond the mere physical thing is not something that can be separated off by itself, not something juxtaposed, but something *in* the physical thing [*an diesem*]. Thus it moves "along with" the thing and acquires its spatial determination by its being *in* something which is itself spatial [*an dem Räumlichen*]. [*Ideen* 11 176; *Ideas* 11 186]

According to Husserl, the living body is distinguished from mere physical things by four fundamental phenomena. First, the living body appears as a *field of sensations*. Feelings of touch, contact, pressure, movement, tension, warmth and cold, pleasure and pain are localized on the surface of the body and in its different organs. Second, the living body appears as the immediate *starting point* of all spontaneous, free movement. The body of an animal is the only thing that the animal can move immediately, without moving some other thing first, and conversely, the animal needs its own body to move all other things. Third, the living body functions as the *fixed point* in our perceptions of direction, distance, and movement. Other material things appear in relation to it: they are near or far, above or below, on the right-hand side or on the left-hand side. These determinations are not just additional figurative language but are presupposed by scientific descriptions of human and animal behavior. Fourth, the living body takes part in *causal relations*: it causes movements, and it reacts to changes, both within itself and in its environment.[14]

These are the main lines of the first description given by Husserl in *Ideas* 11. It is important to keep in mind that what is described here is the body *as* observed by a person living in the natural scientific attitude, for example, a zoologist observing, describing, and explaining the behavior of primates or insects. The description includes directional and theological features which later investigations show originating from another – the personalistic – attitude. However, the naturalist works on the hypothesis that all such features can be explained as features of a complex physical system.

Husserl reminds us about this starting point again and again when he is developing and specifying his description. His remarks aim at excluding fundamental misunderstandings. The order of his exposure is not the order of epistemological or ontological priority. Even though Husserl starts his book by illuminating the natural scientific attitude and its body-object, he rejects the idea that this is the only valid way of relating to the world. In Husserl's phenomenology the natural scientific attitude is secondary, dependent on a more profound connection.

THE LIVING BODY IN THE PERSONALISTIC ATTITUDE

The natural scientific attitude is based on a personalistic attitude that does not explain the behavior of the body but expresses itself in the body and thus addresses other bodies. In this case, our activity and interest are not in predicting the behavior of others but in responding to their movements and gestures. Husserl argues that the living body as an object of biological and psychological sciences is achieved only through the mental activity of abstraction. Originally, we see and hear bodies as full of meaning. This applies both to our own bodies and to the bodies of others, animals and humans.

The personalistic attitude does not posit the body as a research object but presupposes it as a nonthematized horizon of all activity, both everyday dealings and scientific practices. It is the basis for the meaningfulness of action, for its directions and purposes. The phenomenological method makes possible the study and description of this presupposition. Such a study shows that the living body presents itself originally as an expression (*Ausdruck*) of psychic life.

Bodily gestures, postures, and movements are expressions of the soul, of its meaning and the unity composed of these meanings. The soul binds bodily functions and parts together into a unity that cannot be broken up or divided into autonomous parts. Thus, the organs and movements of our bodies form a stylistic unity similar to that of the chapters, paragraphs, and sentences of a book. Husserl introduces the textual analogy as follows.

The thoroughly intuitive unity presenting itself when we grasp a person *as such* (e.g., when we, as persons, speak to them as persons, or when we hear them speak, or work together with them, or watch their actions) is the unity of the *"expression"* and the *"expressed"* that belongs to the essence of all comprehensive unities. This body–spirit unity is not the only one of this kind. When I read the "lines and pages" of a book or when I read in the "book" and grasp the words and sentences, then we are dealing with physical matters. The book is a body [*Körper*], the pages are sheets of paper, the lines are black marks and physical imprints at certain spots of these papers, etc. Is that what I grasp when I "see" the book, when I "read" the book, when I "see" that what is written is written, what is said is said? It is obvious that my attitude is here quite different. [*Ideen* II 236; *Ideas* II 248]

In this other attitude we study the marks on the sheets of paper as a meaningful whole. The personalistic attitude is not restricted to art and aesthetics but is also required in the activities of reading, quoting, referring, and interpreting.

In a similar way, we relate to living bodies. We do not explain or predict the movements of hands, facial expressions, or bodily postures but try to understand them and respond to their appeals, calls, and demands. The primordial relations of the life-world are not causal but motivational.

It is important to realize that Husserl's contribution to the later phenomenology of embodiment is not just in developing the distinction between the living body and the physical thing, or the distinction between objectifying and personalizing attitudes. What is original and pathbreaking in his phenomenology is a strong argument about the relation between the personalizing attitude and the objectifying attitude of the natural scientist. Husserl argues that the scientific attitude and its mere physical object are secondary, *dependent* on the primary personalistic attitude and its expressive objects. The natural scientific description requires that at least some bodies are treated in the personalizing way, full of meaning and intention. We cannot observe or experiment on living bodies – or on anything, for that matter – unless we relate to our own bodies and their organs as purposeful wholes, instruments of will and expressions of soul. This primary relation should not be taken for granted but should be subjected to critical reflection if philosophy is to be a rigorous science.

SEXUAL AND EROTIC BODIES

Husserl's work does not include a phenomenological analysis of sexuality or sexual difference. The problem of "the sexes" is mentioned in the later work, *The Crisis of European Sciences and Transcendental Phenomenology*, but not studied there either. The arguments and

analyses that Husserl develops regarding embodiment imply, however, that we can take three different attitudes toward the sexual
body: the natural scientific viewpoint, the personalistic stance, and
the phenomenological attitude. The last of these, the phenomenological attitude, allows us to study the relations between the two
other attitudes as well as the sexual body as it appears within them.
Such an investigation would form the basis for a phenomenology of
sexuality and sexual difference.

Fragments for such studies can be found in the work of French
thinkers who in the 1930s took their philosophical starting points
in Husserl's phenomenology. The early works of Sartre, Emmanuel
Lévinas, Merleau-Ponty, and Beauvoir all include elaborations of
Husserl's phenomenological description of the living body. What
is common to these thinkers is that they all focus their phenomenologies on affective experiences, on erotic perception, desire, and
love.

We know that Beauvoir studied some of Husserl's works in detail. In her autobiography she mentions reading Husserl's lectures
on internal time consciousness as well as Eugen Fink's interpretations (FA 231, 254; PL 201, 220).¹⁵ However, the main phenomenological influence that we can detect in The Second Sex comes from
Beauvoir's close contemporaries, Sartre, Lévinas, and Merleau-Ponty.
This she says explicitly, as the quote above shows: "in the perspective I am adopting – that of Heidegger, Sartre, and Merleau-Ponty –
if the body is not a thing, it is a situation: it is our grasp upon the
world and the outline of our projects" (DS 1 73; SS 66).

Beauvoir does not mention Lévinas in this context.¹⁶ But she does
point to Heidegger, which suggests the hypothesis that the basic
concepts of embodiment she uses in her analysis of sexuality are to
be found in Heidegger's Being and Time.¹⁷

Heidegger's early work, however, does not include a phenomenological description or analysis of our experience of living bodies.
Heidegger explicitly excludes the problematic of "bodily nature"
(Leiblichkeit) from his topics.¹⁸ He focuses his attention on our
being-in-the-world, a bodily relation, but he does not thematize the
body as an object of experience. Further, as Sartre points out (EN 423;
BN 498), Heidegger's Being and Time bypasses the problem of sexuality as a question of mere factuality. Jacques Derrida argues in two
essays in Psyché that the exclusion is not accidental but necessary

from the point of view of Heidegger's project. Heidegger did not just forget or ignore the topic of sexuality; his definition of phenomenology did not allow for such a study.[19]

Thus, Heidegger's influence on *The Second Sex* is – contrary to Beauvoir's own words – not in providing the concept of the living body, but rather in offering other central concepts, such as concepts of finitude and instrumentality (*DS* I 40; *DS* II 485; *SS* 39, 609).[20] We must look for a basic explication of the living body in the works of Beauvoir's close contemporaries.

Lévinas, Sartre, and Merleau-Ponty all wrote about the living body and its erotic and sexual dimensions. But they disagreed about several questions, both conceptual and methodological, in their readings of Husserl. They also cited and used each other's concepts and arguments, partly confirming and partly criticizing each other's results. Thus the problem of interpretation and influence is complex. What is clear, however, is that we can find two detailed explications of the sexual body in this literature, one presented by Sartre (*Being and Nothingness*) and another developed two years later by Merleau-Ponty (*Phenomenology of Perception*).

My argument is that Beauvoir's discussion of embodiment is more akin to Merleau-Ponty's than to Sartre's. I base this claim on both historical and systematic evidence. First, I show a historical connection between *The Second Sex* and *Phenomenology of Perception*, and second, I argue that we can find similar concepts, arguments, and metaphors in Merleau-Ponty's and Beauvoir's descriptions of the body, which are not found in Sartre's *Being and Nothingness*.

The historical examination helps to bring up an important fact about the goals that Beauvoir sets for *The Second Sex*. Her main aim, I will show, is neither defending women's rights (*DS* I 30; *SS* 28) nor explaining the destiny of the female sex by biological or social facts. Rather, Beauvoir wants to propose an ethical inquiry.

AGAINST NATURALISM AND DUALISM

We know that Beauvoir studied *Phenomenology of Perception* in detail, for she wrote a review of it for *Les Temps modernes* in 1945. Beauvoir begins her review by explaining why she thinks that phenomenology, in general, is a fruitful approach in human sciences. She writes, "One of the great merits of phenomenology is...in its abolishing of the opposition between the subject and the object. It is impossible to define an object apart from the subject by whom and for whom it is the object; and the subject reveals itself only in relation to the objects that it is engaged with" (PPMP 363).

These statements may sound trivial, Beauvoir remarks, but they have far-reaching philosophical implications: one can develop a genuine ethics only by taking the phenomenological understanding of the subject–object relation as the basis. According to Beauvoir, such an understanding is necessary for a sincere ethical commitment (PPMP 363; cf. DS 1 238, SS 172). In the essay *The Ethics of Ambiguity* Beauvoir explains further: what phenomenology shows is that all values are dependent on our activities – no value or end is absolutely given (PMA 21, 27–28, 34; EA 14, 18–19, 24, 49). She writes: "It is desire which creates the desirable, and the project that sets up the end. It is human existence which makes values spring up in the world on the basis of which it will be able to judge the enterprise in which it will be engaged" (PMA 22; EA 15).

Beauvoir rejects the naturalistic view according to which the sense and values of objects are independent of our activities. On the contrary, she argues, it is our activity that creates the sense and value that we find in the world. In *The Second Sex* she makes this claim in the case of sex: "It is by exercising sexual activity that men [human beings] define the sexes and their relations, just as they create the sense and the value of all the functions that they accomplish" (DS 1 39; SS 38; cf. DS 1 73; SS 66).

Beauvoir sees the main merit of Merleau-Ponty's work in its description of the body-subject. For Merleau-Ponty, she writes, quoting his words, the individual "is not a pure for-itself, nor a gap in being, as Hegel wrote, and Sartre repeated, but it is 'a hollow [creux], a fold [pli] which has been made and can be unmade'" (PPMP 367; PP 249; PP(tr.) 215). The contrast to Hegel's philosophy comes from Merleau-Ponty's original text. But the comment on Sartre is Beauvoir's addition. She explains further that Merleau-Ponty rejects Sartre's opposition between the for-itself and the in-itself and describes the bodily subject in its concrete existence and relations. Here her sympathies are clearly with Merleau-Ponty. For Beauvoir, Merleau-Ponty's phenomenological descriptions of the body, its spatiality, motility, sexuality, and expressivity are a "rich" and "convincing" source. Their additional merit is that they are not "violent." On the contrary, they suggest that we should adopt in our reflections the movement of life itself (PPMP 367).

Beauvoir's review testifies to her engagement with phenomenology. But it also shows that she saw clearly the difference between Merleau-Ponty's and Sartre's interpretations of Husserl's work and that she considered, in this phase of her thinking, Merleau-Ponty's nondualistic modification more promising on account of its ethical implications.[21] That she took this position is crucial from the point of view of understanding her aim in *The Second Sex*. I will shortly discuss the implications of Beauvoir's ethical stance for her discussion of sexual difference. The discussion shows that the bioscientific considerations that Beauvoir introduces in the beginning of the book are not the foundation of her explanation of women's position but, on the contrary, a further object of her critical inquiry.

The main problem with the standard reading – in both its feminist and nonfeminist versions – is that it does not recognize Beauvoir's ethical interests and their basis in existential phenomenology. The work is usually read as historical or sociological description or both. Contrary to such a reading, Beauvoir repeatedly states that the main framework of her inquiry is ethical. But for her, ethics is not a normative study based on the concepts of good and right. On the contrary, she argues in *The Ethics of Ambiguity* that ethics can only begin in a suspension of all value positings (*EA* 20–21, 186–87; *PMA* 14–15, 133–34; cf. *DS* I 239; *DS* II 496; *SS* 172, 618). The suspension makes it possible to realize that values depend on our activities. And this realization allows us to take responsibility for the values in force.

In the introduction to *The Second Sex* Beauvoir points out that all epistemic and theoretical projects are based on implicit values. She writes: "It is doubtless impossible to approach any human problem with a mind free from bias. The way in which questions are put, the points of view assumed, presuppose a relativity of interest; all characteristics imply values, and every objective description, so called, implies an ethical background" (*DS* I 30; *SS* 28).

This observation is true also, and especially, of the explanations and theories developed to account for the relations between women and men. In the introduction to her work, Beauvoir discusses three explanatory paradigms: the bioscientific, the psychoanalytic, and historical materialism. She argues that all these paradigms are useful but that they are also inadequate in leaving certain values unproblematized. The bioscientific paradigm takes as given the values of life and physical strength, the psychoanalytic paradigm assumes the supreme value of the phallus, and historical materialism bases its explanations on the value of the tool (*DS* 1 77, 93–95, 99–100, 105–06; *SS* 69, 82–83, 86–87, 91).

Beauvoir does not aim at adding new explanations to these three paradigms. Nor does she present a synthesis of the old ones. Instead, she proposes a radical investigation that questions the values forming the bases of theories and explanations of the relation between the sexes. And, taking one step further, she aims to problematize the activities these values depend on.

In the case of the bioscientific paradigm, this means that Beauvoir questions the goals of survival and reproduction that form the basis of all biological explanations of sexual relations. Woman is not defined by the functions of the womb or ovaries. Chromosomes, hormones, and reproductive organs are biological and biochemical abstractions made for the purposes of explanation and prediction; they are not elements of her concrete living body (*DS* 1 74; *SS* 66–67).

Thus, the bioscientific explanation that Beauvoir introduces at the beginning of her book is not her own. The biological facts of sexual reproduction are not presented naively and accepted, but are introduced for critical study. Beauvoir argues that philosophical inquiry into sexual hierarchy cannot be founded on the values of life, procreation, or physical strength. On the contrary, it must also include a critical examination of these values, how they are constituted, in what kinds of activities they are formed, and how these activities relate to sexuality and sexual difference (*DS* 1 71–77; *SS* 65–69). Beauvoir concludes the chapter on biological givens by writing: "The close bond between mother and child will be for her a source of dignity or indignity according to the value given to the child – which is highly variable – and this bond will be recognized or not according to social prejudices" (*DS* 1 77; *SS* 69).

Thus the basis of Beauvoir's inquiry into sexual difference is not the bioscientific notion of the body. It is, as she explicitly says, the concept of the body-subject. So in order to understand Beauvoir's claims about the specificity of women's bodies, we must study the two discussions of the living body with which she was acquainted, that of Sartre and that of Merleau-Ponty.

INSTRUMENTS AND EXPRESSIONS

The influence of Husserl's notion of the living body in Sartre and Merleau-Ponty is primarily in their common rejection of all naturalistic approaches to bodily activity and sexual behavior. Both aim at identifying the primary level of experience on which causal explanations depend. The body that can take part in causal interaction is a result of a process of objectification. The task of the phenomenologist is to inquire into the basis of this process. On this starting point Sartre and Merleau-Ponty agree.

However, Sartre's and Merleau-Ponty's phenomenologies relate differently to Husserl's writings. Sartre works with Husserl's early publications, and he is strongly influenced by Heidegger's criticism of them. Merleau-Ponty, in contrast, bases his study not just on publications but also on the manuscripts he studied in the Husserl archive in Louvain.

This historical fact helps to account for the main differences in the ways in which Sartre and Merleau-Ponty develop the phenomenological notion of the living body. A further difference is that Sartre's discussion of embodiment and sexuality is an elaboration of his principal distinction between two different modes of being: being-for-itself and being-in-itself. Against this, Merleau-Ponty argues that the distinction between being-for-itself and being-in-itself is an abstraction, a theoretical preconception that leads the pure description of experience astray.

Beauvoir's relation to this controversy is studied in Sonia Kruks' pathbreaking work, *Situation and Existence*. However, the full implications of the disagreement remain hidden as long as we fail to relate the discussion to Husserl's phenomenology of embodiment. From this point of view, the crucial difference between Sartre's and Merleau-Ponty's work is that Sartre discusses the living body mainly under the categories of instrumentality, whereas Merleau-Ponty follows Husserl's argument to its conclusions and ends up describing the body primarily as an expression.

For Sartre, consciousness is a lack of being, a nothingness, constantly surpassing the given order and orientation of things, annihilating it to create a new ordering. It is bound to things precisely because its original project is to transcend them.

The body for such a consciousness is a basic viewpoint and protoinstrument necessary for relating to things and manipulating them. It is not just any viewpoint or any instrument. This is because the body is not originally perceived as an instrument, not given to us primarily in that way. If it were, I could conceive myself using it with some further instrument, which is absurd. In other words, there is no distance between my consciousness and my body. Postulating such a distance would lead to an infinite regress. So instead of using its body, Sartre states, "Consciousness exists its body" (*EN* 369; *BN* 434).

Still, the body's instrumentality is implied by the way things appear to us. According to Sartre, the world is originally given to us as a practical world, composed of materials, tools, and utensils. It is a world structured by ends and means (*EN* 52, 362; *BN* 51, 425).

Here Sartre builds on Heidegger's description of the life-world as an aggregate of equipment (*Zeuge*). In *Being and Time* Heidegger argues against Husserl that we do not encounter the world primarily as just there (*da*), present-at-hand (*vorhanden*), but as ready-to-hand (*zu-handen*). We do not just look at things or listen to them but manipulate them and put them to use (*SZ* 67; *BT* 95), and accordingly, things appear to us primarily in the modes of serviceability, conduciveness, usability, and manipulability: "The wood is a forest of timber, the mountain a quarry of rock; the river is water-power, the wind is wind 'in the sails'" (*SZ* 70; *BT* 100).

Heidegger points out in passing that the body is given in work and production implicitly as the wearer and user of things (*Trager, Benutzer, Verbraucher; SZ* 70–71; *BT* 100). Sartre's analysis builds on this idea. For him, one's own body is a protoinstrument presupposed by the instrumentality of the world. Other bodies, however, are given as full-fledged instruments. They appear as tools that can be used in the making and managing of other tools. They are, "in a word, tool-machines" (*EN* 360; *BN* 422).[22]

For Merleau-Ponty, instrumentality is just one aspect of the living body, and it is not primary.[23] On a more primordial level, we relate to the world in an affective way. Things are not given to us as useful or suitable. Instead, they appear as attractive or repulsive, and we respond to their calls and appeals. A piece of metal is not primarily for hammering. It appears first as attractive to the hand. And the hand is not primarily for grasping or working. It is first given to us in its caressing and fumbling movements. The world is not a practical world of ends and means but an aesthetic world, and our relation to it is dialogical (*PP* 109–10, 161, 366; *PP*(tr.) 93, 139, 317).

The body, as a whole, is the expression of a way of being. It is neither a collection of entities nor an instrument but the revelation of a way of relating to the world, similar to an art work (*PP* 171, 176, 230; *PP*(tr.) 146, 150–51, 197–98).[24]

Beauvoir affirms this notion. In *The Ethics of Ambiguity* she writes, "The body itself is not a brute fact, it expresses our relationship to the world" (*PMA* 60; *EA* 41). *The Second Sex* extends the notion of the expressive body to the study of sexuality: "But if body and sexuality are concrete expressions of existence, it is with reference to this that their significance can be discovered" (*DS* I 87; *SS* 77).

But my body is not just a manifestation of my personal existence. It also expresses the prepersonal, anonymous way in which we all relate to the world. This is revealed in the study of affective perception. Merleau-Ponty argues that the faithful description of perceptual experience requires that we say that someone perceives in me, not that I perceive. I do not experience myself as the subject or agent of my seeing, hearing, and touching; instead, I experience someone in me (*PP* 186, 249, 277; *PP*(tr.) 160, 215–16, 240).

The prepersonal body should not be understood as a distinct entity but as an aspect or a layer of our experience. It is not another entity besides my body, but, rather, the internal fracture of my embodiment. It is the mute basis from which personal projects, decisions, volitions, and judgments are differentiated. Thus understood, the personal is like a figure that stands out from the background of the prepersonal, or, to use Merleau-Ponty's dynamic terminology, it is like a "fold which has been made and can be unmade."

I showed above that this is the main feature of Merleau-Ponty's phenomenology that Beauvoir brings up, in contrast to Sartre's thinking. Merleau-Ponty's work shows her that the individual body can be thought within the phenomenological framework as both separate from other bodies and bound to them. Its uniqueness and particularity do not have to mean opposition or detachment, but can be understood in terms of variation and change. This allows Beauvoir to set herself the task of describing the "common basis from which every singular feminine existence comes off [*s'enlever*]" (*DS* II 9; *SS* 33).

Her aim is not to fall back on bioscientific explanations or to propose a theory of changeless essences but to study the feminine variation of human experience.

LABOR AND LOVE

The Second Sex includes descriptions of instrumental relations between sexual bodies. But it clearly rejects the view according to which the body appears to us merely or primarily as an instrument. Beauvoir argues explicitly against this notion by presenting counterexamples. She aims to show that the instrumentalist notion is inadequate in describing feminine experiences. It exhibits a male point of view: "The world does not appear to woman 'an assemblage of utensils,' intermediate between her will and her goals, as Heidegger defines it: it is, on the contrary, obstinately resistant, indomitable" (*DS* II 485; *SS* 609) and "The masculine apparatus loses its power at the frontiers of the feminine realm. There is a whole region of human experience which the male deliberately chooses to ignore because he fails to *think* it: this experience woman *lives*" (*DS* II 501; *SS* 622).

These statements should be taken in their extreme form. Beauvoir is not just claiming that the world appears to a woman as an obstacle or a broken instrument. Rather, she claims that the conceptual framework of instruments is inadequate as a whole in the description and analysis of feminine experience. Things do not appear as useful or suitable. But neither are they given as useless or unsuitable. The world as revealed through the feminine body is not a practical world ready-to-hand. Instead, it is "dominated by fatality and traversed by mysterious caprices" (*DS* II 485; *SS* 609).

This is true especially of the experience of embodiment. The menstruating, impregnated, and lactating body does not appear to a woman as an instrument for her projects. But neither is it given as a simple obstacle. Instead, it presents itself as an alien vitality:

This mystery of a collar of blood (*fraise de sang*) that changes into a human being inside the mother's belly is one no mathematics can put in equation, no machine can hasten or delay; she feels the resistance of duration that the most ingenious instruments fail to divide or multiply; she feels it in her flesh, submitted to the lunar rhythms, and first ripened, then corrupted, by the years. [*DS* II 485; *SS* 609]

Beauvoir's idea here is not that the feminine body is an invalid body, as some readers have argued. But she does suggest that the feminine body reveals an alien vitality similar to that presented by sickened, diseased, aging, and infantile bodies (*DS* I 65, 400; *DS* II 101; *SS* 60, 286, 361). "Woman as man is her body, but her body is something other than herself" (*DS* I 67; *SS* 61).

Even though alien vitality is evident in the experience of pregnancy, it is not specific to women but belongs to everyone's life. Both men and women use their bodies as instruments of will. But both also experience in their bodies alien intentions (*DS* I 398; *DS* II 166, 658; *SS* 285, 406, 737).

So what is specific to a woman's embodiment is not that it includes forms of experience lacking in a man's experience. Rather, what is peculiar is that in a woman's experience, alien vitality has a different position than it has in a man's. It is not just now or then that alien intentionality is revealed to her, in sickness or in fatigue. Rather, it forms a continuous cyclic vein in the flow of her experiences. So the difference is not a difference in the elements of men's and women's experiences but in the temporal structures of their experiences.

It is not just the maternal body that functions in Beauvoir's argument as a counterexample to the instrumentalist notion of the living body. Beauvoir also describes the body of a loving woman. She argues that, when making love, women relate to their own bodies and their lovers' bodies in a specific way. The body of the beloved is not given to the woman as a tool. Rather, it appears as a possibility of a recreation (*DS* II 208; *SS* 436). Also, her own body lacks the aspects of instrumentality. Its movements are not directed to determinate ends. It does not aim at any specific state, satisfaction, orgasm, or even pleasure. Instead, it lingers in a state of nonsettlement.

Feminine enjoyment radiates throughout the whole body. It is not always centered in the genital system. Even when it is, the vaginal contractions constitute, rather than a true orgasm, a system of undulations that rhythmically arise, disappear and reform, attain from time to time a paroxysmal condition, become vague, and sink down without ever quite dying out. Because no definite term is set, pleasure extends toward infinity. [*DS* II 181–82; *SS* 416]

Thus Beauvoir argues that a woman experiences erotic love in her own specific way. Feminine sexuality "has its original structure"

(*DS* 11 194; *SS* 416). It is misrepresented when described with concepts developed to account for male eroticism (*DS* 1 79–93; *SS* 70–82).

Beauvoir's argument makes it clear that the special character of women's experience of embodiment has remained unrecognized in the traditions of science and philosophy. When men have generalized and theorized about human experience, they have assumed either that women live their bodies in the same way as men or else that the feminine mode of experience can be described as a deviant form of the masculine (*DS* 1 15, 79–81, 92–93; *SS* 15–16, 70–72, 81). Texts in which women describe their experiences have been neglected and ignored.

Male theorists have taken their own experiences as exemplary and have described the feminine not as a variation but as a deviation. Their perception and imagination have been guided by prejudices and habitual evaluations (*DS* 1 402–06; *SS* 288–91). This holds also for accounts of embodiment: "He sees his body as a direct and normal connection with the world, which he believes he apprehends in its objectivity, whereas he regards the body of woman as weighed down by everything peculiar to it, as an obstacle, a prison" (*DS* 1 15; *SS* 15).

One of Beauvoir's main aims in *The Second Sex* is to question the androcentric conception that identifies women with matter and men with spirit. The extensive third part of book 1, "Myths," tracks this opposition down to men's anxiety about their finitude and death.

Beauvoir attacks the notion of an opposition between women and men. But, with equal strength, she rejects the assumption of sameness. Women and men are not opposites, she argues, but neither are they identical. Rather than wavering between these alternatives, we need to start thinking in terms of difference. Beauvoir writes:

there will always be certain differences between men and women; her eroticism, and therefore her sexual world, have a singular form [*figure singulière*] of their own and therefore cannot fail to engender a singular sensuality, a singular sensitivity. Her relations to her own body, to that of the male, to the child, will never be identical with those the male bears to his own body, to the feminine body, and to the child. [*DS* 11 661, *SS* 740]

NOTES

1   *SS*, trans. H. M. Parshley (Harmondsworth: Penguin, 1952); *DS* 1 (Paris: Gallimard, 1993 [1949]); *DS* 11 (Paris: Gallimard, 1991 [1941]).

2 Such a reading is common in feminist discussions of the 1980s. But relatively recent feminist commentators accept it also. See, e.g., Carol McMillan, *Women, Reason and Nature: Some Philosophical Problems with Feminism* (Oxford: Blackwell, 1982), pp. 117-19, 139-40; Nancy Hartsock, "The Feminist Standpoint," in *Discovering Reality*, ed. Sandra Harding and Merrill B. Hintikka (Dordrecht: Reidel, 1983); Genevieve Lloyd, *The Man of Reason: "Male" and "Female" in Western Philosophy* (London: Methuen, 1984), pp. 86-102; Susan J. Hekman, *Gender and Knowledge: Elements of a Postmodern Feminism* (London and New York: Routledge, 1990), pp. 74-78; and Elisabeth Grosz, *Volatile Bodies: Toward a Corporeal Feminism* (Bloomington, IN: Indiana University Press, 1994), p. 15.

3 Maurice Merleau-Ponty, *The Phenomenology of Perception*, trans. Colin Smith (London and New York: Routledge, 1995); *Phénoménologie de la perception* (Paris: Gallimard, 1993 [1945]).

4 Jo-Ann Pilardi argues that the phenomenological influence comes to Beauvoir's work from Sartre's interpretation and criticism of Husserl (*Simone de Beauvoir Writing the Self*, Westport, CN: Greenwood Press, 1999, pp. 6-7, 40). My reading agrees with hers in seeing Beauvoir as a phenomenologist, but differs in arguing that Beauvoir's phenomenology is not Sartrean but is more akin to the philosophy of Merleau-Ponty. See Sara Heinämaa, "Woman – Nature, Product, Style? Rethinking the Foundations of Feminist Philosophy of Science," in Lynn Hankinson Nelson and Jack Nelson, ed., *A Dialogue Concerning Feminism, Science, and Philosophy of Science* (Dordrecht: Kluwer, 1996), pp. 289-308; "What Is a Woman? Butler and Beauvoir on the Foundations of the Sexual Difference," *Hypatia*, 12, 1 (winter 1997): 20-39; and "Simone de Beauvoir's Phenomenology of Sexual Difference," *Hypatia*, 14, 4 (fall 1999): 114-32. My reading joins that of Sonia Kruks in *Situation and Human Existence: Freedom, Subjectivity and Society* (London and New York: Routledge, 1991) in explicating the connection between Beauvoir's work and Merleau-Ponty's phenomenology.

5 This side of Husserl's work has recently been studied closely by several scholars. See, e.g., Natalie Depraz, *Transcendance et incarnation: Le statut de l'intersubjectivité comme altérité à soi chez Husserl* (Paris: Vrin, 1995); Anthony Steinbock, *Home and Beyond: Generative Phenomenology after Husserl* (Evanston, IL: Northwestern University Press, 1995); Dan Zahavi, *Husserl und die transzendentale Intersubjektivität: Eine Antwort auf die sprachpragmatische Kritik* (Dordrecht, Boston, and London: Kluwer, 1996).

6 For this argument, see Margaret A. Simons' essays, collected in *Beauvoir and "The Second Sex"* (Lanham, MD: Rowman & Littlefield, 1999); Eva

Lundgren-Gothlin, *Sex and Existence: Simone de Beauvoir's "The Second Sex"* (London: Athlone, 1996; first edn Swedish, 1991); and Debra B. Bergoffen, *The Philosophy of Simone de Beauvoir: Gendered Phenomenologies, Erotic Generosities* (Albany, NY: State University of New York Press, 1997).

7 Such an argument is developed by Eva Gothlin. See chapter 2 above.

8 Beauvoir describes her relation to phenomenology in her multivolume autobiography. See Heinämaa, "Beauvoir's Phenomenology of Sexual Difference," pp. 119–21.

9 I give my own translations of Beauvoir's text because prevailing translations are misleading and even false. Here Beauvoir's statement is almost a word-for-word quote from Sartre, who says, "Thus the world as a correlate of the possibilities which I *am* appears, from the moment of my upsurge, as the enormous outline of all my possible actions" (*EN* [Paris: Gallimard, (1998) 1943] 362; *BN* [New York: Washington Square Press, 1966] 425). Note, however, that Beauvoir substitutes the plural "our projects" for Sartre's singular "my possible actions."

10 Edmund Husserl, *Thing and Space: Lectures of 1907*, ed. and trans. Richard Rojcewicz (Dordrecht: Kluwer, 1997).

11 Edmund Husserl, *Ideen zu einer reinen Phänomenologie und Phänomenologischen Philosophie, Zweites Buch: Phänomenologische Undersuchung zur Konstitution* (hereafter *Ideen* 11) was redacted by Husserl's assistants Edith Stein and Ludwig Landgrebe. Stein's work was not restricted to the mere editing of Husserl's manuscript and working notes. She revised the manuscripts significantly and independently wrote several sections of the volume, basing her work on her doctoral thesis, *On the Problem of Empathy* (1916, trans. Waltraut Stein, The Hague: Martinus Nijhoff, 1970). *Ideen* 11 was first published in German only in 1952, long after Husserl's death. But Merleau-Ponty studied it as a manuscript in 1937 in the Husserl archive in Louvain. On Merleau-Ponty's relation to Husserl's manuscripts and unpublished works, see Ted Toadvine, "Merleau-Ponty's Reading of Husserl: A Chronological Overview," *Merleau-Ponty's Reading of Husserl*, ed. Lester Embree and Ted Toadvine (Dordrecht: Kluwer, 2001).

12 *Ideen* 11, ed. Marly Biemel (The Hague: Martinus Nijhoff, 1952), p. 25; *Ideas* 11 27.

13 In *Phenomenology of Perception* Merleau-Ponty points out that Husserl's description of the living body is anticipated by René Descartes' discussion of the mind–body union in the *Passions of the Soul* (1649, trans. Stephen Voss, Indianapolis: Hackett, 1989). On this connection see Sara Heinämaa, "From Decisions to Passions: Merleau-Ponty's Interpretation of Husserl's Reduction" in *Merleau-Ponty's Reading of Husserl*, ed. Embree and Toadvine.

14 On the difference between living bodies and mere material things, see Dan Zahavi, "Husserl's Phenomenology of the Body," *Etudes Phénoménologiques*, 19 (1994): 63–84, and Donn Welton, "Soft, Smooth Hands: Husserl's Phenomenology and the Lived-Body," in Donn Welton, ed., *The Body: Classic and Contemporary Readings* (Malden, MA and Oxford: Blackwell, 1999).

15 *La Force de l'âge* (Paris: Gallimard, 1995 [1960]); *The Prime of Life*, trans. Peter Green (Harmondsworth: Penguin, 1981).

16 Beauvoir refers critically to Lévinas' *Time and the Other* (1947, trans. Richard A. Cohen, Pittsburgh: Duquesne University Press, 1987), when discussing the negative meanings given to femininity (*DS* 1 15–16, 304; *SS* 16, 218). For more detailed discussion of Beauvoir's argument against Lévinas, see Heinämaa, "Beauvoir's Phenomenology of Sexual Difference," pp. 124–26. Despite Beauvoir's criticism, she seems to accept Lévinas' anti-Hegelian argument according to which men and women are originally not in relations of opposition or conflict but form non-hierarchical relations, pairs, and couples (*DS* 1 19, 75, 239; *SS* 19, 67–68, 172).

17 *Being and Time*, trans. John Macquarrie and Edward Robinson (Oxford: Blackwell, 1992).

18 *SZ* (Tübingen: Max Hiemeyer, 1927) 108; *BT* 143. Heidegger addressed the "problem of the phenomenology of the body" later in his *Zollikoner Seminare* [1959] (Frankfurt-on-Main: Klostermann, 1987). On his description of the body and its relation to Sartre's and Merleau-Ponty's works, see Richard R. Askay, "Heidegger, the Body, and the French Philosophers," *Continental Philosophy Review*, 32 (1991): 29–35; cf. Maria Villela-Petit, "Heidegger's Concept of Space," in Christopher Macann, ed., *Critical Heidegger* (London and New York: Routledge, 1996).

19 Jacques Derrida, "Le Main de Heidegger: Geschlecht II," *Psyché* (1987) and "Geschlect: différence sexuelle, différence ontologique," *Psyché* (1987).

20 On these connections, see chapter 2 in this volume.

21 Beauvoir took a stand on several disagreements between Sartre and Merleau-Ponty. In 1955 she wrote an article, "Merleau-Ponty et pseudo-sartreanism" ("Merleau-Ponty and Pseudo-Sartreanism"), defending Sartre's ontology and dialectics against the attack Merleau-Ponty launched in "Sartre et ultrabolshevism" ("Sartre and Ultrabolshevism"), *Les Adventures de la dialectique* (1955) (translations of both essays are included in Jon Stewart, ed., *The Debate Between Sartre and Merleau-Ponty*, Evanston, IL: Northwestern University Press, 1998, pp. 448–91 and 355–447). The discussion did not touch upon the phenomena of embodiment, but instead focused on the ideas of subjectivity, freedom, and

temporality that were crucial to Sartre's and Merleau-Ponty's political thinking. Beauvoir's argument was that Merleau-Ponty systematically ignores the philosophical contexts of Sartre's statements and thus ends up misreading them grossly.

22 This is also true of my own body as it appears to the Other. For Sartre these two phenomena are identical: "To study the way in which my body appears to the Other or the way in which the Other's body appears to me amounts to the same thing" (EN 379; BN 455).

23 For a more detailed explication of the differences between Sartre's and Merleau-Ponty's descriptions of the living body, see Martin Dillon, "Sartre on the Phenomenal Body and Merleau-Ponty's Critique," in Stewart, Debate Between Sartre and Merleau-Ponty, pp. 121–43.

24 For the implications of this conception of the body, see Heinämaa, "Woman – Nature, Product, Style" and "What is a Woman?"

4 Beauvoir and Merleau-Ponty on ambiguity

Ambiguity is arguably the most important idea in Beauvoir's philosophy.[1] This chapter argues that Beauvoir's idea of ambiguity has much more in common with Merleau-Ponty's idea of ambiguity than with Sartre's. Beauvoir's philosophy of ambiguity and Merleau-Ponty's philosophy of ambiguity complement each other.

Beauvoir and Merleau-Ponty were friends[2] and knew each other's work. In a 1945 commentary on Beauvoir's *L'Invitée* (*She Came to Stay*), Merleau-Ponty says this novel portrays a genuine morality that does not seek to dispel our fundamental ambiguity.[3] In a later prospectus of his own work, Merleau-Ponty declares that establishing a "good ambiguity" "would...give us the principle of an ethics,"[4] but he never developed that ethics. Shortly after his review of *L'Invitée*, Beauvoir wrote a review of Merleau-Ponty's *Phénoménologie de la Perception* (*Phenomenology of Perception*) in *Les Temps modernes*, a journal that both had helped to found and on whose editorial board both served. There Beauvoir praises phenomenology for "abolishing the subject–object opposition" that education erects in wrenching the living, meaningful world away from children and substituting a universe of frozen, independent objects. Ethics teaches children to renounce their subjectivity in favor of universal laws, yet they retain a sense of personal uniqueness and intimacy with the world in the spontaneous movement of their life. Beauvoir says phenomenology addresses and abolishes this split. She insists that only phenomenology can provide the foundation for an ethics we could embrace "wholly and sincerely" (PPMP 363; my translation).

Beauvoir makes it very clear that this foundational phenomenology is Merleau-Ponty's, not Sartre's. The sentence immediately following her insistence on ethics' need for phenomenology declares: "That's why Merleau-Ponty's *Phenomenology of Perception* [is] ... a book which interests the whole man and every man: the human condition is at stake there." Beauvoir notes that Sartre "stresses primarily the opposition of the for-itself and the in-itself" and the "absolute freedom" of the former, whereas "Merleau-Ponty on the contrary devotes himself to describing the concrete character of the subject who is never, according to him, a pure for-itself." For Sartre, consciousness is "a hole in being," whereas for Merleau-Ponty consciousness is incarnated in a body possessing a prepersonal relationship to the world. Beauvoir emphasizes the importance of Merleau-Ponty's phenomenological description of the lived body and of his analysis of pathological experience. She notes that for Merleau-Ponty, "perception is communication and communion" with the world. By restoring our body Merleau-Ponty also restores the world to us. Beauvoir concludes that besides being convincing, one of the merits of *Phenomenology of Perception* is that "it does not ask us to do violence to ourselves; on the contrary, it proposes that we espouse the very movement of life" (PPMP 363–67). Beauvoir's review clearly sides with Merleau-Ponty's phenomenology – not Sartre's – as providing the basis for an ethics that we could wholeheartedly embrace.

Beauvoir's *Pour une morale de l'ambiguïté* (*The Ethics of Ambiguity*) attempts to construct such an ethics. This work first appeared in four installments in *Les Temps modernes*, approximately one year after her review of Merleau-Ponty's *Phenomenology of Perception*. The first and third installments appeared in the same issues that carried portions of Merleau-Ponty's *Humanisme et terreur* (*Humanism and Terror*). Yet Beauvoir's *Ethics of Ambiguity* does not mention Merleau-Ponty. This silence is all the more striking since Beauvoir refers to Hegel, Marx, Kant, Sartre, Descartes, Kierkegaard, Heidegger, Plato, Nietzsche, Bataille, Montaigne, Husserl, Spinoza, Socrates, and Fichte. Yet *The Ethics of Ambiguity* has more affinity with Merleau-Ponty's philosophy than with that of any philosopher mentioned – including Sartre. In fact, the idea of ambiguity is so central to Merleau-Ponty's philosophy that he is known as the philosopher of ambiguity. As they had not quarreled, the only explanation I can suggest for the glaring omission of Merleau-Ponty's name is Beauvoir's personal commitment to Sartre.

Both in her written works and in interviews Beauvoir consistently and misleadingly portrayed her thought as simply derivative of Sartre's. In *Force of Circumstance* she indicates that her *Ethics of Ambiguity* is based on Sartre's *Being and Nothingness*; and in *The Ethics of Ambiguity* she names Sartre immediately after a passage that echoes Merleau-Ponty perhaps more than any other passage in the work (*FC* 75; *EA* 121–22).[5] I suggest it is precisely because there were such signal reasons to refer to Merleau-Ponty in *The Ethics of Ambiguity* that Beauvoir felt constrained not to do so. She may have thought – or hoped – that not mentioning his name in the work would somehow hide its strong affinity with Merleau-Ponty's philosophy – or at least not draw attention to it. Among the many philosophers mentioned, none was likely to be construed as challenging her commitment to Sartre. The relative paucity of commentaries linking Beauvoir's and Merleau-Ponty's philosophies attests to the success of her strategy.[6] Given this strategic omission of Merleau-Ponty's name, it is not surprising that Beauvoir's explicit descriptions of ambiguity do not adequately convey her idea of ambiguity.

"Ambiguity" comes from the Latin *ambiguitas*, meaning doubt, uncertainty, or paradox. The adjective *ambiguus* means ambiguous, obscure, dark, wavering, changeable, doubtful, uncertain, disputed, unreliable, and untrustworthy.[7] We generally associate ambiguity with lack or failure, and consider these as shortcomings (for example, lack of clarity or specificity, failure to draw distinctions, or failure to "get to the point"). Philosophically, this negative approach to ambiguity draws on the Cartesian project of achieving "indubitable certainty" through a truth criterion of clarity and distinctness. Descartes couples certainty with truth, and links truth with moral virtue and error with moral weakness. He argues that "whatever I clearly and distinctly perceive [by the understanding] is necessarily true." Further, Descartes argues that if I judge what "I apprehend more obscurely and confusedly," "my will... easily turns aside from truth and goodness; and so I fall into both error and sin."[8] Cartesian philosophy strives to eliminate ambiguity, because it considers uncertainty and indistinctness to be highly undesirable epistemologically and ethically.

To appreciate what ambiguity means for Beauvoir and Merleau-Ponty, we must relinquish the traditional approaches and not insist on achieving a completely clear conception of ambiguity in their philosophies. Merleau-Ponty makes this point particularly well in a discussion at an international conference in 1951:

MR. MERLEAU-PONTY: By definition, it seems that there cannot be any consciousness of ambiguity without ambiguity of consciousness... From the moment you assume that consciousness of ambiguity is perfectly clear ... and ambiguity is perfectly ambiguous, there is no more consciousness of ambiguity. You see ambiguity as an omnipotent thought might see it. In your eyes it's no longer ambiguity...

MR. CAMPAGNOLO: Is there a notion of ambiguity which isn't ambiguous?

MR. MERLEAU-PONTY: I said that if one could conceive ambiguity with total clarity, it would no longer be ambiguous. Consequently, you're right.[9]

We must refrain from trying to clarify ambiguity through explanations or definitions. Explanations assume we can "unfold" ambiguity, "spread it out" in front of us, and analyze it.[10] Definitions assume we can circumscribe, capture, and fix it. Such attempted clarifications miss the very meaning of ambiguity. Ambiguity separated from experience is no longer ambiguity. Beauvoir's and Merleau-Ponty's philosophical method is descriptive, letting us understand ambiguity without destroying it. For Beauvoir and Merleau-Ponty, ambiguity is not ambivalence, equivocation, dualism, or absurdity. Ambiguity characterizes our existence and involves an irreducible indeterminacy, and multiple, inseparable significations and aspects.

The epigram and opening sentence of *The Ethics of Ambiguity* both quote Montaigne rather than Merleau-Ponty, and the first few paragraphs construe ambiguity as ambivalence, paradox, and dualism. This suggests – misleadingly – that Beauvoir's idea of ambiguity is simply Sartrian, and her subsequent summary of Sartre's position is designed to confirm that impression. However, Beauvoir's emphasis on ambiguity as paradox enables her to go beyond Sartre's philosophy without appearing to do so. A paradox contains elements that seemingly or actually contradict each other. In her *Ethics of Ambiguity* Beauvoir actually juxtaposes her own idea of ambiguity with Sartre's. Yet that juxtaposition has the appearance of being nothing but an elaboration of Sartre's paradoxical ambiguity. Beauvoir's idea of ambiguity contradicts Sartre's in certain important respects, but also retains some of its elements. Her conception emphasizes attachment, joy, and a positive bond with others, whereas Sartre's emphasizes uprooting, nausea, and conflict with others. Focusing on ambiguity as paradox allows Beauvoir to mask the evident incompatibility of these two conceptions – or at least to render it less obvious – by implying that both conceptions are merely elements of an elaborated Sartrian view.

Beauvoir asserts that "the most fundamental" ambiguity of the human condition is the tragic paradox "that every living movement is a sliding toward death." Those who face this paradox also find "that every movement toward death is life ... thus the present must die so that it may live"(EA 127, 7). This most basic ambiguity subtends several other paradoxical ambiguities of the human condition. We are each a consciousness of the world, yet are part of it and feel crushed by things. Each one of us is a sovereign and unique subject, yet we share this with everyone else. All are simultaneously subjects for themselves and objects for others. Although sovereign subject, each is an individual who depends on the collectivity. Beauvoir points out that Sartre's Being and Nothingness defines us by ambiguity as beings "whose being is not to be." For Sartre, we make ourselves "a lack of being" so that being might be. Our anguished awareness of ourselves as "a lack of being" prompts us to strive for an impossible synthesis of being for-ourselves and in-ourselves. Sartre declares that we are a "useless passion" because that attempt fails.

Beauvoir acknowledges that Sartre stresses this inevitable failure above all; yet she insists this does not imply pessimism or unhappiness. She argues that the failure is itself ambiguous. It involves a choice (the attempt itself), makes an ethics possible, and enables us to create meanings, values, goals, and reasons that justify our existence. We thus "deny the lack as lack," "take delight" in attempting the unrealizable synthesis, and experience success by affirming ourselves joyfully "as a positive existence" (EA 9–15). Under cover of merely indicating the implications of Sartre's philosophy of ambiguity, Beauvoir has juxtaposed her own, which is in fact at odds with his.

To appreciate how Beauvoir's idea of ambiguity differs from Sartre's, it is worth summarizing Sartre's position. In Being and Nothingness Sartre argues that because consciousness is always consciousness of something, there is necessarily a noncoinciding, a gap, between consciousness and its object. As conscious beings we are aware of ourselves (we are "for-ourselves") and aware of the world (an "in-itself"). This awareness means that we do not coincide with ourselves or the world, that we "wrench" ourselves away from both precisely so as to be this consciousness. Consciousness is this uprooting, this "nihilating spontaneity" – the sheer activity of bringing about the noncoincidence with its object. The "surging up" of consciousness as sheer nihilation is the creating of "a hole" in being and the revealing of being as the object of consciousness.

For Sartre, nihilating and disclosing are one and the same activity, which is consciousness. This sheer spontaneity, this noncoinciding, disclosing activity of consciousness, is absolute freedom. As such, consciousness lacks a foundation, and we experience this ineradicable lack in anguish. Hence we seek to appropriate a foundation for ourselves – to fill up the "hole" in being – without eliminating our existence as a consciousness (i.e., as a freedom). This endeavor, which necessarily fails, may involve various strategies of "bad faith," whereby we attempt to deceive ourselves about existing as a freedom. Lack also characterizes our relation to time, to our body, and to other people. Thus we are our past, present, and future; yet we are not reducible to (that is, do not coincide with) any one of these. We are our body; yet our body is also an object in the world, and we as consciousness are not that object. Sartre says: "A dull and inescapable nausea perpetually reveals my body to my consciousness" (BN 804; see also pp. 563, 126, 408, 434).[11] The "taste" of our necessary connection with our past and with the world is nausea. Nausea is the "taste" of our existence as freedom – a "taste" that Sartre's 1938 novel Nausea describes more fully.

For Sartre, our presence in the world is a "fall," a "degeneration"; our existence is an "exile" amidst things whose primary meaning is "adversity and utilizable instrumentality." Our relations with other people are characterized by "insecurity, danger, confrontation" and "conflict." Sartre asserts that "the very meaning" of freedom is to surge up in the world as "confronting others," and that these others try to objectify us. Our only recourse is to respond by attempting to objectify them instead. We are thus irremediably caught in a circle of constantly seeking to enslave the other and to escape such enslavement ourselves. Others inevitably impose an alien meaning on us and limit our freedom. Once again there is a gap, a noncoincidence. This time it is between our existence as consciousness and our being for other people who try to reduce us to the body as object. We are the alienating image others have of us; yet we are not reducible to our "being-for-others." Our existence as consciousness requires "negating" the others; hence unity with others is theoretically and practically "unrealizable" (*BN* 802 ["Facticity"], 126, 651, 377, 472–77, 555, 568–71, 617, 623, 651–57, 671–74, 784, 797).

According to Sartre, "The essence of the relations between consciousnesses is not the *Mitsein* [Being-with]; it is conflict" (*BN* 555). We cannot escape this conflictual, alienating situation, despite the fact that it exists only through our freedom. Sartre calls this the "paradox of freedom": "there is freedom only in a situation, and there is a situation only through freedom" (*BN* 598–99). Sartre says that "the situation is an ambiguous phenomenon in which it is impossible... to distinguish the contribution of freedom from that of the brute existent" (that is, the "given") (*BN* 597). Our fundamental project in this situation is the vain attempt to give ourselves a foundation by objectifying and appropriating others. Our inevitable failure "dooms" all our activities to "equivalence," so that solitary drinking and leading a country amount "to the same thing" (*BN* 797, 472–77).

Sartre's philosophy of ambiguity as set out in *Being and Nothingness* is thus extremely negative in its emphasis on uprooting, nausea, conflict, lack, and failure. The ambiguity is predominantly paradoxical, focusing on the contradictory incorporation of being and not-being that is involved in the phenomenon of noncoincidence. In describing the situation as "an ambiguous phenomenon," Sartre gives another meaning to ambiguity: the indistinguishability of components – be they aspects, or factors, or elements. However, this type of ambiguity is more prevalent in Beauvoir's and Merleau-Ponty's philosophies of ambiguity than in Sartre's.

In her *Ethics of Ambiguity* Beauvoir refers to "uprooting or tearing away," and to conflict, lack, and failure. This gives the impression that her philosophy of ambiguity is simply an extension of Sartre's, whereas it in fact counters the latter in important respects and is fundamentally positive. Beauvoir retains the idea of lack and agrees that this lack is ineradicable. However, she insists it is a mistake to define us as a lack as such, rather than "as the positive existence of a lack." She argues that we can transform the "negativity" of noncoinciding, which we are "originally," into an exact coinciding with ourselves "as a positive existence." Although we never lose "the desire to be that being of whom [we] have made [ourselves] a lack," we can choose to enjoy this permanent "tension" of desiring "an impossible possession." In doing so, we negate the lack as negativity, as "lack." We affirm ourselves positively, and transform our original noncoincidence into an exact self-coincidence (*EA* 57, 118–19, 12, 13). In Sartre's philosophy of ambiguity, such exact self-coincidence would spell the death of consciousness.

In arguing for the possibility of self-coincidence, Beauvoir emphasizes the idea of disclosure. Ostensibly merely noting the implications of Sartre's position, she distinguishes between desiring being and desiring the disclosure of being. She declares that unlike the desire to be, the desire to disclose being is realizable. Beauvoir asserts that fulfillment here does not eliminate the lived distance required for disclosure. Hence we can delight in disclosing being without trying to "trap" it. This desire to disclose being involves "uprooting" ourselves so as to bring about its presence to us, and our presence to it. Beauvoir indicates that paradoxically, "uprooting" ourselves from the world enables us to "root" ourselves in the world. Further, the meaning of our situation "surges up" only in virtue of our disclosing rupture, and this disclosing rupture is the very movement of freedom. By actively willing it we "root" ourselves in the world, while retaining the tension necessarily involved in the lived distance of disclosure. Beauvoir adds that willing freedom is the same choice as willing to disclose being (*EA* 12, 30, 19, 20, 23–24, 70, 78, 66).[12]

Beauvoir returns repeatedly to the theme of "disclosing being," perhaps because it plays a major part in Sartre's *Being and Nothingness*.[13] Retaining its centrality reinforces the misleading impression that her *Ethics of Ambiguity* is purely Sartrian. Perhaps owing to her personal commitment to Sartre, Beauvoir attempts to transform the disclosure of being from a negative into a positive notion, under the guise of simply explicating Sartre's position. However, the idea of disclosure and its coupling with the notion of rupture are fundamentally at odds with her positive philosophy of ambiguity. Disclosure implies passivity or unresponsiveness on the part of the disclosed, rather than the communication and communion with the world that Beauvoir commended in her review of Merleau-Ponty's *Phenomenology of Perception*. Disclosure suggests the subject–object opposition and the world of independent, frozen objects that she deplored.

Beauvoir praised the *Phenomenology of Perception* for not asking us to do violence to ourselves. The Sartrian linking of disclosure with rupture – which Beauvoir retains – requires that we do violence to ourselves. As Merleau-Ponty shows, tearing ourselves away from being precludes becoming rooted, engaging freedom in the world, and creating meaning. Rupture with being produces a hole and destroys a lived distance. It eliminates any possibility of establishing the intimacy with the living, meaningful world that Beauvoir esteemed in her review of Merleau-Ponty's book. Unfortunately, she cannot succeed in her attempt to convert uprooting into rooting, rupture into bond, and nihilating spontaneity into engaged freedom.[14] Rooting, bonding, and engagement require that the Sartrian notion of disclosing rupture with being be abandoned.

Despite this significant flaw, Beauvoir's philosophy of ambiguity differs profoundly from Sartre's and repeatedly tacitly contests his. For Beauvoir, unlike Sartre, our presence in the world is not inevitably a degeneration, exile, and defeat; the resistance of things sustains our actions "as air sustains the flight of the dove." Contrary to Sartre, Beauvoir contends (problematically, as indicated above) that we can convert negativity into positivity by "assuming" and positively concretizing our original, sheer spontaneity. Consequently, we can make our presence in the world a self-fulfillment, joy, and "triumph." Beauvoir asserts that original, absolute freedom is not only "completely inner and...abstract," but also "stupid" and "absurd" when considered simply "as a pure contingency," "a given spontaneity." If we are "[t]o exist genuinely," we must "refuse to lose [ourselves]" in that sheer spontaneity (EA 81, 25–28, 12–14).

Beauvoir insists (problematically) that we must engage freedom in the world by converting purely "natural freedom" into "ethical freedom" through an act of will (simultaneously disclosure), in which we make freedom the goal of a concrete and particular action. We thereby create a legitimation for our will and a foundation for our existence. If we consistently choose to confirm this act of will, our freedom will be "a creative freedom [which] develops happily." Far from being doomed to equivalence, our actions can confirm or deny "ethical freedom." If we "choose not to will [ourselves] free," we forego experiencing the joy of "a creative freedom," and fail to fulfill our existence (EA 78, 24–28, 32–34).

Willing and acting imply temporality. For Sartre, temporality is the subjective process whereby consciousness as "nihilating spontaneity" continuously brings about a noncoincidence with its object. Sartre describes this ongoing project of "nihilating" noncon-scious being (the "in-itself") as a ceaseless fleeing, on the part of con-sciousness, from its past toward its projected future. Unlike Sartre, Beauvoir emphasizes the profoundly positive character of temporal-ity. Thanks to temporality we are able to develop our will, choose a goal, decide on a course of action, implement our decisions, confirm our freedom, and justify our existence. Beauvoir describes the con-version of sheer spontaneity into creative freedom as a supremely positive process: "The creator leans upon anterior creations in or-der to create the possibility of new creations. His present project embraces the past and places confidence in the freedom to come, a confidence which is never disappointed" (*EA* 28).

Creative freedom presupposes that we exist as bodily beings, since a pure consciousness would lack any hold on the world. A disem-bodied consciousness would seem to know everything and to act on everything. Yet as Beauvoir points out, that would dissolve the phe-nomena and destroy the meaning of action. Sounding remarkably like Merleau-Ponty, she adds that

between sky and earth there is a perceptional field with its forms and colours; and it is in the interval which separates me today from an unforeseeable future that there are meanings and ends toward which to direct my acts . . . If one denies with Hegel the concrete thickness of the here and now in favour of universal space-time . . . one misses with Hegel the truth of the world. [*EA* 121–22]

That "concrete thickness" implies bodily being. Like Sartre, Beau-voir asserts that "the body itself is not a brute fact. It expresses our relationship to the world" (*EA* 41). While Sartre considers that rela-tionship to be fundamentally negative, Beauvoir regards it as funda-mentally positive.

For both Sartre and Beauvoir the body's ambiguity is inseparable from the ambiguity of our situation, since our situation is our en-gagement in the world, and the body is its expression. For Sartre the body is paradoxically ambiguous, in that we simultaneously are and are not our body. It is both subject for us and object for others, and our relations with others are irremediably confrontational. For Beau-voir our embodiment makes conflict and oppression always possible, but not irremediable. "The fundamental ambiguity of the human condition will always open up to man the possibility of opposing choices," she says. Thus there is "the permanent possibility of violence" (*EA* 118, 99). Yet bodily being also makes possible our "attachment to existence" and the establishing of positive bonds with other people.

Beauvoir argues that instead of trying to objectify and appropriate others to provide a foundation for ourselves, we can create our own foundation and regard them as crucial contributors to our creative freedom. That freedom requires an open future, and it is other people who open it to us. Without other people's confirmation, our acts become nothing but "a stupid and opaque fact." Beauvoir notes that as she argued in *Pyrrhus et Cinéas*, we need others to keep our goals alive beyond our own lifetime (*EA* 158, 71, 82, 27). Others' confirmation requires that we seek their freedom and happiness, rather than enslaving them. Beauvoir notes that such "generosity" is "more valid the less distinction there is between the other and ourself and the more we fulfill ourself in taking the other as an end. That is what happens if I am engaged in relation to others" (*EA* 144). Beauvoir stresses that although we are different and separate beings, we are all bound to each other. While our interdependence never rules out oppression, "such sentiments as love, tenderness, and friendship" have "a valid existence" (*EA* 18, 82, 108).

Since fulfilling relations with others are possible and valid, why is oppression widespread? Beauvoir argues that the answer lies in nostalgia for the world of our childhood. Children are a "living affirmation . . . an eager hand held out to the world" (*EA* 102), and normally their experience is primarily positive. They are unaware of their freedom, and think that values are absolute, "ready-made things," rather than human creations. They experience the world as not demanding anything of them except obedience to adults who take care of them. Consequently, they feel happily carefree and protected as they play. Yet they feel defenseless against mysterious powers, which they imagine are ruling the course of events. Though free, children are not held accountable for their actions, because they lack the knowledge and experience to foresee possible consequences. Their situation is therefore paradoxically ambiguous: they feel simultaneously protected and defenseless; they can set and attain goals joyfully and act egoistically with impunity, yet they feel their actions are puerile and insignificant; they are free, yet are unaware of their freedom and exercise it heedlessly. Without realizing it, children are forming their own characters through their actions.

In adolescence, individuals discover their freedom and its repercussions, and must choose how to respond to this discovery. They feel simultaneously anguished by an as yet unjustified freedom, and joyful at no longer being the prey of obscure forces. Thus their situation is also paradoxically ambiguous. They respond to the discovery of their freedom – and its accompanying responsibility – in accordance with the character they have formed. Adolescents may choose to retreat from their discovery back into some form of infantile existence by adopting various self-deceptive attitudes ("bad faith"). Alternatively, they may decide to live honestly by embracing their freedom and concomitant responsibility. Either way, they must continue to choose between these alternatives for the rest of their lives. Beauvoir argues that the first alternative is the more common, because we all remain nostalgic all our lives for the happy irresponsibility and security of childhood.

Self-deceptive attitudes are paradoxically ambiguous, because we simultaneously know and do not know what we hide from ourselves. While remaining implicitly aware of our unfounded freedom and concomitant responsibility, we may try to perpetuate an undemanding, ready-made, infantile world by adopting an apathetic attitude. Or we may posit absolute values and endow ourselves with inalienable rights, though tacitly aware of our unfounded freedom and its preclusion of such values and rights. Then again, we may acknowledge that our freedom is unfounded, but refuse to admit that we create values. Alternatively, we may joyfully embrace our unfounded freedom and the relativity of values, but refuse to recognize others' freedom and our fundamental interdependence. Or we may seek security by trying to turn another freedom into an object to possess absolutely. Then again, we may claim to possess a total, timeless, universally valid, securely objective truth. Yet we are implicitly aware that our own choice actually defines this truth as such. Finally, we may respond to the discovery of our unfounded freedom by taking refuge in intellectual or artistic activity and refusing to acknowledge our basic bond with others. These dishonest attitudes are egoistic in being indifferent to other people or actively negating their freedom. Oppression springs from such attempts to perpetuate childhood irresponsibility and security.

Despite our lifelong nostalgia for childhood, its experience of joyfully setting and pursuing goals need not induce us to regard ourselves as absolutely independent and our life as an egoistic adventure. Instead, childhood joy can encourage us to choose the joy of fulfilling our existence as adolescents and adults. This means acknowledging and transforming our original, unfounded freedom into an ethical, founded freedom. Beauvoir argues that to accomplish this conversion[15] we must actively will not only our own freedom, but also that of all others, because our freedom is bound up with theirs. We must implement our will – and continually confirm it – in concrete and particular actions aiming at this goal of universal freedom. Moreover, we must accept responsibility for the repercussions of our actions on others. Beauvoir stresses that the world of our actions "is a human world in which each object is penetrated with human meanings. It is a speaking world from which solicitations and appeals rise up" (*EA* 74). In responding, we must strive for universal freedom.

This honest way of living means embracing ambiguity rather than denying it. It involves experiencing not only paradoxical ambiguity, but also the ambiguity of multiple, inseparable aspects and significations, of indistinguishable components, and of an irreducible indeterminacy. The ambiguities I described earlier concerning our embodied consciousness, our situation, our freedom, our temporality, and our relations with other people all merge in that ongoing, dynamic experience that is our concrete existence in the world. Consciousness, body, situation, temporality, willing, choosing, acting, creating meaning, and relating to others are all inextricably and indistinguishably bound up together.

Living honestly, we experience this multifaceted ambiguity most keenly in attempting to translate our goal of universal freedom into concrete, particular actions. Our fundamental ambiguity precludes any recipes or certainties here. Unlike Sartre in *Being and Nothingness*, Beauvoir insists that people can be mystified and have their freedom destroyed. She argues that we cannot be ethically neutral here: we either work actively to achieve universal freedom, or we tacitly contribute to oppression through inaction. Taking liberatory action precludes adopting an external, detached standpoint. Instead, we must recognize the indissoluble bond linking us with other people, and our destiny with theirs. In this nexus each individual has an absolute, irreplaceable value. Consequently, we must make the individual's good, or the good of a group of individuals, an absolute goal of our action. Yet we cannot accord this absolute value to oppressors, because they refuse to recognize it in their victims. Nor can we accord it to their mystified – and hence oppressed – accomplices, who thus become the innocent victims of our action. As we sacrifice these oppressed accomplices, their oppressors, and possibly also ourselves in acting to liberate oppressed others, do we not become oppressors? And do we not undermine our goal of achieving universal freedom? Beauvoir argues that such dilemmas are unavoidable. Means and goal perpetually contest each other, and we must commit ourselves unconditionally to the pursuit of universal freedom without ever being able to justify our actions absolutely. Our will, choices, actions, and relations with others are thus irreducibly ambiguous.

The interdependence of present means and projected end adds further facets to this ambiguity. Beauvoir argues that our choice of means effects both the definition and the realization of our goal, because the goal is defined all along the way. Consequently, means and end are inseparable and must be judged together. We can achieve liberation only if we employ means that do not destroy its very meaning – yet there can be no liberation without the use of oppression. We cannot appeal to the future to justify our present action, because the present shapes that future, and the outcome is always uncertain. In trying to achieve a balance between our action and its goal, we have only probabilities – never certainties. Not only is our own action inherently ambiguous, but it meshes or interferes with others' actions in unforeseeable ways. The meanings and values created through our actions are therefore not knowable in advance – yet we must act. Beauvoir stresses that violence is both outrageous and unavoidable. Failure to take action perpetuates the violence of existing oppressive conditions; and acting to abolish such conditions itself involves violence. We must strive to inflict less violence than that which we try to forestall or eliminate. Our choice is thus a choice between different forms of violence. Beauvoir discusses Marxist politics and the 1937 Moscow Trials from this perspective. She asserts that political choices are ethical choices, and that "morality resides in the painfulness of an indefinite questioning" (*EA* 133).

However, Beauvoir stresses that we must not let this anguish overshadow the joy of existence, for liberatory action loses its *raison d'être* in the absence of that joy: "in order for the idea of liberation to have a concrete meaning, the joy of existence must be asserted in each one, at every instant...If we do not love life on our own account and through others, it is futile to seek to justify it in any way" (*EA* 135–36). While emphasizing the inevitability of conflicts and the reality of present oppressions, Beauvoir holds out hope for a future that is free of oppression: "Perhaps it is permissible to dream of a future when men will know no other use of their freedom than this free unfurling of itself; constructive activity would be possible for all" (*EA* 81). Beauvoir's complex philosophy of ambiguity is thus profoundly positive.

In *Humanism and Terror* Merleau-Ponty makes many of the same assertions as Beauvoir, but does not mention her. He emphasizes the importance of loving our times, the inherent "impurity" and ambiguity of action, the interdependence of present means and future end, and the impossibility of always respecting everyone's absolute individuality. Like Beauvoir, Merleau-Ponty considers conflict with others as a constant, and declares: "We do not have a choice between purity and violence but between different kinds of violence. Inasmuch as we are incarnate beings, violence is our lot."[16] Merleau-Ponty says this violence can be minimized and it may be possible to eliminate institutionalized violence. However, in working toward that end one must sacrifice those who threaten it, because abstaining from violence toward oppressors means becoming their accomplice. Yet there is no absolute justification for actions. Their outcome is always uncertain; there are only probabilities. Again like Beauvoir, Merleau-Ponty stresses we are not a plurality of juxtaposed for-itselfs, although we encroach on each other and can treat one another as objects. Unlike pure consciousnesses, we "blend" with, and compose, a common situation – an intersubjectivity. Further, we feel the need for others' recognition. Given the sameness of so many of their assertions, Beauvoir and Merleau-Ponty evidently influenced each other.

In discussing institutionalized violence in *Humanism and Terror*, Merleau-Ponty fails to account for its pervasiveness. His assertions (that we encroach, and can treat others as objects) make the existence of oppression comprehensible, but do not elucidate why it has become widely institutionalized. Moreover, his hope regarding the possible elimination of institutionalized violence despite the ineradicability of conflict, shows that conflict cannot account for institutionalized violence or its pervasiveness. What is needed here is Beauvoir's description of childhood and of our nostalgic attempts to recapture it. Beauvoir's philosophy of ambiguity also fills another gap in supplying the main features of a viable ethics. Merleau-Ponty notes approvingly that Marxism does not consider ethics only in individuals' hearts, but also in human coexistence – and specifically in proletarian action. Yet *Humanism and Terror*'s discussions of Marxist politics and the 1937 Trials do not constitute an ethics – nor does Merleau-Ponty provide one elsewhere. Given the affinities between their philosophies, Beauvoir's *Ethics of Ambiguity* implicitly highlights this gap and suggests how one might remedy it.

For its part, Merleau-Ponty's philosophy of ambiguity implicitly highlights problems with Beauvoir's ideas of disclosure and bond. It also develops important aspects of Beauvoir's philosophy of ambiguity. Earlier I argued that Beauvoir's idea of disclosure precludes forging that intimate bond with the living, meaningful world, which she values in Merleau-Ponty's *Phenomenology of Perception*. Further, in stressing that we need to justify our existence, and can do so only through others, Beauvoir implies that our bond with others is merely egoistic. She recognizes this implication and attempts to dispel it, by asserting that mutual concern is "an irreducible truth" and that "The me–others relationship is as indissoluble as the subject–object relationship" (*EA* 72). As I have shown, Beauvoir also says the less the distinction between us, the more we fulfill ourselves in taking the other as an end. However, this idea of a more intrinsic relationship remains undeveloped in *The Ethics of Ambiguity*. In his *Phenomenology of Perception*, Merleau-Ponty describes our ambiguous, intrinsic bond with the world and with others in detail. In doing so, he develops these and other vital aspects of the multifaceted ambiguity that forms the core of both their philosophies: corporeal consciousness, situatedness, temporality, freedom, and the creation of meaning. To appreciate this multifaceted ambiguity, we must abandon an "objective" thinking, which actually distorts lived experience. Such thinking finds its crassest expression in positivistic sciences' efforts to reduce the world and our bodies to quantifiable objects observed by an unsituated spectator-manipulator. In exposing the bias of "objective" thinking, Merleau-Ponty seeks to awaken us to the inherent ambiguity of lived experience and our inextricable interrelatedness with the world and with others.

Unlike the "objective" body constructed by mechanistic physiology and intellectualist psychologies or philosophies, the lived body is prereflectively bound up with the lived world. Neither body nor world is an object. Both come into being in an ambiguous movement that forms an ongoing, prepersonal "dialogue" underlying all reflection and objectification. It is impossible to demarcate body and world in this ambiguous exchange. Corporeality is not a mechanistic system of parts externally related in "objective" space. Nor is the lived body a container for a pure consciousness or "ego." Whether prereflective or reflective, consciousness is thoroughly corporeal – it is the lived body, situated in a world that is indistinguishably natural and cultural.

For Merleau-Ponty world and body-subject intertwine in a continual dialectic of corporeal intentionality and worldly solicitation. The bodily senses are themselves inseparably intertwined, forming an "intentional arc" that projects an anticipated world; and the world simultaneously draws forth this bodily intentionality. This dialectical movement not only creates lived temporality and lived spatiality, but also ceaselessly brings into being a web of multiple, inseparable meanings. Since it occurs at the prereflective level, this marvelous, ambiguous intertwining of body-subject and world usually goes unnoticed. Merleau-Ponty draws it to our attention with the help of examples, such as playing an instrument or using a cane. In learning to play an instrument, we prereflectively establish and incorporate a lived spatiality specific to this activity. Without having to reflect or relearn, accomplished organists quickly adjust to various organs having different stops. Not thinking about their fingers or feet, they lend themselves to the solicitation of the music and become one with the instrument while playing it. Similarly, users of white canes incorporate them into their bodily spatiality.

Merleau-Ponty stresses that learning to play an instrument or use a cane "is to be transplanted into them, or conversely, to incorporate them into the bulk of the body itself."[17] Acquiring such habits is neither an intellectual analysis and reconstruction, nor a mechanical recording of impressions. It is a corporeal comprehension and incorporation. It is only when this organic relationship between body and world becomes impaired (as in certain pathologies) that we must resort to intellectual analysis and reconstruction. Because "the body is essentially an expressive space" (*PP* 146), particular expressive spaces (such as those of the organ) can come into existence and be incorporated into it. Through this dynamic bodily spatiality a meaningful world comes into being.

This ambiguous spatiality inherently involves an ambiguous, lived temporality. As fundamental project, the body has a temporal structure, such that its present activities simultaneously draw on its past acquisitions and outline an expected future. That anticipated future is not a representation, and the past acquisitions are not collections of memories. Past, present, and future are inseparable aspects of that ambiguous, ceaseless movement that is constitutive of the lived body. In projecting itself towards a perceptual world, the body experiences itself in an amorphous, prepersonal awareness that makes possible the self-reference of specifically personal existence. Rupturing the primordial "dialogue" of body-subject and lived world destroys both terms, spelling the destruction of freedom and meaning. Freedom presupposes a corporeal rootedness, since absolute freedom would lack any hold on the world. Merleau-Ponty emphasizes that freedom "gears" itself to the situation, and that the situation is primordially intersubjective. We exist as an "intersubjective field," and Merleau-Ponty considers this point so important that he ends his *Phenomenology of Perception* by quoting Saint-Exupéry: "Man is but a network of relationships" (*PP* 456). By assuming these relationships and carrying them forward, we realize our freedom.

Traditionally, we have postulated a realm of subjectivity consisting of pure thought, allegedly distinct from the body and inaccessible to others – who were therefore considered extrinsic. Merleau-Ponty overturns this tradition by describing an intrinsic relationship between thought and the body, and between ourselves and others. He shows that in attempting to divorce thought from speech, traditional theorists failed to understand aphasia. They were puzzled by patients' inability to find in gratuitous language words available to them in concrete situations, or to categorize color samples, though able to name the colors. Merleau-Ponty shows that for such patients words have lost the living meaning that normally inhabits them, and the link between language and thought has been broken. We usually regard speech as incidental to an autonomous thought. This arises from our failure to note that allegedly "pure thought" is actually a monologue using already acquired meanings created by earlier acts of expression. In fact, there is no pure thought prior to speech. Thus we can learn something new during conversation with others. We are mutually present to one another and have no need to decode each other's words. Our lived bodies "gear" into each other in conversation. Since there can be no personal self-awareness in the absence of language, and since language is inherently intersubjective, our fundamental relationship with others is not extrinsic, but intrinsic. It shares in the multifaceted ambiguity that characterizes our existence as body-subjects.

Merleau-Ponty's philosophy of ambiguity thus highlights problems with Beauvoir's ideas of disclosure and an extrinsic bond with others. Simultaneously, it develops the idea of a multifaceted ambiguity in which we are intrinsically related to the world and to others. For its part, Beauvoir's philosophy of ambiguity fills in two significant gaps in Merleau-Ponty's philosophy. Phenomenologists have recognized Merleau-Ponty as a philosopher of ambiguity. Let us now also celebrate Beauvoir as a philosopher of ambiguity.

NOTES

1 cf. Debra B. Bergoffen, *The Philosophy of Simone de Beauvoir: Gendered Phenomenologies, Erotic Generosities* (Albany, NY: State University of New York Press, 1997), p. 4.

2 cf. Margaret A. Simons, "Two Interviews with Simone de Beauvoir," *Hypatia*, 3, 3 (winter 1989): 25. See also Simone de Beauvoir, *Letters to Sartre*, trans. and ed. Quintin Hoare (London: Radius, 1991) pp. 356–57, 393, 423, and Edward Fullbrook and Kate Fullbrook, *Simone de Beauvoir: A Critical Introduction* (Cambridge, MA: Polity Press, 1998), p. 21.

3 Maurice Merleau-Ponty, "Metaphysics and the Novel," in *Sense and Non-Sense*, trans. Hubert L. Dreyfus and Patricia Allen Dreyfus (Evanston, IL: Northwestern University Press, 1964), pp. 26–40.

4 Maurice Merleau-Ponty, "An Unpublished Text by Maurice Merleau-Ponty: A Prospectus of his Work," in *The Primacy of Perception and Other Essays*, ed. James M. Edie (Evanston, IL: Northwestern University Press, 1964), p. 11. I have retranslated "*réunit*" as " reunites," rather than "gathers together."

5 *Force of Circumstance* (Harmondsworth: Penguin, 1968).

6 Among the most noticeable exceptions are Sonia Kruks, *Situation and Human Existence: Freedom, Subjectivity and Society* (London: Unwin Hyman, 1990); Bergoffen, *Philosophy of Simone de Beauvoir*; and Fullbrook and Fullbrook, *Beauvoir: Critical Introduction*.

7 *Webster's New World Dictionary of the American Language*, ed. David B. Guralnik (New York: World Publishing, 1972), pp. 42–43; and John

C. Traupman, *The New College Latin and English Dictionary* (New York: Bantam Books, 1966), p. 14.

8 René Descartes, *Philosophical Writings*, ed. Elizabeth Anscombe and Peter Thomas Geach (London: Thomas Nelson & Sons, 1970), pp. 63, 96–100, 107.

9 "Deuxième entretien privé," *La Connaissance de l'homme aux XXe siècle. Rencontres Internationales de Genève*, 1951 (Neuchâtel: Editions de la Baconnière, 1952), pp. 220–21. My translation.

10 Hugh Silverman, "Merleau-Ponty's Human Ambiguity," *Journal of the British Society for Phenomenology*, 10, 1 (January 1979): 29.

11 See also Jean-Paul Sartre, *Nausea*, trans. Hayden Carruth (New York: New Directions, 1964).

12 Note the translation error p. 70 line 13: "in order to desire being" should read "to reveal [dévoiler] being."

13 cf. Hazel E. Barnes, "Sartre's Ontology: The Revealing and Making of Being," *The Cambridge Companion to Sartre*, ed. Christina Howells (Cambridge: Cambridge University Press, 1992), pp. 13–38.

14 Bergoffen, by contrast, interprets the activity of disclosing *per se* as positive. She argues that Beauvoir opens a new direction by introducing the joy of disclosure. See Debra Bergoffen, "Toward a Feminist Ethic: First Steps," *Simone de Beauvoir Studies*, 8 (1991): 163–65; and Bergoffen, *Philosophy of Simone de Beauvoir*, pp. 76–82. In the latter, Bergoffen argues that Beauvoir's unique philosophical perspective arises from her redescription of intentionality, and that Beauvoir participates in "a three way conversation with Sartre and Merleau-Ponty." Surprisingly, Bergoffen focuses far more on Merleau-Ponty's last work, *The Visible and the Invisible*, than on the *Phenomenology of Perception* in describing Merleau-Ponty's position.

15 As I argued earlier, such conversion is problematic, given Beauvoir's linking of freedom and disclosure.

16 Maurice Merleau-Ponty, *Humanism and Terror: An Essay on the Communist Problem*, trans. John O'Neill (Boston: Beacon, 1969), pp. 187, 109.

17 Maurice Merleau-Ponty, *Phenomenology of Perception*, trans. Colin Smith (London: Routledge and Kegan Paul, 1962), p. 143. I have altered Smith's translation to accord with the French text.

5 Bergson's influence on Beauvoir's philosophical methodology

The topic of this chapter, the early philosophical influence of Henri Bergson (1859–1941) on Simone de Beauvoir, may surprise those who remember Beauvoir's reference to Bergson in her *Memoirs of a Dutiful Daughter* where she denies Bergson's importance. She writes there of her interests in 1926: "I preferred literature to philosophy, and I would not have been at all pleased if someone had prophesized that I would become a kind of Bergson; I didn't want to speak with that abstract voice which, whenever I heard it, failed to move me."[1]

But in this case, as in so many others, Beauvoir's diaries present a very different picture. Her unpublished diary of 1926, written when she was 18 years old and beginning her study of philosophy, contains several pages of quotations from Bergson's *Time and Free Will: An Essay on the Immediate Data of Consciousness* (1889),[2] which she describes, in an entry dated 16 August, as "a great intellectual intoxication." The entry continues:

whereas in reading other philosophers I have the impression of witnessing more or less logical constructions, here finally I am touching palpable reality and encountering life. Not only myself, but art, the truths suggested by poets, and everything that I studied this year is magnificently explained. Simply a call to intuition...in short the method that I spontaneously apply when I want to know myself and the most difficult problems disappear. How many things [there are] in the 180 pages of Bergson's *Time and Free Will: The Immediate Givens of Consciousness*.[3]

Intrigued by this diary passage, I began analyzing Beauvoir's early philosophy for evidence of Bergson's influence, focusing on Bergson's three most important texts: *Time and Free Will* (1889), *Matter and Memory: An Essay on the Relation of the Body to the Mind* (1896),[4] and *Creative Evolution* (1907).[5] My analysis uncovered evidence of Bergson's influence in several of Beauvoir's important early texts, especially *She Came to Stay*, Beauvoir's metaphysical novel written from 1937 to 1941,[6] but also in her essays on existential ethics and *The Second Sex* (1949).[7] Indeed, Bergson now seems to me to be a key to understanding the roots of Beauvoir's philosophy. In this chapter I will narrow my focus to Bergson's philosophical methodology and its influence on *She Came to Stay*, identifying three Bergsonian elements of Beauvoir's philosophical methodology. First of all, Beauvoir takes seriously Bergson's criticism of intellectual understanding and accepts his implicit challenge to do philosophy through the novel. Secondly, Beauvoir shares with Bergson a methodological interest in exposing distortions in perception and thinking. Finally, they both rely on a methodological turn to immediate experience, which discloses our freedom.

Beauvoir did not follow Bergson completely or uncritically. She did not follow him, for example, in the vitalist system-building of *Creative Evolution* or the mysticism of his later work, *Two Sources of Morality and Religion*.[8] In Beauvoir's short story cycle *When Things of the Spirit Come First*, written from 1935 to 1937,[9] which she describes as "clarifying the genesis" of her later work (*QPS* viii), she satirizes her early intellectual passions, including Paul Claudel's morality of feminine self-sacrifice, André Breton's surrealism, and Bergson's philosophy. Furthermore, Beauvoir's early work, including *She Came to Stay*, focuses on an aspect of reality ignored by Bergson's early work, namely, the problem of the opposition of self and Other.

Beauvoir's interest in this problem is already evident in her diary of 1926, where she discusses the necessity of serving both self and others and the temptations of egoism and self-abnegation: "[It is] very difficult, because turning in on oneself readily turns into egoism; while on the other hand, when one goes out of oneself, it's indeed rare that one does not go too far and that one is not diminished. What I'm proposing is to achieve [*réaliser*] this equilibrium" (CA26 1). Later in the diary, Beauvoir defines the problem with an ontological distinction between "two parts in my existence: one for others [*pour autrui*]," "the links that unite me with all beings," and another "part for myself [*pour moi-même*]" (CA26 85). In her diary of 1927 Beauvoir vows to "deepen those problems that have enticed me... The theme is almost always this opposition of self and other that I have felt since beginning to live."[10] This theme and the 1926 distinction between "for others" and "for myself" point to an early Hegelian influence, although the diary passages make no reference to Hegel. But her student diaries do show that Beauvoir's interest in the theme of the opposition of self and Other predates Bergson's own discussion of the problem in *Two Sources of Morality and Religion*, first published in 1932, a full discussion of which must await a study of Beauvoir's moral philosophy.

PHILOSOPHY AND THE NOVEL

Given our focus on Beauvoir's metaphysical novel *She Came to Stay*, we should begin with Beauvoir's Bergsonian criticisms of the limitations of philosophy's traditional reliance upon intellectual understanding and Bergson's admiration for the novelist. For Bergson, reality is fundamentally a temporal process: "Matter or mind, reality has appeared to us as a perpetual becoming" (*CE* 296). Matter is characterized by "inertia," and mind by spontaneity, unforeseeability, and freedom. Consciousness, although capable of perceiving the constant flux of reality, has a practical focus that distorts reality. As intellect, our consciousness delimits the world by identifying useful qualities in the chaos of changing impressions and fixing them into manageable units. But consciousness has the capacity to grasp reality in its temporality through intuition. "Consciousness, in man, is eminently intellect," Bergson writes in *Creative Evolution*, "It might have been, it ought ... to have been also intuition" (*CE* 291).

In *Time and Free Will* Bergson celebrates the novelist as unveiling this "absurd" reality of changing impressions inaccessible to the intellect and distorted even by naming. He asks us to imagine

some bold novelist, tearing aside the cleverly woven curtain of our conventional self show[ing] us under this appearance of logic a fundamental absurdity, under this juxtaposition of simple states an infinite permeation of a thousand different impressions which have already ceased to exist the instant they are named ... Encouraged by him, we have put aside for an instant the veil which we interposed between our consciousness and ourselves. He has brought us back into our own presence. [*TFW* 133, *DIC* 101].

But despite his celebration of the novelist, Bergson did not attempt to write philosophy in novels.

In her diary of 1927, Beauvoir declares her intention to write philosophy in literary form: "I must . . . write 'essays on life' which would not be a novel, but philosophy, linking them together vaguely with a fiction. But the thought would be the essential thing" (CA27 54–55). Belying her later claim in her *Memoirs* never to have been interested in doing philosophy, Beauvoir avows her commitment to philosophy in a 1927 diary entry:

> Oh! I see my life clearly now . . . a passionate, frantic search . . . I didn't know that one could dream of death by metaphysical despair; sacrifice everything to the desire to know . . . I didn't know that every system is an ardent, tormented thing, an effort of life, of being, a drama in the full sense of the word, and that it does not engage only the abstract intelligence. But I know it now, and that I can no longer do anything else. [CA27 133–34]

These early references to doing philosophy are strikingly Bergsonian, rejecting the conception of philosophy as engaging only the abstract intelligence.

In "Littérature et métaphysique" (1946) Beauvoir gives a Bergsonian critique of intellectual understanding, arguing that the novelist can "unveil" reality: "Since reality is not defined as graspable by the intelligence alone, no intellectual description is capable of giving an adequate expression of it. One must try to present it in its integrity, as it unveils itself in the living relation that is action and feeling before it makes itself thought."[11] Existential philosophers thus aspire to do philosophy in the novel: "The more vividly a philosopher underscores the role and the value of subjectivity, the more he will be led to describe the metaphysical experience under its singular and temporal form" (LM 101).

> A metaphysical novel . . . seems to me . . . the highest achievement, since it strives to grasp man and human events in their relation with the totality of the world, and since it alone can succeed where pure literature like pure philosophy fails, in evoking in its living unity and its fundamental living ambiguity, this destiny which is ours and which is inscribed both in time and in eternity. [LM 105–06]

Beauvoir's first published work, *She Came to Stay*, takes up Bergson's implicit challenge to philosophers to become novelists. In the novel, as I shall show, she traces the philosophical odyssey of a woman writer, Françoise, as she confronts the limitations of her intellectual grasp of the world.

EXPOSING DISTORTIONS IN PERCEPTION AND THINKING

A second area of Bergson's apparent influence on Beauvoir's philosophical methodology is their shared methodological interest in exposing distortions in perception and thinking. Beauvoir's most well-known exposé of such distortions is in *The Second Sex*, where she describes the distortions in men's image of woman as the Other. But Beauvoir's methodological focus on the deceptions of what she terms "bad faith," or self-deception, is evident in her earliest literary-philosophical texts, including *She Came to Stay*.

According to Bergson, distortions in perception arise when our utilitarian consciousness singles out features of interest from the mass of changing sense impressions: "Our needs are so many search lights which, directed upon the continuity of sensible qualities, single out in it distinct bodies" (*MAM* 262). The result is a diminution of reality, since the effect of perception is "to obscure some of its aspects, to diminish it by the greater part of itself" (*MAM* 28). Bergson describes consciousness as "tormented by an insatiable desire to make distinctions" and to perceive reality through symbols and words. Language thus distorts our perception and thoughts as it "arrests [their] mobility" (*TFW* 128–29, *DIC* 97–98): "the word...which stores up the stable, common, and therefore impersonal element in the impressions of mankind, overwhelms...the delicate and fugitive impressions of our individual consciousness" (*TFW* 131–32).

The distortions of utilitarian consciousness cause problems for philosophers who mistakenly assume that words and symbols represent ontological distinctions rather than simply practical conveniences. "[I]t may be asked whether...by merely getting rid of the clumsy symbols round which [philosophers] are fighting, we might not bring the fight to an end" (*TFW* xx).

A distortion of perception and thinking that is of particular concern to both Bergson and Beauvoir is the distortion of human freedom. According to Bergson, such distortions are so common that "free acts are exceptional" (*TFW* 197). Our intellect, in analyzing our feelings and naming them, distorts their living reality, with the result that our consciousness "gradually loses sight of the fundamental self" (*TFW* 128, *DIC* 97). We accept these distortions "for the convenience of language and the promotion of social relations." When "our most trustworthy friends" advise us to take some important step, "the sentiments which they utter with so much insistence lodge on the surface of our self and ... form a thick crust which will cover up our own sentiments; we shall believe that we are acting freely, and it is only by reflecting on it later on that we shall see how much we were mistaken." Thus language and the intellect distort freedom by distorting the perception of our feelings. The formation of habits also inhibits our freedom, enabling us to act as "a conscious automaton" (*TFW* 167–69, *DIC* 127–29). In *Creative Evolution* Bergson describes freedom as "dogged by automatism": "Our freedom, in the very movements by which it is affirmed, creates the growing habits that will stifle it if it fails to renew itself by a constant effort ... The most living thought becomes frigid in the formula that expresses it. The words turn against the idea" (*CE* 141).

So, this first, negative step in Bergson's method exposes distortions in perception and thought caused by the "insatiable desire" of utilitarian consciousness to impose an order on the chaos of fleeting impressions. Philosophical problems result when the utilitarian intellect breaks up reality, including our self and our feelings, into distinct, spatially oriented objects immobilized by language and symbol. A particularly serious result of these distortions is an erosion of our freedom.

EXPOSING DISTORTIONS OF REALITY: *SHE CAME TO STAY*

In *She Came to Stay* Beauvoir traces the philosophical odyssey of a woman writer, Françoise, away from the distortions of utilitarian consciousness. In the opening pages, set in pre-World War Two France, Françoise is hard at work in a theatre office late at night revising a play. Her utilitarian consciousness is evident first in Françoise's exaggerated awareness of her orientation in space and her tendency to define herself by her work and the objects surrounding her: "I wonder what he thinks of me ... this office, the theater, my room, books, papers, work" (*SCS* 15, *LI* 17). Habitually denying her feelings and forcing herself to work, Françoise denies her physical exhaustion and her sexual desire for the young man, Gerbert, who is working beside her.

Françoise's view of her inner life has been defined and solidified in response to social conventions, much as Bergson describes. To protect her image of herself as happy and free in her relationship with her partner, Pierre, the play's director, Françoise refuses to acknowledge any feelings that threaten it, including her sadness at the denial of the desired intimacy with Gerbert: "In her heart rose a sadness as bitter and glowing as the dawn. And yet she had no regrets; she had not even a right to that melancholy which was beginning to numb her drowsy body" (*SCS* 18, *LI* 21). In *When Things of the Spirit Come First* Beauvoir uses the term "bad faith" (*WT* 210, *QPS* 246) to describe acts such as Françoise first noticing and then denying a disturbing reality. Bergson anticipates the concept of bad faith in his description of our tendency to "thrust... back into the darkest depths of our being," "feelings and ideas which are not unperceived, but rather which we do not want to consider" (*TFW* 169, *DIC* 129–30).

The habitual nature of Françoise's denial of her feelings is evident in scene after scene of the novel, as she chooses to deny her own feelings rather than inconvenience others. For example, Françoise, we are told, "loathed tomatoes," but when offered them responds, with resignation: " 'They look delicious' " (*SCS* 137). Françoise's concern with social convention is also apparent in her preference for language over experience: "nothing that happened was completely real until she had told Pierre about it... [S]he no longer knew solitude, but she had rid herself of that swarming confusion. Every moment of her life that she entrusted to [Pierre] was given back to her clear, polished, completed, and they became moments of their shared life." Françoise sees herself as merged with Pierre, " 'We are simply one' " (*SCS* 26, *LI* 30), and feels anguish at their separation: "separation was agony" (*SCS* 108).

Françoise also experiences an inhibition of her freedom:

She ought not to thrust responsibility for herself upon someone else... If she were to take full responsibility for herself, she would first have to want to; but she didn't want to... An act that bespoke of genuine independence, an act that was self-initiated and had no connection with [Pierre], was beyond her imagination. This, however, did not worry her; she would never find it necessary to call upon her own resources against Pierre. [*SCS* 113]

Bergson describes freedom as inhibited by "some strange reluctance to exercise our will [à vouloir]" (TFW 169, DIC 129): "we often resign our freedom... by inertia or indolence" (TFW 169, DIC 129). In Creative Evolution Bergson describes a "tendency... toward the vegetative life," where "torpor and unconsciousness are always lying in wait" (CE 125).

Françoise can experience the world of fleeting impressions at odds with her utilitarian consciousness: "There was nothing but this passing sound, the sky, the hesitant foliage of the trees... there was no Françoise any longer." But this brief interlude only serves to highlight her utilitarian consciousness: "She jumped to her feet. It was strange to become someone again... a woman who must hurry because pressing work awaited her, and the moment was only one like so many others in her life" (SCS 12–13). With the return of a substantive self, Françoise denies the unique characteristics of this moment, dismissing it as interchangeable with other instants, thus reflecting, in Bergsonian terms, a utilitarian consciousness of time as interchangeable units in "a duration whose moments resemble one another" (TFW 221). Moments of time, for Bergson, are not interchangeable but irreplacably unique, differing qualitatively – as a moment in a museum differs from a moment in a dentist's chair.

When, in another scene early in the novel, Françoise is unsettled by a contemptuous glance from a young woman, her body signals her anxiety: "her throat was dry; her heart beat a little faster than usual." But Françoise uses her intellect to analyze away these troubling sensations: "This malaise brought her no pathetic revelation; it was only one accident among others, a brief and quasi-foreseeable modulation which would be resolved in peace. She no longer ever took such instants violently; she knew well that none of them had any decisive value" (SCS 32, LI 37). Beauvoir's use of Bergsonian terminology highlights Françoise's utilitarian consciousness in this scene, dismissing her feeling as "quasi-foreseeable," a quasi-mechanistic reaction, rather than a unique and spontaneous creation, just as she dismisses this poignant moment as interchangeable with any other.

Bergson tells us that utilitarian consciousness produces philosophical problems when applied to metaphysical questions and Françoise is no exception. She retreats to subjective idealism in order to suppress the regret that accompanies her dutifulness: "'It used to break my heart to think that I'd never know anything but one poor little corner of the world... But now it doesn't bother me... because I feel that things which do not exist for me, simply do not exist at all... [They have] no reality. [They are] nothing but hearsay.'" Trying to keep change at bay, she refuses to acknowledge the dire possibilities soon to confront her: "[Illness and war] could never happen to me. Those things only happen to others" (SCS 14–16, LI 15–17). In a later scene at a night club, Françoise denies her embodiment, imagining herself to be a disembodied, sovereign subject: "I am there, impersonal and free. I contemplate at once all of these lives, all of these faces. If I were to turn away from them, they would disintegrate at once into a deserted landscape" (SCS 29).

Françoise cannot help but notice the existence of the external world, since she experiences reality as overflowing her perception of it. But she denies it, wanting to regard reality as wholly encompassed by her perception. Walking through the empty theatre, in the novel's opening scene, Françoise senses her power to "revive things from their inanimateness." But she also notes the limitations of her point of view: "She would have to be elsewhere as well... she would have to be everywhere at the same time" (SCS 12). In Matter and Memory Bergson argues that "[O]ur actual perception [is] always only a content in relation to a vaster, even an unlimited, experience which contains it" (MAM 186). "In our perception we grasp a state of our consciousness and a reality independent of ourselves – this mixed character of our immediate perception... is the principal theoretical reason we have for believing in an external world which does not coincide absolutely with our perception" (MAM 270). That Bergson presents this theory of appearances for proof of the existence of the external world challenges the view that the theory was originated by either Beauvoir or Sartre, as scholars have claimed.[12]

Unlike Bergson in his early work, Beauvoir in She Came to Stay is interested in the problem of the existence of other minds. In the first few pages of the book Beauvoir portrays Françoise as denying in bad faith her experience of the existence of other consciousnesses separate from her own. Interestingly, these encounters with the Other occur within relations of intimacy and dependency. In the first example, Françoise discovers herself as an object in the eyes of Gerbert, who sees her life as "rather well regulated." Françoise's response to his judgment is twofold. She first attempts to deny their separateness: "They were enclosed alone in this circle of rosy light; for both of them, the same light, the same night." Then she takes refuge in solipsism, denying the metaphysical possibility of a separate consciousness: "'One cannot realize that other people are consciousnesses that sense themselves from within as one senses oneself,' said Françoise. 'When one glimpses that, I find it terrifying. One has the impression of being nothing more than an image in someone else's head. But that almost never happens, and never completely.'" She refuses to acknowledge the reality of the Other's judgment: "For me their thoughts are exactly like their words and their faces: objects in my own world" (SCS 15–17, LI 17–18). So Françoise denies, in bad faith, the uncomfortable experience of being judged by the Other.

A second example of the bad faith denial of other minds arises in Françoise's relationship with Xavière, a naive young woman from the provinces whom Françoise has taken under her wing. Françoise is enchanted by Xavière's impulsiveness and sensuality, that is by Xavière's difference from herself. But Françoise's response is to deny their separateness: "what was especially wonderful was her having attached this pathetic little being to her own life. For...now Xavière belonged to her." Françoise savors the sense of being a sovereign consciousness: "Xavière's gestures, her face, her very life depended on Françoise for their existence" (SCS 20, LI 23). Thus Françoise denies, in bad faith, the very source of Xavière's attraction, her ability, as a separate existent, to open up a new world of experience to Françoise.

A third example also concerns Françoise's relationship with Xavière. Françoise vows to help her escape the stifling confines of her family in the provinces: "That can't go on." When Xavière sullenly rejects Françoise's plan – "'It will go on,' Xavière said" (SCS 21, LI 24) – Françoise is bewildered and disconcerted by this expression of independence. Yet it is only as a separate existent that Xavière can require Françoise's help and thus necessitate Françoise's life, allowing her to be useful on a human scale.

A fourth example of Françoise's bad faith refusal to acknowledge the existence of other minds comes in an encounter with Pierre, who praises her rewriting of the play: "'That's good,' he said, 'really good.' 'Do you mean it? Oh, I'm so glad!'...said Françoise. 'I thought I'd never manage to lick that third act.' 'You've done some excellent work.' He came over to the couch, leaned over and kissed her" (SCS 22–23, LI 25–26). Only a separate consciousness can provide recognition and acknowledgment for one's contribution to a shared project. Thus Françoise's satisfaction with Pierre's praise entails her recognition of his separate existence. But she then denies, in bad faith, their separateness: "'We are simply one,' she murmured" (SCS 26, LI 30).

Thus Beauvoir opens her metaphysical novel by exposing the intellect's distortions of reality, echoing Bergson's criticism that the intellectual narrowing of our perceptions by utilitarian consciousness inhibits our awareness of the external world and our freedom. But Beauvoir's interest in the bad faith attempt to deny our dependence upon others and the existence of other minds moves outside Bergson's early work.

THE TURN TO IMMEDIATE EXPERIENCE

The third Bergsonian element in Beauvoir's philosophical methodology is a turn to immediate experience, a turn that reveals human freedom. In *Matter and Memory* Bergson explains that exposing distortions is only the beginning: "To give up certain habits of thinking, and even of perceiving, is... but the negative part of the work to be done." The next step is "to seek experience at its source, or rather above that turn where, taking a bias in the direction of our utility, it becomes properly human experience" (MAM 241). "This method... attributes a privileged value to immediate knowledge" (MAM 245), which entails attending not to the intellect but to the feelings and impressions of our embodied engagement in the world. Since philosophical problems are caused by the intellect's misapplication of utilitarian consciousness to philosophical questions, Bergson's methodological turn to immediate experience is also meant to resolve or dissolve philosophical problems, such as the dilemmas of realism versus idealism and freedom versus determinism.

In *She Came to Stay* the challenge to Françoise's solipsism and her turn to immediate experience are driven both by the force of circumstances that disrupt her work and by her desire to experience the world differently. One of the circumstances that undermines Françoise's utilitarian consciousness is the approaching war and Pierre's loss of interest in their collaborative work: "'Don't you realize?' [said Pierre], 'We may have war within the next six months. And here I am trying to reproduce the color of dawn...I feel about as big as an insect.'" Françoise protests helplessly: "It was Pierre who had convinced her that the greatest thing in the world was the creation of beauty. Their whole life together had been built on this belief. He had no right to change his opinion without warning her" (*SCS* 55).

But it is not only the force of external circumstances that drives the turn to immediate experience. Beauvoir also presents Françoise as desiring an escape from the confines of her utilitarian consciousness. This desire is represented as an attraction to Xavière, a sensualist whose life seems to personify elements of both a Bergsonian ideal and the *femme-enfant* muse of Surrealism: "[Xavière] leaned her head back, half closed her eyes and lifted the glass [of aquavit] to her mouth. 'It burned all the way down my throat,' she said, running her fingers along her lovely slender neck. Then her hand slipped slowly down the length of her body. 'And it burns here. And here. It's odd. I feel as if I were being lighted up inside'" (*SCS* 55). Xavière is like the dreamer whose quality of perception Bergson contrasts with that of the 'man of action' in *Creative Evolution*: "in the almost instantaneous perception of a sensible quality, there may be trillions of oscillations which repeat themselves." The "man of action" is able to "embrace trillions of these oscillations in...[his] simple perception," and thus dominate them, while the dreamer is able, like some lower beings, to "vibrate almost in unison with the oscillation of the ether" (*CE* 327–28). In Beauvoir's novel, Xavière's body trembles in response to a dancer: "'I wish I could dance like that,' said Xavière. A light tremor passed over her shoulders and ran through her body" (*SCS* 19, *LI* 21).

Xavière also mirrors Bergson's interest in the body, and especially "the surface of our body – the common limit of the external and the internal," "the only position of space which is both perceived and felt" (*MAM* 58). In a scene in a bar, "Xavière was engaged in gently blowing the fine down on her arm which she was holding up to her mouth." "'It's funny the feeling it gives you when you touch your eyelashes [Xavière said]... You touch yourself without touching yourself. It's as if you touched yourself from a distance'" (*SCS* 60–61).

Beauvoir's contrast between Françoise and Xavière also encompasses Bergson's distinction between utilitarian memory and pure memory, "where our mind retains in all its details the picture of our past life" (*MAM* 323). "'I never forget anything,' [Xavière tells Pierre scornfully]... 'But I don't give a damn about understanding with my mind alone,' Xavière cried with unexpected violence. And with a kind of sneer, she added, 'I'm not an intellectual'" (*SCS* 62). Françoise, the intellectual, refuses to attend to memories unrelated to her projects. Nor is she willing to probe too deeply into her feelings. When hurt by a thoughtless remark, Françoise suppresses her feelings: "What disturbed her was this feeling... she had discovered in herself, and which had not yet completely dissipated. She hesitated, and, for a moment, she was tempted to try to analyze her uneasiness; but she did not feel like making the effort. She bent over her papers" (*SCS* 114). Françoise's denial of her feelings contributes to the inhibition of her freedom, as Bergson argues.

Where Françoise is dutiful and social, Xavière is spontaneous, refusing to be bound by social obligations. "'You make appointments and then don't keep them,' said Françoise. 'You might also ruin some real friendships by going through life that way.'... 'Well, that's just too bad,' said Xavière. She pouted disdainfully. 'I've always ended up by quarreling with everyone'" (*SCS* 57). Xavière, who criticizes Françoise for giving people rights over her, refuses all social demands: "'I'd rather live alone in the world and keep my freedom'" (*SCS* 103). Xavière also has contempt for work and the kind of utilitarian concerns that rule Françoise's life: "'I never like to take trouble over anything'... 'How can anyone endure living according to a plan, with timetables and homework?...I'd rather be a failure'" (*SCS* 55, 57).

Reflecting Bergson's description of language as forcing conformity to social convention, Xavière refuses the demands of language, often choosing to remain silent: "There was a kind of intimacy that one could never achieve with Xavière...Xavière said nothing" (*SCS* 47). For Xavière, as for Bergson, language and words overwhelm and thus distort fleeting impressions and feelings: "'The trouble is,' Xavière drawled, 'that big words immediately make everything so oppressive.'" "'It's like a strait-jacket around me,' she trembled from head to foot" (*SCS* 202–04, *LI* 253–55).

Françoise's involvement with Xavière challenges Françoise's solipsism, since in Xavière she confronts a consciousness that stubbornly refuses to be joined. Through her various attempts to relate to Xavière, we see Françoise increasingly turn to immediate experience, attending to her feelings and memories and losing her faith in language. In the process, Françoise witnesses the collapse of her initial sense of self as a sovereign consciousness and discovers her freedom. But the collapse of Françoise's metaphysical solipsism, with her realization of Xavière's existence as a separate consciousness, presents her with a new philosophical problem, as I shall show.

In the first stage of her attraction to Xavière, Françoise views Xavière as her possession. The difficulties begin when Xavière refuses to be controlled. Françoise is irritated "to feel this small, hostile, stubborn mind beside her." "Xavière's resistance was real and Françoise now wanted to break it down" (SCS 34). When Pierre becomes infatuated with Xavière, Françoise is forced to see Xavière differently: "[Xavière's] demands, her jealousies, her scorn, these could no longer be ignored, for Pierre had mentioned them and that was enough to lend them importance" (SCS 68). If Pierre takes Xavière more seriously, Françoise must do so as well. Thus the problem of solipsism arises for Françoise within the context of dependency and a fused identity with the other.

As Pierre becomes obsessed with Xavière, idolizing her, Françoise cedes Xavière to him: "From then on, Xavière belonged to Pierre." But her painful feelings of exclusion and exile are not easily analyzed away. They even disrupt her sense of time, which she now experiences as composed of qualitatively unique moments. At her parents' apartment, while Xavière and Pierre meet elsewhere, Françoise feels that "time was spread out all around her in a quiet, stagnant pool. To live was to grow old, nothing more." Then as Françoise leaves to meet Gerbert, "time had begun to move again. She was going to meet Gerbert; that at least gave some meaning to these moments" (SCS 117–19).

Françoise's sense of exclusion and exile challenges her solipsism, her sense of being the sole knowing subject: "Ordinarily, the center of Paris was wherever she happened to be. Today... [t]he center of Paris was the café where Pierre and Xavière were sitting, and Françoise felt as if she were wandering about in some vague suburb." Her feelings are so intense that her ordinary means of distorting and suppressing them fail. Even language seems inadequate: "Pierre would tell her the whole story that night, but for some time now she had less and less confidence in words" (SCS 119–20).

Unable to suppress her feelings, Françoise awakens a troubling childhood memory.

She felt a sudden anguish...she began to delve deep into the past to unearth a similar malaise. Then she remembered...The old jacket was hanging over the back of a chair...It...could not say to itself, 'I'm an old worn jacket'... Françoise tried to imagine what would happen if she were unable to say 'I am Françoise; I am six years old'...She closed her eyes. It was as if she did not exist at all; and yet other people would...see her, and would talk about her. She opened her eyes again; she could see the jacket, it existed, yet it was not aware of itself...[S]he could look at the jacket...and say very quickly, 'I'm old, I'm worn'; but nothing happened. The jacket stayed there, indifferent, a complete stranger, and she was still Françoise. Besides, if she became the jacket, then she, Françoise, would never know it. Everything began spinning in her head and she ran downstairs. [*SCS* 120, *LI* 146]

The jacket, which is "indifferent" to her, defies Françoise's consciousness, thus challenging her belief that the world is wholly enclosed within her consciousness.

Xavière and Pierre also exist "without her being there," but this time "she couldn't say, 'It doesn't know it exists, it doesn't exist.' For it did know...Xavière, with rapt attention, was devouring every word Pierre uttered" (*SCS* 123). In *Memoirs of a Dutiful Daughter* Beauvoir recounts the same childhood experience as confronting her with the reality of her death, when she will be reduced to an unknowing object, like the old jacket. "In...the silence of inanimate objects I had a foreboding of my own absence" (*MD* 49, *MJF* 69). This experience thus threatens her subjective idealism as she realizes that the world exists without her consciousness of it, that it extends beyond the reach of her consciousness.

In order to dispel her anguish, Françoise allows the bond uniting the instants in Pierre's meeting with Xavière to dissolve: "They had smoked cigarettes...and had spoken words; and those sounds and the smoke had never been condensed into mysterious hours of forbidden intimacy that Françoise might envy...Nothing existed except...the eternal present." But with a sudden anguish Françoise sees the dissolution of her relationship with Pierre as well: "If Pierre's and Xavière's friendship was no more than a mirage, then neither did her love for Pierre and Pierre's love for her exist. There was nothing but an infinite accumulation of meaningless moments, nothing but a chaotic seething of flesh and thought... 'Let's go,' she said abruptly" (SCS 129-30, LI 157-58). Françoise's anguish, which spurs her flight from immediate experience, is aroused by the thought of her separation from Pierre.

Françoise tries to lessen their separation by assuming Pierre's view of Xavière: "she almost wanted to believe in this seductive figure. If she often felt herself separated from Pierre, these days, it was because... [t]heir eyes no longer saw the same things. When she beheld only a capricious child, Pierre saw a wild and exacting soul." "The only way she could bring herself nearer to Pierre was by... trying to see [Xavière] through his eyes" (SCS 134-35, LI 164). But Xavière's jealous demands interfere with Françoise's relationship with Pierre.

Françoise is no longer reassured by Pierre's words, "We are one," describing them in Bergsonian terms as a crust over reality: "'Your feelings... [are] like the white sepulchers of the Holy Bible... They're firm, they're faithful, they can even be whitewashed periodically with beautiful words.' She was again overcome by a flood of tears. 'Only, they must never be opened, because you'll find only dust and ashes inside.'" Françoise's revelations are accompanied, as Bergson would have predicted, by strong emotions. When Pierre appeals to her reason – "'Stop crying,' he said. 'I'd like to talk reasonably'" – Françoise rebels: "Presently he would find a whole slue of lovely arguments, and it would be so easy to give in to them. Françoise did not want to lie to herself... She loathed the thought of that moment when she would cease crying and return to the world of merciful deception" (SCS 162, LI 199-200). Language and intellect have become a means of deception and distortion for Françoise, who now trusts her feelings more than Pierre's words.

When Pierre and Xavière rebel against her efforts to make them work, Françoise feels powerless: "all her happiness rested on his free will, and over that she had no hold" (SCS 172, LI 213). Françoise is aware of her lack of freedom: "For many years now she had ceased to be an individual... Our past, our future, our ideas, our love... never did she say 'I.' And yet Pierre disposed of his own future and his own heart" (SCS 175, LI 216). Françoise's philosophical odyssey out of deception is also a search for self and freedom. According to Bergson, "To act freely is to recover possession of oneself, and to get back into pure duration" (TFW 231-32).

Françoise's experiences continue to undermine her subjective idealism. Carried from her hotel room on a stretcher, after developing pneumonia, "Françoise was hardly more than an inert mass... She was carried down the stairs, head first, nothing more than a heavy piece of luggage that the stretcher-bearers handled in accordance with the laws of gravity and their own personal convenience." Beauvoir's use of Bergsonian terms highlights Françoise's embodied experience of herself as an "inert" object subject to natural "laws of gravity." With her illness, Françoise discovers herself as swept up in an external world whose existence she had denied: "Sickness, accidents... war; these impersonal misfortunes could not happen to her... And yet there she was stretched out in an ambulance" (*SCS* 179, *LI* 222).

Françoise declares her love to Xavière, in a bad faith effort to create a trio and "cling obstinately to the past" (*SCS* 209, *LI* 262). "She had been slowly drying up in the security of the patient constructions and leaden thoughts... One naive look from Xavière had sufficed to destroy this prison, and now... a thousand marvels would come to life, thanks to this exacting young angel... 'My precious Xavière,' said Françoise" (*SCS* 211, *LI* 264–65). Xavière remains elusive, but in her longing and regret Françoise discovers satisfaction in the emotional richness of the moment: "wholly drawn toward this infinitesimal golden head which she was unable to seize... [h]er happiness was shattered, but it was falling around her in a shower of impassioned moments" (*SCS* 250, *LI* 314). Time is no longer composed of objectively measurable, interchangeable instants of time. Focused on her desire, her feelings, Françoise has entered the world of immediate experience.

Françoise experiences the further erosion of her intellectual solipsism in a scene at a night club where Xavière, facing Pierre's jealousy over her relationship with Gerbert, deliberately burns her hand with a cigarette: "The girl was pressing the lighted end against her skin, a bitter smile curling her lips... Françoise flinched. It was not only her flesh that rose in revolt... Behind that maniacal grin was a danger more definitive than any [Françoise] had ever imagined" (*SCS* 283–84, *LI* 354). What terrifies Françoise is the experience of Xavière's consciousness, an experience confirmed by Xavière's jealousy later in the evening: "Facing Françoise... an alien consciousness was rising. It was like death, a total negation, an eternal absence, and yet, by a staggering contradiction, this abyss of nothingness could make itself...exist for itself with plenitude...Françoise...was herself dissolved in this void, the infinity of which no word, no image could encompass" (SCS 291, LI 363-64). Françoise later explains her experience to Pierre: "'I discovered she has a consciousness like mine. Has it ever happened to you to feel another's consciousness as something within?' Again she was trembling... 'It's intolerable, you know'" (SCS 295, LI 369).

As Edward Fullbrook argues, the originality of Beauvoir's demonstration of the existence of other minds is that it does not rely on the traditional argument from analogy, but "on the phenomenological event of experiencing oneself as the object of another's consciousness."[13] Bergson's influence is apparent in Beauvoir's privileging of immediate experience over the theoretical: "'What surprises me is that you are touched in so concrete a manner by a metaphysical situation,'" Pierre says. "'But it is something concrete,' said Françoise... '[F]or me, an idea is not theoretical...It is experienced [s'éprouve], or, if it remains theoretical, it doesn't count'" (SCS 301, LI 375-76).

The collapse of Françoise's metaphysical solipsism does not, however, free her from her attraction to Xavière, whom Françoise continues vainly to pursue. But as Pierre's passionate relationship with Xavière is rekindled, "their dual rejection" awakens in Françoise a new feeling towards Xavière: "with a kind of joy [Françoise] felt stirring within her something black and bitter...something powerful and free was bursting at last. It was hate" (SCS 357, LI 445). Beauvoir's description of Françoise's hatred echoes Bergson's description, in Time and Free Will, of the free act as "the deep-seated self rushing up to the surface" and bursting through the "the outer crust" of social convention (TFW 169). So, in Bergsonian terms, this emotional revelation is reflective of Françoise's freedom and deepest self, a view that suggests that the dissolution of Françoise's metaphysical solipsism has presented her with a new problem, that of moral solipsism.

The emergence of Françoise's freedom is also evident on a walking tour with Gerbert, where she musters the courage to tell him, hesitatingly, of her desire for him, and invites his embrace. "A few moments later, Françoise incredulously ran her hand over this smooth, young, firm body that for so long had seemed beyond reach." "'I've always been crazy about you,' [Gerbert] said... 'I'm so glad I wasn't discouraged,' she said. 'So am I.' He put his warm lips to her mouth and she felt his body cleave tightly to hers" (*SCS* 368–71, *LI* 458–62). Françoise's acting on her desires is rewarded with a miracle of our ambiguous condition when our embodiment enables us to unite with another embodied consciousness thus overcoming, ever so briefly, our separation. The body is philosophically significant for Bergson, who describes the body as a "privileged image," "the seat of affection and... the source of action, which I adopt as the centre of my universe and as the physical basis of my personality" (*MAM* 64). Françoise's hesitant decision, after so many months of desire for Gerbert, also mirrors Bergson's description of a truly free act as one in which "a self... lives and develops by means of its very hesitations, until the free action drops from it like an over-ripe fruit" (*TFW* 176–77, *DIC* 136).

Pierre, whose affair with Xavière has ended, insists that Françoise's affair with Gerbert be kept secret, since Pierre has convinced Xavière to love Gerbert exclusively. Françoise gloatingly agrees: " 'I've won,' thought Françoise triumphantly. Once again she existed alone, with no obstacle at the heart of her destiny... Xavière was now but a futile, living pulsation" (*SCS* 375, *LI* 467). Xavière, having rejected Françoise's love, has won her hatred.

Several months later, with the war begun and the men gone, Françoise brings Xavière to Paris, out of a nostalgia that reeks of bad faith: "There was no longer any future. The past alone was real, and it was in Xavière that the past was incarnate" (*SCS* 387–88, *LI* 481–82). Xavière, breaking into Françoise's desk, discovers Gerbert's love letters and the secret affair. Françoise feels herself "crushed by a deadly weight. Her love for Gerbert was there before her, black as treason." Françoise begs Xavière to understand; Xavière refuses: "With horror Françoise saw the woman Xavière was confronting with blazing eyes, this woman who was herself... 'I was jealous of her. I took Gerbert from her'... 'I did that, I.' " As long as Xavière exists, Françoise's betrayal exists: " 'My guilty face exists in the flesh'.... 'Either she or I. It shall be I' " (*SCS* 399–402, *LI* 497–501).

Françoise walks to the kitchen and turns off the gas meter, then she returns to Xavière's room: " 'Give me a chance not to feel odiously guilty.' " Xavière scoffs at her: " 'I would rather drop dead.' " Françoise puts her hand on the gas range and turns the valve. " 'I'm imploring

you,' she said. 'Imploring!,' Xavière laughed. 'I'm not a noble soul.'"
Françoise leaves the room; Xavière bolts the door.

Alone...Relying now solely on herself...[Françoise] walked into the
kitchen and put her hand on the lever of the gas meter. Her hand tight-
ened...Face to face with her solitude, beyond space, beyond time, stood
this enemy presence that had for so long crushed her with its blind shadow:
Xavière was there, existing only for herself...she was absolute separation.
And yet it was only necessary to pull down this lever to annihilate her...
[H]ow was it possible for a consciousness not her own to exist? In that case,
it was she who did not exist. She repeated. "She or I," and pulled down the
lever...Françoise was alone...She had acted alone...No one could condemn or absolve her. Her act was her own...It was her will that was in
the process of accomplishing itself, nothing could separate her from herself
any longer. She had finally chosen. She had chosen herself. [SCS 403–04,
LI 502–03]

Beauvoir's focus on Françoise's hand as it tightens first on the lever
of the gas meter and then on the valve on the stove, mirrors Bergson's
focus on muscular effort in *Time and Free Will*, where he discusses
the effort "to clench the fist with increasing force" (*TFW* 24) and
in his discussion of human freedom in *Matter and Memory*, where
he also focuses on the movement of the hand (*MAM* 246). Bergson
is interested in freedom's reliance on the body, which has "the sole
function of preparing actions" (*MAM* 82). But is this murder a free
act, or is it a product of deception and bad faith, denying the moral
reality of the Other's existence as Françoise had earlier denied its
metaphysical reality? Consider Bergson's description of the free act,
in *Time and Free Will*:

in the depths of the self, below the most reasonable ponderings over most
reasonable pieces of advice, something else was going on – a gradual heat-
ing and a sudden boiling over of feelings and ideas...We find that we have
decided without any reason, and perhaps even against every reason. But, in
certain cases, that is the best of reasons. For the action which has been per-
formed...agrees with the whole of our most intimate feelings, thoughts and
aspirations...and this absence of any tangible reason is the more striking
the deeper our freedom goes. [*TFW* 169–70]

Beauvoir portrays the murder in Bergsonian terms, as an act of genuine freedom – instinctual, irrational, and asocial. Françoise, once
the personification of conventional morality, sees her suppressed

hatred break through the crust of social convention. Françoise experiences the murder, which goes against every reason, as the choice of herself, thus as the expression of her deepest self.

NOTES

I gratefully acknowledge the research support of a summer research fellowship from the Graduate School of Southern Illinois University Edwardsville. Earlier versions of this chapter were presented at one of the University's philosophy department colloquiums and also at the 9th International Simone de Beauvoir Society Conference held at St. John's College, Oxford, on 20–22 July 2001. My research has also benefited from discussions with Brett Carroll, Ron Carter, Belinda Clark, James Crockett, Pam Decoteau, Kate Fullbrook, Christian Hainds, Ashley Harp, Rebecca Jeyes, Janet Novosad, Rhonda Penelton, Anne Valk, Tricia Wall, and Steven Williams, and from the unfailing encouragement and patience of Claudia Card, for which I am deeply grateful.

1 Simone de Beauvoir, *Mémoires d'une jeune fille rangée* (Paris: Gallimard, 1958), p. 288; *Memoirs of a Dutiful Daughter*, trans. James Kirkup (New York: Harper & Row, 1959), p. 208; my revised translation.

2 Henri Bergson, *Essai sur les données immédiates de la conscience*, 6th edn (Paris: Félix Alcan, [1908] 1889), hereafter *DIC*; *Time and Free Will: An Essay on the Immediate Data of Consciousness*, trans. F. L. Pogson (New York: Macmillan, 1913), hereafter *TFW*; my revised translation.

3 Simone de Beauvoir, 2e cahier [1926], holograph manuscript, Manuscript Collection, Bibliothèque Nationale, Paris, pp. 7–8; my transcription and translation. "Cahier" hereafter given as CA.

4 Henri Bergson, *Matière et mémoire: Essai sur la relation du corps à l'esprit*, 10th edn (Paris: Félix Alcan, [1913] 1896); *Matter and Memory*, trans. Nancy Margaret Paul and W. Scott Palmer (London: George Allen & Unwin, 1911), hereafter *MAM*; my revised translation.

5 Henri Bergson, *L'Evolution créatrice*, 6th edn (Paris: Félix Alcan, [1910] 1907); *Creative Evolution*, trans. Arthur Mitchell (New York: Modern Library, [1944] 1911), hereafter *CE*; my revised translation.

6 Simone de Beauvoir, *L'Invitée* (Paris: Gallimard, 1943); *She Came to Stay*, trans. Yvonne Moyse and Roger Senhouser (New York: Norton, 1954); my revised translation.

7 Simone de Beauvoir, *Le Deuxième sexe*, 2 vols. (Paris: Gallimard, 1949); *The Second Sex*, trans. H. M. Parshley (New York: Knopf, 1952); my revised translation.

8 Henri Bergson, *The Two Sources of Morality and Religion*, trans. R. A. Audra and C. Brereton with W. H. Carter (New York: Henry Holt, 1935).

9   Simone de Beauvoir, *Quand prime le spirituel* (Paris: Gallimard, 1979);
     When Things of the Spirit Come First: Five Early Tales, trans. Patrick
     O'Brian (New York: Pantheon, 1982); my revised translation.

10   Simone de Beauvoir, 4e carnet [1927], holograph manuscript, Manu-
     script Collection, Bibliothèque Nationale, Paris, p. 94; transcribed by
     Barbara Klaw, Sylvie Le Bon de Beauvoir and myself; my translation.

11   Simone de Beauvoir, "Littérature et métaphysique" (Literature and
     Metaphysics), in *L'Existentialisme et la sagesse des nations* (Paris:
     Editions Nagel, 1963), pp. 102–03; my translation. Originally published
     in *Les Temps modernes*, 1, 7 (April 1946).

12   For an argument that Beauvoir, rather than Sartre, originated this theory,
     see Edward Fullbrook, "*She Came to Stay* and *Being and Nothingness*,"
     Hypatia, 14, 4 (1999): 58–60.

13   ibid., 53.

6   Philosophy in Beauvoir's fiction

A critic of the currently popular genre "Reality TV" sums up the enterprise: the basic idea is that the watchers and the watched will more or less forget about the cameras, "and the result will be raw, emotion-packed – and tedious."[1] Having pointed out that the extensive editing of such programs to adapt them to the respective tastes of Europe and America means that viewers are surely not in fact getting an unadorned slice of reality, this critic hypothesizes that "reality TV" is in principle an oxymoron. The general hypothesis may be wrong; *Road Rules* and *Real World* seem to show that normal teenagers discussing their feelings can forget all about the cameras and behave naturally. Still, the very availability of the kind of information supplied by "Reality TV" raises an important question, one which was anticipated by Simone de Beauvoir in her 1965 contribution to the forum, *Que peut la littérature?* She describes reading *Children of Sánchez*, an account put together from tapes that recorded the daily conversations of a father and his four children off and on over an eight-year period.[2] The advantage of this format of collecting and presenting information, she observes, is that the reader receives a presentation of family life from multiple viewpoints, the sort of thing that literary works frequently try to do. One could, she says, produce more works of this kind – technologically we could record and present information about the daily inner workings of all sorts of social units. If we did so, she asks, "Would literature still have a role to play?" Beauvoir's answer is "Yes" (*QPL* 74–75). The difference between information and literature, she says, has to do with the basic features of the human condition and with the distinctive way in which literature functions.

Each of us is "situated" in an absolutely individual – or "singular" – relationship with the world, which is a single world for all of
us by virtue of being "the interplay of all the individual situations
as they overlap and envelop each other." There is a plenitude which
is being, and it is that being to which I and others are related by our
situations, in which we are involved by our actions. We experience
the world as common, and we experience others as claimants on it
and as involved in it.

The singularity of our individual situations is in a sense "irreducible." I have got my particular "view" or "involvement" in the
world, which is never experienced as completely confounded with
yours. "I" never means for you what it means for me; neither, for
that matter, can "green" or "anguish" be assumed to refer to identical experiences for the two of us.

Still, despite the irreducible singularity of our individual situations, the most fundamental features of our separate existences –
and *a fortiori* of our separate involvements in the world – are the
same; for each of us there is a unique "taste of our own life," an irreducible separation from the others by virtue of having a particular
and singular point of view or involvement *vis-à-vis* the whole world,
a unique and separate death (*QPL* 77). This sameness means that
our individual situations are not completely closed with respect to
each other. Language gives us a means of communicating precisely
because the basic features of our individual situations are every time
the same; you can understand what I mean by "I," just as you can
understand my references to red and green (*QPL* 77–79).

All genuine literature, autobiography, novel, or essay, has an ine-
liminable role to play because it allows us to bridge our "irreducible
separation" from each other. Authentic literature thus distinguishes
itself sharply from what Beauvoir calls "information." When "information" is communicated to me, I "annex" something to my own
situation, to my world. When I read about the Sánchez family, my understanding of the world comes to include a more articulated Mexico
and the members of the family who live there, in place of my previous indeterminate sense that the world more or less keeps going
on south of Texas. "Literature" functions differently: "This is the
miracle of literature and is what distinguishes it from information:
it is that a truth which is *other* becomes mine without ceasing to be

other. I give up my 'I' in favor of the 'I' of the person who is speaking; and nonetheless I remain myself" (*QPL* 82).

The special power of literature is thus that it allows us to pass beyond our separation from one another – precisely by remaining aware that we are separate, although we coinhabit a point of view. The expression "point of view," says Beauvoir, is open to the objection that it is "a little idealistic . . . as if our relationship to the world were simply one of reflecting it in consciousness" (*QPL* 80–81). It is preferable to talk about one's "situation," which denotes the active and involved relationship of each consciousness to its world. When I read literature, then, I remain perfectly aware that I am not Kafka or Balzac; yet, I adopt the novelist's situation, so to speak, from the inside out.

For the writer, literature has a double importance. It confers upon the writer's transient situation-in-progress a certain immortality (*QPL* 89); insofar as Beauvoir's "irreducibly singular," transient anguish or happiness is expressed in literature, it can become the situation for you or me as reader, albeit a situation shared only in the imagination. That unique relationship to reality in its irreducible singularity then exists anew. Moreover, for every genuine work, the writing is one's attempt, as a writer, to work out and make comprehensible the relationship between two "incomplete totalities": the world and one's experience. Literature thus enables one, as a writer, to achieve self-understanding through a comprehension of one's situation, and in adopting the writer's "I," I thereby adopt that "investigation" of the writer's world and share the writer's discovery of self and world (*QPL* 84).[3]

These ideas about the general role of literature are a constant in Beauvoir's thinking. She sees a difference, however, between fictive literature and other kinds of literature. She addresses this question first in her essay of 1946, "Littérature et métaphysique," in which she distinguishes between writing metaphysics and writing a "metaphysical novel" as two different ways in which, as a writer, one can express to the reader the ideas suggested by one's lived contact with concrete things and events, a contact that is in itself inexhaustible and colored by action, emotion, and feeling (*LM* 1154). In writing a metaphysical essay, one forces oneself to express some universal meaning in abstract language, then to impose these ideas on the reader (*LM* 1154). In contrast, even the "novel of ideas" makes a more radical appeal to freedom. In reading a novel, readers go through the experience of things and events in imagination; they exercise their freedom to judge, interpret, and react – as if the world of the novel were reality itself (*LM* 1154–55). For the author as well, the novel is more of an experiment than the metaphysical treatise. The characters of a novel do not, of course, literally wander about the writer's room, exercising their freedom to the astonishment and consternation of the writer. Nevertheless,

> If he wants the reader to believe in the creations he puts forward, it is neces-
> sary that the novelist believe in them strongly enough to discover in them
> a meaning which bounces back against his original idea; this will give rise
> to unforeseen problems, twists and turns, and developments. Thus as the
> narrative continues to unroll, he watches truths appear whose faces are un-
> familiar to him, and questions arise to which he has no answer. [LM 1157]

Another source of information about the relationship between Beauvoir's fiction and her nonfictional writing is her multivolume autobiography, published beginning in 1958, in which she describes how she worked through and discovered the meanings of crises of her life experience through her novels, by "transposing" real occurrences into a fictional world.[4] The volumes of the autobiography are retrospective in relation to the writing of the novels, and Beauvoir's recollections of her own intentions and motivations are sometimes suspect. Still, because of the remarkable juxtaposition of literary autobiography, "metaphysical fiction," and philosophical reflection, Beauvoir offers us a rare opportunity to examine the relationship between the "novel of ideas" and the author's philosophical writings in the light of her own views about what she was attempting to do in each genre, what she accomplished, and what each accomplishment meant.

It is clearly Beauvoir's view that her novels and her philosophical essays have a common field of reference in the historical events and people of her life experience. In her case, the "metaphysical novels" are as much *about* her life experience *in their own way* as her autobiography and philosophical essays are. For example, her novel *The Mandarins* is described by Beauvoir in the third volume of her autobiography, *The Force of Circumstance*, as an attempt to understand and come to terms with "shattered illusions" (*FC* 274). For Beauvoir, this meant, first of all, a sense of personal failure connected to the disintegration of the Left in postwar France; she had come to realize that instead of an organized and unified opposition to the combination of bourgeois values, rigid class structure, and societal and governmental repression, which she associated with the situation of prewar France, there would be a climate of sustained acrimony and rejection by wartime ideological allies. Less obviously, perhaps, in the story of Anne's love affair with an American writer, *The Mandarins* is an attempt on Beauvoir's part to come to terms with her own decision to define herself within this French intellectual world and in terms of her life with Jean-Paul Sartre. She composed the characters and their interactions, she says, in order to "step back from my recent experiences to see them better...I was interested in all the things that made our world...To talk about myself, I had to talk about *us* in the sense in which we used that word in 1944" (*FC* 275).

The Mandarins is not really a philosophical novel. Its political-historical story is told in terms of individual passions, friendships, and rejections; in writing it Beauvoir did not put forward a large-scale philosophy of history.[5] Perhaps more importantly, although the familiar themes of Beauvoir's philosophical position are everywhere in evidence in the novel, they are not essential to understanding the characters' motivations, and they are not themselves at issue. At one point, Anne's awareness that she and her husband are now living parallel lives crystallizes; she remembers seeing him that morning and finding her gaze arrested by his teeth, "the only constant thing about a body." Fairly soon, she realizes, she could find herself alone looking at Robert stretched out on a bed, "his skin waxen, a false smile on his lips." "They can mix our ashes together," she thinks, "but they won't unite our deaths...each of us is alone, imprisoned in his body, with his arteries hardening under his withering skin...with his death which ripens noiselessly inside him, and which separates him from everyone else."[6] This fairly typical existentialist insight reveals the extent of Anne's sense of isolation; yet it is not this apprehension of each individual's essential existential separation that brings Anne near to suicide, but rather her sense of futility in the face of the fallout from the war and its aftermath and her realization that who she has become cuts her off from becoming the person she wants to be. She is turned aside from death by the thought that she has no business leaving the baby alone in the garden in order to come up to her room and take the chloral, then by the wider thought that she has no business imposing her corpse and her death on her family. "I would die alone," she thinks, "yet it's the others who would live this, my death" (*M* 759). Again, Anne's thinking about her death is almost formulaically existentialist. Still, what turns her away from suicide is not this metaphysical insight but her own personality: Anne is someone who is who she is through and for others. In the end, the fact that she has nothing to live for personally is not a good enough reason for killing herself.

By contrast, Beauvoir's earlier, more "metaphysical" novels are integrally related to the basic themes of the philosophical position made current by herself and Sartre and by such writer-philosophers as Merleau-Ponty and Camus. In these novels, basic existentialist ideas and their consequences are actively under investigation. This is particularly true of the 1943 novel *L'invitée* (*She Came to Stay*), in which the main character confronts "the scandal of the Other."

SHE CAME TO STAY: THE STUFF OF A MURDERESS?

She Came to Stay is an intense and beautiful novel that ends with a singularly aseptic and fairly unpremeditated murder. Standing outside Xavière's apartment with the door bolted behind her, Françoise envisions Xavière inside:

She was there, existing only for herself, entirely turned in upon herself, reducing to nothing everything she excluded; she enclosed the entire world in her own triumphant solitude, she expanded outwards without limit, infinite and unique; everything she was she drew from within herself; she rejected every hold on her; she was absolute separation. And nonetheless it would be enough to pull down this handle to annihilate her. Annihilate a consciousness. "How could I?" thought Françoise. But how could there be a consciousness which was not her own? In that case, it would be she who did not exist. She repeated, "She or I?" She pulled down the handle. [*LI* 418; cf. *SCS* 403–04][7]

Looking back upon this scene in the second volume of her autobiography, *The Prime of Life*, Beauvoir says that she did not much care whether Françoise's murder of Xavière is the right solution or not – *She Came to Stay* is not a novel written to prove any point. Indeed, Beauvoir describes Françoise as someone who "has given up on looking for an ethical solution to the problem of coexistence."[8] She would consider herself satisfied, Beauvoir says, "if those who are wholly opposed to her decision nonetheless believe in it" (PL 340; FA 123). What is at issue, then, is whether the reader can follow the events of the narrative to the point of finding it credible in that final moment that turning the gas on, leaving Xavière behind her locked door with the gas jet open, is exactly what Françoise would do to save herself whole and free from threatened dissolution – so that it becomes clear that this dramatic ending to the story of Françoise, Xavière, and Pierre is not just Beauvoir's contrived and desperate way of stopping a novel she could not figure out how to finish, but "the very motor force behind the novel, and its reason for being" (PL 340; FA 123).

On a flat retelling of the story of Françoise, Xavière, and Pierre, prospects look dim for establishing this sort of credibility for the dramatic climax of She Came to Stay, for on the face of it these are normal people tracing their way through the ordinary complexities of an everyday sort of situation. Pierre and Françoise have found their way to a life together with Pierre's revolutionary work in the theatre as their common goal. Their intimacy has drifted into habit. The teenage Xavière attaches herself first to Françoise, then increasingly to Pierre, offering uncertainty, and excitement, to both of them. To Pierre in particular she offers a chance to see everything anew in a fresh and critical light. In his attempts to attract Xavière, Pierre betrays his understanding with Françoise in a thousand ways. He flirts with Xavière's dismissive attitude towards his own values and achievements and exhibits crude and unreasoning sexual jealousy when Xavière goes behind his back to start up a flirtation with Gerbert. Xavière comes to dislike and resent Françoise and demands that Pierre give up his relationship with her. Françoise begins her own affair with Gerbert. In the end, Xavière turns on Françoise in a jealous rage, and Françoise, jealous of the way Xavière attracts Pierre, and confused and guilty about her own affair with Gerbert, responds by turning on the gas and leaving Xavière to die. If that is all there is to the story of Françoise, Xavière, Pierre, and Gerbert – an everyday string of melancholy inevitabilities – then the novel ought to have an ordinary ending.

Beauvoir is surely able to write an everyday ending to an ordinary tale of loss and disorientation. In the final scene of The Mandarins

Anne comes downstairs to rejoin her family, hoping that their lives will somehow give her a reason to live her own life for the next ten years or so. In "A Woman Destroyed," a middle-aged woman comes to realize finally that she has no place in life; her husband is wrapped up in the possessive demands of his young mistress, and her children are living their own lives without her. Finally she sits alone facing the connecting doors of their apartment and feels the future crouching behind the door like some hideous presence. "The door to the future will open," she thinks; "There is only this door and what is watching behind it. I am afraid. And I cannot call anyone to help me. I am afraid" (FR 250–51; cf. WD 220).[9]

These are everyday resolutions in ordinary lives that have come unstuck: Living for others. Paralysis. Resignation. If Xavière is just an everyday threat to Françoise in her middle-aged life, then the story ought to have some such ordinary ending. Killing someone, however, is not a commonplace action, as Beauvoir comments in The Prime of Life (PL 339); Beauvoir worries that Françoise as she is presented is just not the sort of person who would actually kill someone, that Xavière is not a sufficiently malign presence to excite so violent a reaction (FC 339). Perhaps, she speculates, she ought at least to have set the story in the provinces, where a tale of ordinary emotions that acquire violent intensity and tragic dimensions would be more credible (FC 343).

The narrative of She Came to Stay offered Beauvoir several opportunities to end things in some ordinary way. When Françoise is first stricken by the realization that Pierre and Xavière are coming to an understanding that closes her out, she is desolated by the loss of the reciprocity of vision with Pierre that gave her world its meaning. For Françoise, "It was as if the world had been emptied out; there was nothing more to fear, but nothing more to love either. There was absolutely nothing. There was nothing but an ill-defined accumulation of indifferent moments, nothing but a disordered swarm of flesh and thought, with death at the end" (LI 133; cf. SCS 130).

Beauvoir might have ended She Came to Stay with Françoise's moment of paralysis, but the narrative goes on. During Françoise's bout with pneumonia, Pierre and Xavière draw closer; upon her recovery, the carefully balanced triangle with Xavière disintegrates. Françoise is shattered by the realization that Xavière has long since ceased to be a mere complementary part of her universe and has become instead a living, hating source of jealousy and resistance and an implacable arbiter of Françoise's own existence. She has become an "irreducible and alien consciousness." Françoise feels herself completely excluded; she has allowed herself to dissolve in this vast universe in which she has no part. "Why should it be she rather than I?," Françoise asks herself. "Never before had she achieved with such perfect lucidity her own annihilation" (*LI* 302; cf. *SCS* 292).

She Came to Stay could have ended here, like "A Woman Destroyed," with a vivid vision of annihilation, but Beauvoir goes on with her story. Eventually Françoise discovers that she has encouraged a reconciliation between Pierre and Xavière, only to find that Xavière has used the brief moment of mutual understanding to draw Pierre into betraying his "love of devotion" for herself. Finally, and dramatically, she allows her feelings towards Xavière to focus into something, "powerful and free, opening out at last without constraint; it was hate" (*LI* 369; cf. *SCS* 357). If Beauvoir was bent on finding Françoise a way of extricating herself from the trap of a destructive triangle with Pierre and Xavière, surely this powerful moment of emotional crystallization could have served as a conclusion for the novel.

Yet the ultimate ending of *She Came to Stay* seemed necessary to Beauvoir when she wrote the novel; she reached Françoise's moment of paralysis, her instant of annihilation, the point at which her hatred of Xavière crystallizes – and continued her story. There was, it seems, a kind of dynamic inner logic to the story of Françoise that demanded the ending the novel got. Beauvoir explains that the murder of Xavière had deep personal meaning for her because it allowed her to work out her hostility towards Sartre and Olga (cf. *PL*, 238–43, 254–61, especially 340). But as Beauvoir herself says, fiction comes from pulverizing the resources of real life so that something new, the work, comes out of them (*FC* 280). The novel has got to work and have meaning, if it does, because of its own narrative logic.

Looking back on her works, Beauvoir says of *The Mandarins* that she avoided ending it, as she did *She Came to Stay*, by assigning to her protagonist a final action "motivated by purely metaphysical reasons" (*FC* 283). In order to understand what makes the murder of Xavière inevitable, then, it seems that we need to bring into sharper focus a second, "metaphysical" layer of narrative. The metaphysical framework by means of which Beauvoir organized reality

段组织

in 1943 was the existentialist phenomenology that she sums up in her first published philosophical essay, *Pyrrhus et Cinéas*, in which the central point of discussion is the confrontation of consciousness with the Other, the "*scandale de l'autre*," and the necessity of violence.

METAPHYSICAL NARRATIVE: INCARNATION, VIOLENCE AND RECOVERY

On a deeper, "metaphysical" level, *She Came to Stay* is the story of Françoise's incarnation. At the start of the novel, Beauvoir says, Françoise has "literally no 'moi'" (*PL* 338). She has no sense of herself as someone with definite outlines over against the world and others. She experiences herself as a sort of pure and transparent sentience from which the world extends unproblematically outwards. "I am at the heart of my world," she thinks, "I am here at the heart of my life...wherever I go, the rest of the world moves with me" (*LI* 13; cf. *SCS* 14–15). She has no sense of her own reality in the world, or of her presence to others; her face "was always an agreeable surprise to her when she encountered it in a mirror – ordinarily she was not even aware of having one" (*LI* 21; cf. *SCS* 22). Her "happiness" with Pierre gives her no sense of herself as a person, because she thinks of herself and Pierre as perfect reflections of each other. Everything that has reality for either of them has a place in the seamless, common world they share. Others, like Gerbert and Xavière, are simply part of her world; with everyone except Pierre, whose appearance she hardly notices any more than her own, she is extraordinarily conscious of hair, of eyes, of the feel of physical contact; she sees their lives and experiences, when she thinks of them, as an extension of her own experience. In the café with Xavière, she reflects that "what most delighted her was to have annexed this pathetic little existence to her life; for now, like Gerbert, like Ines, like Canzetti, Xavière belonged to her; nothing ever gave Françoise so much joy as this kind of possession" (*LI* 19; cf. *SCS* 20).

The first palpable sign that this world is disintegrating is Françoise's discovery that she and Pierre do not see Xavière's behavior in the same light. They have both been shocked to discover that Xavière has told Gerbert that the three of them sneaked off without him for an evening of fun; but Françoise finds that Pierre takes quite a favorable view of what Xavière has done and her very suspect account of why she did it:

> "She isn't entirely lying, either; it is necessary to interpret what she says," said Pierre. One would have thought he was talking about the Pythian oracle.
>
> "Where are you going with this?" said Françoise impatiently. Pierre gave a crooked smile.
>
> "Doesn't it strike you that she was in the end reproaching me with not having seen her since Friday?"
>
> "Yes," said Françoise, "That shows that she is beginning to like you."
>
> "With that young lady to begin and to go to the end are the same thing, I think," said Pierre.
>
> "What do you mean?"
>
> "I think that she likes me very much," said Pierre with an air of smug complacency which was partly assumed, but in part revealed an inner satisfaction. Françoise was shocked at it. Ordinarily Pierre's calculated coarseness amused her. But he respected Xavière, the fondness which had shone in his smiles at the Pôle Nord had not been feigned; his cynicism made her uneasy. [*LI* 117–18; cf. *SCS* 115]

Françoise has lost her sense of complete metaphysical complicity with Pierre. She sees him preening himself, fatuously overcomplicating Xavière in his attempt to construe her behavior as a response to him. His attempt to distance himself through a play of facetious crudity shows that he is more interested in Xavière than he is willing to admit. She has become aware, too, that Xavière is manipulating her and using her to interact with Pierre. Françoise is thus becoming aware of herself as something in the world, present to other people as something to be assessed, used, and abused. From this point on, Françoise is increasingly conscious of herself as definite and limited; she is a woman who has never learned to dance and has never shot the Colorado in a canoe (*LI* 150; cf. *SCS* 149). She becomes acutely aware that others have a separate presence to the world, which she sees only from the outside. She is set up for that terrible moment of disorientation when she discovers that she is exiled from the world about which she said happily, "I am at the heart of my world"; she is annihilated as the pure, transparent center of that world, and has fallen into the world and into genuine involvement with others. Beauvoir describes this first stage of Françoise's incarnation as a fall from a kind of "absolute subjectivity": "One thing consoled her for her downfall; limited and vulnerable, she became a human creature with precise contours, and situated precisely at a certain point on the earth" (*PL* 338).

This kind of "downfall" is described by Beauvoir in philosophical and abstract terms in *Pyrrhus et Cinéas*. We are first of all "for ourselves," consciousness, "the fact of transcendence which goes before every goal or purpose"; "it is not for others that each of us transcends himself" (*PC* 96). But we are in fact in the world; we must also on some level be aware that we are not pure transcendence; "we also desire to escape from this contingency, from the arbitrariness of pure presence" (*PC* 96). It is over against others and their projects that we ourselves and our actions and our achievements have being as part of the world (*PC* 96); "We need others in order for our existence to become grounded and necessary" (*PC* 96). We have being for others insofar as we affect their projects positively or negatively; "For the Other we are thus nothing but a means, even when we pose an obstacle" (*PC* 86). Others can play this role in our existence only on the condition that we understand them as consciousness, as present to themselves as we ourselves are for ourselves. The encounter with the Other brings me face to face with a world which is not mine, which is not organized in accordance with my values and objectives; the Other thus presents me with a metaphysical "affront," or "scandal" (*PC* 89).

"Obstacle" and "scandal" are thus technical terms for Beauvoir. "Scandal" has considerable latitude. In the narrower sense, that we affront the Other with "scandal" denotes a particular coexistential strategy against the Other; "we demand that he grasp that his project is separate from ours; we attempt to become for him an object of ridicule and hatred; thus there can be no more complicity between us" (*PC* 106–07). Yet Beauvoir also uses "scandalous presence" or "scandalous existence" in an extremely broad sense, which denotes the presence to consciousness of anything that it is not, but most particularly the presence of a consciousness that it is not. I am such a scandalous existence for the Other just by virtue of the fact that "whatever I undertake, I exist before him. I am there for him. I am blended with the scandalous existence of everything which he is not; I am the facticity of his situation" (*PC* 89).

Beauvoir later criticizes *Pyrrhus et Cinéas* for being too subjectivistic and idealistic, for treating existence for the Other as something encountered more or less as an accident by the fully formed individual engaged in his fully and independently formulated project in the world. In her judgment, *Pyrrhus et Cinéas* thus falls victim to the very philosophical individualism it was trying to avoid (*FC* 549). *She Came to Stay* succeeds as a novel where *Pyrrhus et Cinéas* is flawed as a philosophical treatise, precisely because Beauvoir instinctively presents Françoise's original state of innocence as a kind of false consciousness. Françoise has had an occasional intimation of the significance of others as centers of consciousness like herself; she has had the fleeting fear that she herself is "nothing more than someone else's mental image" (*LI* 15; cf. *SCS* 16). More importantly, in her unguarded moments she is dissatisfied with her lack of involvement in the world – she envies Xavière for her rapturous involvement in the "sharp and unforgettable taste" of the here and now; and she envies Elizabeth, Pierre's unhappy sister, for a suffering that is "violent and real" (*LI* 31; cf. *SCS* 32). She wonders if she is not in reality slightly bored by her happiness with Pierre; "imprisoned in happiness" (*LI* 31; cf. *SCS* 32), she thinks – then hastily thrusts the thought away.

Xavière intrudes with convincing force into this unstable world. As soon as she and Pierre disagree about Xavière, Françoise recognizes that she was wrong in thinking that they had reached a state of perfect reciprocity. Instead, she realizes, she has tried to submerge herself in Pierre, who has always retained a certain independence – which he is quick to reassert as soon as his objectives diverge from hers, as they do immediately when he begins his attempt to attach Xavière to himself. Françoise quickly becomes dependent on Xavière's separate vision of her, because it gives her an authentic sense of herself as "a human creature with precise contours" (*PL* 338) and not merely as a pure and disembodied spectator or as Pierre's reflection. It is this dependence that lays her open to a shattering vision of Xavière as "scandal," as an irreducible Other arising with annihilating force, existing in its own freedom for itself:

Day after day, minute after minute, Françoise had fled the danger, but it had happened; she had finally met with the insuperable obstacle of which she had had indistinct intimations from her earliest childhood. Through Xavière's maniacal joy, through her hatred and jealousy, the scandal burst upon her as monstrous and definite as death. Facing Françoise, and nevertheless without her, everything existed as a condemnation without possibility of appeal:

free, absolute, irreducible, an alien consciousness was rising. It was like death, a total negation, an eternal absence; and nonetheless, in shocking contradiction, this abyss of non-being could make itself present to itself and make itself exist for itself in its fullness. The entire universe was engulfed by her, and Françoise, forever dispossessed of her world, herself dissolved in this void, whose infinity no word and no image could encompass. [*LI* 301; cf. *SCS* 291]

Pierre is struck with something between wonder and amusement that Françoise is so concretely affected by the realization that someone else has a consciousness like hers: what surprises him, he says, is that she is touched so concretely "by a metaphysical situation" (*LI* 311; cf. *SCS* 301).

Given a chance to break off the affair between Pierre and Xavière, Françoise does not do so. In part, she is surely afraid that if she asks Pierre to give up the relationship, he will resent it. And in any event, she cannot go back to her sense of innocent complicity with Pierre. Pierre has addressed her sharply; she has noticed the little jut of his lips when he does not get his way, the fatuous little smile on his face when he has made some trifling advance with Xavière; she has taken to concealing much of her thought from him. These facts cannot be unmade. But in part, too, Françoise is unwilling to demand that the affair be broken off, because she cannot return to being a pure and uninvolved spectator. She has come to crave being immersed in a flow of intense self-consciousness, the cycle of conflict and reconciliation, and the struggle for control.

Dependence on the Other and its consequences are a central concern of *Pyrrhus et Cinéas*. Human projects are separate, and even opposed; yet my own projects attain substance and being only insofar as they exist for another. As a result, I must sometimes feel that I am condemned to be divided between my vision of myself as a process oriented towards my future and the Other's vision of me as fact in the world in which his projects are to be realized. It is unavoidable that for each of us interaction with the Other has a fundamental element of struggle for control, each of us attempting to co-opt the Other in order to establish control of who we are and how the world will be (*PC* 111). Moreover, the very fact that we are separate, with distinct projects, means that as we each attempt to bring about a future that is aligned favorably with our respective projects, those projects twist together in a complicated interplay of strategy and counterstrategy (PC 105–06). "It is necessary to me that the Other project me towards a future that I recognize as my own; I am checked decisively if my action achieves significance by virtue of becoming useful to my enemies" (PC 106).

Pyrrhus et Cinéas is deeply ambivalent about the transition from this inescapable interplay of strategic checks and counterchecks to violence. On the one hand, justification for my own actions, she says, requires that others freely recognize the value of my actions. Violence is simple negation of the Other as consciousness; it embodies the determination to interact with the Other as Object. To the extent that I simply negate the projects of others, I treat them as "obstacles"; I lose the possibility of significant recognition and acceptance on their part, thus losing any possibility that my own actions be justified. "I give up being able to treat them as free, and I correspondingly restrict what I can be" (PC 116). Violence is thus self-defeating because the Other as pure Object is of no use to me in my project of self-validation.

On the other hand, at the time she wrote Pyrrhus et Cinéas Beauvoir was strongly attracted to the idea that if struggle with others is ubiquitous and unavoidable, then to that extent violence is inevitable as well. So long as there are individuals in their necessary struggle against each other, she says, "We are condemned to check and be checked because we are condemned to violence. We are condemned to violence because man is divided and opposed within himself, because men are separate and opposed to each other" (PC 117).

It is hard to see exactly how this sweeping conclusion that we are condemned to violence is reached here. The argument looks to be backwards. It seems that Beauvoir ought to argue here from the unavoidability of opposition to each other to the conclusion that the situation of checks and counterchecks is inevitable and that violence is a necessary realization of this unavoidable situation. It is also somewhat unclear what the conclusion means in real terms, for "violence" seems to be a semitechnical term with a troublesome latitude of meaning. It can be used very broadly simply to denote conflict of interest, it seems – in this sense there is "violence" whenever my project is incompatible with yours, perhaps whenever we both espy the same pair of sale-priced shoes, and certainly when we both stretch out our hands for them. In such a case I need not, it seems, fail to recognize you as another consciousness. Indeed, a normal level of conflicting objectives seems to be, as Beauvoir says elsewhere in *Pyrrhus et Cinéas*, compatible with cooperation and communication with others. But "violence" can also be used in a narrower sense to designate the situation in which I use some sort of force to eliminate you as a significant Other. Violence in the broader sense is inevitable, it seems; but this conclusion is not particularly shocking to anyone who has shopped in bargain basements. In the stronger, narrower sense violence seems to be one strategy of coexistence among many, and it is hard to see why it should be inevitable in every situation, even if Beauvoir were right about the metaphysical necessity of conflict of interest.

Still, in 1944 Beauvoir clearly tended to think that violence in the stronger, narrower sense was an inevitable realization of the state of struggle that is the unavoidable condition of our coexistence with others, even if she also recognized that violence was in some sense self-defeating. Indeed, she went further in her positive assessment of the significance of violence: "By violence one makes an infant a man and a horde into a society. To renounce the struggle is to renounce transcendence, to renounce being" (*PC* 117). Thus violence can give rise to an evolution from a lower to a higher level of consciousness. This is precisely because violence is the actualization and real expression of the Self's definition of itself and its projects.

It is no accident that *She Came to Stay* ends with an act of violence. As the quintessential Other, Xavière invites violence. She is entirely wrapped up in herself; she repeatedly expresses her contempt for any way of seeing things or acting that is other than her own. At any given moment, Xavière is completely consumed by whatever desire or attitude seizes her. When she is balked of any objective, no matter how trifling her interest in it, she responds with blind rage and condemnation. When she is irritated by attempts to impose schedules upon her or expectations that she will defer pleasures or act from decency and devotion, she is completely consumed by her contempt for Françoise.

It can happen that my disregard encompass the entire person, and not just some particular area of competence. It is the project of his being as a whole which we reject, against which we fight. Thus my disregard becomes contempt. I am entirely indifferent to the opinion of someone for whom I have contempt. Out of contempt, one says, "I do not want your opinion," and even "I am not speaking to you," for every time I speak, every time I express myself, I make an appeal. True contempt is silence. It removes the last trace of contradiction, of scandal. [PC 106]

In the earlier scene in which Françoise has her terrifying vision of Xavière as malign Other, Xavière has retreated into one of her alienated silences. Her silence has annihilated Françoise, who thinks of Xavière as "a beautiful face with a scandalous presence lurking behind it" (LI 301; cf. SCS 291). But on that earlier occasion, Pierre was present to mediate the moment of conflict. In the final scene of the novel, Pierre and Gerbert have gone off to war, leaving Xavière and Françoise alone with each other. Xavière flies into a fury of contempt at Françoise, and her rejection of Françoise carries over into action: she refuses to speak with Françoise any more and bolts the door behind her. "She or I?" Françoise asks. And this time she resorts to violence; by turning on the gas she ensures that behind that door, where Xavière is now sleeping, there will soon be no "scandalous presence."[10]

Alone. She had acted alone. As alone as if in death. One day Pierre would know. But even he would know this act only from the outside. No one could condemn her or absolve her. Her act belonged to her alone. "It is I who willed it." It was her will which was being done; nothing separated her from herself anymore. She had finally chosen. She had chosen herself. [LI 418; cf. SCS 404]

The original title of Beauvoir's novel, which she gave up at her publisher's insistence, was Légitime défense; the implication of the title, surely, is that the violence against Xavière is justifiable. Moreover, it is difficult to read this final scene other than as a triumphant emergence of Françoise as an authentic individual. From pure spectator at the start of the narrative she has developed through her struggle with Xavière into a free agent actively incarnate in the world, with an authentic consciousness of herself in separation from others. It is Françoise's will that is being done. By violence she has freed herself.

AMBIGUITY

She Came to Stay does not end with a vision of Françoise stricken by the awareness that she has eliminated her own possibility for justification in eliminating Xavière's destructive vision of her. What has become of Beauvoir's understanding of violence as a self-defeating strategy?

For one thing, of course, within the story Françoise still projects the reaction of the absent Pierre as Other. More importantly, the very nature of fiction undercuts Françoise's view that there is no one to witness her action. She is also present to the reader, whose access to the events of the story is mediated through a kind of narrative presence, described by Beauvoir in *The Force of Circumstance* as an underlying "monologue" that occurs in the present, "permitting me to break into the narrative, elide it and comment freely on it" (*FC* 283). In the course of the novel Beauvoir's "monologue" has frequently undercut Françoise's vision by inviting the reader to reinterpret what she sees. For example, in the scene in which Pierre and Françoise disagree about the significance of Xavière's behavior, Françoise is genuinely shocked and puzzled by his attitude. The reader, by contrast, is neither puzzled nor shocked; the events in the Pôle Nord – as seen by Françoise, but not appreciated by her – have established that she gives Pierre too much credit. Only someone as determined as Françoise not to face facts could fail to see that Pierre is a hardened and thoroughly invested seducer with an extremely practiced and transparent technique.

It is principally Beauvoir's monologue that gives *She Came to Stay* its eerie ambiguity. At every turn we are reminded that alongside the metaphysical narrative, alongside events as "enacted on the tragic level" (*PL* 241) by Françoise, there is another narrative, in which everything we see from Françoise's perspective is a depressingly ordinary story of two middle-aged intellectuals who are blowing their fling with a fairly boring and self-absorbed little teenager out of all sane proportion. The ordinary also finds a knifelike expression in Elizabeth's acid reflections, where the drama of Pierre, Françoise and Xavière is reduced to "derisory proportions" (*PL* 241). The reader enters the second part of the novel through Elizabeth's eyes. Given the ridiculous way in which Pierre and Françoise are falling over each other to please Xavière, she thinks, it is no wonder the child thinks she is a goddess (*LI* 225; cf. *SCS* 219). Pierre loses all sense of proportion when he is besotted, she thinks – otherwise how could he be so taken with the very ordinary looking Xavière (*LI* 224; cf. *SCS* 218). Throughout the novel the metaphysical narrative is constantly destabilized by the presence of a second, commonplace level of narrative. It is this ambiguity that gives the novel its air of clear-eyed and self-aware integrity. It also draws the reader into a sustained attempt to disentangle the commonplace from the metaphysical, which gains solidity and credibility from being played off against the ordinary.

In the final moments of *She Came to Stay*, however, it is the metaphysical vision that prevails. The "monologue" does not undercut Françoise's vision. The reader is not invited to see a mundane reality beyond Françoise's desperate sense that she has nowhere to turn, that she is threatened beyond bearing, and that she cannot refrain from this action without herself being destroyed. The ordinary Françoise would perhaps not have been a credible murderess. But in the final scene of *She Came to Stay* it is the metaphysical Françoise, who has undergone incarnation and finds herself in danger of dissolution, who confronts us. This Françoise is entirely credible in her moment of triumph. Precisely in choosing the ultimate violence, by choosing to reduce Xavière literally to an object, Françoise achieves a new level of her own being. Only after the final chord of the novel fades does the reader turn to the sobering task of trying to sort out the conflicting claims of the metaphysical and the ordinary.

By 1963 Beauvoir had doubts about whether she had brought off the narrative of *She Came to Stay* convincingly. These doubts are largely without foundation; Beauvoir had found an ingenious way of exerting the essential power that she attributed to literature and especially to fiction. Precisely because of the oscillation of the ordinary and the existential points of view, *She Came to Stay* draws the reader ineluctibly into a thick and substantial world open to alternative interpretations and thus into Beauvoir's philosophical vision of intimate politics between the Self and the Other, of their suffocating interdependence, and of the significance of violence for self-definition, with a power and intensity that is pretty unlikely to be matched by Reality TV.

NOTES

1 Ed Cullen, "What's so Real about Reality TV?," *The Advocate*, 11 June 2000, H1.

2 Oscar Lewis, *The Children of Sánchez: Autobiography of a Mexican Family* (New York: Random House, 1961).

3 "Investigation" (*recherche*) is not precisely a technical term, but it has both scientific connotations and resonances with Proust's literary self-explorations.

4   *FC* (Harmondsworth: Penguin, 1968) 279.

5   In *Force of Circumstance*, especially pp. 276–84, Beauvoir describes in detail how she crafted the characters and constructed the narrative of *The Mandarins* so as to illuminate the world of post-war French intellectuals, and even to some extent to "redeem" it.

6   *M* (London: Fontana, 1960) 758.

7   All translations from *L'Invitée* are my own. Compare corresponding pages in *She Came to Stay* (New York: Norton, 1990).

8   *PL* (Harmondsworth: Penguin, 1965) 340.

9   All translations from *FR* are my own. Compare corresponding pages in *WD*.

10 It is with a sure instinct for credibility that Beauvoir makes the violence consist of the disturbingly commonplace action of depressing the gas lever from the aseptic distance of the corridor.

7 Complicity and slavery in *The Second Sex*

In the introduction to *The Second Sex* Simone de Beauvoir characterizes the category of the other as primordial (*SS* 16; *DS* 1 16).[1] To understand the relations between social groups, including men and women, we must follow Hegel's insight that there is "in consciousness itself a fundamental hostility to every other consciousness; the subject can be posed only in being opposed – he sets himself up as the essential, as opposed to the other, the inessential, the object" (*SS* 17; *DS* 1 17). Here, Beauvoir presents a framework for explaining the relations between the sexes that makes them continuous with other human relationships. That man should strive to subjugate woman is not in itself unexpected, since it exemplifies a universal disposition also manifested in the behavior of nations and races and even in that of three travelers who share a compartment and make vaguely hostile "others" out of all the other passengers on the train (*SS* 17; *DS* 1 16). What is surprising, however, is the extent of man's success. For while domination is usually an unstable and temporary achievement upset by war, potlatch, trade, or treaties, woman has been subordinate to man throughout history, and the sheer persistence of this state of affairs therefore needs to be accounted for. Beauvoir here sets out to examine a difference not of kind but of degree. Among the social relations that express the primordial dynamic between subject and other, man's domination of woman is an extreme case; it lies at one end of a spectrum of more or less persistent forms of domination (although its immutability makes it appear ahistorical), and its tenacity is what renders it puzzling. Why, we are encouraged to wonder, is the relation between man and woman not more volatile and changeable and thus more like the relations between other groups of

149

people? Or as Beauvoir puts it, whence comes this submissiveness in the case of woman (SS 18; DS 1 17)?

Although she initially poses the problem in these terms, Beauvoir does not always stick to a comparative approach. She sometimes explores a view of woman's domination to which struggles between men are irrelevant. Man, as this strand of argument portrays him, is unremittingly transcendent in all aspects of his life. In addition to dominating woman, he belongs to the social spheres of work, politics, and intellectual life, where he exists as one transcendent being alongside others and where his subject position is unequivocally affirmed. In representing the broader social world as a region where men confront one another as free agents, Beauvoir draws a veil over the struggles for domination that occur within it. The invincibly transcendent creature who figures in her more highflown descriptions of masculinity is worlds away from those men who find themselves in the position of the other, whether by virtue of their beliefs, class or color, with the result that their experience of immanence is simply not acknowledged.

The portrayal of man as transcendent, which serves to make the domination of woman a unique and unparalleled problem, crops up at various points in *The Second Sex*. But it is balanced elsewhere in the book by Beauvoir's recognition that members of both sexes suffer subjection and also that men's experience of domination can shape their behavior towards women. In dominating his wife, she argues, a husband makes up for "all the resentments accumulated during his childhood and his later life, those accumulated daily among other men whose existence means that he is brow-beaten and injured – all this is purged from him at home as he lets loose his authority upon his wife" (SS 483; DS 11 297). He looks to her to be his double and to repair his self-esteem "after a hard day of struggle with his equals, of yielding to his superiors" (SS 483; DS 11 296). Moreover, where her admiration is not enough, he enacts his power by resorting to tyranny and violence. Here we are allowed to glimpse the complexity of the male world, which reveals itself, in Hegelian vein, not simply as a realm of transcendent subjects, but as one where men, like women, can be rendered immanent. In both realms, then, the struggle that Beauvoir construes as that between master and slave is to be found. In both realms some individuals are confined to otherness. On this account, the crucial difference between them is not that the public realm contains uniformly transcendent men, while the private one contains both transcendent men and immanent women. Rather, transcendence and immanence are to be found in each; but whereas a man who is subordinated in the public realm can dominate woman in the private one and can thus occupy both subject and object positions, this possibility is denied to women. With the important exception of women who assert their transcendence by dominating their children (*SS* 527; *DS* 11 370), woman has no other. There is no social arena where she can be recognized as a subject, and her struggle to become transcendent is therefore invariably blocked.

This second strand of Beauvoir's argument returns her to the comparative approach from which she begins, and to the question it raises: if men are not invincibly transcendent, and if, as she asserts, "the temptation to dominate is the most truly universal, the most irresistible one there is" (*SS* 483; *DS* 11 297), what prevents women from becoming subjects, either by objectifying other women or by objectifying men? Beauvoir answers with two interconnected arguments, one broadly social and psychological, the other more abstractly philosophical. The first charts the cultural images of masculinity and femininity in the light of which men and women understand themselves, together with the possibilities and obstacles that their self-understandings contain. The second applies Hegel's master–slave dialectic. Man, as master, establishes himself as a free subject by subjugating woman, who serves as his other and remains mired in immanence.

Through the use of this second argument, Beauvoir places her work in a Hegelian framework and instructs her readers to understand it in Hegelian terms. However, as a number of writers have pointed out, it is difficult to see exactly how Beauvoir conceives the analogy of man and woman to master and slave.[2] This is partly because there are incompatibilities between Hegel's doctrine and Beauvoir's debts to Sartrean existentialism which she does not disentangle,[3] and partly because it is not clear how she herself understood Hegel.[4] In addition, interpretation is complicated by tensions between the philosophical framework Beauvoir adopts and her detailed social and psychological analyses of woman's predicament. By investigating these tensions, feminist philosophers have revealed a series of points at which Beauvoir departs from both Hegel and Sartre. Two of the most important of these are her connected interpretations of complicity and embodiment. Beauvoir's famous admission "that the males find in woman more complicity than the oppressor usually finds in the oppressed" (*SS* 731; *DS* 11 649) draws attention to a central feature of oppression for which there is no room in Hegel's account of the relation between master and slave. According to Hegel, the slave has been defeated in a battle in which both he and his opponent have risked their lives. There is thus nothing voluntary about the slave's subordination. When Beauvoir discusses woman's complicity, she sometimes presents it as an instance of Sartrean bad faith, as a voluntary refusal of freedom and acceptance of domination. However, her sophisticated analysis of the position in which woman finds herself is at odds with such a reductive diagnosis and illuminates an aspect of oppression to which neither Hegel nor Sartre seem to do justice. In her arresting account, complicity is conceived as a condition of an embodied self whose abilities, and therefore options, have been formed by its social circumstances. Once again, her interest in the way our experience works upon our bodies and shapes what we can do goes beyond Hegel's interpretation of the relations between master and slave, and once again, there is a discrepancy in *The Second Sex* between Beauvoir's understanding of embodiment and her Sartrean conception of humans as split between transcendence and immanence. Although Beauvoir continues to work with the Sartrean conception, her own account pulls against it, thus undermining the assimilation of complicity to bad faith.

The insight, convincingly established in recent research, that Beauvoir's conceptions of embodiment and complicity cannot be squeezed into the philosophical framework she herself adopts,[5] raises the issue of her place in the history of philosophy. If her work goes beyond the legacies of Hegel and Sartre, how might we position it? As completely novel? As indebted to Merleau-Ponty? As shaped by Nietzsche? Many possibilities are suggested by Beauvoir's own range of reference. I offer a reading of *The Second Sex* that places it in the context of an older tradition of philosophical inquiry into the character of social hierarchy and into the passions that create and sustain it. Since this tradition is a long one, I only attempt to discuss a part of it, although it is a part with which Beauvoir was undoubtedly familiar. In French philosophy of the late seventeenth century, I show, hierarchical social relations are widely held to depend on the affects of admiration and contempt, which are understood to operate on and through the body. In the resulting economy of the passions, people are construed as complicitous in their domination in a sense that comes very close to the one articulated by Beauvoir. At the same time, the writers of this period are aware that being dominated can amount to servitude. Like Beauvoir, they are sensitive to the mechanisms by which people become effectively enslaved. In early modern discussions of social hierarchy we therefore find a collection of interrelated themes that recur in Beauvoir's work and in some ways illuminate it more clearly than the Hegelian context in which it is usually set. My argument consequently draws attention to a strand of discussion that has largely been neglected, but which may help us to understand the preoccupations of both Beauvoir and some of her philosophical contemporaries.

Beauvoir's analysis of the relations between man and woman assumes that all human beings desire esteem or admiration and that they can only gain it from other human beings. This view is deeply embedded in seventeenth-century moral psychology, where it is dramatized by Arnauld and Nicole in a thought experiment designed to uncover the limitations of *l'homme machine*.[6] Imagine a world in which there is only one person and in which every other apparently human creature is in fact a mechanical statue. The lone person knows perfectly well that the statues, which outwardly resemble him, are entirely devoid of reason and thought. But he is able to control their movements and can make them behave in a thoroughly human fashion. Although he may amuse himself by getting the statues to display admiration for him, their outward shows of respect will never nourish his self-esteem, since what is needed to arouse this passion is not mere behavior but the passionate responses of other human beings capable of conscious thought. Three features of this example are relevant here. First, Arnauld and Nicole are concerned with the role of subjectivity in social relations; although they do not use the language of transcendence and immanence, they share Beauvoir's conviction that our desire for an other can only be satisfied by human beings. Second, they focus on the *passionate* interactions between people. Finally, they concentrate on the particular passions of admiration and self-esteem that, as I show, likewise play an important part in Beauvoir's argument.

Among seventeenth-century philosophers, the passions are widely regarded as manifestations of a natural and functional sensitivity to the harms and advantages that people, objects, and states of affairs may bring to us. To fear something, for instance, is to perceive it as potentially damaging. Moreover, unlike sensory perceptions, our passions prompt us to act, and it is thus by virtue of our fears, hopes, and loves that we respond to the world.[7] In classifications of the affects to which early modern philosophers are so attached, a central position is often given both to esteem or admiration and to contempt or disdain.[8] These passions are evoked by aspects of the world that we perceive as possessing *grandeur* and *petitesse*, both thickly descriptive terms that can apply to things by virtue of their size, brilliance, birth, age, wisdom, virtue, and so forth. Malebranche, for example, explains that we are inclined to admire things that strike us as large, such as the night sky or monumental buildings, and to disdain things that are small, such as insects. Equally, we are inclined to feel admiration or esteem for people whose power or rank exceeds our own and contempt for those below us on the social scale.[9] Admiration and contempt can thus be excited by both people and objects; but because only people can return these passions, the most elaborate and consequential analyses of them deal with human relationships. In a particularly rich account, Malebranche explains that our passions are simultaneously mental and physical; fear, for example, is constituted both by a feeling and by a configuration of the body, a constellation of facial expressions, gestures, and postures that allows the passions to be read and evokes answering passions in those who read it. In some cases, such transmissions of feeling are roughly mimetic; for example, if I perceive that someone is desperate, I too may become distressed (*RV* II 92–93; *ST* 351). But in other cases, including the exchange of scorn and esteem, the process is more complex.

Malebranche offers a full account of the effects of these passions, which can be most easily conveyed through an invented example.[10] Imagine a petitioner who comes before a prince. When the petitioner perceives that the prince's *grandeur* is superior to his own, he feels himself to be base and experiences a kind of humility. He also gives his passions bodily expression, manifesting his *petitesse* in his supplicating stance, his bent head and respectful countenance. These changes have an effect on the prince, who feels contempt for the petitioner's *petitesse* but at the same time recognizes his submissive air as a response to his own *grandeur*. The petitioner's countenance and bearing provide the prince with sensible evidence of his comparative greatness, and upon perceiving this he feels pride and self-esteem, passions which he in turn expresses by drawing himself up to his full height, staring at the space above the petitioner's head, or swelling out his chest. Finally, these changes have a further effect on the petitioner, who feels, alongside the baseness we have already examined, a kind of self-esteem. Some of the prince's *grandeur* rubs off on him, so to speak, and his connection with a person greater than himself increases his sense of his own worth. As he leaves the court, he stands a little straighter, and his stride is a little longer.

Malebranche emphasizes that this self-reinforcing dialogue is mechanical, by which he means that our bodies are structured in such a way that we express our passions and are moved by those of others without having to think about it (*RV* II 121–22; *ST* 377). To some extent we can learn to control and modify these reactions. But the mutual dependence bred by our disposition to admire and scorn people for their *grandeur* is one of the chief mechanisms that binds us together into hierarchical communities where each stratum feeds off those above or below it and depends on them for its sense of worth. It is easy to be reminded of the dependence of Hegel's master on his slave when one reads Malebranche's claim that "the general of an army depends on all his soldiers because they hold him in regard. It is often this slavery that produces his *générosité*, and the wish to be esteemed by all those who see him frequently causes him to sacrifice other desires that are more pressing and more rational" (*RV* II 84; *ST* 343, translation modified). But whereas Hegel presents the master's dependence as an unwanted consequence of his subjugation of the slave, Malebranche sees it as an aspect of a functional and divinely ordained social order. He is concerned with hierarchical relations between men – princes, courtiers, magistrates, peasants, philosophers – who need to be admired and are highly sensitive to the esteem and contempt that others feel for them. Their sensitivity consists in an attunedness to the ways in which these passions are embodied, together with a natural disposition to embody the changing levels of their own self-esteem and self-contempt. Their ability to act is shaped by the passions directed toward them, and they are thus bound into a system of exchange that makes them vulnerable but is at the same time potentially empowering.

The central features of this seventeenth-century discussion all recur in Beauvoir, who allots an important place to admiration in her analysis of the hierarchical relations between man and woman. In her role as other, woman sustains man's self-esteem by reflecting back to him an image of himself; but the image must be an admiring one. Men "seek to find in two living eyes their image haloed with admiration and gratitude, deified" (*SS* 217; *DS* I 302). The look or gaze that is so central to Beauvoir's account is significant. Man searches for his image in two human eyes, he looks to woman's facial expression for confirmation of his own worth, and it is through her body that she makes her admiration manifest. This passion may have many objects, some of them coinciding with the forms of *grandeur* that interest philosophers such as Malebranche; for example, woman may admire man for his strength, power, wealth, munificence, or learning. Thus, the relation between man and woman resembles that between man and man insofar as it is a relation between haves and have-nots. A man's wealth may win him the esteem of a man who is poor, and an educated man may be esteemed by one who lacks learning. Because the women Beauvoir portrays are mainly excluded from the public realm, they lack the valued qualities it can supply. Ill-educated and financially dependent, their admiration for males who possess these qualities is a form of passionate exchange that also occurs between men. At the same time, however, there are forms of admiration that man gains specifically from woman, forms of *grandeur* to which only woman is responsive. Some of man's qualities, "and among others his vital qualities, can interest woman only; he is virile, charming, seductive, tender and cruel only in reference to her. If he sets a high value on these more secret virtues, he has an absolute need of her; through her he will experience the miracle of seeming to himself to be another, another who is also his profoundest ego" (*SS* 216–17; *DS* I 301–02). Man's need to be esteemed for his sexual and erotic powers lies at the heart of his relation with woman, and here, too, as Beauvoir illustrates throughout *The Second Sex*, woman is called on to admire what she herself lacks. The activity and independence of the male body and of masculine sexuality, as contrasted with the passivity and immanence of woman, set the terms of a relationship in which woman finds traits to admire in man that he cannot admire in her. *Grandeur*, as Beauvoir constructs it, is explicitly masculine; it is available only to the transcendent and thus denied to woman. "How could one expect her to show audacity, ardor, disinterestedness, grandeur? These qualities appear only when a free being strikes forward through an open future, emerging far beyond all given actuality" (*SS* 616; *DS* II 493). Woman's life, devoted to cooking and washing diapers, is "no way to acquire a sense of *grandeur*" (*SS* 615; *DS* II 492).

If woman creates man's self-esteem by admiring him, how does he respond to her? While Beauvoir allows that men sometimes sustain their sense of their own value by disdaining women (she cites Montherlant as an author who needs to render women abject so that he can feel contempt for them [*SS* 238; *DS* I 331]), she is alive to the fact that the admiration of a thoroughly degraded person is usually unsatisfying; hence, "man aspires to clothe in his own dignity whatever he conquers and possesses" (*SS* 113; *DS* I 136). Drawing on a wide range of sources, she enumerates the qualities that can make woman's esteem worth having and arouse an answering passion in man. He may esteem her for her willingness to satisfy his demands and for the many ways in which she makes herself useful to him (*SS* 660; *DS* II 557); for her ability to give him erotic pleasure; for her beauty; for her ability to understand him and enter into his projects (*SS* 637; *DS* II 520); for her ability to enlarge the realm of his experience; for her willingness to argue with him and yet be defeated; and so on. It is helpful here to return for a moment to Malebranche, who identifies two kinds of exchange of esteem. In some situations, people esteem one another for different reasons, as when a nobleman esteems a philosopher for his wisdom and the philosopher esteems the nobleman for his rank. The forms of *grandeur* that are in play may not be on a level (Malebranche complains that social rank is regarded as more impressive than the wisdom of philosophers), but each is recognized as admirable. In other situations, esteem is nonreciprocal; a prince may find nothing to esteem in a servant, although his recognition of the servant's esteem for him may evoke a different passionate response, such as a feeling of mild benevolence. Even here, however, Malebranche argues that the servant may derive some self-esteem from his relation with the prince, if it allows him to perceive himself as sharing the prince's *grandeur*. Thus the lesser members of a household, a court, a guild, or a profession may acquire self-esteem by association with the great.

Beauvoir takes it that both kinds of exchange occur between man and woman. Because the sexual and social forms of *grandeur* to which the highest value attaches belong to man (either by virtue of his masculinity or by virtue of woman's exclusion from the public realm), woman has comparatively little to give and is particularly dependent on association for her self-esteem. A woman gains her social status, wealth, and connections from her relationship with a man; at the same time, she admires him for one set of qualities and is admired by him for another. Beauvoir's discussion of this form of exchange departs from the framework supplied by early modern authors such as Malebranche, who inhabit a world where the comparative values of different kinds of *grandeur* are hotly contested – where the claims of virtue are regularly played off against those of status, and true wisdom competes with false philosophy. By contrast, the forms of *grandeur* available to man and woman are, as Beauvoir articulates them, monolithic, and because the most valuable are stacked firmly on the masculine side, the admiration of man for woman is not qualified by any challenge to his social or sexual superiority. Beauvoir here draws attention to an aspect of hierarchy that early modern writers overlook. In their anxiety to vindicate a society organized around widely differing degrees of power, Malebranche and many of his contemporaries conceive esteem and contempt as passions that pass smoothly up and down the vertical scale running from *petitesse* to *grandeur* and serve to unite the members of different social ranks into a relatively harmonious social whole. They are therefore untroubled by the fact that there may be points at which the standards of *grandeur* and *petitesse* alter in such a way as to make mutuality of esteem impossible. Such blockages can occur in the relations between men, as Beauvoir points out in an aside about race (*SS* 289; *DS* 1 403), but she is, of course, most interested in the divide between man and woman.

Since Beauvoir's insights into the multifarious ways in which this division is constructed have been widely discussed, we need only note some of the principal strategies she identifies. Contrasting understandings of man as active (and thus as transcendent and in control of himself) and of woman as passive (and thus as immanent and out of control) are rooted in their bodily differences. The softness of woman's body, the secretions that flow from it, the doubling and blurring of boundaries that occur during pregnancy, the uncontrollability of conception, her penetration during sexual intercourse, and the diffuseness of her sexual pleasure are all understood to make her, by contrast with man, inert and passive. By the same token, the comparative hardness and containedness of man's body, the neatness and visibility of his sexual organs, his well-defined erotic climax, and his role in intercourse contribute to the association of masculinity and activity. Each sex understands and evaluates itself with reference to the other, and the superiority and inferiority of the self-images that man and woman internalize are heightened by a range of further interpretative devices. First, bodily differences that are a matter of degree are imagined as oppositions; for example, although man is prey to uncontrollable bodily secretions, these are obliterated in the contrast with flows of menstrual blood, amniotic fluid, and so forth, so that woman alone emerges as leaky and unbounded. Secondly, "the categories in which men think of the world are established from their point of view, as absolute"; for example, although bodily differences render each sex mysterious to the other, mystery attaches only to woman. "A mystery for man, woman is considered to be mysterious in essence" (*SS* 286; *DS* I 399–400). Finally, the indefeasibility of bodily differences serves to naturalize them, so that the superiority of man and the inferiority of woman appear inevitable. While colonial administrators or generals could escape from the unjust hierarchical relations in which they were involved by giving up their jobs, "a man could not prevent himself from being a man. So there he is, culpable in spite of himself and laboring under the effects of a fault he did not himself commit; and here she is, victim and shrew in spite of herself" (*SS* 732; *DS* II 652–53). Society inculcates in individual men and women a normative understanding of their own bodily and above all sexual powers; moreover, because these are affirmative for men and diminishing for women, the scene is set for admiration and contempt.

As I have shown, Beauvoir's emphasis on embodiment works with an understanding of the self that had already been central to French philosophy in the seventeenth century. Like writers of this period, Beauvoir takes it as given that our properties and powers are emotional and that our passions are both constituted by, and manifested in, our bodily states and abilities. In the hierarchical social order discussed by Malebranche, people's self-esteem is expressed in their habitual postures, movements, or tones of voice and in their responses to those they encounter. Moreover, these traits shape what they can do and also what they can be. Analogously, Beauvoir articulates an account of the way men's and women's experiences of themselves as embodied human beings constitute their passions and capacities. As passive, woman admires man and suffers feelings of humiliation and self-disgust, and her identity also shapes and limits her actions.

In each of these accounts two complementary interpretations of the complicity of people at the bottom of the heap in the power of those above them can be found. First and most important, the acceptance of social subordination is to be explained by the ways in which differences of power are embodied and therefore shape the way we understand ourselves, the way others understand us, and what we can do. Just as a man of low rank who tried to behave like a prince would not exact esteem but would be regarded as vainglorious and ridiculous, so a woman who tries to act like a man is viewed as outlandish (SS 692; DS 11 601). To this extent – and here *The Second Sex* implicitly departs from Sartre's account of bad faith – complicity is not a matter of choice. As Beauvoir summarizes her argument, "all the main features of [woman's] training combine to bar her from the roads of revolt and adventure" (SS 730; DS 11 649). At the same time, the psychic benefits that go along with social subordination produce a further knot of affects and interpretations. The *grandeur* of a prince rubs off on a petitioner, and woman "may fail to lay claim to the status of subject because she lacks definite resources, because she feels the necessary bond that ties her to man regardless of reciprocity, and because she is often very well pleased with her role as the other" (SS 21; DS 1 21–22). The self-esteem gained from associating with those who possess *grandeur* is still self-esteem. But this way of getting it depends on psychological strategies that have their own costs. Since woman is "doomed to dependence, she will prefer to serve a god rather than obey tyrants" (SS 653; DS 11 547) and will therefore project her desires on to her relationship with man; "she is quick to see genius in the man who satisfies her desires" (SS 628; DS 11 509); she "judges her judge, and she denies him his liberty so that he may deserve to remain her master" (SS 665; DS 11 563). At the same time, her sense of sexual abasement reinforces her need for esteem; "nothing but high admiration can compensate for the humiliation of an act she considers a defeat" (SS 658; DS 11 554). Beauvoir here explores woman's *ressentiment* in Nietzschean terms but also echoes her early modern predecessors, who are equally familiar with the relation between our desire for self-esteem and our disposition to project. As Malebranche remarks,

The dependence men have on the great, the desire to share in their greatness, and the perceptible glamour surrounding them, often causes men to render divine honours to mere mortals . . . For if God gives authority to princes, men give them infallibility, but an infallibility not limited to certain subjects, nor to certain occasions, and not attached to certain ceremonies. The great know everything by nature; they are always right, even if they decide questions about which they know nothing. To examine what they propose is not to know how to live, to doubt them is to lack respect, to condemn them is to rebel, or at least to exhibit oneself as foolish, extravagant and ridiculous. [*RV* ii 333; *ST* 168]

Hierarchical relations, whether or not they are between men and women, thus provide the subordinate with a motive for forming illusory beliefs about their dominators. Yet this illusion is not complete and is in perpetual conflict with the more realistic recognition that the great have their weaknesses.

Beauvoir vividly portrays this split and the suffering to which it gives rise. Woman is locked into the subordinate position described so far but at the same time distanced from it, so that, confronting man, she

is always play-acting; she lies when she makes believe that she accepts her status as the inessential other, she lies when she presents to him an imaginary personage through mimicry, costumery, studied phrases. These histrionics require a constant tension; when with her husband, or with her lover, every woman is more or less conscious of the thought: "I am not being myself." [*SS* 557; *DS* ii 411]

As she simultaneously lives and acts out her existence as other, woman is hypocritical, abject, resistant, and servile by turns and experiences an associated range of passions. She is deceitful and hypocritical toward man, who demands that she give herself over to him and sincerely recognize the superiority of his merits.

She lies to hold the man who provides her daily bread; there are scenes and tears, transports of love, crises of nerves – all false – and she lies also to escape from the tyranny she accepts through self-interest. He encourages her in make-believe that flatters his lordliness and his vanity; and she uses against him in turn her powers of dissimulation. [*SS* 626; *DS* ii 506]

She is humiliated by sex and rendered abject by her lover's judgmental gaze. "It is not given to woman to alter her flesh at will: when she no longer hides it, she yields it up without defense ... and is unable to take arrogant pride in her body unless male approval has confirmed her youthful vanity" (*SS* 402; *DS* 11 159–60). Her knowledge of her disadvantage makes her cruel and spiteful, and "she will even be very happy if she has occasion to show her resentment to a lover who has not been able to satisfy all her demands: since he does not give her enough, she takes savage delight in taking back everything from him" (*SS* 732; *DS* 11 652). Finally, she is servile.

> Woman wears herself out in haughty scenes, and in the end gathers up the crumbs that the male cares to toss to her. But what can be done without masculine support by a woman for whom man is at once the sole means and the sole reason for living? She is bound to suffer every humiliation; a slave cannot have the sense of human dignity; it is enough if a slave gets out of it with a whole skin. [*SS* 615; *DS* 11 492]

This dispiriting catalog of female stratagems is strikingly contin-uous with early modern interpretations of the corrosive effects of subordination. Seventeenth-century analysts of esteem recognized perfectly well that its role in a harmonious social hierarchy can be undermined by contrary passions, and believed that one way to hold these at bay is to maintain a certain distance between ranks. People who only glimpse a monarch on ceremonial occasions may carry away an undisturbed image of his *grandeur*.[11] But – and this is a particularly acute problem in relation to servants and courtiers – esteem is easily destroyed by intimacy. A courtier who observes the illnesses, weaknesses, and tyrannies of a prince is unlikely to view him with unadulterated esteem, and in fact writers regularly por-tray the courtier as trapped in a position strictly comparable to that of Beauvoir's woman. In the same way that woman is overwhelm-ingly dependent upon man, the courtier's self-esteem depends to an unusual extent on the *grandeur* of the prince; in this respect he is no more than a glorified version of the *valet de chambre*, who, as La Bruyère tartly points out, judges himself by the fortunes of the people he serves (*C* 264.33; *Ch* 148.33). Much as the hierarchical re-lation between man and woman appears ineluctable to them both, courts set store by differences of rank that assure the supremacy of the prince, so that the courtier's subordination cannot be overcome. Much as woman admires man, while appreciating the gap between the image she esteems and the reality, so it is with the courtier. His investment in the prince's *grandeur* may make him "render divine honours to mere mortals" (*RV* II 333; *ST* 168), but his simultaneous knowledge of and contempt for the prince's weaknesses give rise to the very range of strategems that Beauvoir attributes to woman. The courtier is hypocritical; he subscribes to all the opinions of the prince regardless of how quickly they change (*RV* I 333; *ST* 168), he dissimulates constantly (*C* 221.2; *Ch* 116.2), and he is an inveterate flatterer (*C* 224.18; *Ch* 118.18). Abject before the prince, he compensates himself for his own abasement by dominating others, and like woman, he is servile. "Men are willing to be slaves in one place if they can only lord it in another. It seems that at court a proud, imperious and commanding mien is delivered wholesale to the great for them to retail in the country; they do exactly what is done unto them, and are the true apes of royalty" (*C* 222–23.12; *Ch* 117.12).

Seventeenth-century accounts of the courtier's habitual vices illuminate two connected aspects of his servitude. First, he is dependent on the arbitrary will and accompanying passions of the prince for the outward aspects of his social status and his self-esteem. This dependence makes him deferent, so that he follows the prince's opinions and tastes rather than developing or standing by any of his own. Second, while he invests in the *grandeur* of the prince, he is also aware of its limitations and consequently finds himself split between a range of passions that are self-deceiving, such as excessive admiration, and a range that are demeaning, such as self-contempt. How, though, do these traits make the courtier a slave? According to a neo-Roman tradition of republican thought that was important in seventeenth-century politics, one is enslaved if one is subject to the arbitrary will of another, for instance, if one is subject to a king who possesses discretionary powers. The fact that such a king has the power to impose arbitrary restrictions on one, regardless of whether he does so, is enough to remove one's liberty, which can therefore be realized only in a republic of free citizens.[12] The early modern writers I have been discussing are not, of course, republicans; Malebranche, for example, argues that, as well as head and heart, the body politic must have hands and feet, "small people as well as great, people who obey as well as those who command" (*RV* II 72; *ST* 333). Nevertheless, they share with this republican tradition a conception of and disdain for the vices that monarchies and comparable constitutions engender. As they see it, courtiers suffer an extreme form of dependence, which tends to undermine their virtue and makes them incapable of the straightforwardness, courage, or proper pride that are among the qualities of an *honnête homme*. Even though the courtier is not in their view deprived of *political* freedom, he is nevertheless socially and psychically unfree, and this is why it is appropriate to describe him as a slave.

Beauvoir's insistence that relations between the sexes are unlike other forms of oppression hinges on her claim that woman is subordinated by virtue of a bodily difference that she cannot escape. The barrier that prevents a courtier from becoming a prince is a social one. But the fact that woman's inferiority is written on her body makes it uniquely ineluctable and thus creates a form of subordination that is qualitatively unlike any other. Moreover, whereas there are various forms of *grandeur* to which a courtier may aspire, such as elegance or wit, none are available to woman. The seventeenth-century philosophers I have discussed offer a view that implicitly challenges both these claims and is at the same time conformable with a divergent strand of argument to be found in *The Second Sex*. According to this view, some forms of *grandeur* are more ineluctable than others, so that although a courtier may reasonably aspire to become a little wiser, there is nothing he can do about his lack of royal blood. He inhabits a milieu where this deficiency is an inescapable and defining mark of inferiority, which shapes his passions and his body, so that he is as much formed by his domination as is woman. At this stage in the argument, Beauvoir would probably point out that although the courtier can retire to the country or go abroad, woman cannot retire from womanhood (*DS* 11 653). Here she is on strong ground, but her objection nevertheless turns its back on the fact that, insofar as the subordination of both woman and the courtier is embodied, the differences in their oppression are of degree rather than kind. The dispute is half-hearted, however, because Beauvoir should be sympathetic to this view. As many commentators have pointed out, her insistence on the ineluctability of woman's bodily inferiority is at odds with her claim that our passionate evaluations of our bodies are socially constructed and susceptible to change. Torn between this conviction and the desire to explain why women have always been dominated, she sometimes represents the bodily differences between man and woman as discontinuous with those between men (and for that matter with those between women). But, as she also occasionally acknowledges (see, for example, *SS* 372; *DS* 1 402), there is little in her overall position to warrant such a divide. Men's *grandeur* and *petitesse* are written on their bodies, and the same is true of man and woman; moreover, bodily differences of various kinds – between races, nationalities, sexes, or classes – may contribute to interpretations of inferiority or superiority and thus to oppression or subordination. Finally, oppression can amount to slavery, and men as well as women sometimes find themselves enslaved.

For a number of seventeenth-century philosophers, as much as for Beauvoir, slavery is defined by a range of psychological and social traits organized around the passions of esteem and contempt. To this extent, they draw on a common and deeply embedded understanding of servitude. However, an author such as Malebranche is comparatively tolerant of subordination; although he condemns the extreme deference of the courtier, he regards social hierarchy as an inevitable and proper price of social order and does not appear to think that dependence is intrinsically incompatible with freedom (*RV* II 122; *ST* 377). A man who is dependent on his patron, a servant who is dependent on his master, or a tenant who is dependent on a landowner may all be formed by habits of deference, but this need not make them slaves. Beauvoir, however, takes an altogether different line, arguing in a republican spirit that freedom can only exist between equals who are not bound by relations of dependence. Her view thus sets the threshold for slavery much lower, making slaves of many of us, male as well as female. Much of the fascination of *The Second Sex* lies in its analysis of the self-images available to woman and the resulting psychic bind in which she finds herself. Divided between admiration and contempt for man and for herself, she struggles for forms of self-respect that are precarious and liable to be self-defeating. Like the courtier who strives to be witty or elegant, the forms of *grandeur* available to her are systematically inferior to the ones from which she is excluded; and, as with the courtier, equality of esteem is beyond her reach. Beauvoir's conception of what it is to be a slave is thus continuous with one to be found in seventeenth-century discussions of social hierarchy. Like her, early modern philosophers were deeply interested in the ways that servitude is maintained and in the complicity that it involves. Like her, they explained complicity as a set of embodied and affective attitudes that contribute to our identities, and, like her, they regarded esteem and contempt as passions central to our struggles for power. Their analysis of slavery is, I believe, much closer to Beauvoir's than the Hegelian one with which she allies herself. Unlike Hegel, Beauvoir does not cast any light on the origin of slavery – there is no battle, as in the Hegelian story of master and slave. Nor does she propose a way out of it – there is for woman no equivalent of the labor that allows Hegel's slave to transform his domination. It is therefore helpful to see *The Second Sex* in a longer historical context, as extending to woman an existing interpretation of servitude, with dramatic and revolutionary effect.

NOTES

1 *SS* (Harmondsworth: Penguin, 1972); *DS* i and ii (Paris: Gallimard, 1976).
2 For recent discussions of this point, see Tina Chanter, *Ethics of Eros: Irigaray's Reading of the Philosophers* (London: Routledge, 1995), p. 65; Catriona Mackenzie, "A Certain Lack of Symmetry: Beauvoir on Autonomous Agency and Women's Embodiment" in *Simone de Beauvoir's* The Second Sex: *New Interdisciplinary Essays*, ed. Ruth Evans (Manchester: Manchester University Press, 1998), pp. 123–24.
3 On the relation of Beauvoir's philosophy to that of Sartre, see Kate Soper, *Humanism and Antihumanism* (London: Hutchinson, 1986) and Sonia Kruks, *Situation and Human Existence: Freedom, Subjectivity and Society* (London: Unwin Hyman, 1990).
4 On Beauvoir's knowledge of Hegel, see Eva Lundgren-Gothlin, *Sex and Existence: Simone de Beauvoir's Second Sex*, trans. Linda Schenck (London: Athlone, 1996). Lundgren-Gothlin argues that Beauvoir follows Hegel in regarding women as outside the struggle between master and slave. This is the sense in which woman is man's absolute Other. However, this leaves open the question of how Beauvoir accounts for woman's complicity, and I shall argue that, in dealing with this theme, it is helpful to see her as drawing on philosophies other than Hegel's.
5 See, e.g., Judith Butler, "Gendering the Body: Beauvoir's Philosophical Contribution," in *Women, Knowledge and Reality*, ed. A. Garry and M. Pearsall (Boston: Unwin and Hyman, 1989), pp. 253–62.
6 Antoine Arnauld and Pierre Nicole, *Logic or the Art of Thinking*, trans. and ed. Jill Vance Buroker (Cambridge: Cambridge University Press, 1996), p. 55.
7 These assumptions are shared by a wide range of seventeenth-century authors. For further discussion see Susan James, *Passion and Action: The Emotions in Seventeenth-Century Philosophy* (Oxford: Clarendon Press, 1997).

8   For example, Descartes describes them as species of wonder, which, in his classification, is the first of all the passions. See René Descartes, *Passions of the Soul*, in John Cottingham, Robert Stoothoff, and Dugald Murdoch, eds., *The Philosophical Writings of Descartes* (Cambridge: Cambridge University Press, 1985), II: 54; *Les Passions de l'Ame*, ed. G. Rodis Lewis (Paris: Gallimard, 1988), II: 54.

9   Nicolas Malebranche, *De la recherche de la vérité* (hereafter *RV*), ed. G. Rodis Lewis, 3 vols., in *Oeuvres complètes*, 2nd edn, ed. A. Robinet (Paris: Librairie Philosophique J. Vira, 1972), I: 91, II: 127. Malebranche, *The Search After Truth* (hereafter *ST*), trans. Thomas M. Lennon and Paul J. Olscamp (Columbus, OH: Ohio State University Press, 1980), pp. 31, 382.

10   The example distills Malebranche's discussion at *RV*, II: 120 ff.; *ST* 377 ff.

11   La Bruyère, *Les Caractères* (hereafter *C*), ed. R. Garapon (Bordas: Classiques Garnier, 1980), p. 222. La Bruyère, *Characters* (hereafter *Ch*), trans. Henri Van Laun (Oxford: Oxford University Press, 1963) p. 116.6.

12   On this conception of liberty see Quentin Skinner, *Liberty Before Liberalism* (Cambridge: Cambridge University Press, 1988) and Philip Pettit, *Republicanism: A Theory of Freedom and Government* (Oxford: Oxford University Press, 1977).

8　Beauvoir on Sade: making sexuality into an ethic

"MUST WE BURN SADE?"

There are many surprising aspects to Beauvoir's consideration of the Marquis de Sade. Beauvoir is a feminist, and Sade is one whose name gave rise to the phenomenon of sexual sadism. Beauvoir has written copiously on the empowerment of women; Sade sought, through sexual means, to punish and control women and then to write, in the form of fiction and essays, a detailed account of his form of libertinism. In asking why Beauvoir reads Sade, and why it is a question whether or not he must be burned, we are asking what, if any, encounter there might be between a philosophy of feminism that grounds itself in freedom, as Beauvoir's clearly does, and a philosophy – and practice – of sexual libertinism that for the most part assumes the pleasurable aspects of the domination of women within heterosexual practice?

There are many tricky questions here, and it will serve us well to consider some of them. When Beauvoir asks whether we should burn Sade, she is referring to Sade the author. Should we burn his books? This is an incendiary title in more ways than one. To ask the question is to recall the burning of heretics and saints, including Joan of Arc. It is also to recall the burning of books, mainly Jewish and heretical, that took place during the Inquisition in Spain in the late fifteenth and early sixteenth centuries in Spain. Published in 1951, the essay poses the question shortly after World War Two, a period in which human beings in the millions were destroyed by gas and fire as well as by other means, and books were incinerated in ritualized efforts to purify the German Nazi state of its unwanted others (Jews, Gypsies, homosexuals, communists, the physically challenged, the non-Aryan, resistance fighters). As Beauvoir herself points out, his son is said to have burnt the ten volumes of Sade's final opus, *Les Journées de Florbelle* in an act of repudiation. If we burn Sade, then we will be burning books and, perhaps, by implication, associating ourselves with those who seek to achieve forms of social purity by violently expelling parts of the population and what they believe.

Among others, Albert Camus, whose politics belong to that of the left resistance, identifies Sade as one who prefigures the massive and systematic cruelty of the Nazi regime. In his view, published before Beauvoir's, it makes no sense to romanticize Sade, as some in the surrealist movement had done, as an antiauthoritarian philosopher of liberty: "Two centuries in advance and on a reduced scale, Sade exalted the totalitarian society in the name of a frenzied liberty that rebellion does not in fact demand. With him the history and tragedy of our times really begin."[1] Although Beauvoir does not respond directly to Camus' essay, she clearly does not agree that Sade belongs to the inaugural moments of modern fascism. Indeed, she takes distance from both fascist tactics and left moralism when she refuses to burn Sade. Refusing to burn his work is a way of insisting on the importance of the challenge to thought that his work delivers. Clearly, for Beauvoir, "burning" works that are disturbing is no solution for feminism or, indeed, for the existential humanism and progressive politics she espoused. By posing the question in this way and at that time, Beauvoir makes it clear that feminism and philosophy ought not to participate in anti-intellectual trends, that it ought to distance itself from inquisitorial practices, and that its intellectual task is to remain open to the difficulty and range of the human condition.

The question of whether or not we burn Sade's books thus becomes a question as well, in American parlance, of "First Amendment" rights. Ought we to accept as part of the public exchange of ideas the promulgation of views that we find difficult to accept or even abhorrent? Must we burn Sade or can we, without accepting his views, nevertheless learn from them? Must we burn Sade, or can we read him and find there something of importance for a feminist philosophy of freedom, including a philosophy of sexual freedom? To read Sade is not to accept as true or right what he writes, but to consider that we might, through reflection on his work and its aims, consider anew the human condition in its fundamentally sexual and gendered dimensions, and thus to come to know ourselves better and decide our aims with greater deliberateness.

We might expect that as a feminist Beauvoir would condemn Sade's cruel treatment of women, his refusal to engage in sexuality as a sphere of mutual respect, his practice of domination and violence in sexual domains. But Beauvoir clearly thinks we should read Sade, and she does actually, in her essay,[2] provide a reading of him for us. In reading him, she makes clear only that he is *worth reading*. She does not, as it were, take him to bed, or suggest that we condone him, take him as a model for action, or think he is exemplary of sexual freedom as she understands it. In the end, she claims that he makes the mistake of construing rebellion as a purely individual act, missing the very meaning of "action," and refusing to surrender a cultural elitism that supports his sexual and literary strategies. Although not a model, he provides the occasion for reflective insights into sexuality, in particular, whether an individual can attain an absolute and sovereign status in that domain, whether something like radical singularity can be achieved there. Related to this question is another: can one reach another being through the flesh? Can passionate engagement yield another's will? Beauvoir makes it clear that Sade is of interest for thinking critically and constructively about sexuality and ethics. This view may seem paradoxical. Sade hardly seems concerned with ethics. We might be tempted to presume that his behavior is unethical and that his disposition is pathologically criminal. Beauvoir is, however, unwilling to rest with such an explanation. A surprising aspect of her reading is that Sade's behavior, as well as his writing (after all, another form of behavior), are structured by ethical concerns. Even his "sadism" – to use the coinage anachronistically – must be understood as impelled and shaped by ethical preoccupations. She notes that Sade is always *justifying* himself, offering a defense of crime in light of the social conditions of the day, appealing to others to understand and accept his choice, and offering himself as a critical example to follow.

SADE'S CAREER

Before I consider further Beauvoir's view of Sade, let us consider who Sade was, what he did, and for what he is known. This will help us to understand who the "Sade" is to whom Beauvoir refers in her title and her essay. Born in 1740, Sade grew up in a Provençal family whose paternal side maintained aristocratic lineage. His mother belonged to the reigning "Bourbon" family in France. In 1724, before his marriage to Sade's mother, Sade's father was arrested on sodomy charges (in the Tuileries gardens). In 1733 Sade's parents were married, and his father purportedly began an affair shortly after. In 1740, after the death of a younger sister, "Sade" was born (Donatien-Alphonse-François, Marquis de Sade). His mother suffered chronic illness during his childhood, and he was raised in Avignon and near Versailles by various attendants. After having been tutored by an *abbé*, he attended school in 1750 in Paris. Then he joined the army and rose to the rank of captain of the Bourgogne cavalry. In the army his "dissolute" behavior was noted, and by 1763 he had contracted venereal disease through a liaison with someone not his fiancée. He married Renée-Pélagie de Montreuil that same year, reluctantly, and soon started renting a cottage to pursue other sexual liaisons. By 1765 he was deeply in debt. In 1768 the famous "Arcueil affair" broke out. Sade kept a small house in the village of Arcueil and brought people, mainly women, there for sexual encounters of various kinds, most of which he paid for. He spotted a working-class woman, Rose Keller, and lured her, with the promise of employment, to his *maison* in Arcueil. There, according to her testimony, he forcibly tied her down and whipped her; she is said to have screamed uncontrollably as he dropped hot wax on her back where he had made small incisions with a knife. After his reportedly tumultuous orgasm, he locked Rose Keller in a room from which she escaped (she found her way over a garden wall and landed on a street, where a group of women found her and took her to the police). The subsequent investigation produced a scandal that came to be reported in newspapers throughout Europe. Sade was imprisoned for six months and then released as a result of special pleas made on his behalf by family members with access to the reigning authorities. After this, Sade fought against social ostracism, accumulated debts, and became involved in illegal duels. Then, in 1772, he was accused of sodomizing and poisoning five prostitutes. He evaded the law for several months but was then caught and incarcerated. He escaped from prison in 1773, only to be reincarcerated in 1777, after having, with the aid of his wife, employed as domestic servants young girls who were said to have been abused by him. He remained imprisoned at Vincennes for twelve years. From 1778 to 1789 he wrote several important literary works, including plays. During the storming of the Bastille, where Sade was retained, he is said to have helped incite the crowd on the street from his prison window. Afterwards, he was transferred to another prison and then released in 1790. In 1791 he published one of his most enduring works, *Justine ou les malheurs de la vertu* (Justine, or the Illnesses of Virtue). He published tracts on libertinism and against the restrictive use of laws and was arrested again in 1793 for his political views. In 1795 he published *La Philosophie dans le boudoir* (Philosophy in the Bedroom), one of his most important tracts. In 1799 he published *La Nouvelle Justine* (The New Justine), after which he was imprisoned again on charges of pornography. In 1803, however, he was transferred to an asylum at Charenton. In 1807 *Les Journées de Florbelle*, his last novel, a ten-volume tome, was immediately seized by the police and later burned by his son. And in 1811 Bonaparte himself refused an appeal by Sade for release. In 1814 Sade died at Charenton, during a time in which he was paying for a sexual liaison with a 17-year-old woman.[3]

SADE'S SEXUAL THEORY

Although Sade is a novelist, many scenes in his novels are considered to be realistic accounts of his sexual practice, detailed and systematic, accompanied by didactic disquisitions on freedom, sexuality, law, and nature. Baroque and sometimes tedious descriptions of debauchery, they are interrupted by political and philosophical disquisitions. They all contain this strong didactic dimension, counseling the public on the mandates of nature, the irrepressibility of impulse, the damage done by civilization and morality to the sexual life force of human beings. Although one may well conclude that Sade has little in common with feminism, it is important to note that he defended sexual freedom and the expressive impulses of individuals. Moreover, Sade did not believe that sexuality was meant only to satisfy the requirements of procreation.

Beauvoir remarks, in fact, that for Sade, "sexuality not a biological matter, but a social fact" (*MBS* 43). She refers to the fact that there are always scenes of people to arrange for sexuality to take place for Sade. But she understands as well that, for him, sexuality was part of a "nature" that is not reducible to biological impulse. She notes that he uses the term "nature" variously, sometimes inconsistently. Sexuality, for instance, has a natural dimension, although nothing in its natural organization mandates procreation as its exclusive or privileged social form. For Sade, there are two kinds of natural impulse: the first is unbridled, energetic, and expressive; the second is self-preserving, seeking to ward off the destruction of the organism. The self-preservative impulse is most often in the service of civilization and morality. As a result, it tends to war with the energetic or expressive impulse. Sade objects to the force of civilization, and its laws, to repress and damage the energetic side of human beings. He promotes sexual freedom, under the name of libertinism, to counter the damaging effects of civilization. For Sade, according to Beauvoir, the laws set up to curtail nature and its cruelties not only make matters worse but propagate cruelty in the name of "justice": "laws, instead of correcting the primitive order of the world only aggravate its injustice" (*MBS* 62). She paraphrases Sade, "In erecting scaffolds, society, far from mitigating the cruelty of Nature, merely aggravates it. Actually, it resists evil by doing greater evil" (*MBS* 63).

The philosopher Michel Feher puts the matter this way: "If Sadian libertinism promotes reprobate pleasures – sodomy, tribadism, cruel passions, murderous orgies, and so on – this is first and foremost to fight the 'ecological' disequilibrium produced by a repressive civilization and unnatural morality."[4] To the degree that primary nature rebels against secondary nature, energy seeks to counter the repressive force of "preservation." To preserve the organism, according to Sade, does not require repressive laws, however. In this way, Sade prefigures the famous Freudian distinction between Eros (pleasure) and Thanatos (death) in *Beyond the Pleasure Principle* (1920) whereby Eros – or libido – is countered by a death drive, which is associated with repetition, compulsion, and sadism. For Freud, sadism is not primarily about pleasure but about a return, through repetitive means, to a deindividuated state of the human organism, a return to primary nature. Sade associates sadism with individuality but also with nature. But for him nature itself is twofold. He considers the primary and energetic impulse to be expressive and potentially destructive, but he also understands that this first nature cannot limit its potential destructiveness on its own. In a sense, Sade's "first nature" contains the energy of Eros as well as the destructiveness of Thanatos. Significantly, for both thinkers, "civilization" emerges not only to bind affect, in Freud's terms, but to limit its destructive potential as well. In this way, Sade prefigures Freud's critique of the psychic and libidinal costs of "civilization" in *Civilization and its Discontents* (1930). But whereas Freud comes out in favor of civilization and its channeling of the death drive, Sade continues to stand for the twofold power of natural Eros to counter the unnaturally repressive social law of "civilization." In Feher's terms, according to Sade, "the rejection of procreation and the destruction of organized beings are thus the forms of human conduct most worthy of nature" (35). For Sade, there are no natural laws of prohibition: prohibition is, by definition, always unnatural and, thus, always suspect.

Sade's libertinism is not simple hedonism: he does not celebrate sexual sensation as such but rather offers a systematic approach to sexual gratification, a sexual science in application, an architectonic of the sexual encounter. Beauvoir insists that Sade is crafting his sexual encounters and that a strange but undeniable operation of "principle" is at work in his sexual planning and the execution of his sexual and criminal deeds. Indeed, he is, in her words, a "cold, cerebral lover" (*MBS* 33). Whereas we might be tempted to think of him as exercising a merely "frenzied freedom," as Camus maintains, unthinking and impulsive, it is perhaps more perplexing, and more disturbing, to recognize that there is method in his "madness," a deliberate and calculated effort to achieve certain effects. The immediacy of his feeling is always taken up by a plan. Not only is he intensely interested in the technology of bodily pain, on which his writings report in detail, but he also engages in his own brand of sexual science, predicting and exacting pain and pleasure at definite intervals through specific means. He achieves a certain mastery in this process, one he considers at once "natural" and scientific. He seeks not only to craft the pain and pleasure of his sexual partner but to produce himself as a perfect instrument and a sovereign will.

Although his cruelty cannot be said to be ethically good, it becomes part of an ethic because a plethora of justifications arrive to support its practice. He argues, in effect, that under conditions of bourgeois morality, where the interchangeability and indifference of individuals reign, sexual cruelty is a way to reestablish individuality and passion. According to Beauvoir, Sade interrogated the fundamental relations of self and Other, seeking to know their limits and the conditions of their possibility. "This behavior," she writes, "compensates for separateness by deliberate tyranny" (*MBS* 33). It is not just that he does evil, or writes about it. He offers elaborate justifications for evil's supremacy; he has, Beauvoir maintains, "a profound conviction that crime is good" (*MBS* 74). He says quite clearly in 1795 that he hopes only to have "contributed in some way to the progress of enlightenment" (cited at *MBS* 47). Beauvoir summarizes his view in this way: "virtue deserves no admiration and no gratitude since, far from reflecting the demands of a transcendent good, it serves the interests of those who make a show of it" (*MBS* 68). Thus, Sade objects to the hypocrisy of bourgeois morality, entering a position of moralism himself. He objects to the indifference that bourgeois morality fosters, to the blindness to their own violence that such abstractions as universality and equality inflict, the destruction of nature and life that abstract morality performs. She writes: "he could not excuse the Terror: When murder becomes constitutional, it becomes merely the hateful expression of abstract principles, something without content, inhuman" (*MBS* 26). Through recourse to distinct values – opposition to false equality, to violence done through false abstraction – he justifies his own crime and cruelty. He chides himself for not following the imperatives of nature adequately and in this way engages in a moralistic self-beratement as well. In this sense, perhaps perversely, he becomes for Beauvoir a philosopher of freedom:

it is as a moralist rather than as a poet that Sade tries to shatter the prison of appearances. The mystified and mystifying society against which he rebels suggests Heidegger's 'the one' [*das Man*] in which the authenticity of existence is swallowed up. For Sade, too, it is a question of regaining authenticity by an individual decision. [MBS 75]

Indeed, Beauvoir insists upon the counterintuitive claim that Sade is everywhere concerned with ethics. Moreover, she remarks that his life gives us occasion to think about how ethics becomes sexualized in sadism and what forms of self-assertion are possible within sexuality when social conditions work against self-assertion in other domains. In effect, the questions Beauvoir poses regarding his life are not moral questions of the sort, "should one act in this or that way." She questions whether what Sade ultimately does – as a person, an author, a political figure – truly qualifies as "action," by which she means a transformative intervention into the collective conditions of existence. Yet the question, for her, is not only what he "does" but what his action seeks to accomplish, whether it transcends the activity of pure negation, whether it can be said, in whatever way, to be creative and to alter the common conditions of life. Whereas some critics might seek to explain Sade's political actions and literary productions in terms of his sexuality, thereby using sexuality as the key to understanding the tacit psychological aims of his work, Beauvoir refuses this view. Sexuality is not the key, since sexuality itself must be explained. The way to explain it, however, is not only through recourse to childhood events or influences, but rather to situate all of these in terms of a larger project that structures and animates his life.[5] This project is not always in accord with what an individual might say or think it is. It is a matter of interpretation. Beauvoir offers us an example of this kind of analysis as she reconsiders Sade. She opens up the question of how to understand this life in light of how he made it, how, in his various writings and actions, he took up a specific relation to himself.

EXPLAINING SADE

What can we know about Sade? Beauvoir remarks that he is, first and foremost, an author and that he is also known as a "sexual pervert." Does she use the word "pervert" ironically? Does she subscribe to certain sexological categories available to her in the early 1950s? Or is she simply telling us that "perverted" is how he was and is regarded? She makes clear that his sexuality reveals the human condition and should not be considered as idiosyncratic or aberrant in that sense. There is a relationship between his authorship and sexuality: "it is neither as author nor as sexual pervert that Sade compels our attention: it is by virtue of the relationship which he created between these two aspects of himself" (*MBS* 12). Indeed, Beauvoir does not try to explain his sexuality, to give an account of his desire to dominate prostitutes, his predilection for various forms of sexual torture. It seems that sexology, law, and psychiatry have amassed many such explanations, and finally, it seems, they do not interest her, at least not as ways of getting to something true about Sade. Indeed, she is interested in the relationship between sexuality and explanatory systems, in how one gives rise to the other. But she does not seek to "explain" Sade. "Sade's aberrations begin to acquire value when, instead of enduring them as fixed nature, he elaborates an immense system in order to justify them" (*MBS* 12). At the same time, and conversely, if we look at his writings and seek to know what of his life is being communicated there, we find that the writings fail to communicate the life and that the life remains incommunicable. This is not because of some existential fact about life and communication, but rather because "he [Sade] is trying to communicate an experience whose distinguishing characteristic is, nevertheless, its will to remain incommunicable" (*MBS* 12). Indeed, whereas some literary critics have sought to dismiss Sade as a second-rate writer whose literary works are finally "unreadable" (*MBS* 12), Beauvoir takes this very unreadability as an important symptom of his personhood and work. What kind of person seeks to become incommunicable in the act of communication? How are we to understand his writing to the public but refusing them at the same time? He is publishing but making himself difficult, if not impossible, to understand. He is laying bare another body, subjecting it to his control, but does not yield to a reciprocity. Through obscurity, he retains his sovereign individuality.

There is clearly a relation at work here between sexuality and writing. But it will be important to avoid two pitfalls: the first would be to reduce the writing to the sexuality, as if sexuality could provide the explanatory principle for the writing; the second would be to explain the sexuality through the writing, which was apparently Sade's explicit aim. So we cannot use the writings to explain the sexuality, and we cannot use the life to explain the writings, since the life is what remains incommunicable in the writings. And we cannot, as some psychoanalysts would attempt to do, use the sexuality to explain the life and the writings. How, then, are we to proceed? Sade wills not to communicate his life in his writing. What does this tell us about his life, his sexual life in particular, and his writings? It tells us that even though the writings seek to justify the life, they conceal the life, protect it, enshroud it. And in this way they must fail to accomplish their task, for how can one justify a life that never quite clearly comes into view? Even though the life is conducted according to "principles," it cannot be understood exactly by the terms through which it is presented. For Beauvoir, there is something specifically obscure about Sade, some way in which he withholds himself. "He is trying to communicate an experience whose distinguishing characteristic is, nevertheless, its will to remain incommunicable" (*MBS* 12). But for Beauvoir, there is something which, in general, is also inexpressible about a life, and that is a certain operation of freedom. We see its effects; we discern its presence; but freedom is never fully defined by the phenomena in which it is manifest and by which it is discerned. There is a gap between the freedom to which we refer, which we cannot see or grasp, and the expressions by which it is known, always and only indirectly. To be a biographer is always to stay attuned to this double truth, namely, *that freedom is what structures the life and that freedom in its autonomy and purity cannot directly be apprehended.*

Beauvoir also assumes that sexuality is the expression of freedom and that it is, in particular, the expression of freedom for Sade. We are perhaps used to thinking of sexuality as a drive, an urgency, something unconscious, physical, beyond conscious control, an upsurge of nature, or a preconscious psychic domain of need and desire. Beauvoir knows these theories in the early 1950s, and her essay tacitly and insistently contests them. To claim that sexuality belongs to the realm of freedom is not to say that one sits back and, from an instrumental distance, *decides* what one's sexuality will be. Freedom is not the same as deliberate and instrumental choice. Indeed, I would be tempted to say that freedom itself has an unconscious dimension for her and that the workings of freedom are not there on the surface for us to understand without an attendant act of interpretation. One acts, one produces, and there in the result – the deed, the work – is the trace of a freedom that was – must have been – operative all along. One does not know one's freedom until after the fact, and this is why we are at once responsible and unknowing about ourselves.

Two different aspects of Sade's freedom are noteworthy: on the one hand there is the resolution of freedom into sexual self-assertion, against the law, but in the name of an "ethics" carefully crafted; on the other hand there is a will to communicate in such a way that something of him remains incommunicable. To the extent that freedom is always expressed in or as a displacement, Sade works the very invisibility of freedom to his advantage, concealing himself in and through the act of communication. Self-concealing language, sexual sadism: what is the connection? What formation of the will informs both activities?

When Beauvoir seeks to understand Sade, she does not probe the inner "causalities" of his psyche, his motives, what might have caused his desire to take the form that it did. She is less interested in causes than in aims. She asks instead what he endeavors to achieve through sexuality and how it is that sexuality became, as it were, the domain of achievement for him. How does she go about doing this?

Beauvoir is clearly interested in historical circumstances, and she makes use of them in trying to give an account of Sade. She explains that he belongs to a "fallen aristocracy" and that his bourgeois life was one in which no special distinction or singularity was available to him. She even argues that he becomes something like a "feudal despot" in the imaginary realm of his sexual life, that this position of resurrected sovereignty is compensation for an irreversibly deteriorating class position. After all, he is writing during the period of the French Revolution (1789) and the Terror. His own aristocratic roots are figured as the enemy of revolutionary forces. He comes to oppose the evolution of the revolution into the Reign of Terror and its brutal application of "universal" principles. The Terror became the occasion on which Sade decried the "legal" application of murder; citizens who fell out of line with the regime were routinely executed in the name of "law," "universality," "equality," and "justice." Beauvoir locates Sade in this historical predicament. He cannot recover his class privilege, and he is living at a time when sovereignty and aristocratic privilege are becoming undone by social and political forces. Not only can he no longer inhabit an aristocratic position, but aristocracy is for him, even as a child, part of a past dream, an identity already lost, an increasingly imaginary position. Indeed, when he comes to oppose the Terror, he does so in the name of nature and freedom, not in the name of a lost aristocracy. But something else happens in the domain of sexuality, something perhaps not quite compatible with his political beliefs.

In Beauvoir's view, Sade's sexual practice is inspired by a desire to rehabilitate feudal power in the midst of bourgeois life: "Scions of a declining call [the aristocracy] which has once possessed concrete power, but which no longer retained any real hold on the world, they tried to revive symbolically, in the privacy of the bedchamber, the status for which they were nostalgic, that of the lone and sovereign feudal despot" (MBS 15). So, in this sense, the sovereign position of the aristocrat cannot be actually inhabited by him in his actually existing social world: it can only be assumed in an imaginary way. Sexuality, Beauvoir argues, is the venue by which that assumption takes place. Beauvoir does not use Sade's class position as the explanatory cause of his character. But it is there, as a loss, as a dream, and Sade takes it up in his own way. It is in relation to it that he must form himself, but it does not define him. He is clearly in a certain historical predicament. But he also seeks to resolve this predicament in his own way. In Beauvoir's view, facts alone are never explanatory, and, in this case, it turns out that we do not have many facts, or that they are inconsistent. "Value is not to be found in information, but in the value the facts assume for Sade himself." What we do know is that "he made of his sexuality an ethic," the erection of "tastes into principles" (*MBS* 15).

To understand how Sade makes his sexuality into an ethic, we have to ask how sexuality becomes the venue, the means, by which his imaginary solution to a lost social station takes place. He is, we learn from Beauvoir's account, a conformist who honors his commitments in the realms of both work and household at the same time that he moves into brothels in order to work out the refusal or negation of bourgeois norms he otherwise obeys. So Sade obeys outside of the sexual realm; and within the sexual realm, he demands obedience.

Thus, Beauvoir is clear that he lived in a certain bourgeois world, one in which he participated (prior to his criminalization) not only as a "normal" citizen but as a citizen who, in her view, desired to craft a life that satisfied social convention in every way.[6] As a good citizen, he experiences the norm in his person and his action and becomes, in this respect, interchangeable with others. Beauvoir, then, concludes that sexuality became for him a privileged site of freedom, where he could still achieve singularity: "there was only one place where he could assert himself as such...in the brothel where he bought the right to unleash his fantasies" (*MBS* 16). To the extent that he is able to buy his pleasure there, he still operates firmly within a commodity system. To the extent that it is his "right" to pleasure which he buys there, he is instating a certain liberal bourgeois individualism, even as he apparently strays from its norms. Sade is clearly engaging his history, his context, at the same time that he is trying to defy the normalization required by bourgeois social life. He shows no sign of trying to exceed the bounds of normality *within* bourgeois life, according to Beauvoir, no aspiration to become a great entrepreneur or distinguish himself within the market or its social world: "we are struck by the fact that beyond the walls of his 'little house' it did not occur to him to 'make full use of his strength.' There is no hint of ambition in him" (*MBS* 15). Indeed, sexuality becomes produced as the domain in which he will assert himself. This assertion is at once an assertion of "himself as such," his singularity, but also of a former time, a time now lost, the time of the feudal despot. So he asserts his singularity but always through a set of norms that show the historical conditions and aims embedded in his own desire.

If at first Sade appeared to be mastering and managing his various selves, his various practices, keeping them at a significant distance from one another, after he was arrested for lewd and cruel acts (the Arcueil affair), he lost not only his control but his bourgeois respectability. Where is he when he is in these various "places" in his life? Is he ever at home when he is at home? Is he ever at work when at work? Would it be right to say he is fully present at the brothel? Or can we assume that this self, partitioned, is always never where he is, always eluding the site where he might be constituted? Is there a specific operation of freedom in this constant sliding from place to place? What kind of freedom might this be? And what happens when, by his own action, he is finally delivered over to the police and becomes the occasion for public scandal?

Beauvoir tries to understand Sade at this juncture. But understanding him means *imagining* him. And so she tells his story, but in the mode of a conjecture: perhaps it happened like this, he probably thought that. She writes sometimes without marking this conjectural character of her account, offering instead a point of view that claims special access to his perspective. At the same time, she will not precisely take him at his word, accept his own account of what he was doing with his life – and he left many. Her writing is an effort to reconstruct him, to reestablish what the world was for him from a point of view that is at once imagined as his and avowed as her own. Thus the writing sometimes appears to forfeit her own point of view, and she writes from a sympathetic third-person perspective that presumes some kind of access to his own reality. At other times, her point of view marks the limit of its own access: she was born a century after his death, she is hampered by no direct access to him;

she is constrained to reconstruct him from extant legal documents and his written texts.

So sometimes she reports on his feelings at the time, as if she knows what they were, and with an air of certainty. After his exposure and arrest, she writes for instance, "Sade reacted at first with prayer, humility, and shame. He begged to be allowed to see his wife, accusing himself of having grievously offended her. He begged to confess and open his heart to her. This was not mere hypocrisy. A horrible change had taken place overnight; natural innocent practices, which had been hitherto sources of pleasure, had become punishable acts" (*MBS* 19). Beauvoir then imagines that he may have experienced from his mother something of what it is to be a scandal but that after 1763, the year of his arrest, "Sade had a foreboding that he would henceforth and for the rest of his life be a culprit" (*MBS* 19).

BEAUVOIR'S CRITICAL SYMPATHY

To try to explain Sade is not only to find out the historical facts about him, to read all the words he has left behind, but, quite literally, to imagine oneself in his place, as if he were utterly present to one's own consciousness. To reconstruct a life is to admit that life into human imaginability. To try to understand Sade is to recognize that if nothing human is foreign to us, even Sade will have to cease to be unimaginable. By imagining him, Beauvoir is exemplifying a task of (a postwar) humanism, making a choice of her own, establishing as well, and in a timely way, what it takes to overcome the difficulty of imagining others who are disgusting or difficult to apprehend. "To sympathize with Sade too readily is to betray him" (*MBS* 79), she writes, for sympathy is what he seeks to resist, in the name of a "natural" disposition to inflict pain and incite the flesh. So Beauvoir, in her nearly uncanny ability to sympathize with Sade, betrays him in order, precisely, to know him and present him to us. She differs from him explicitly on this point, maintaining that although both prize the individual, they subscribe, finally, to different views on how far individuals can overcome their individuality. Just as, for Beauvoir, "action" in the normative sense engages the collective or shared conditions of existence and their transformation, so she faults Sade finally for failing to emerge from the sensual tactics of the individual into a common world. Thus, she writes, "it is in the name of the individual that it seems possible to raise the most convincing objections to Sade's notions; for the individual is quite real, and crime does him real injury. It is here that Sade's thinking proves to be *extreme*: the only thing that has truth for him is that which is enveloped in my own experience; the inner presence of other people is foreign to me" (*MBS* 76). This last claim is one that Beauvoir could not utter in her own name. For what she does in this patient elaboration of Sade is to show that the inner presence of his being, bequeathed in his writings and what is written about him, is *not* foreign to her. She shows that we would be making a mistake if we failed to take into account Sade as a definite human possibility, one that is, therefore, at least potentially, ours. Indeed, her entire effort to apprehend him through biographical means would be threatened if his view, disputing the possibility of sympathy with others, prevailed over hers.

Whereas Sade maintains that the individual can rely only on his (*sic*) own sensations and feelings, Beauvoir counters that "the only sure bonds among men are those they create in transcending themselves within a common world by means of a common project [se transcendant dans un monde commun par des projets communs (*FB* 1224)]" (*MBS* 76, my translation).

Beauvoir does not quite accept Sade's explicit proclamation that humans share nothing in common, that they are each, individually, potential or actual sovereigns. She shows, for instance, how in Sade's sexual practice he presumes that everybody is vulnerable to pain and to pleasure. And when he appeals to his audience, offering reasons and examples to justify his crime, he assumes that by virtue of living in a common linguistic world he will, to a degree, be communicating effectively to them. But there is also a way in which Beauvoir accepts Sade's view of the individual's potential solipsism. She writes, for instance, that Sade is only disputing the existence of an a priori relationship between oneself and an Other (*MBS* 76–77) and that it is not possible to accept this relation as an abstract reality that is in place prior to action. Like Beauvoir, Sade does not dispute the possibility of making such a relationship. We might tentatively conclude that both believe that relationality is always achieved through action and that a shared world is the special dispensation of action. If there is to be an ethical recognition of the Other, it will not be through recourse to an abstract scheme of human equality or universality that enfolds us all. For Sade, the connection with the Other will have to travel through the body, conceived as a limit that is only overcome, if it ever is, through a passionate and violating sexual action.

Although Beauvoir makes clear that she understands "action" in the normative sense to be collective, she seems to share with Sade an insight into the limits of collectivity. He treats the human body as a limit that must be destroyed, a limit beyond which resides a noncorporeal person or will, always isolated, never fully reached. Beauvoir seems to countenance this view when she writes: "Each mind bears witness only for itself as to the value it attributes to itself and has no right to impose this value on others. But it can, in a singular and vivid manner, demand recognition of such value in its acts" (*MBS* 77). One might expect her to object to this view of the body as an enclosure and a limit and to offer a notion of the flesh as that which articulates both the will in its corporeality and its interconnectedness with others. But here it seems that it is not, finally, the body that releases us from solipsism to intersubjectivity but "action," which impels us into a common project which, ideally, will not efface the singular individuals who make that common reality possible.

The question remains, though, whether the body, which Beauvoir describes in *The Second Sex* as "a situation," does not as well imply an intersubjective world and offer a way out of solipsism and, by implication, out of sadism as well. She does not give us that reassurance in this essay. But in her discussion of sadomasochism she makes clear her difference from the Sadean account (and the Sartrean as well).[7] We might consider that here she identifies passivity as the link between the sadist and the masochist, the common predicament of embodiment, one that offers an alternative to the presumption of solipsistic ontology that Sade offers.

Beauvoir offers an original reading of Sade's eroticism, arguing that he is incapable of the experience of self-loss: "never in his stories does sensual pleasure appear as self-forgetfulness, swooning, or abandon" (*MBS* 32). Along with a passionate desire for erotic contact, Sade is also, as if constitutionally, alone. She notes this "emotional apartness" as "the key to his eroticism" (*MBS* 32). Paradoxically, although Sade champions nature and justifies his various acts through recourse to nature, even berating himself for not following the dictates of nature more rigorously, "he never, for an instant, loses himself in his animal nature; he remains so lucid, so cerebral, that philosophical discourse, far from dampening his ardor, acts as an aphrodisiac" (*MBS* 32). Just as Sade fails to achieve an "action" that is collective and transformative, according to Beauvoir, so in sexual encounters he lacks the necessary experience of intoxication. Beauvoir clearly thinks that intoxication is essential to the sexual encounter, but finds that Sade resists intoxication fully and effectively. Without intoxication, there can be no passivity, which means that the boundaries of the self fail to give way to the "ambiguous unity" of lovers in sexual exchange. Without the capacity to lose his lucidity, to undergo intoxication and passivity, Sade remains remote, cut off, "sovereign," and finally self-referential or, in her words, "autistic" (*MBS* 33). This autism, the psychic correlate of philosophical solipsism, was what prevented Sade from acknowledging the genuine presence of another human being. Indeed, in Beauvoir's view, only through an intoxicated and passive "forgetting of oneself" does one come to apprehend the genuine presence of the Other.

Sade's position is thus differentiated from Beauvoir's precisely on this point. He cannot overcome his lucidity, his separateness. In her view, his forms of sexual tyranny are an effort to compensate for his incapacity, his refusal of passivity and intoxication. He is, as it were, always at a distance from his body, its capacity for yielding, for overwhelming the lucidity of consciousness. So the only way to return to the body he refuses is through the corporealization of the Other: "a cold, cerebral lover watches eagerly the enjoyment of his mistress and needs to affirm his responsibility for it because he has no other way of attaining his own fleshly state" (*MBS* 33). Beauvoir is clear that Sade takes no pleasure in the infliction of pain on an inert or unfeeling body. In a paraphrase of his logic, Beauvoir writes: "in order for me to become flesh and blood through the pains I have inflicted, I must recognize my own state in the passivity of the other" (*MBS* 34). So if it appears, at first, that Sade seeks to differentiate himself from his lovers by being the sovereign will who acts upon another's body, it turns out that the only way the "sovereign will" can take pleasure in its actions is by imagining, even if only vicariously and through displacement, the dissolution of its own sovereignty and will. That Sade sometimes arranged for his own flagellation offers further proof, for Beauvoir, of the inexorability of this dialectic. Similarly, although he performs acts on others, he often arranges these scenes so that he is *seen* performing these acts, whereby he becomes a spectacle within the scene. Beauvoir thus speculates: "By contemplating the flesh to which he had done violence[,] the violence which he himself had borne, he repossessed himself as subject within the being of his own passivity [en contemplant sur une chair qu'il violente les violences qu'il supporte, il se ressaisit comme sujet au sein de sa passivité (*FB* 1031)]" (*MBS* 43–44, my translation).

Beauvoir thus shows how Sade interrogates this dialectic and seeks to refuse its claim upon him. But she also shows how, through the example of the man who refuses to acknowledge the presence of the Other, she can demonstrate the very structure of human intersubjectivity as it appears within sexual exchange. By insisting on understanding Sade, by giving herself over, through a method of critical sympathy, to the logic of his conduct, Beauvoir refutes Sade's thesis that the Other is not to be understood. By betraying his dictates in this way, Beauvoir is able to illuminate what she takes to be the human condition, which is always at issue in his action and writing. Beauvoir maintains that although Sade wrote about murder he opposed the death penalty, and that his eroticism depended not only on the continuing life of his victims but on their responsiveness as well: "In order to derive pleasure from the humiliation and exaltation of the flesh, one must ascribe value to the flesh" (*MBS* 26). With regard to his sexual exploits, she makes allowances for Sade that may well seem questionable. She writes: "He was sure, in any case, that a man who was content with whipping a prostitute every now and then was less harmful to society than a farmer-general" (*MBS* 64). Is it Beauvoir in an act of critical sympathy who offers this point of view? Or Sade? Have their voices merged? Is she, as it were, so given over to his voice at this point that we cannot finally tell whether Beauvoir is here making an ethical distinction between sexual cruelty and political injustice? If he bought the right to unleash his fantasies in the brothel, then surely the women who worked there ought to have had rights to decent work conditions, health care, and protection from violence. The ethical point is not to oppose prostitution *per se* but to accept it as a social institution for which collective responsibility is required. Sade may well have helped to avow the social reality of prostitution, but the critical supplement to Sade must defend the rights of prostitutes against unwanted violence. Under these conditions sexual cruelty is part of what must be properly situated within the sphere of political justice. The right to sex, which Sade made so clear, must be complemented with a right to sexual protection. It is this last point that Beauvoir does not identify as part of the domain of justice, although we might have suspected that she would.

What she makes clear from the start of this essay is that she seeks neither to romanticize nor to vilify Sade. To understand the ethical significance of Sade, one must suspend judgment about him and adopt the critical sympathy of the biographer. The ethical question for her is not whether such conduct should or should not be condoned, but what such conduct tells us about who we are and how we might come to know the full range of human possibility. In response to the ethical injunction to know oneself, one must, as it were, undertake to know Sade, even if – or precisely because – he assumed that no such knowledge of the Other was finally possible.

NOTES

1 Albert Camus, "L'Homme revolté," in *Essais d'Albert Camus*, ed. R. Quillot and L. Faucon (Paris: Gallimard-Pléiade, 1965), p. 457.

2 Simone de Beauvoir, "Must We Burn Sade?," in *The Marquis de Sade: An Essay by Simone de Beauvoir*, trans. Annette Michelson (New York: Grove, 1953); "Faut-il brûler Sade?," *Les Temps modernes*, 74–75 (Dec. 1951–Jan. 1952): 1002–33, 1197–230.

3 For a complete chronology of Sade's life, see Laurence Bongie, *Sade: A Biographical Essay* (Chicago: University of Chicago Press, 1998), pp. 271–80.

4 Michel Feher, "Introduction: Libertinisms," in *The Libertine Reader: Eroticism and Enlightenment in Eighteenth-Century France*, ed. Michel Feher (New York: Zone Books, 1997), p. 35.

5 Critics such as Pierre Klossowski offered influential psychological readings focusing on the passions of Sade's childhood, especially his putative hatred for his mother. "The principal events of his life seem to have singularly favored the more rare and generally less manifest complex of hatred of the mother. Traces of this are easily recognized at every moment of his work; we can even consider it the constant theme of Sadean ideology." Pierre Klossowski, "The Father and Mother in Sade's Work," trans. Alphonso Lingis, in *Sade My Neighbor* (Evanston, IL: Northwestern University Press, 1991), pp. 127 ff.

6 Recent biographies have called this assumption into question. See Laurence L. Bongie, *Sade: A Bibliographical Essay* (Chicago: University of Chicago Press, 1998). In France, the monumental *Vie du Marquis de Sade, avec un examen de ses ouvrages*, written by Gilbert Lely, was published the year after the first installment of Beauvoir's essay, in 1952, and then in 1957. More recently, a vindication of Sade's life and work has appeared.

See Annie Le Brun, *Soudain un bloc d'abîme, Sade* (Paris: J.-J. Pauvert, 1986) and *Sade, aller et détours* (Paris: Plon, 1989).

7 For Jean-Paul Sartre's account of sadomasochism, see "Concrete Relations with Others," *BN* (New York: Philosophical Library, 1956) 361–412. Beauvoir does not cite Sartre here, and it is clear that her recourse to passivity, autism, and intoxication constitute an original contribution to the theorization of sadism.

9 Beauvoir and feminism: interview and reflections

INTERVIEW[1]

BRISON: Yesterday, you agreed that it's not enough for women to put themselves in exactly the same situation as men in order for them to be liberated. But you didn't say what you think we need to do now. I'd like to ask you the same question that you asked Sartre, a question it seemed to me he avoided: "Should women completely reject the masculine universe or should they find themselves a place in it? Should they steal their tools or change them? I'm thinking of science as well as language, the arts. Every value is marked with the seal of masculinity."[2]

DE BEAUVOIR: That's a lot of questions in one. I think that feminists, at least those I'm involved with, want to change not only women's situation but also the world. That is, these are women who would like to see a certain dismantling of society and who think that if feminism were victorious, if the oppression of women were completely eliminated, well, society would be shaken to its foundation. This cannot be accomplished without other kinds of action, for example, actions supporting class struggle and immigrants, in other words, all the actions one can imagine in favor of society. They must all be linked. So, it's a matter not of women taking men's place in this world, but of their being emancipated in such a way as to simultaneously change this world. OK, you asked a second question, namely, can certain parts of this world, like science, literature, the arts, which were largely, very largely, developed by men in a masculine world – can we use these, or should we reject them altogether? I think we should use them – I think I said it yesterday, we should naturally use them with a great deal of precaution, because, for example, we're not going to recreate language from one day to the next on the basis of personal initiative. Language is never created that way, in any country at any time. So of course we must seize upon language, but in doing so we must remain aware that language bears the mark of men. It's universal but also singular. For instance, there are words like "virile" that have a positive meaning for men that women have no reason to accept. You could find a lot of others. Similarly, for science, sure, 2 and 2 is 4 for men as for women. But the orientation given to science is obviously very different according to whether it is men or women who direct the research. Men have never taken much interest in specifically female biology or medicine. If women were to undertake serious research, they could, they should, do it much more in the way of . . . well, to serve their sex as such. Same for language, for science, for art, and for literature. You can, indeed, steal the tools and use them, but you have to use them carefully and, for that matter, nothing prevents you from changing them at the same time.

BRISON: In *The Second Sex* you wrote that the woman who is culturally conditioned into womanhood doesn't know how to make use of the sort of technical training that would allow her to control (material) things. She doesn't find any usefulness in masculine logic. But couldn't that be considered rather as a positive feature in women? The "knowledge of domination" has proven to be so destructive that now it is essential to preserve its contrary, that is, to foster a real desire to interact with the natural world and with others. As Hélène Cixous has written: "It's not a question of appropriating their instruments, their concepts, their places, or their position of mastery . . . Let's leave all that to the anxious ones, to masculine anguish and its obsessional relation to mastery, to domination, to knowing 'how it works' in order to 'make it work.'"[3] I think you're in agreement with her.

DE BEAUVOIR: Yes, the point is not for women simply to take power out of men's hands, since that wouldn't change anything about the world. It's a question precisely of destroying that notion of power. That's it. On this I completely agree: women must master many, many things, but not in order to seize power and to dominate others. I'm certain, in fact, that this idea of domination is one of the features of the masculine universe that must be totally destroyed, that we must look for reciprocity, collaboration, etc.

BRISON: So, some features of the masculine universe must be destroyed. It seems to me that there are also certain traditionally feminine features that ought to be preserved in both men and women, as you yourself say to Sartre: "If we consider ourselves as possessing certain positive qualities, isn't it better to convey them to men rather than suppress them in women?"[4] I wonder what qualities you had in mind.

DE BEAUVOIR: Precisely because they don't generally have power, women don't have the flaws that are linked to the possession of power. For example, they don't demonstrate the self-importance, the fatuousness, the complacency, the spirit of emulation that you find in men. Women have more irony, more detachment, more simplicity. They play fewer roles, wear fewer masks, and I think the kind of truthfulness you find in many women is there because, in a sense, they have to have it, and that's a quality they should keep and should also transmit to men. There are also qualities of devotion. Devotion is very dangerous because it can become a way of life and can devour people sometimes, but it has its good sides, if it's what we think of as altruism. There is often, in women, a kind of caring for others that is inculcated in them by education, and which should be eliminated when it takes the form of slavery. But caring about others, the ability to give to others, to give of your time, your intelligence – this is something women should keep, and something that men should learn to acquire.

BRISON: If one doesn't want to define woman negatively in relation to man – woman as an inferior man, a failed man – how can one define her positively? As Cixous has written: "They've stuck us between two horrifying myths, between Medusa and the abyss."[5] It seems to me that Sartre, as well, has identified woman with the "viscous," with what blocks the transcendence of the in-itself...

DE BEAUVOIR: Sartre didn't say that; I'm the one who spoke of woman as immanence. But I did so in considering the role she has been made to play. It's not by nature that she is reduced to immanence; she's been reduced to it by men, who prevent her from acting, creating, transcending herself, as we put it during the era of existentialism, as I would still put it today.

BRISON: I was thinking of somewhat more symbolic things, for example, of the words he chose in describing the female as "slimy" and "viscous."

DE BEAUVOIR: It's possible that he had some "macho" prejudices, as he says in the dialogue with me in *L'Arc*. It's his whole education, his whole past, all of that which gave him at once a lot of sympathy for women and a way of looking at them as different, even better, in his eyes, but indeed, different from men. A positive definition of "woman"? Woman is a human being with a certain physiology, but that physiology in no way makes her inferior, nor does it justify her exploitation.

BRISON: You explained in *The Second Sex* that women grant a great deal of importance to sensual pleasure because of their immanence. Perhaps that's true. But now, is the goal to devalorize sensuality or to rediscover it at the very center of both sexes?

DE BEAUVOIR: Well, the writer of *The Second Sex* says both things. I also said that there are an awful lot of women who were completely frigid. Frigid, in any case, with men. And on the other hand, there are some who, having discovered pleasure, grant it enormous importance. But I think that if they consider the physical to be so important, it's not because of some physiological destiny, but precisely because they are deprived of so many other things in life. They have so little of real interest in their lives that they are led to confer much value to the part, let's say, the sexual, sensual part of their existence. This goes as well for relations with children, with the newborn, etc. They take pleasure in breastfeeding, etc., and all of this is very important for them largely because they have so little else.

BRISON: But even if women could transcend their immanence, they should still preserve their sensual nature.

DE BEAUVOIR: Well yes! Of course, for men and women, sexuality should be something that is really free and fulfilling.

BRISON: You said yesterday that you refuse to accept the notion of a uniquely feminine style of writing, that we have to get rid of "macho" words but that it's not a question of creating a new language.

DE BEAUVOIR: Yes, that's what I was just saying a moment ago, too, because a language is never really created by individual initiative. Language is not voluntaristic. It's something constituted through circulation, in the mass of people, in reciprocity, in all of that, and if you try to create a language artificially you'll never manage to make a real language out of it, and you'll cut off communication with others. I find that many of Cixous's books, for example, are virtually impossible to read because they sever communication with others.

BRISON: But perhaps it's necessary for really innovative writers to be, initially, a bit incomprehensible, like James Joyce in *Finnegan's Wake*.

DE BEAUVOIR: I don't know. They're not always incomprehensible. If they try to be, as James Joyce did in *Finnegan's Wake*, their work becomes very, very hard to read. But, in *Ulysses*, you find a lot that is quite accessible in spite of everything.

BRISON: I agree completely with what you said yesterday about how "every woman has the right to shout, but the cry must be heard and listened to..."

DE BEAUVOIR: Right, that's it.

BRISON: But what do you think of the idea of "women's writing" – "women's" in the sense of "feminist," that is, a writing that rebels in order to lead us toward liberation?

DE BEAUVOIR: Ah, yes! I'm totally in favor of that. I think that women can write, and even should write – perhaps not all women, but still – that they should write feminist books, books that reveal women's condition, that revolt against it and lead others to revolt. I mentioned to you, for example, that I really like Kate Millet's book, *Flying*. I even like it much more than her first book, the theoretical one, because here she really puts her experience as a woman on the table and everybody can read it and see how a woman tries to manage with her sexual tendencies as well as with society, etc. I think that women certainly have new things to say, unique things, and that they must say them. What I don't approve of is the choice of a language that is completely different from common language because I think it cuts off communication. In a feminist book like Kate Millet's, the language is normal, understandable for everyone. To the extent that there are new things to say, they must be said in a way that's accessible.

BRISON: Many critics have asked why you haven't portrayed truly liberated women in your novels. The stress is placed on your female characters' love lives. Even a character as liberated as Anne in *The Mandarins* is depicted primarily through her love life rather than through her interest in her work or in political life. Yet your portraits of male characters don't seem to follow this pattern. Does this mean that there is no point in portraying liberated women and ideal relationships? Does it mean that, in a society where women are still conditioned to assume the traditionally feminine attributes of submission and self-effacement, it's not useful to portray liberated women and ideal relationships?

DE BEAUVOIR: I wanted to describe women such as they are, and not as they should be. Actually, there are very, very few truly liberated women. I don't know if there's a single one. I don't know if there are even any men who are really completely liberated. Everybody is alienated in some way or other. But, anyway, I wanted to take typical women, like the ones I know, as they are, and not an ideal woman. In other words, what you suggest goes in the direction of socialist realism, where there must always be positive heroes. I didn't want to have positive heroines. That genre of writing – too moralizing, too didactic – irritates me. I've been much more interested in women who are much more divided, that is, more in conformity with the way women generally are. I didn't want to portray really exceptional women.

BRISON: Among the many reasons that you have given for writing, is that you have felt the need "to conserve, to save the past," "to recuperate" your life, as well as to communicate your experience. But was it also your intention to establish a new way of living, if only through its absence, as in, for example, your most recent novels, in which you describe an intolerable society and destructive, traditional relationships?

DE BEAUVOIR: You know, I've looked for different things in writing. After all, my books are spread out over a lot of years. There are, of course, books in which I seek to recount the past: for example, my memoirs and also to some extent *The Mandarins*, in which I tried to capture a period I'd lived in, and also somewhat in *She Came to Stay*. There are autobiographical elements everywhere. But I've also tried to describe the society around me – outside of me – to describe how things are in the present. For example, in *Les Belles images* I tried to describe society or, in any case, to make its way of speaking heard, as I said somewhere. I tried to show society such as it unfortunately is today. And then, in *The Woman Destroyed*, I told the story of a woman very different from myself. In the monolog and in my depiction of the "broken woman" I was actually inspired by women I'd known, whom I'd met, whose plight I have seen up close, for example, in the drama of breaking up. But at that point I was no longer engaged in autobiography, in remembering the past. I also try to describe, to grasp, the world as I see it, as I sense it.

BRISON: But do you envision a new way of living?

DE BEAUVOIR: Perhaps, if you wish. But *Les Belles images* is a denunciation, as it were: a denunciation of that society, a certain consumer society, snobbism, false relationships, etc. Certainly.

BRISON: Is it desirable to assume a political position in writing novels? Or is there a risk of literature becoming propaganda?

DE BEAUVOIR: I think that you write with everything you are, including political opinions, including your situation as a woman. You write on the basis of your situation, even if you don't talk about it. Obviously, in *Les Belles images* there is never really any explicit position on politics, but one could say all the same when reading the book that there is a whole bourgeois world that I find horrible and want nothing to do with. So, negatively, it can make you think of another, more fraternal, truer world. But there's no propaganda side to my novels.

BRISON: More generally, in your opinion, is the goal of art to show things as they are or to "make possible" a new world?

DE BEAUVOIR: Sartre has spoken of this very well in his articles on literature, when he showed how revealing things through words is already to act on things. When you give a name to oppression, to stupidity, to justice, you've already made them felt and that leads to a desire for change. It's certainly not a question of simply showing things in an entirely external manner, as in the new novel, for example;

it's not at all that, our notion. The idea of committed literature is perhaps the notion of literature not only as a commitment, but as an act, a certain act, without of course exaggerating the possibilities of literary action. One shouldn't exaggerate the political effect of writing. Take, for example, *The Second Sex*. I know that it's widely read today in America and in France because, twenty years after its publication, feminist movements emerged. So, these movements find in *The Second Sex* a theoretical confirmation of their spirit. But at the time of its publication, *The Second Sex* reached a number of women individually without creating a feminist movement. It's once the movement exists that the book assumes a certain value.

BRISON: One of the greatest problems for contemporary feminists is that expressed by Sartre: "They have no base in the masses and the task now, it seems to me, is to achieve it."[6] But how?

DE BEAUVOIR: It's very difficult, but there are certain things that affect all women. Take, for example, our success in the area of abortion rights. Every women is affected by that – a rich woman (a bit less so, because she is rich and can go to Switzerland or elsewhere, but after all that's not very pleasant) as well as her housemaid. There are things we're trying to do in France right now – I'm not sure about America – but we're trying to focus on things that interest more or less all women. For example, the anti-rape movement is of concern to the working woman down at the corner no less than to woman in the factory or to the girl still living at home, who can get raped like any other. So actions against rape can interest a whole lot of women. It's the same thing with protests against domestic violence – this is also very important to all women because there are victims of such abuse in all the social classes, including the middle class. One mustn't think that a lawyer or a doctor doesn't beat his wife just like a farmer or a worker does. I even think that the farmer is the one who does it less because his wife works, she is useful, he doesn't want to break her arm or leg. So, we have to find issues all women can be interested in and, on that basis, make them understand that their problems are experienced by all women, not only them, and give them a sense of solidarity. This is what we managed to do with abortion, by receiving women in abortion centers before the law was passed: when they had abortions, we explained why we were doing this and they realized they weren't alone in the world, that there were problems. They saw other women and sometimes they joined the movement and helped out. But for now it's certain that in France – I think it's the same thing in America – the big problem is that we don't reach women who are exploited in additional ways, whether directly, in the factory, or else because they're the wives of workers and exploited as such. The choice of action depends on the circumstances. In the examples I just mentioned, rape and domestic abuse, the movements against these happened because there were trials going on, inquiries, polls, and so women began to speak out a bit, they were encouraged to speak out, and the more they spoke the more it became clear what a crime sexual violence is – a very, very common crime that really concerns all social classes. So we need to find the points where the interests of women of all classes intersect. That, I think, is what feminists should be seeking.

BRISON: A somewhat more personal question: what are your current projects?

DE BEAUVOIR: Right now, I'm primarily working on some projects in film. They're making a film of *The Woman Destroyed*. That's for television, Channel 3. And then I have a really big project, making a film based on *The Second Sex* with a Swedish director named Mai Zetterling, who's done some excellent feminist films. She did a film called "The Girls." You haven't seen it? Well, it's really beautiful. So, we're going to take two years to do it and try to look at different aspects of the condition of woman. I'm really interested in it. We're going to collaborate on it and I'm really looking forward to it, since film, if it's done well, has a very strong impact on people. It can make women aware of a lot of things, more than books can, and it can easily reach workers' wives, wives of employees, since everybody has TV nowadays. It's a way of speaking to all women; one can do this more effectively through film or television than one can do in a book that they're not going to read. Reaching them through books is a bit too difficult. I'll be busy with this during the coming year, maybe even two years because it will take a long time to make, since *The Second Sex* covers the entire condition of women.

BRISON: And what are Sartre's projects right now?

DE BEAUVOIR: You know, Sartre can't see very well anymore. At least he can't read or write. He's working with a secretary who is also a friend and they're trying to write a book together, a book on the question of "power and freedom." The problem of power seems to interest everyone right now and so they're tackling it; his friend reads to him, they have conversations, his friend takes notes, etc. They're studying the huge subject of power and freedom: what exactly is power? And how can you reconcile a certain kind of power with freedom? Or must all power be completely suppressed? For example, in French feminist movements – the same problem comes up in America – feminists refuse all hierarchy, all bureaucracy, practically any organization whatsoever. Well, everything's disorganized and, for that reason, it turns back on itself, it's not a real democracy, because those who speak loudest, or with the greatest ease, talk all the time, and the others can't make themselves heard. That's pretty horrible, too, and it creates a lot of difficulty for the feminist movement. It's hard because it ends up being always the same ones who are the leaders, almost in spite of themselves. But they are still the leaders and have a certain power. Some are very happy with that; some, however, don't like it because it's draining, it requires too much responsibility, and then of course it reproduces masculine patterns to the very extent that they have tried to avoid them. Very difficult, this question of power. Yes.

REFLECTIONS: THEORY AND PRACTICE IN BEAUVOIR'S LATER FEMINISM

Although *The Second Sex*, first published in 1949, had inspired women around the world to rethink their situations and change their lives, it was ignored or disparaged by a surprising number of feminists during the so-called "second wave" of the women's movement in the 1970s, especially in France. Simone de Beauvoir was not even mentioned in the early feminist writings of Hélène Cixous, Luce Irigaray, and Julia Kristeva.[7] Suzanne Lilar declared, in a book published in France in 1970, "it is high time to lose respect for Simone de Beauvoir, it is high time to desecrate [*profaner*] *The Second Sex*,"[8] and Jean Leighton, in a book published in the United States in 1975, accused Beauvoir of "misogyny"[9] and of writing "a diatribe against the female sex."[10] According to Leighton, "*The Second Sex* staunchly insists that transcendence, action, creativity, and power are the masculine virtues par excellence, and these are what determine human value... Action and transcendence are male and good; being and immanence are feminine and bad. Unless women renounce 'femininity' and equal men on their own terms, they will continue to be inferior."[11]

Beauvoir was attacked by feminists not only in academic texts, but also in activist circles. Anne Tristan and Annie de Pisan describe a meeting (in Paris in 1970) of the nascent French women's liberation movement (the Mouvement de Libération des Femmes, or MLF) at which the announcement that Simone de Beauvoir had agreed to sign a manifesto calling for legalized abortion was met with the response: "'What's that got to do with anything? We don't want any of that kind of feminism here. *The Second Sex* is old hat.'"[12]

The main arguments being raised at the time against *The Second Sex*, and against Beauvoir herself, who was assumed to hold the same views roughly twenty-five years later, were that Beauvoir valorized "masculine" values and disparaged "feminine" ones and that she held that women needed simply to achieve the positions of power currently held by men in order to be truly liberated. Beauvoir did little to counter these charges. On the contrary, she reinforced these views, primarily by refusing to reply to critics, but also by suggesting, in interviews and publications, that her views *hadn't* changed since publishing *The Second Sex*. In 1972 she wrote that "As far as theory is concerned my opinions are still the same; but from the point of view of practice and tactics my position has changed."[13]

One might fault her for allowing these misperceptions to proliferate. Alternatively, one might give her credit for remaining above the fray in French feminist politics – a rather nasty one and soon to become worse. One of the first feminist groups in Paris, "Psychanalyse et Politique" (or "Psych et Po"), led by Antoinette Fouque, a psychoanalyst, dedicated itself to the celebration of feminine difference and disparaged Beauvoir as a reactionary masculinist. They founded the press Des Femmes and succeeded in legally registering the labels "Mouvement de Libération des Femmes" and "MLF" as commercial trademarks, in effect prohibiting anyone who was not part of their organization from calling herself a member of the women's liberation movement. The animosity of Psych et Po to Beauvoir's brand of feminism never abated. When Beauvoir died, in 1986, Antoinette Fouque wrote a piece in *Libération*, ascribing to

Beauvoir an "intolerant, assimilating, sterilizing universalism, full of hatred and reductive of otherness."[14]

Although there were deep ideological disagreements between Psych et Po and Beauvoir, the charge of intolerance was unfounded (not to mention ironic, given Psych et Po's trademarking of the very name of the women's liberation movement). In the mid-1970s Beauvoir's comments about feminism indicated precisely the opposite: an openness to the unexpected and exciting directions the movement would take. Her preface to the early collection of feminist essays, *Les Femmes s'entêtent*[15] (*Women Protest*, also a pun meaning women without a head) begins with the exhortation "perturbation, ma soeur" ("disruption, my sister"), signaling her nearly anarchic rejection of hierarchies, her refusal to be the leader of this movement without leaders. When *L'Arc* (a journal that devoted each issue to the work of a famous intellectual figure) decided to do a special issue about her in 1975, Beauvoir insisted that it be entitled *Simone de Beauvoir et la lutte des femmes* (*Simone de Beauvoir and Women's Struggle*), that other women appear on the cover with her, and that it consist of essays (not about Beauvoir) by a range of feminist theorists. It was in this volume that Hélène Cixous' essay "The Laugh of Medusa," praising "écriture féminine" ("feminine writing") first appeared. The editors of the volume write in their introduction that they wanted to convey Simone de Beauvoir's "inimitable way of being open to others."[16]

In the spring of 1976 I wrote to Simone de Beauvoir asking if I could meet with her. It seemed to me that the charges against her being made by a considerable number of French feminists were unfounded, and I wanted to know how she would reply to them. I would have been surprised to learn that her views about feminism had not evolved at all since 1949 (when she did not describe herself as a feminist). She had, in a 1966 interview with Francis Jeanson, called herself a "radical feminist" and discussed a wide range of ways of being a radical feminist. And when Beauvoir wrote, in 1972, that she stood by her argument in *The Second Sex* ("that all male ideologies are directed at justifying the oppression of women, and that women are so conditioned by society that they consent to this oppression"), she added that her view that "'You are not born a woman; you become one'... only require[d] completing with the statement 'You are not born a male; you become one.' For masculinity is not given at the beginning, either."[17] It seemed unlikely to me that she (still) advocated (if she ever did) that women simply become more like men. I told her that I wanted to ask her about, among other things, her current relationship to the women's movement in France and elsewhere and the ways in which her views might have changed since the publication of *The Second Sex*. I wanted to know what kinds of political actions she thought offered the greatest chance of radically transforming society. I had been reading Cixous[18] on *l'écriture féminine* and I wanted to ask her about her views on the revolutionary potential of writing – in particular of women's writing. And, with the adolescent audacity of a 21-year-old, I offered to tell her about my experiences with feminism in the United States, suggesting to her that certain generalizations she had made regarding the combativeness (*vis-à-vis* men) of *la femme américaine* (American women) were not, in fact, justified.[19]

I also wrote (with a now quite embarrassing forthrightness) that I was perplexed by her concepts of "essential" and "contingent love." If, as Sartre had written, there was no such thing as love apart from the deeds of love,[20] how could a so-called "essential love" that supposedly became an ineradicable part of one's self-definition be anything other than an illusory act of faith? Even in love, I wrote, every individual remains radically free to choose new projects, new futures, and every relation constantly evolves, sometimes in unpredictable ways. So how is a love that is both "essential" (necessary, permanent, and unchangeable) *and* authentic possible? What I didn't write was that I was also concerned, from a moral standpoint, about the position of those who were relegated, by both Beauvoir and Sartre, to the status of contingent loves. I had recently read Nelson Algren's review of Beauvoir's memoir *Force of Circumstance* (in which she had recounted her "contingent" affair with Algren) as well as some painfully caustic interviews with him on the subject of his relationship with Beauvoir. "Anybody who can experience love contingently has a mind that has recently snapped," he wrote. "How can love be *contingent*? Contingent upon *what*?"[21]

Beauvoir agreed to meet with me. I got a fellowship to spend the summer of 1976 in Paris researching recent trends in French feminism. In September I met Beauvoir in Rome at the Albergo Nazionale, where she and Sartre had spent the latter part of the summer for many years.

She greeted me cordially, and I was struck (as other young feminists were at the time) by her very proper, indeed feminine, demeanor – and her bright red nail polish. She asked me if I would like a scotch ("un whisky"). I'll never know whether this was because her time with Algren in Chicago had convinced her that all Americans liked scotch or because I seemed really nervous. In any case, I had my first taste of whisky, and I started asking her questions.

It quickly became clear that she had, indeed, revised her views about feminism since writing *The Second Sex*. She didn't think that the point of women's liberation was for women to become more like men or to assume their positions of power in a capitalist society. Nor did she think that the advent of a socialist society would automatically ensure equality for women. She thought that writing could help to change the world, but she completely rejected the idea of a *l'écriture féminine* that was premised on distinctively, essentially, feminine values.

We talked about the political potential of *la littérature engagé* (committed literature) and about the limits of writing as a catalyst for social transformation. I asked her about the philosophical and personal difficulties of having "contingent" love relationships while sustaining an "essential" one and she replied, tersely, "yes, it's difficult," or something to that effect, so I dropped the subject. After a couple of hours, I asked if I could do a more formal, tape-recorded interview with her the following day. That she was willing to spend another afternoon talking with a young student who was simply interested in her work was a sign of her extraordinary generosity.

In the interview that followed, Beauvoir replied to those who said that she was urging women to become more like men: "it's a matter not of women taking men's place in this world, but of their being emancipated in such a way as simultaneously to change this world." Far from advocating that women assume men's positions of power, she asserted that "the point is not for women simply to take power out of men's hands since that wouldn't change anything about the world. It's a question precisely of destroying that notion of power."

She acknowledged that, precisely because of the ways women have been oppressed, they "don't have the flaws that are linked to the possession of power." And yet she rejected the notion that women have some positive, essentially feminine, traits worth promoting: "A positive definition of 'woman'? Woman is a human being with a certain physiology, but that physiology in no way makes her inferior, nor does it justify her exploitation."

This is far from the valorization of feminine difference found in other French feminist writers of the time. Although she acknowledged that the physical, the sensual, should be a source of pleasure for women as well as for men, she also asserted that if women

consider the physical to be so important, it's not because of some physiological destiny, but precisely because they are deprived of so many other things in life. They have so little of real interest in their lives that they are led to confer much value to the part, let's say, the sexual, sensual part of their existence. This goes as well for relations with children, with the newborn, etc. They take pleasure in breastfeeding, etc., and all of this is very important for them largely because they have so little else.

It is not hard to see why she did not agree with Cixous that women should be encouraged to write in a distinctively feminine voice, "in white ink," with their mothers' milk.

And yet Beauvoir was "totally in favor" of feminist writings – "books that reveal women's condition, that revolt against it and lead others to revolt" – provided that they were written in accessible language. "To the extent that there are new things to say," she maintained, "they must be said in a way that's accessible." For Beauvoir, writing is a kind of political action, a way of changing the world by revealing it. As Sartre writes, "The 'committed' writer knows that words are action. He knows that to reveal is to change and that one can reveal only by planning to change."[22] Language is not, for Beauvoir, a mere expression of thought. Nor does it merely reflect some preexisting reality. "No work that has reference to the world can be a mere transcription, since the world has not the power of speech," she writes. "Facts do not determine their own expression; they dictate nothing. The person who recounts them finds out what he has to say about them through the act of saying it."

Although Beauvoir thought writing had political potential, she also warned against overestimating the power of literary action. From the early 1970s on she was concerned with direct action, with legislative reform, with the actual, everyday problems of real women. This was in contrast with the agenda of Psych et Po, whose "primary battle," according to Claire Duchen, "was against the masculinity in women's heads; not against the material conditions of women's

204 SUSAN J. BRISON

lives, or against discrimination that can be changed through legis-
lation, but, as feminist Nadja Ringert says... against the 'phallus in
our heads.'"[23] In an article written in 1972, the Psych et Po collective
distinguished masculine and feminine power in the following way:

Women's power isn't legal, patriarchal, sadistic, pederastic, it isn't concerned
with representation, with leadership, with names, with rape, repression,
hatred, avarice, knowledge, order, individualism, with abstractions.

It's a non-power of the matrix, of birthings, givings, chaos, differences, of
collective freedoms, of openings, of bodies, of recognitions, of lifting censorships, of pleasure, outside the law, it's a power-to, act-think-do, by/for all
women, all.[24]

Beauvoir had little use for the sort of revolution from within being proposed by the adherents of feminine difference. After all, it's
what people *do* that counts. In her interview with John Gerassi, on
"*The Second Sex*: Twenty Five Years Later," published in early 1976,
after describing how she realized, after 1968, that the class struggle
did not eliminate the need for the sex struggle, Beauvoir acknowledges that, increasingly, leftist groups "feel compelled to keep their
macho male leaders in check. That's progress. Here in our newspaper,
Libération, the male-oriented majority felt obliged to let a woman
become its director. That's progress. Leftist men are beginning to
watch their language, are...," at which point Gerassi interrupts to
ask: "But is it real? I mean, I've learned, for example, never to use
the word 'chick,' to pay attention to women in any group discussion,
to wash dishes, clean the house, do the shopping. But am I any less
sexist in my thoughts? Have I rejected the male values?" To which
Beauvoir replies: "You mean inside you? To be blunt, who cares?
Think for a minute. You know a racist Southerner. You know he's
racist because you've known him all his life. But now he never says
'nigger.' He listens to all black men's complaints and tries to do his
best to deal with them. He goes out of his way to put down other
racists. He insists that black children be given a better-than-average
education to offset the years of no education. He gives references
for black men's loan applications. He backs the black candidates in
his district both with money and with his vote. Do you think the
blacks give a damn that he's just as much a racist now as before 'in
his soul'?" She goes on to add: "A couple of generations feeling that
they have to appear nonracist at all times, and the third generation

will grow up nonracist in fact. So play at being nonsexist, and keep playing."[25]

Beauvoir valued clarity, precision, accessible language, and action; a politically engaged intellectual, she was aware of the limits of the life of the mind – and of the power of the pen. When I met her, she was attending demonstrations, going to meetings of groups fighting against rape and domestic violence, and lobbying for legislative change. She had largely stopped writing and was devoting herself to film and television projects that would reach a wider audience of women. For the last decade of her life, the most influential French feminist theorist of the twentieth century dedicated herself to political practice.

I have sorely missed her brand of feminist activism when it has seemed to me that feminist theorists have tended to give abstract theory priority over the actual experiences of real women, to the detriment of both their scholarship and their political agenda. I came across a startling example of this in the spring of 1992, when I was in France doing legal research to prepare for the trial of the man who had raped and nearly murdered me in the south of France in 1990. I went to what is still the largest feminist bookstore in Paris, the Librairie des femmes (founded by Psych et Po). While there was an entire bookcase (with several shelves) devoted to Etudes lacaniennes, I found only two books in the store by French authors on violence against women (and one was a reprint of a 1978 transcript of a well-known French rape trial).

A libertarian colleague of mine defines "freedom" as lawlessness. When I think of lawlessness, I think of being trapped in a ravine by a man trying to kill me who looks like he's going to get away with it. Freedom is something else altogether. Current debates within US feminism about freedom and the power of the state remind me of the conflict in the 1970s between Beauvoir and the feminists who located women's emancipatory potential outside the laws of the state, beyond the male-dominated systems of discourse and knowledge, in "the non-power of the matrix... of lifting censorships, of pleasure, outside the law."

Beauvoir refused this version of a feminist utopia; she rejected the dichotomies presupposed by those who asked: should women use or reject masculine "tools" – language, science, art, law – for understanding and controlling the world? Her response to this question is a call to action that breaks through the kind of aporia induced, at times, by relentless theorizing: "You can, indeed, steal the tools and use them," she replied, "but you have to use them carefully and for that matter," she added, "nothing prevents you from changing them at the same time."

NOTES

1   This interview of Beauvoir by Susan J. Brison took place in Rome on 7 September 1976. It was translated by Thomas Trezise and Susan J. Brison in July/August 2001. This chapter was written by Susan J. Brison in 2001.

2   "Simone de Beauvoir interroge Jean-Paul Sartre," in *Simone de Beauvoir et la lutte des femmes, L'Arc,* 61 (1975): 3–12, 11.

3   Hélène Cixous, "Le rire de la Méduse," in *Simone de Beauvoir et la lutte des femmes, L'Arc,* 61 (1975): 39–54.

4   "Simone de Beauvoir interroge Jean-Paul Sartre," 12.

5   "Le rire de la Méduse," 47.

6   "Simone de Beauvoir interroge Jean-Paul Sartre," 12.

7   See Toril Moi, *Simone de Beauvoir: The Making of an Intellectual Woman* (Oxford: Blackwell, 1994), pp. 182–83 and Elaine Marks, *Critical Essays on Simone de Beauvoir* (Boston: G. K. Hall, 1987), pp. 1–5.

8   Suzanne Lilar, *Le Malentendu du deuxiéme sexe* (Paris: Presses Universitaires de France, 1970), p. 14 (my translation).

9   Jean Leighton, *Simone de Beauvoir on Woman* (Cranbury, NJ: Associated University Presses, 1975), p. 221. Both Leighton and Lilar identified themselves as feminists.

10 ibid., p. 118.

11 ibid., p. 213.

12 Anne Tristan and Annie de Pisan, "From Beauvoir to the Women's Movement," in Toril Moi, ed., *French Feminist Thought: A Reader* (Oxford: Blackwell, 1987), p. 48.

13 Simone de Beauvoir, *All Said and Done* (New York: Warner Books, 1975), p. 462.

14 Quoted in Moi, *Simone de Beauvoir,* p. 182.

15 Simone de Beauvoir, preface to *Les Femmes s'entêtent* (Paris: Gallimard, 1975), pp. 11–13.

16 The expression they used was "poreuse aux autres" (porous to others), which suggests an even greater degree of relationality, indeed intermingling, with others. *L'Arc,* 61 (1975): 2.

17 *All Said and Done*, pp. 462–63.

18 Cixous, *"Le rire de la Méduse."*

19 For example, in an interview with Francis Jeanson in 1966, Beauvoir described the feminist stance of treating men as adversaries as "très 'femme américaine'" (very "American woman") and "extrèmement irritant." Francis Jeanson, *Simone de Beauvoir ou l'entreprise de vivre* (Paris: Editions du Seuil, 1966), p. 264.

20 Jean-Paul Sartre, "The Humanism of Existentialism," in *The Philosophy of Existentialism*, ed. Wade Baskin (New York: Philosophical Library, 1965), p. 48.

21 Nelson Algren, "The Question of Simone de Beauvoir," review of *Force of Circumstance, Harper's Magazine* (May 1965): 136. For recent discussions of the problematic nature of Beauvoir and Sartre's distinction between essential and contingent love, see Melanie C. Hawthorne, ed., *Contingent Loves: Simone de Beauvoir and Sexuality* (Charlottesville: University of Virginia Press, 2000) and Bianca Lamblin, *A Disgraceful Affair* (Boston: Northeastern University Press, 1996).

22 Jean-Paul Sartre, *"What is Literature?" and Other Essays* (Cambridge, MA: Harvard University Press, 1988), p. 37. In the above interview, Beauvoir cites, with approval, Sartre's discussion of committed literature.

23 Claire Duchen, *French Connections: Voices from the Women's Movement in France* (Amherst: University of Massachusetts Press, 1987), p. 48.

24 From *Le Torchon brûle*, 3 (1972), quoted in Claire Duchen, *Feminism in France: From May '68 to Mitterrand* (London and New York: Routledge & Kegan Paul, 1986), p. 36.

25 John Gerassi, "Simone de Beauvoir: *The Second Sex* 25 Years After," *Society*, 13, 2 (Jan./Feb. 1976): 81–82.

10 Life-story in Beauvoir's memoirs

> A life is such a strange object, at one moment translucent,
> at another utterly opaque, an object I make with my own
> hands, an object imposed on me, an object for which the
> world provides the raw material and then steals it from me
> again, pulverized by events, scattered, broken, scored yet
> retaining its unity; how heavy it is and how inconsistent:
> this contradiction breeds many misunderstandings.[1]

THE MAKING OF A LIFE-STORY

In the Interlude that comes between parts I and II of *Force of Circumstance*, Simone de Beauvoir's third autobiographical volume,[2] she reflects on what a peculiar object a life is. The peculiarity accrues when it is viewed not so much as a thing lived, but rather as an object of ongoing written representation – an object amenable to that double publicity entailed by the telling of one's own life-story in a published memoir. For the author, some of this peculiarity must inevitably be reflected back onto the life lived, because as the project of writing a memoir gets under way and life infuses the page, so will the prospect of the written record begin to infuse the experience of living. Certain experiences will take on the aspect of a theme, certain events the significance of an aberration, a confirmation of a pattern, a turning point, a nemesis, and so on, even while they are being spontaneously lived. We know that even as a little girl, if out of sheer romanticism, Beauvoir thought of her life as a "lovely story" in the making. Later, when relating her and Sartre's only slightly more mature sense of total personal freedom, she says, "I still wanted my life to be 'a lovely story that became true as I told it to myself,' and touched it up improvingly here and there in the telling" (*PL* 363). This feeling was finally tempered during the German Occupation, when she describes herself as being "at last prepared to admit that my life was not a story of my own telling, but a compromise between myself and the world at large" (*PL* 484). Whether as "lovely" and embellished, or as radically free, or as a compromise with circumstance, then, it seems that Beauvoir consistently entertained a sense of her own life as a living story.

This is nothing if not appropriate for a writer with existentialist commitments, although the life-as-life-story stance is really only an exaggerated version of what it is in any case like to live a meaningful life – a life with a particular narrative shape. The storylike shape of any life means that the appropriate method of understanding and representing it is as narrative in form. Thus it is to be conceived not synchronically in terms of Being but diachronically in terms of Becoming. And how else might one hope to understand the nature of a Becoming than by *narrating* it? This conception of life is in tune with Beauvoir's antiessentialist insight, which gains its most famous expression in the opening line of the second book of *The Second Sex*, "One is not born, but rather becomes a woman."[3] This is the mature version of her early suspicion of essentialist identity categories, which expressed itself in impetuous form when she was a young teacher:

One day she [Olga] asked what it *really* meant to be a Jew. With absolute certainty I replied: "Nothing at all. There are no such things as 'Jews'; only human beings." Long afterwards she told me what an impression she had created by marching into the violinist's room and announcing: "My friends, none of you exist! My philosophy teacher has told me so!" [*PL* 165]

This is an important marker in Beauvoir's intellectual development, for it presents us with the naive precursor to her mature view. She recalls her ill-judged remark with embarrassment (460), but she also explains:

I was right to reject essentialism; I knew already what abuses could follow in the train of abstract concepts such as the "Slav soul," the "Jewish character," "primitive mentality," or *das ewige Weib*. But the universalist notions to which I turned bore me equally far from reality. What I lacked was the idea of "situation," which alone allows one to make some concrete definition of human groups without enslaving them to a timeless and deterministic pattern. But there was no one, outside the framework of the class struggle, who would give me what I needed. [PL 165–66]

Beauvoir's presentation of the incident as a stage in personal intellectual development exemplifies the manner in which she shapes her self-narrative with the contours of storytelling. One of the most important ways in which she crafts the story of her life is by recounting intellectual commitments, or their passing, as phases in a development, a maturation. Furthermore, the story told gains a special sonorousness through a counterpoint between such personal developments and events on the grander scale of world history. Momentous world events are in a kind of harmony with personal ones because the individual is affected by and responsive to them, and the result is that Beauvoir's individual life-story is punctuated by the rhythms of history.[4] The very advent of war, for instance, is not only symbolically but causally connected with the dawning of historical consciousness for her:

With all the naivete of a child who believes in the absolute vertical, I thought that there was an absolute truth governing the world ... In the peace which had been granted us, justice and reason worked like a yeast. I built my happiness on firm ground and beneath immutable constellations.

What a misapprehension this was! It was not a fragment of eternity I had lived through but a transitory period, the pre-war years. [PL 599]

If representing a life requires presenting a story, then while this does not altogether preclude a thematic presentation (as is given in *All Said and Done*), it does make a plain chronological telling the more natural. Sticking to chronology allows the passage of the years to tell its own tale; it minimizes the role of the writer-as-interpreter who would telescope and reorganize her glimpses of self to create an overall self-portrait, and instead it emphasizes the idea of temporal process and transformation – the passage from then to now. Beauvoir touches on this in the interlude to *Force of Circumstance*:

why have I subjected myself to chronological order instead of choosing some other construction? I have pondered this matter, and I have hesitated. But what counts above all in my life is that time goes by; I grow older, the world changes, my relation with it varies; to show the transformations, the ripenings, the irreversible deteriorations of others and of myself – nothing is

more important to me than that. And that obliges me to follow obediently
the thread the years have unwound. [*FC* 276]

In the prologue to her final volume of memoirs, *All Said and Done*,
Beauvoir's attitude to her life becomes almost completely retrospective, with little sense of an ongoing journey, a future with promise;
so it is fitting that she should abandon the chronological form there
for a thematically organized narrative with a distinctly "closing" feel
to it: "I no longer feel that I am moving in the direction of a goal,
but only that I am slipping inevitably towards my grave." But in the
earlier volumes, the different discipline of chronological mapping is
called for. Particularly in *Memoirs of a Dutiful Daughter* and *The
Prime of Life*, which account for her childhood and early adult life,
the distance of age between the mature author and her former selves
strongly recommends the chronological approach. No longer having
direct access to the girl or young woman she once was, the literal-
minded discipline of chronological documentation allows Beauvoir
responsibly to locate her subjects within a shared personal history. It
allows her to place them in a single Becoming, and thus to rediscover
her former selves in their proper context. This narrative strategy is
well designed to allow the thread of years to be rewoven, while pre-
serving the integrity of the little girl or younger woman she once was.

In *Memoirs* the young Simone's girlish sense of great things to
come generates a skipping teleological momentum in the narrative,
and this is enhanced time and again by Beauvoir's authorial shaping
of her story. *Memoirs* constructs the young Simone as a figure of
deep-felt yet frustrated rebellion against the arbitrary constraints of
bourgeois propriety. Thus, for instance, one evening while staying
at La Grillière, Simone is as usual out alone in the countryside, but
this time returning home late and almost missing supper. As a pun-
ishment her mother prohibits her from going beyond the bounds of
the estate all the next day:

I spent the day sitting on the lawns or pacing up and down the avenues with
a book in my hand and rage in my heart. Over there, outside, the waters of
the lake were ruffling and smoothing, without me, without anyone to see:
it was unbearable. "If it were raining; if there were *some* reason for this silly
prohibition," I told myself, "then I could resign myself to it." Here, once

more, boiling up inside me, was the rebelliousness that had expressed itself in furious convulsions during my early childhood.[5]

This sort of rage is made more bearable through the passionate alliance with her beloved friend Zaza. But the intimacy with Zaza itself has its special narrative import bestowed upon it less through the presentation of their living common front against the irrationalities of a bourgeois upbringing, than through the significance given to Zaza's death and the superseding of this female–female intimacy by the female–male intimacy of her and Sartre. As Ursula Tidd points out, each of these couples – Simone and Zaza, Beauvoir and Sartre – is founded upon an opposition to bourgeois values, so that "Beauvoir constructs her autobiographical representation of selfhood... through two different relations to the Other: reciprocity (with Zaza and Sartre) and conflict (in opposition to the bourgeoisie)."[6]

Symbolically, what Zaza succumbs to in death is the suffocating weight of bourgeois convention. She dies, from it is unclear quite what, at a time of unsustainable anguish on her part over her conventionally inappropriate love match with Jean Pradelle (Maurice Merleau-Ponty). As a qualification, it should be said that Beauvoir's presentation of Zaza's demise as connected to bourgeois restrictions is not black and white. Although the symbolic connection is undoubtedly there,[7] it is not created at the expense of fairness to the people concerned. It should not be overlooked that Beauvoir is careful to cast the mothers of both Zaza and Pradelle in a flexible and humane light. It is just that these qualities come too late:

Madame Mabille put her [Zaza] to bed and called the doctor; she had a long talk with Pradelle: she didn't want to be the cause of her daughter's unhappiness, and she was not opposed to their marriage. Madame Pradelle wasn't against it either; she too didn't want to cause anyone unhappiness. It would all be arranged. But Zaza had a temperature of 104° and was delirious. [*MD* 359]

This due fairness dispensed, *Memoirs* closes with the death of Zaza and with Beauvoir's testimony to her experience of what these days we might identify, glibly perhaps, as a kind of "survivor guilt":

The doctors called it meningitis, encephalitis; no one was quite sure. Had it been a contagious disease, or an accident? Or had Zaza succumbed to exhaustion and anxiety? She has often appeared to me at night, her face all yellow under a pink sun-bonnet, and seeming to gaze reproachfully at me. We had fought together against the revolting fate that had lain ahead of us, and for a long time I believed that I had paid for my own freedom with her death. [*MD* 360]

Whatever the clinical explanation of Zaza's death, it marks the end of Simone's dependence on adults and the end of a female–female intimacy that makes way for an alliance with a man who is destined to become Beauvoir's new primary "Other." Shortly before recounting the events culminating in the death of Zaza and preparing the way for the sense of transition with which the book ends, Beauvoir quotes her diary entry regarding her first meeting with Sartre, so as to make it very clear how important a figure he is to be in her life: " 'Why am I overwhelmed by this meeting, as if something had *really* happened to me at last?' Something *had* happened to me, something which indirectly was to shape the whole of my life to come: but I wasn't to know that till later" (*MD* 311). Thus the end of *Memoirs* is no kind of closure but precisely an opening up to an exciting future that promises a new alliance, although one where Beauvoir's excitement – and even her experience of the freedom in store – remains indelibly tinged with a pained awareness that such an escape to independence is not the fate of every young girl.

One might be tempted to link the mournful inflection attending Beauvoir's new-found independence with her acute and lifelong fear of death,[8] but the loss of Zaza and the mark it leaves on Beauvoir's experience of freedom is not recounted in these terms. The bereavement is a tragic offense against the passionate solidarity that grounded the two young girls' personal relationship; it has nothing to do with the horror of mortality *per se*. It is not until much later, during the war, that a particular death is to cause Beauvoir the experience of being confronted as if for the first time by the absolute finality of our mortal condition. It comes with the news of the death of her young neighbor and friend, Bourla: "Never before had I been brought up against the ghastly uncertainty of our mortal state in so irrefutable a way" (*PL* 579). The significance of Zaza's death is less abstract than this, less about the human condition and more about the particular social condition of helplessness in the face of bourgeois constraints which Simone and Zaza suffered together in solidarity. Thus the loss of Zaza is both more personal and more political than any abstract shock of the mortal. It took a feat of political imagination to regard the bourgeoisie as waging a war on women, whereas the outrages of the actual war that stole Bourla from the world took a more readily recognizable form.

In these subtly different presentations of her encounters with death, as in the depiction of her childhood rages and ultimate passage to personal independence, we see Beauvoir making a storyteller's use of chronology – shaping and coloring her self-narrative as she goes.

MECHANISMS OF SELF-NARRATIVE

Beauvoir knows not simply to tell a "lovely story," but rather to tell a broadly truthful[9] story of a situated personal development, a life in history – a Becoming. The telling of a life-story where there is psychological distance between author and subject opens up a space for irony as a means of comment and criticism. Irony is the key technique of self-narration for Beauvoir, and this is so most of all in the earlier two volumes, where there is the greatest distance of age and outlook between author and narrated self. In *Memoirs* the irony often takes an openly self-mocking (though always affectionate) form. She writes, for instance:

I went round sticking the flags of the Allies in all the flower vases. In my games I was always a valiant Zouave, a heroic daughter of the regiment. I wrote everywhere in coloured chalks: *Vive la France!* The grown-ups admired my devotion to the cause. "Simone is an ardent patriot," they would say, with proud smiles. I stored the smiles away in my memory and developed a taste for unstinted praise. [*MD* 27]

Here, of course, she is mocking not only herself but also the grown-ups whose attitudes the young Simone's behavior reflects.[10] Later, in *The Prime of Life*, the irony is also often mocking in tone, though perhaps less indulgently so, for she is talking about young adults now. For example, she describes her and Sartre's brattish idealism in suitably sardonic tones: "Man was to be remoulded, and the process would be partly our doing. We did not envisage contributing to this change except by way of books: public affairs bored us. We counted on events turning out according to our wishes without any need for us to mix in them personally" (*PL* 15). The ironical tone is the channel for the critical attitude needed to spice the chronology, and it generates the wry intellectual personality that breathes the life into these volumes. Without it there would be little critical tension between author and narrated self, and the life-story would be flattened into laborious linear documentation. The wry smile of Beauvoir the ironist is a crucial counterbalance to the earnestness of Beauvoir the documenter.

The particular mechanism of irony involves three parties: the author whose irony it is, the reader who shares the joke, and the narrated subject who is thereby cast in a certain light. But the overall mechanics of storytelling, of which irony is a part, involves a fourth essential party, and that is the constructed reader. Any actual reader may take a different interpretive view of things from that of the reader-position constructed for her in the text. For example, when Beauvoir explains her lifelong assumption that her husband would have to be her "superior," the author explains:

Why did I insist that he should be superior to me? I don't for one moment think I was looking for a father-image in him; I valued my independence... we would be two comrades. Nevertheless the concept I had of our relationship was influenced indirectly by the feelings I had had for my father. My education, my culture, and the present state of society all conspired to convince me that women belong to an inferior caste... If in the absolute sense a man, who was a member of the privileged species and already had a flying start over me, did not count more than I did, I was forced to the conclusion that in a relative sense he counted less: in order to be able to acknowledge him as my equal, he would have to prove himself my superior in every way. [MD 145]

Emphasized here are the conditioning influences of education, culture, and society, but previous glimpses of Beauvoir's relationship with her father make plain the more personal psychological mechanism by which it came to be that her self-esteem depended upon a certain identification with him. For the manner in which her father encouraged and praised Simone's intellectual achievements relied upon a symbolic annihilation of her feminine person: "Papa used to say with pride: 'Simone has a man's brain; she thinks like a man; she *is* a man.'" (121). Further, the objectivist classification "superior" – and its inevitable counterpart, "inferior" – reflects an essentializing style of judgment (perhaps especially characteristic of French culture, although certainly not exclusive to it) that makes peculiarly treacherous territory for a budding woman intellectual. Such a categorial, objectivist frame of reference for intellectual ability is one which well-nigh forces serious students to rank themselves in these judgmental terms; and in a climate where the woman intellectual is an interloper into a symbolically and actually masculine territory it would take an astonishing ego to categorize oneself as among the nascent superiors of the game, let alone to withstand the hostility such boldness would be likely to inspire. This quite general feature of the intellectual culture surrounding Beauvoir seems likely to be a significant factor in her repeated and sincere pronouncements of her inferiority to Sartre. I think this is part of the explanation why she found it "comfortable" to insist on looking up to him, even with respect to a characteristic as dull as his "stubbornness" over an avowed ambition to keep up the writing no matter what: "As I saw it, the resolution which Sartre displayed set him above me. I admired him for holding his destiny in his own hands, unaided; far from feeling embarrassed at the thought of his superiority, I derived comfort from it" (PL 26).

There is one episode in particular where any reader with a smidgeon of feminist consciousness (especially if one has had experience of life as a philosophy student) will surely find that the reader position that Beauvoir constructs is sadly, if instructively, uncomfortable. The episode in question is the "discussion" of the young Simone's nascent ideas about ethics with her equally young fellow-philosophy student, Jean-Paul. Here the actual reader may long for a tone of critical irony to be directed against the young Sartre from the mature Beauvoir, but instead one finds only ingenuousness. The incident occurs at the Medici Fountain in the Luxembourg Gardens, and it features in *Memoirs of a Dutiful Daughter* as a pivotal moment in the intellectual trajectory of the young Beauvoir. It has been given a powerful feminist reading by Michèle Le Doeuff, and the scene will be most efficiently set by a quotation from Le Doeuff that begins with the relevant passage from *Memoirs*:

"Day after day, and all day long I measured myself against Sartre, and in our discussions I was simply not in his class. One morning in the Luxembourg Gardens, near the Medici fountain, I outlined for him the pluralist morality which I had fashioned to justify the people I liked but did not wish to resemble: he ripped it to shreds. I was attached to it, because it allowed me to take my heart as the arbiter of good and evil; I struggled with him for three hours. In the end I had to admit I was beaten; besides, I had realized, in the course of our discussion, that many of my opinions were based only on prejudice, bad faith [oh] or thoughtlessness, that my reasoning was shaky and my ideas confused. 'I'm no longer sure what I think, or even if I think at all,' I noted, completely thrown. My pride was not involved. I was by nature curious rather than imperious and preferred learning to shining."

There follows a very sad page which shows her "suddenly uncertain of [her] true abilities" and fascinated by the gang formed by Sartre, Nizan, Aron and Politzer who "impressed" her for all sorts of reasons, some better than others. It is an astounding tale, which shows that even if one knows an enormous amount of philosophy, one never knows enough to remember, at the right moment, that "shining" or "impressing other people" is not the point of it. "Not being sure" and "learning" come closer to what is called "thinking" in the ethics of the discipline.[11]

Le Doeuff's interpretation perspicuously portrays the absurdity of one young man's wholly convincing one young woman, in a single conversation in a park, of the utter worthlessness of her thoughts towards a pluralist ethics. And it brings out the pathos inherent in the older feminist giant of an author's recounting the episode in a way which shows that she remained convinced (hence the factive "realized") that he was quite right and that her younger self was indeed guilty of "bad faith" *et cetera* in her short-lived hopes for a project in which she aimed – ridiculous! – to take her "heart as the arbiter of good and evil." But perhaps we can make a further observation here that adds a new dimension to the pathos. The reason the constructed position may not be comfortable for today's reader is largely thanks to the enhanced feminist consciousness and the increased feminine participation in academic life which Beauvoir did so much to pioneer. Any woman who has had the experience of being a philosophy student among a majority of young men will find a particular poignancy in the scene recounted, for it is so obvious what is going on. What female philosophy student has not had *that* discursive experience with some clever young man ready to be one's superior if one gives him the least encouragement? One finds oneself audience to a dress-rehearsal of another's emerging intellectual authority, and this experience typically involves being on the receiving end of a (perhaps naively enthusiastic) barrage of competitive energy still so automatic in many young men and so alien to so many young

women, who may or may not have the political and emotional resources to experience the exchange for what it is. Beauvoir did not
have these resources – although she had plenty of personal grit and
intellectual discipline to come out of it well – and so she could not
do what one now knows the young woman philosophy student really
must do to survive: avoid those conversations, or (better) neutralize
their impact by writing them off as "one of those" – think of them
like the rain. This is imperative, for either one finds the resources to
resist colluding in a social-intellectual dynamic whereby he is cast
as the clever one (if only so that one may avoid the indignity, indeed
the tedium, of repeated competitions), or else one risks becoming
alienated from the whole enterprise. If one takes such experiences
half as seriously as they feel at the time, half as seriously as it felt
to Beauvoir, then one will gradually come to think "philosophy is
not for me." This is why it now reads so especially poignantly that
that is basically what Beauvoir came to think. She soon moved to
identify herself not as a philosopher but as a writer instead.

   That this discursive battering at the hands of an intellectually
boisterous friend named Jean-Paul (whose fateful upper hand here
incites one to a spiteful reminder that he, unlike her, failed his
agrégation first time around [see *MD* 275]) should have been a pivotal moment in the young Beauvoir's intellectual path, brings to the
fore the enormous debt that female intellectuals owe to this woman.
It was gender that made her need to be with a man she could regard
as her superior, and it was gender that saw to it that she got one. We
are significantly indebted to Beauvoir for the better conceptual and
hermeneutical resources we now have to see such quotidian philosophical crushings for the banal gender performances they are. It is, I
think, particularly this aspect of the episode that justifies Le Doeuff's
sinister interpretation of Sartre's comment, "From now on, I'm going
to take you under my wing" (*MD* 339). For I think it shows that we
can accept the interpretation without commitment to Sartre's personally having any sinister motivations. One must not forget, after
all, that he was as subject to gender as she was (if never so disadvan-
taged by it) and consequently stood to lose a great deal in any failure to deliver the discursive performance of a self-styled superior –
indeed, according to Beauvoir's account of her own psychology, he
would have risked losing *her*. Gender is the sinister force at work
here; less so the ebullient Jean-Paul. There is perhaps a certain

poetic equilibrium in all this: if Zaza paid for Simone's freedom, there is a sense in which Beauvoir paid for ours.

It seems, then, that Beauvoir moved to identify as a writer rather than as a philosopher in significant part because of what the Medici incident encapsulates. Nonetheless, her decision was surely a good one all told, not least because she had an excellent intellectual complaint against the philosophical enterprise as it presented itself to her:

In this field a genuinely creative talent is so rare that queries as to why I did not attempt to join the elite are surely otiose: it would be more useful to explain *how* certain individuals are capable of getting results from that conscious venture into lunacy known as a "philosophical system," from which they derive that obsessional attitude which endows their tentative patterns with universal insight and applicability. As I have remarked before, women are not by nature prone to obsessions of this type. [PL 221]

She is committed to the irreducibly ambiguous nature of reality and thus to its native resistance to philosophical systematization. A stronger version of this idea is explicit in a comment from *The Prime of Life*, where the point is more general in that it is directed to the inherently systematizing nature of language itself: "I maintained that reality extends beyond anything that can be said about it; that instead of reducing it to symbols capable of verbal expression, we should face it as it is – full of ambiguities, baffling, and impenetrable" (PL 145). Thus her skepticism about systematization seems to extend to writing quite generally: the fundamental ambiguity of the world, of life, means it will elude any attempt to pin it down in words. Nonetheless, whereas philosophy as she found it – as calling forth the endowment of "tentative patterns with universal insight and applicability" – is essentially incapable of making room for ambiguity, more literary forms are better able to leave ambiguity in the picture. Thus, she can say of her own memoir: "I have attempted to set out the facts in as frank a way as possible, neither simplifying their ambiguities nor swaddling them in false syntheses, but offering them for the reader's own interpretation" (PL 368).

Beauvoir is quite clear, then, that she "didn't want to speak with [the] abstract voice" of the philosopher (MD 208), though there is more to be said about the particular motivations behind her writings of the self. Dissatisfaction with philosophy is a general negative reason; but the expressed positive reasons are numerous and often specific to the particular volume. One of her aims in writing *Force of Circumstance*, for instance, was simply to set the record straight as against the mendacious publicity brought by her and Sartre's celebrity. Towards the end of the book, discussing the lies spread about her in the press, she writes, "It was my desire to establish the truth of these matters that was largely responsible for my writing these memoirs, and many readers have in fact said that the ideas they entertained of me beforehand could scarcely have been more false" (*FC* 648–49). There again, in *The Prime of Life* she says she hopes to do her readers the service of showing them the biographical background to her work: "No book takes on its full meaning without the reader knowing the circumstances and background of its inception, and having some acquaintance with the personality of its author. By addressing my readers directly I hope to perform this service for them" (*PL* 8). After that, she goes on to make a further case, this time for memoir as having a universal significance that can be instructive: "if any individual . . . reveals himself honestly, everyone, more or less, becomes involved. It is impossible for him to shed light on his own life without at some point illuminating the lives of others" (*PL* 8). These various expressed motivations for writing about her life have a somewhat incidental feel, and although they are no doubt genuine, they do not, I suspect, go particularly deep. There is, however, a deeper and more subtle underlying motivation for her extended self-narrations. I read Beauvoir as most fundamentally driven to tell her life-story by an essentially ethical motivation: to achieve solidarity with the other selves who lived different chapters of the selfsame life.

MOTIVATIONS FOR WRITING: MEMOIR OR AUTOBIOGRAPHY?

If Beauvoir is motivated to document the events of her life but also to narrate the self by shaping these events as a story, then her writings move between the distinct genres of autobiography and memoir. It would be pointless to pretend that these are precisely differentiated genres on whose boundaries there is unanimity. Nonetheless, I agree with Catharine Savage Brosman's sensible observation that the wide variation in conceptions of autobiography need not obscure the common purpose of true autobiographies: not just to re-count a life but to illuminate it. By that is meant identifying and scrutinizing those elements which shape a destiny and thereby plumbing the meaning of the self in its temporal trajectory... The point is that the linguistic process of verbalizing... becomes the means of, and is one with, the writer's project of self-understanding; the self is "inscribed" in the text, thereby attaining a new reality that both reproduces and extends the self.[12]

By contrast, the purpose of memoir is "to recount the subject's ex-periences and associated events but to do so without subordinating these to the search for, or portrait of, an inner self. In other words, memoirs are principally the record of what happened to and around the self, not the interpretation of the self."[13] On this view of the distinction between the genres, all of Beauvoir's narrations of the self might be more or less categorized as memoirs. However, it is clear that – despite its being the only volume that includes the word "memoir" in its title – *Memoirs of a Dutiful Daughter* comes very close to being autobiographical in Brosman's sense. Indeed Beauvoir's own description of her project there echoes Brosman's idea of the autobiographical subject becoming "inscribed" in the text: "I took that child and that adolescent girl, both so long given up for lost in the depths of the unrecalled past, and endowed them with my adult awareness. I gave them a new existence – in black and white, on sheets of paper" (*PL* 7). It is only in *Memoirs* that Beauvoir really creates a new persona, through the recreation of the little girl she once was, and only there that one has the sense of Beauvoir search-ing for an "inner self" in the person of that seemingly long-lost girl. However, these genuinely autobiographical features of the book are in a certain way more the result of necessity than design. They result principally from the great temporal and psychological distance be-tween mature author and young subject, which distance means that Beauvoir's memory itself cannot do nearly as much work in recre-ating this phase of her life as it can the later phases. The distance obliges Beauvoir to reconstruct much more than to recall, and (al-though there must always be some reconstruction in recollection) this is what brings the persona of the *jeune fille rangée* to be at one with the text in the way that is, as Brosman says, special to autobiography.[14]

But there is another important difference between autobiography and memoir. It is surely essential in memoirs, whose primary source must be memory, that they are written by the subject. That author and subject are one and the same person is not merely true by definition; it is crucial to the point of memoir as a genre and to the standards by which we may judge its quality and interest. Indeed it is a perfectly excusable feature of memoirs that they might never transcend a keenly subjective outlook – that is their distinctive prerogative. By contrast, autobiography is simply the auto-version of biography. The auto-biographer will naturally have a more privileged access to the resource of memory than the biographer, but that is merely an advantageous side effect of the (so to speak) chance identity of author and subject. In auto-biography, this identity does not affect either the point or the received virtues of the genre, which are fundamentally those of biographical writing in general: objectivity, impartiality, explanation, illumination. If this is right, then autobiography is to be conceived as biography that happens to be written by the subject, whereas in memoir it is essential that author and subject are one and the same. This is not unconnected to the distinction that Brosman emphasizes: the project of creating a persona, a portrait-in-words of an inner life, is a project one can take on from a fairly objective (if thoroughly informed) stance; whereas the project of recounting experiences drawn from memory must start with a distinctly subjective stance – the stance of the person who had those experiences first-hand. Although shaped with hindsight and recounted with the writer's sense of story, it is crucial to the point of memoirs that they originate in that first-hand participation in a life that constitutes its being one's own.

It should be clear that the necessarily first-hand, subjective origin that I am claiming is essential to memoir and inessential to autobiography has nothing to do with any claim that the first-hand stance brings any special access to the truth of the life. On the contrary, Beauvoir is right to infuse her text with a sense of the opacity of memory and the special difficulties of self-understanding. This explains why she often emphasizes that her project is precisely not to *know* herself, or to present an *interpretation* of the self – self-portrait is the autobiographer's burden – but, rather, simply to present her story so that readers may come to their own interpretations. Indeed, there is some reason to think of the reader as having better access to the subject of memoir than the author herself:

I still believe to this day in the theory of the "transcendental ego." The self (*moi*) has only a probable objectivity, and anyone saying "I" only grasps the outer edge of it; an outsider can get a clearer and more accurate picture. Let me repeat that this personal account is not offered in any sense as an "explanation." Indeed, one of my main reasons for undertaking it is my realization that self-knowledge is impossible, and the best one can hope for is self-revelation. [*PL* 368]

Acknowledging the opacity of the self, then, she aims to make her own acquaintance over time by telling her story and making her past selves exist for others through the publicity of the written word: "I wanted to make myself exist for others by conveying, as directly as I could, the taste of my own life: I have more or less succeeded" (*AS* 463). These twin motives of getting to know herself by acquainting others with her story constitute Beauvoir's principle means of establishing solidarity with past selves. The task of telling her story, however, depends upon a more straightforward project of self-inquiry: there are gaps to be filled, questions to be answered. Indeed, it is as if she is repeatedly drawn to extend her memoirs on to the next volume by the allure of as yet unanswered questions – notably, for instance, those implicitly posed at the end of *Memoirs of a Dutiful Daughter*. This is reflected in the preface to *The Prime of Life*, where she explains:

I had no plans for taking this project any further... When I had completed my *Memoirs of a Dutiful Daughter* no voice spoke to me out of my past, urging me to continue the story. I made up my mind to turn to some other task; but in the event I found myself unable to do so. Beneath the final line of that book an invisible question mark was inscribed, and I could not get my mind off it. Freedom I had – but freedom to do what? What new direction would the course of my life take as a result of all this fuss and commotion, the pitched battle that had culminated in victorious release? [*PL* 7]

Moved by the appetites of a reader, Beauvoir-the-author is repeatedly impelled to embark on the next chapter of her life-story.

UNITY IN SOLIDARITY

Getting to know oneself through opening oneself up to others can be a difficult task. That "strange object" – that "scattered, broken" thing that is a life – is all one has to go on, and Beauvoir certainly seems to have had a sense of a self that was broken up and unintegrated. Not necessarily in a bad way, however. At one time she experiences a sense of fragmentation simply as a result of her emerging public persona. On the warm reception of her first novel, *She Came to Stay*, she recalls: "One literary columnist, discussing new books from Gallimard, referred to me as 'the firm's new woman novelist.' The words tinkled gaily around in my head. How I would have envied this serious-faced young woman, now embarking on her literary career, if she had possessed any name other than my own – but she *was* me!" (*PL* 558). This happy, everyday self-alienation does not go very deep, and the strangeness of public recognition is dispelled by plain habituation: "I had grown used to living inside a writer's skin and nowadays scarcely ever caught myself looking at this new character and saying: It's me" (*FC* 46). Self-alienation occurs in a less happy form, however, when the experience of being "old" crashes in on her: "One day I said to myself: 'I'm forty!' ... The stupor that seized me then has not left me yet ... When I read in print Simone de Beauvoir, it is a young woman they are telling me about, and who happens to be me" (*FC* 656).

Self-alienation, then, can be positive or negative for Beauvoir, but if one is specifically looking for connections between her sense of unintegrated identity and the nature of her "memorialist"[15] project, then a remark about her past selves in *All Said and Done* is particularly telling. Referring to her project of regathering all the fragments of her life in retrospect, she says: "I am behaving as though my life were to carry on beyond my grave as I have managed to regain it in my last years. Yet I know very well that 'I can't take it with me.' I shall *all* die" (*AS* 40). She shall *all* die, as she has *all* lived. Her narratives of the self are most fundamentally a project in gathering together all these selves and, mediated by intersubjective exchange with the reader, generating both a serial intrapersonal connection and an ethical-political alliance. The connection with the reader and the connection with past selves are part and parcel of the same project, for it is through the special publicity of her life-story being read by others that Beauvoir may escape solipsistic entrapment in her present.

This seeking of intrapersonal alliance is where Beauvoir's sense of an unintegrated self finds its most positive role and its ethical point. For Beauvoir, the possibility of an ethical attitude towards

others – the possibility of solidarity with them – is intimately connected with the disintegration of the self. This, for instance, is how
she describes the transformation that a sudden awareness of history
caused her to undergo: "History burst over me, and I dissolved into
fragments. I woke to find myself scattered over the four quarters of
the globe, linked by every nerve in me to each and every other individual" (PL 369). That the establishment of solidarity with past
selves through the publicity of memoir is a fundamental motivation
for Beauvoir's story is perhaps most obvious in her attitude towards
the child she once was: "I was thinking about my childhood, and one
of my earliest memories returned to me: the flower I was accused of
picking in Aunt Alice's garden. I thought how much I would love, one
day, to write a book that evoked the shade of this little girl from the
distant past – never dreaming that I would get the chance to do so"
(PL 326). In that episode the little Simone (prior to the intervention of
her parents – who come off rather well here, since they rightly take
their daughter at her word) has the frustrating experience of being
unjustly disbelieved by her aunt over the picking of a flower. This
episode resonates with an ambition intrinsic to memoirs: to disclose
oneself to a suitably trustful audience.[16] The conditions for this are
constructed in the very mechanism of the memoir text, so as to explain the most literal sense in which the reader is involved in the
relations of solidarity that are being sought: the reader, the author,
and the subject of the memoir are all placed in those relations of trust
that are necessary for successful personal testimony. Beauvoir bears
witness to her life, telling the story of past selves so that they may
be properly understood and, where necessary, their various "distress
signals"[17] vindicated. Memoir is in this way premised upon the sort
of trust that ideally attends all kinds of personal disclosure, and this
trust facilitates the author's solidarity with her past selves via the
reader who joins the author in bearing witness. Needless to say, this
is not an empirical point about whether or not one might believe
everything that is written in memoir, but rather a point about the
relations between the positions of author, reader, and subject that
are constructed in the memoir text.

I hope to have shown that bearing witness by documenting and
shaping the different chapters in a single life-story is, for Beauvoir,
most fundamentally a way of establishing lines of solidarity with
her past selves. I have offered a reading of her memoirs as a project

of intrapersonal alignment, both psychological and ethical. The self-narrative aligns the mature author with those younger women with whom she shares a unique life and to whose experiences of frustration and injustice she aims retrospectively to bear public witness. Thus while the life-story told is hers alone, still it possesses a special ethical significance, for Beauvoir's commitment to establishing relations of solidarity with the others of her own past exemplifies her feminist commitment to female solidarity quite generally. It is this ethical impetus at the heart of her self-narrative that ultimately integrates Beauvoir's story. Indeed it is what integrates her very self, for the achievement of solidarity finally restores the "unity" to that "scattered, broken" object that is her life.

NOTES

1 *FC* (Harmondsworth: Penguin, 1965) 276.
2 There is perhaps some leeway in deciding which of Beauvoir's writings count among her autobiographical volumes, but it is not, I think, controversial to categorize the following four as comprising her complete memoir: *Memoirs of a Dutiful Daughter*, *The Prime of Life*, *Force of Circumstance*, and *All Said and Done*. She also wrote two semi-autobiographical works, *A Very Easy Death* and *Adieux - A Farewell to Sartre*.
3 *SS* (Harmondsworth: Penguin) 295. The French is better: "On ne naît pas femme: on le devient" (*DS* 1 285).
4 In the introduction to *FC* she says, "the way in which history has happened to me day by day is an adventure quite as individual as my subjective development" (v–vi).
5 *MD* (Harmondsworth: Penguin, 1959) 126.
6 Ursula Tidd, *Simone de Beauvoir: Gender and Testimony* (Cambridge: Cambridge University Press, 1999), p. 130.
7 Later, Beauvoir refers to Zaza's death in very strong terms, as a "murder by her environment, her milieu" (*AS* [New York: Paragon House] 10).
8 For example, "One afternoon, in Paris, I realized that I was condemned to death. I was alone in the house and I did not attempt to control my despair: I screamed and tore at the red carpet" (*MD* 138); and in *PL* (Harmondsworth: Penguin, 1962) 578–79, where she talks of "Night's black terrors"; and see *PL* 603.
9 Truthfulness does not entail total disclosure, for it is compatible with (indeed, considered as a virtue it implies) discretion: "I must warn... [readers] that I have no intention of telling them everything. I described my childhood and adolescence without any omissions. But though I have,

as I hope, managed to recount the story of my life since then without excessive embarrassment or indiscreetness, I cannot treat the years of my maturity in the same detached way ... There are many things which I firmly intend to leave in obscurity" (*PL* 8).

10 On Beauvoir's use of irony, see Tidd, *Simone de Beauvoir*, pp. 112-16, and Jo-Ann Pilardi, *Simone de Beauvoir: Writing the Self - Philosophy Becomes Autobiography* (Westport, CN: Greenwood Press, 1999), pp. 49-52.

11 Michèle Le Doeuff, *Hipparchia's Choice: An Essay Concerning Women, Philosophy, Etc.*, trans. Trista Selous (Oxford: Blackwell, 1991), p. 136. The "oh" is Le Doeuff's.

12 Catharine Savage Brosman, *Simone de Beauvoir Revisited* (Boston: Twayne, 1991), p. 134.

13 ibid., p. 135.

14 Note too in this connection Beauvoir's comment that *Memoirs of a Dutiful Daughter* has a "fiction-like quality lacking in the later volumes" (*AS* 14).

15 She coins this term in *FC* (vi); the French, too, is "un mémorialiste."

16 I therefore agree with Tidd that Beauvoir's autobiography is fundamentally testimonial, rather than confessional; see Tidd, *Simone de Beauvoir*, chapter 6.

17 "I had long wanted to set down the story of my first twenty years; nor did I ever forget the distress signals which my adolescent self sent out to the older woman who was afterward to absorb me, body and soul" (*PL* 7).

11 Beauvoir on the ambiguity of evil

Life in itself is neither good nor evil.
It is the place of good and evil,
according to what you make it.

[Montaigne¹]

For Simone de Beauvoir, both men's and women's lives are fundamentally marked by historical events. In reference to her own life she said: "the Resistance, the Liberation, the war in Algeria...these are the things that marked eras, at least for me...That's what marked the big epochs in our lives, it's the historical events, the historical involvements one has in these larger events. It's much more important than any other kind of difference."²

From her first writings published during World War Two, Beauvoir's work is marked by an awareness of these historical crises and the dilemmas that they pose. What is one to do with the knowledge of the Nazi death camps? Is forgetting a betrayal of the dead, or is surrendering to the pain of remembering a betrayal of the living? What action is necessary in the face of the Nazi occupation of France? How can one reconcile the need for terrorist actions with the implacable knowledge that no calculation of means and ends can erase the loss of a human life? Could the Soviet labor camps be compared with the Nazi concentration camps, or did they have some positive meaning or justification? How can one live in an occupied city when the occupiers are one's own countrymen, as during the Algerian war? How can one live when one sees oneself "through the eyes of women who had been raped twenty times, of men with broken bones, of crazed children."³

Beauvoir's reflections on these events hinge on the concepts of freedom, action, and responsibility that she uses in her philosophical, literary, and sociological/historical essays. Never does she seek to systematically justify her use of the concept of evil; nonetheless this term appears repeatedly through these writings during what she has termed her "moral period" following the Nazi occupation in France in 1940.[4] I propose that the concept of ambiguity that she explicitly addresses in *The Ethics of Ambiguity* provides a key for understanding her approach to the problem of evil in her time. The ambiguity of evil in Beauvoir's work is manifested on three distinct levels of analysis: (1) in terms of ontology, that is, how both the facticity and risk of evil are present in the fundamental structures of human existence; (2) in terms of the evils of social and political oppression, injustice, and misery; (3) in terms of cultures' symbolic representation of evil, which links evil in particular with the feminine.

EXISTENTIAL ONTOLOGY AND EVIL

In *The Ethics of Ambiguity* Beauvoir introduces the concept of ambiguity as central for existentialism, which she considers "the only philosophy in which an ethics has a place" (*EA* 34). Human existence is caught in a tragic paradox: humans know themselves to be mind, consciousness, intentionality, to be an end in themselves; at the same time human beings are matter. They cannot free themselves from their natural condition, cannot escape being an object or instrument for others. They are crushed by uncontrollable forces and ultimately their life-work is the building of death (*EA* 7-9). Previous philosophers and the ethics they have proposed have approached this paradox through denial. They have sought to affirm one or the other half of this relation either by reducing humans to mind, inwardness, or eternity or by affirming instead the sensible world, externality, and transitoriness. Hegel approached this dilemma in the spirit of reconciliation: nature itself can be preserved and transformed by its spiritualization. Beauvoir views all of these philosophical strategies as acts of cowardice. Instead of seeking to flee from the complexity of the human condition, we should "try to look the truth in the face... to assume our fundamental ambiguity" (*EA* 9). And it is existentialism that has been able to define itself as a "philosophy of ambiguity."

It has taken seriously the element of failure in the human condition. It defines human beings first of all as a negativity. She writes, "He [sic] is first at a distance from himself. He can coincide with himself only by agreeing never to rejoin himself. There is within him a perpetual playing with the negative, and he thereby escapes himself, he escapes his freedom" (EA 33).

Because humans are not objects that are given in nature, because they have a relation to themselves, question themselves, and can either affirm or seek to escape their freedom, there is failure involved in the human condition. And, Beauvoir notes, "without failure, no ethics" (EA 10). Only existentialism gives "a real role to evil" (EA 34). In the philosophy of Socrates, Plato, and Spinoza evil is explained as error. No one is willfully bad; only adequate knowledge is necessary to avoid the error of evil. It is also difficult for Kantian ethics to explain how autonomous subjects, who give the moral law to themselves, can expressly reject this law. Optimistic forms of humanism view the world and human beings as complete in themselves, and thus can give no account of evil.

According to Beauvoir only existentialism can give an account of how a "perverted willing" or an "evil will" is possible, because it puts as primary the structure of negativity in human existence. Only through the possibility of bad willing, this escape from freedom, can it be meaningful to speak of virtue, victory, wisdom, or joy. And thus only through an understanding of human failure and the possibility of evil can one carry out ethical reflection on good as well as bad and all the values in between that mark the reality of human existence.

There is one aspect of the human condition in which we face not only the inescapability of failure but the complete negation of our existence. That aspect is the inevitability and finality of death. Beauvoir cites Montaigne in her opening sentence of the Ethics: "The continuous work of our life is to build death" (EA 7). Humans can be said to be born dying, and decay is already present in the first hour of life. The emphasis on death as the defining characteristic of human existence is found in other existentialist philosophers as well. In The Second Sex Beauvoir cites the importance for Sartre's Being and Nothingness of Heidegger's dictum that the real nature of man is bound up with death. Without death, the relation of humans to themselves and to the world would be profoundly disarranged; thus the statement "Man is mortal" must be understood as much

more than an observational claim.[5] Indeed, Beauvoir's own texts are
filled with the painful and irrevocable presence of death, from the
death of Louise's baby in *The Blood of Others*, which the narrator
describes as his confrontation with "the original evil,"[6] to the death
of the 16-year-old Diego in *The Mandarins*, who was killed by the
Nazis in Paris without a tombstone or a date of death, despite the
fact that he had claimed, "A Nazi victory doesn't enter my plans,"[7]
and the death of Beauvoir's own mother in *A Very Easy Death*. Death
is irrevocable – Beauvoir repeatedly writes that the dead stay dead.
Even Christianity acknowledges that "the earthly meaning of eternal
life was death."[8]

The evil of death appears to lie in its reduction of humans to their
animality and the annihilation of their life-projects.[9] Death nullifies our freedom at the same time as it is that which marks us as
human. Thus death is also that which makes the human condition
ambiguous, and the evil linked to death must be an ambiguous one.
It can never be discussed apart from the concrete circumstances in
which it is inflicted, as no feature of the human condition can be –
hence the importance of Beauvoir's historical and political discussions. Circumstances circumscribe the degree of the evil of death.
For example, Beauvoir calls lynching "an absolute evil... it is a fault
without justification or excuse" (*EA* 146).[10] But even natural deaths,
like the death of her elderly mother, are not entirely free of human
beings inflicting torture and deception on others.[11]

Thus, the problem of evil is not merely a question of evil willing. It is also fundamentally rooted in the conditions of human existence, in death as an evil that can be accentuated or diminished but
from which we will never be reprieved. Evil is also immanent in the
human condition through the me–others structure of consciousness
that is the source of opposition and violence, although it can also be a
source of solidarity. In *The Ethics of Ambiguity* Beauvoir writes that
the "me–others relationship is as indissoluble as the subject–object
relationship" (*EA* 72). This theme is evident from her earliest reflections, as noted in her 1927 diary, where she writes: "The theme is
almost always the opposition of oneself and the other that I have
felt from the beginning of my life." Beauvoir describes herself as
"waiting impatiently for the day when there will be no longer the
other nor *me*, but only definitively *us*."[12] For Beauvoir, the reality of human conflicts would be incomprehensible if one sought to

comprehend human society merely as *Mitsein* or as fellowship based on solidarity; it is only by understanding the fundamental character of opposition that social conflicts become comprehensible. Beauvoir follows Hegel in viewing this conflict between me and others as an expression of interdependency. It is the simultaneity of interdependence and opposition that explains how "Only man can be an enemy of man; only he can rob him of the meaning of his acts and his life." She adds: "It is this interdependence which explains why oppression is possible and why it is hateful" (*EA* 82).

Beauvoir considers this splitting of the world into the oppressor and the oppressed as an "evil which divides the world" (*EA* 97). Thus, the oppositional–interdependency structure of human relations is a condition for the existence of division and violence and explains why "the world has always been at war and always will be" (*EA* 119).[13] Although the oppositional–interdependency structure of human relations forms the horizon for human existence, oppression and enslavement are not inevitable. Beauvoir writes: "It is possible to rise above this conflict if each individual freely recognizes the other... in a reciprocal manner." But to attain reciprocal recognition through friendship and generosity requires a "struggle unceasingly begun, unceasingly abolished" and leaves a man "incessantly in danger in his relations with his fellows" (*SS* 158). In other words, although opposition and division – which Beauvoir elsewhere describes as evil – are immanent in human existence, they can also be met with a constant effort of resistance.

Therefore, on the ontological level, Beauvoir approaches the issue of evil through an analysis of the fundamental structures of the self and of human existence. Human beings exist as negativity, they exist in relation to themselves with the constant possibility of misrelation. Their actions always involve failure, although there are moments of reprieve. It is failure that makes evil possible, but failure is also that which makes ethics as such meaningful. Evil is an ineradicable reality in the human condition, as in the evil of death that constantly haunts life. Evil is also an ineradicable possibility, because of the me–others structure of consciousness which creates conflict and opposition in relation to others and also in relation to one's own self. But in all of these senses, evil must be acknowledged as ambiguous as well. Death is also that which makes human life human, and although the me–others relationship is a source of

conflict, this conflict can be met in the spirit of resistance by friendship and generosity in order to move towards human solidarity.

SOCIAL EVIL

In both the *Ethics of Ambiguity* and *The Second Sex* Beauvoir identifies social oppression and the enslavement of human beings with the
concept of evil. In *The Second Sex* she refers to the loss of liberty that
she identifies as immanence in the following terms: "This downfall
represents a moral fault if the subject consents to it; if it is inflicted
upon him, it spells frustration and oppression. In both cases it is an
absolute evil" (*SS* xxxiii). In this sense, Beauvoir's discussions of the
different forms of social oppression can be understood as a discourse
on evil. I shall now consider how Beauvoir's concept of ambiguity
inflects her discussion of social oppression.

Although her novels and essays are filled with references to contemporary social evils and the dilemmas of action that they pose,
it is in her discussion of sexism and of racism in the United States
that she develops analyses of concrete forms of oppression. Since
I discuss *The Second Sex* below in reference to representations of
evil, I focus here on her reflections on racism during her four-month
stay in America in 1947, published in *America Day by Day*.[14] Beauvoir's reflections contribute to a phenomenology of oppression that
traces the political dimension of relations between individuals. In
this sense her analysis of social oppression belongs to a discourse
shared by Richard Wright, in *Native Son*, Jean-Paul Sartre, in *Anti-
Semite and Jew*, and Frantz Fanon, in *Black Skin, White Masks*.[15]

In *America Day by Day* Beauvoir takes up the problem of racism
as a problem of white people in their attitudes toward themselves and
toward black people, as well as a problem for blacks. She agrees with
Myrdal's analysis in *An American Dilemma* that the black problem
is first of all a white problem.[16] It is white people's own self-hatred
and fear that leads them to project onto blacks images of animal
sensuality and naturalness. White people's fear of blacks – as in the
refusal by most New Yorkers to enter Harlem – is the reverse of their
own self-hatred and remorse. White people live the privileges of their
skin in bad faith; "It's themselves they're afraid to meet on the street
corners" (*AD* 46). Whites in the lower ranks of the social hierarchy
use their racial privileges to feel superiority over *somebody*, and in

this way they do not try to improve their own position (AD 243).[17] Whites rationalize their view that blacks *are* inferior by reference to the so-called given, natural features of race and hence fail to understand the significance of the verb *to be*, that this situation is one that has evolved (AD 237). While traveling through the South by bus and experiencing the segregation of blacks in bathrooms, restaurants, waiting rooms, and buses, Beauvoir writes: "it was our own skin that became heavy and stifling; its color making us burn" and "we are the enemy despite ourselves, responsible for the color of our skin and all that it implies" (AD 204, 228). The arrogant hatred of whites does not prevent them from having an attitude of ambivalence towards blacks. Although white southerners would never eat at the same table as blacks, they eat the food blacks have prepared and entrust their own children to the care of blacks (AD 237). Even though Beauvoir underlines that whites are responsible for the privileges of their skin color, many white students and intellectuals in America do not feel themselves responsible for anything, because they do not think that they can do anything (AD 102). Beauvoir experienced this same sentiment when she didn't dare offer her seat in the front of a bus to a black woman who had fainted, because "the whole bus would oppose it, and she would be the first victim of their indignation" (AD 231).

In describing the attitude of blacks, Beauvoir follows Wright's injunction that, for blacks, every moment of their lives is penetrated by the social consciousness of being black, by the consciousness of the white world from which black takes its meaning (AD 67). This racial consciousness results in the black person's double-face, in which one side is meant expressly for whites (AD 240).[18] Thus she notes that although blacks are famous for their laughter, an apparent sign of their happiness in their situation, this is a mask put on by the black person because it is expected of him. The other side of the double-face is a silent hatred of whites, in protest against the economic and political dependencies that entrap them. Beauvoir notes that in the paternalistic economy of the South, which still prevailed in 1947, blacks depended exclusively on their master's goodwill for a living (AD 211). Although the attitude of blacks is basically one of protest and refusal, they must adapt themselves to the conditions in which they find themselves. Hence, the attitude of blacks "oscillates between submission and revolt" (AD 245). She notes, though, that since World War Two, when many blacks were the very soldiers who helped liberate Europe, blacks have increasingly expressed a will to revolt (*AD* 216).

Beauvoir's journey through America revealed to her not only neon lights, drugstores, smiles, and prosperity, but also another truth, "the truth of poverty, exhaustion, hatred, cruelty, revolt – the truth of evil" (*AD* 89). Of what signifcance is it that she conjoins the term *evil* with the phenomenology of racial oppression that she sketches in this text? What does this phenomenology reveal about her concept of evil? I think it indicates that evil is not something that exists abstractly, for an Other. This abstract attitude did indeed mark many Americans, who refused to believe in German atrocities and maintained a humanism based on denial (*AD* 74). This view of evil as something that concerns someone else, but not oneself, is linked to a conception of good and evil as distinct and opposing categories. It is this attitude that can lead to the view that the Japanese, for example, are the devil incarnate and hence can justify the internment of Japanese living in the US during World War Two. Such an attitude denies the "ambiguity of judgment," denies that one might ever be obliged *"to take the side of Evil"* (*AD* 76, 379). Such an attitude denies that problems may be so complex that there are no innocent or virtuous solutions. By maintaining the moral term *evil* in reference to social oppressions and miseries, Beauvoir insists that evil is part of our lived realities, that it inflects human attitudes and actions, whether one is on the side of the oppressor or on the side of the oppressed. The existence of evil is present in the way in which a white woman treats a black woman in a bus, in the way a black jazz musician hears the applause of the white audience, knowing that he would not be welcome to sit amongst them. It is in reference to the existence of these social evils that the complexity of human attitudes and actions must be understood.

Beauvoir develops a phenomenology of oppression in relation to sexual relations as well. Her discussions of both racial and sexual relations articulate a philosophical anthropology that posits an interdependency and reciprocity between individuals, following Hegel's account of the master–slave dialectic. The master needs the slave both for economic conquest and for recognition of his own mastery. It is on the basis of this need that Beauvoir portrays the attitudes of the oppressor as defined fundamentally in relation to the oppressed.

White racists need to feel superior to blacks in order to exist in their own eyes.

Other accounts of the evil of oppression, however, indicate that interdependency is not always at play in the relation between oppressor and oppressed. In *Eichmann in Jerusalem* Hannah Arendt portrayed Eichmann's attitudes as defined primarily in relation to his family and superiors in the Nazi regime, which accounted for the "banality" or thoughtlessness of his attitude toward the Jews.[19] Zygmunt Bauman in *Modernity and the Holocaust* underlines the process of rationalization and modernization that was a precondition for the Holocaust.[20] The Nazis did not derive their self-recognition in relation to the Jews so much as detach themselves from human interaction with them. Ervin Staub, in the *Roots of Evil*, shows how individuals' moral behavior moves along a continuum.[21] If one is trained to be cruel toward Jews or Muslims or Serbs, then one typically integrates this behavior into one's self-identity by removing these others from the category of human beings with whom one may have a possible moral relationship. Thus, contrary to Beauvoir, I suggest that the philosophical analysis of human conflict through the dialectic of recognition is inadequate to account for how human beings create extreme situations of evil, such as that of genocide. Beauvoir's philosophical anthropology can account for *perverted* forms of recognition, that is, the misrelation of the self, as in the case of white racial superiority. But this account does not address the ability of human beings to detach themselves from relations of interdependence with the oppressed in a way that enables them to commit atrocities. Eichmann, for example, may have found recognition as father and loyal bureaucrat from his family and Nazi colleagues. But did he seek recognition from the Jews he helped annihilate? As Arendt underlines in *Eichmann in Jerusalem*, his attitude to his Jewish victims was rather one of indifference and detachment.

How can Beauvoir's emphasis on the ambiguity of human action be reconciled with her claim that some actions, like lynching, are an *absolute evil*? In *The Ethics of Ambiguity* she describes absolute evil as "a fault without justification or excuse." Here she contrasts lynching with the suppression of 100 members of the opposition, which "may have a meaning and a reason; it is a matter of maintaining a regime which brings an immense mass of men a bettering of their lot" (*EA* 147). In other words, she is not condemning all forms of murder or execution, but only those that are not necessary, those committed uselessly – hence the debate in *The Mandarins* over whether the Soviet labor camps were necessary, or whether they were a mistake (*M* 406–07). But since one cannot know in advance the consequences of one's actions, since one may always be mistaken in the wager of action, it is difficult to condemn any form of violence as *absolute* evil. This implication is difficult for Beauvoir, since she does not want to minimize atrocities or oppression by calling them ambiguous. A minimizing attitude is too closely linked to the efforts to justify injustices as errors, or to *integrate* them as productive for human creativity.[22] But in order to justify the term *absolute evil* Beauvoir needs to shift from discussing the logic of action to discussing the logic of history. Lynching represents an "obsolete civilization ... a struggle of races which has to disappear," whereas suppressing the opposition supports a regime that is building a future (*EA* 146).

But in terms of the logic of human attitudes and actions one cannot avoid the ambiguity of evil, the fact that now and then one does take the side of evil. This is the case when one accepts as natural the privileges of one's race (such as the white person in racist America) or the privilege of one's national identity (such as the French citizen who has the knowledge that the French government cooperates with torture, rape, and the miscarriage of justice in its colonies). But siding with evil can also occur when one seeks at the same time to resist evil. It is this dilemma that marked the Resistance to the Nazi occupation in France and which is exemplified by the dilemma of violence.

In *Pyrrhus et Cinéas* Beauvoir refuses to call violence evil. In this text she writes that the danger posed to my own freedom justifies treating those who would silence me as objects. When persuasion fails, then violence is a necessary resort (*PC* 116).[23] In this early text Beauvoir does not consider that violence can be a deprivation of one's lived subjectivity. Although she later acknowledged that in order to be free, one's freedom must be *concretely* realized, she still maintained that violence is inevitable in the ambiguity of freedom and that it is sometimes justifiable. In the *Ethics of Ambiguity* she writes: "Thus, we challenge every condemnation as well as every a priori justification of the violence practiced with a view to a valid end. That must be legitimized concretely" (*EA* 148).

Violence is always an outrage, but sometimes it is a justifiable and even a necessary outrage. The dilemma of violence is a central theme in Beauvoir's novel *The Blood of Others*, as well as in *The Mandarins*. Can terrorist violence against Nazi soldiers during the occupation be justified, given that "all means are bad" (*BO* 190)? Is violence against the collaborators who were not brought to justice by French courts after the liberation justified? Both examples exemplify the *ambiguity* of action. But ambiguity in this context seems to vacillate between two distinguishable positions: that violence is sometimes justifiable, hence violence is not evil; that violence is sometimes justifiable, but it is also evil. The latter position is exemplified by Albert Camus in *The Rebel*, where the paradoxical condition of the rebel is that he is good but does evil.[24] Beauvoir seems to adopt the first position in *Pyrrhus et Cinéas* and *The Ethics of Ambiguity*, but she seems to adopt the second position in *America Day by Day* and *The Mandarins*. In the latter texts she admits that "the complexity of various factors creates problems that go beyond all virtuous solutions" (*AD* 79) and in relation to politics, "evil intervenes" (*M* 588). Thus, whether through complicity or active intervention on the side of good, as in fighting the injustices and atrocities of fascism, one also may be siding with evil.

In Beauvoir's discussion of social evil, her emphasis on the interdependency of individuals and on the ambiguity of judgment and action makes it difficult for her to account for what she also calls absolute evil. In Beauvoir's texts this concept appears when she detaches herself from the perspective of the agent and moves to a discussion of the logic of history. I have also suggested that other forms of detachment might be necessary to explain evil in its extremity, that is, a detachment that takes place within concrete human relations. It should be noted that when Beauvoir later does briefly discuss atrocities, such as the Holocaust in her prefaces to Jean-Francois Steiner's book *Treblinka* and to the text of Claude Lanzmann's *Shoah*, or when she describes in detail the rape and torture in police custody of the young Algerian girl, Djamila Boupacha, she does not invoke the terms *evil* or *ambiguity* at all. Instead she uses terms like *horror, injustice,* and *dehumanized world*.[25] The concept of the ambiguity of evil that she uses in her "moral period" is apparently inadequate to the lived realities of these extreme horrors.

REPRESENTATIONS OF EVIL

In *The Second Sex* Beauvoir develops another dimension of her analysis of evil, namely cultural *representations* of evil. Her encyclopedic study is an analysis of how human cultures have created an imagery of evil as the feminine in order to defend against the threats of evil and of ambiguity that are inescapable in the human situation. And, Beauvoir notes, "Representation of the world, like the world itself, is the work of men" (*SS* 161). These representations of evil have of course contributed to the production of social evil, which she also analyzes extensively in this text in relation to women's oppression. Thus, the concept of evil is a central thread through *The Second Sex*, although the index of the English translation gives just a single page reference (*SS* 90).[26]

While death is an evil inherent in the human condition, it is the representation of death in terms of woman that marks much of human dreams, fears, and idols. Woman becomes man's intermediary with nature, and it is in nature that "he is born of her and dies of her" (*SS* 162).[27] It is through woman's own fecundity that she gives birth to an infant and thus dooms man to death. Beauvoir notes, "In most popular representations Death is a woman, and it is for women to bewail the dead because death is their work" (*SS* 166). In love, man also abandons himself to his flesh, which is destined for the tomb, and thus once again "the alliance between Woman and Death is confirmed" (*SS* 186). Beauvoir indicates that it is through the representation of death as woman that man seeks to split off the natural, fleshly, mortal dimension of his own existence from his pure, intellectual and spiritual aspirations.

The ontological risk of evil present in the me–others structure of consciousness is also represented in terms of the feminine, for it is through this dynamic of opposition and interdependency that woman is marked out as Other in human culture. In the preface to *The Second Sex* Beauvoir notes that according to Hegel every consciousness sets itself up as the essential, as opposed to the Other, which is the inessential (*SS* xx). But whereas the Other sets up a reciprocal claim to define itself as essential, in relations between the sexes this reciprocity is lacking. Woman becomes The Other. Beauvoir explictly links the representation of woman as other with evil. She writes of Eve and Pandora, "The Other – she is passivity confronting activity, diversity that destroys unity, matter as opposed to form, disorder against order. Woman is thus dedicated to Evil" (SS 90). *The Second Sex* can be read as an extensive argument for the claim "women's oppression is evil," which coheres with Beauvoir's discussion of both ontological and social evil. But the cultural *representation* of woman as evil does not embody the claim "women's oppression is evil." Instead, it embodies the claim "women are evil." What does the cultural reduction of the claim "women's oppression is evil" to the claim "women are evil" signify? Beauvoir approaches this problem through both the concept of ambiguity and the concept of ambivalence, which she uses in the following paragraph in reference to woman's contradictory attributions.

And her ambiguity is just that of the concept of the Other; it is that of the human situation insofar as it is defined in its relation with the Other. As I have already said, the Other is Evil; but being necessary to the Good, it turns into the Good; through it I attain to the Whole ... And here lies the reason why woman incarnates no stable concept; through her is made unceasingly the passage from hope to frustration, from hate to love, from good to evil, from evil to good. Under whatever aspect we may consider her, it is this ambivalence that strikes us first. [SS 162]

Beauvoir claims that woman's ambiguity is the ambiguity that is in the idea of the Other. The Other can be said to refute the logic of identity. It has multiple placeholders, for example, blacks, Jews, and women. But women can never vacate that category. Because women are specially linked to the category of Other, they seem to retain the same qualities of this category, that is, to refute the logic of identity by being a placeholder filled by multiple and contradictory characteristics. But how does the representation of women as ambiguous, as multiple, explain the cultural image of woman as evil? Beauvoir here invokes the psychological logic of projection: men attempt to resist the ambiguity of the human condition by allotting it only to women: "He projects upon her what he desires and what he fears, what he loves and what he hates" (SS 223).

But in addition to explaining the attribution to women of evil by a psychological logic, Beauvoir suggests something akin to a logic of symbolic systems. The ambiguity of woman becomes separated out into distinct positions: woman as devoted mother, woman as perfidious mistress. Beauvoir writes: "She represents in a living carnal way all the values and anti-values that give sense to life... Between these clearly fixed poles can be discerned a multitude of ambiguous figures, pitiable, hateful, sinful, victimized, coquettish, weak, angelic, devilish" (SS 217). And, "She incarnates all moral values, from good to evil, and their opposites" (SS 223). Beauvoir makes no effort to clarify the relation between the two concepts – ambiguity and ambivalence – that she invokes to explain the conjuncture between woman and evil. But it appears that when Beauvoir refers to the images of persons that we meet in literature and life, that is, the agent perspective, then she uses the term *ambiguity* to refer to the multiplicity of possibilities. But when she refers to a bipolar conceptual system, the opposites of evil and good, hate and love, she invokes the term *ambivalence*.[28] There seems to be a logic within this conceptual system of instability that drives each concept to turn into its opposite.

In other words, in order to address the cultural reduction of the claim "women's oppression is evil" to the claim "woman is evil," Beauvoir implicitly relies on both the concepts of ambiguity and ambivalence. Ambiguity refers to the agent perspective, to men's projection of their multiple fears and dreams on to women. But it does not explain the constant question: why is this projection not reciprocal? Just as in her discusssion of lynching she had to move beyond an agent perspective to the logic of history in order to judge this act as absolutely evil, in *The Second Sex* she has to move beyond the agent perspective to another level of discourse to explain the "absolute evil" of women being defined as Other, object, immanence (SS xxxiii). Her invocation of ambivalence in reference to woman as Other gives her another tool of analysis. The logic of opposing concepts can elucidate how certain representations of women become sedimented in culture, despite and even because of their contradictory character.[29] Thus, the question of why otherness is not reciprocal between the sexes is no longer merely a question to women's psychology. Women's attempt or failed attempt to project their fears and desires onto men becomes secondary in relation to the way in which the logic of ambivalence in the concept of otherness attributes to women the opposing and mutually necessary concepts of good and evil. Thus, in order to understand the cultural reduction in the claim "women are evil" it is necessary to understand how evil is an unstable concept that is necessary to the good and turns into the good and thus is marked by ambivalence. Beauvoir's use of the term *ambivalence* does not explain *why* women are identified with evil, but it does explain *how* this identification is maintained despite the simultaneous representations of woman as the virgin or good mother.

The representation of evil in terms of the feminine has had, of course, negative repercussions on the situation of women and thus has contributed to social evil. The most obvious consequence of such myths is that they produce a complicity by women with their own deprivation of liberty. Beauvoir notes that the Cinderella myth, by which a young girl looks to expect her fortune and happiness from some Prince Charming, "is a thing of evil because it divides her strength and her interests" (SS 153–54). Moreover, because women are deprived of possibilities for genuine action, they themselves take up a skewed conception of evil. Beauvoir describes women as taking up a Manicheist position that clearly separates good and evil as coexisting and discrete entities. Such a worldview, which Beauvoir notes characterizes the attitude of the housewife in her war against dirt, is contrasted with a recognition of the "ambiguousness of all solutions" (SS 675). Myths of woman as evil play a role in other forms of oppression and violence as well. It is well known that lynching in the South often occurred when black men were suspected of having sexual relations with white women. In these incidents it was not only the image of woman as good or pure who must be protected and avenged that was at play, but also the image of woman as evil or polluted who was suspected of enjoying her degradation. Representations of woman as evil may also be suspected of playing a role in the outright physical violence and torture of women, as in war rape and the torture of women accused of working with colonial insurrectionists. Thus the representation of evil as feminine is at play in the confrontation with ontological evils present in the human condition, as well as in the social evils by which, for example, women, blacks, and those working for national liberation movements are oppressed.

CONCLUSION

What are the implications of Beauvoir's analysis of the moral concept of evil in terms of ambiguity? As I have tried to show above, she works through the presence of evil on three levels of analysis: in terms of the ontological conditions of negativity, death, and the me–others structure of consciousness; in terms of the social realities that incarnate evil as relations of oppression between individuals; and in terms of the representation of evil in the form of the feminine. On all of these levels Beauvoir shows that the problem of evil must be thought through in relation to the ambiguity of the human condition.

The centrality of the concept of ambiguity for Beauvoir indicates the primacy of the agent's perspective in her reflections on ethics. It is from the point of view of the individual confronting the dilemma of action and complicity that ambiguity becomes a concept rich with explanatory potential. However, as I have also sought to show, there are two borders at which this agent-based approach to ethics breaks down, both of which touch what Beauvoir has termed *absolute evil*. In one case, as in the example of lynching, she turned to a perspective based on the dynamics of historical development to justify moral judgment. In the other case, in terms of the persistence of the oppression of women, she turned to the logic of representations in order to explain how the representation of woman in terms of evil has been sustained.

But at this point one might well pause to consider the adequacy of her concept of ambiguity to address the agent's perspective in ethics. By way of contrast, I point briefly to the way in which Claudia Card has conceptualized the problem of evil in terms of what she calls *the atrocity paradigm*. Her strategy is to focus on atrocities, which include genocide, slavery, torture, rape as a weapon of warfare, biological and chemical warfare, spousal battery and child abuse. Card argues that "the core features of evils tend to be writ large in the case of atrocities, making them easier to identify and appreciate."[30] She underlines two central features of atrocities: they are both perpetrated and suffered. She thus provides the following definition of evil: "an evil is harm that (1) is reasonably foreseeable (or appreciable), (2) culpably inflicted (or tolerated, aggravated, or maintained) and that (3) deprives, or seriously risks depriving, others of the basics that are necessary to make life possible and tolerable or decent (or to make a death decent)."[31] Card's approach, like Beauvoir's, can be said to be based on the perspectives of the agents, although she takes as her starting point the situations of extremes. Card analyzes the position of the perpetrator, that is, the agent who knowingly inflicts a harm, as well as the position of the victim or sufferer of the harm. Both of these perspectives can be aligned with Beauvoir's analysis of the relation between the oppressor and the oppressed. With Beauvoir's reference to ambiguity, the perspective of the perpetrator of a harm is shown to be a complex one. One need no longer speak of a good will, or a bad will, but instead is forced to address the question of an ambiguous will, of one that is both good and bad at the same time. This approach does address appreciably the complexity of the perspective of the perpetrator of a harm. But ambiguity breaks down in reference to situations of extreme harm, where perpetrators have detached themselves from interaction with their victims and have knowingly taken actions that will bring suffering or death to victims. The term *ambiguity* also reveals the complexity of the perspective of the oppressed, for example, the dynamic of complicity and the double-mask as a survival strategy. But it is less fruitful in relation to the perspective of the sufferer of harm in extreme situations. Instead, ambiguity has a connotation that seems to devalue the extremity of harm inflicted. In this sense, it is important to focus on the nature of suffering in extreme situations, as Card does in her analysis.[32]

Extreme situations that generate the use of the term *absolute evil* reveal the limits of Beauvoir's concept of ambiguity. On the one hand, her use of ambiguity presupposes the demand for mutual recognition. Thus, it cannot address the attitudes and behaviors of individuals when recognition is not invoked. On the other hand, extreme situations reveal that the agent perspective in ethics is limited as such. But as Beauvoir indicates, there are other resources available to address the problem of ethics in extreme situations: a discourse of historical dynamics and a discourse of symbolic representations. These discourses contribute not only to the descriptive task of ethics, of understanding how situations of extremes are generated. They also contribute to the normative work of ethics, of making judgments about these situations. The historical discourse underpins the invocation of emancipatory values in ethics. The discourse of symbolic representations underpins the analysis of ambivalence in the representation of evil as feminine, as well as strategies of disruption or subversion with regard to these representational forms. Thus, the concept of ambiguity that Beauvoir explicitly develops needs to be supplemented by these other resources, which she implicitly invokes. Developing this dimension of Beauvoir's legacy can lead to a multilayered analysis of ethics that can address the problem of evil in extreme situations.

NOTES

1 Quoted at the beginning of *The Ethics of Ambiguity*.
2 Wenzel, Hélène Vivienne, "Interview with Simone de Beauvoir," in *Simone de Beauvoir; Witness to a Century* (special issue of *Yale French Studies*, 72 [1986]: 5–32), 25.
3 *FC* (New York: Putnam, 1965) 369.
4 Margaret Simons, *Beauvoir and the Second Sex* (Lanham, MD: Rowman & Littlefield, 1999), p. 168.
5 *SS* (New York: Vintage Books, 1954) 7–8.
6 *BO* (Harmondsworth: Penguin Books, 1964) 10.
7 *M* (New York: Norton, 1956) 32.
8 *VED* (New York: Pantheon Books, 1965) 60.
9 Beauvoir describes the difficulty her mother had in using a bed-pan while she lay in a nursing home before her death. "Yes," her mother replied, "The dead certainly do it in their beds." Beauvoir adds, "In this prim and spiritualistic woman it was also a form of courage to take on our animality with so much decision" (*VED* 54).
10 Notably, Beauvoir does not condemn violence, or killing as such, as evil. She expresses the ambivalence of the French intellectuals towards violence in the wake of the Resistance and the post-war revelation of the Soviet labor camps. Some forms of violence that result in death may have a "justification or excuse," and some may represent "that necessary element of failure which is involved in any positive construction." I return to the discussion of violence below.
11 Beauvoir writes of her mother's treatment in the nursing home, "A race had begun between death and torture...An evil all-knowing spirit, I could see behind the scenes, which she was struggling, far, far away, in human loneliness...Despairingly, I suffered a transgression that was mine without my being responsible for it and one that I could never expiate" (*VED* 58).
12 See Margaret Simons, "From Murder to Morality: The Development of Beauvoir's Ethics," *International Studies in Philosophy*, 31, 2 (1999): 1–20.
13 Economic, political, and social factors – such as capitalism, racism, and sexism – are decisive, however, as to whether conflicts become institutionalized and rigidified.
14 In *Beauvoir and the Second Sex*, pp. 167–84, Simons has shown that Beauvoir's analysis of racism in this text – as well as her analysis of sexism in *The Second Sex* – is profoundly influenced by Richard Wright's work and by her friendship with him. Beauvoir first read Wright's book *Native Son* shortly after its publication in 1940, she met Wright in Paris

in 1946, and he served as her host and guide during much of her visit to America in 1947. *America Day by Day* is dedicated to Ellen and Richard Wright. Simons argues that Wright's intellectual influence on Beauvoir is found in his concept of the oppressed Other, in his phenomenological approach to the study of oppression, in his redefining a model for struggle against oppression that rejects both orthodox Marxism and liberalism, and in his concept of cultural identity as a basis for political engagement.

15 Richard Wright, *Native Son* (New York: Harper, 1940); Jean-Paul Sartre, *Anti-Semite and Jew*, trans. George J. Becker (New York: Schocken, 1948 [1946]); Franz Fanon, *Black Skin, White Masks*, trans. Charles Lam Markmann (New York: Grove, 1967 [1952]).

16 *AD*, trans. Carol Cosman (London: Phoenix, 1999) 302.

17 Sartre gives a similar analysis of anti-Semites in *Anti-Semite and Jew*.

18 Beauvoir cites here Wright's *Black Boy*, as well as "John Dollar, *Caste and Class in a Southern Community* [sic]."

19 Hannah Arendt, *Eichmann in Jerusalem: A Report on the Banality of Evil*, revised and enlarged (New York: Viking, 1965).

20 Zygmunt Bauman, *Modernity and the Holocaust* (Ithaca, NY: Cornell University Press, 1989).

21 Ervin Staub, *The Roots of Evil: The Origins of Genocide and Other Group Violence* (Cambridge: Cambridge University Press, 1989).

22 Note Henri's contempt for Louis' claim that "Art is an attempt at integrating evil" (*M* 289).

23 See Debra Bergoffen's discussion in *The Philosophy of Simone de Beauvoir* (Albany, NY: State University of New York Press, 1997), pp. 54 ff.

24 In *The Rebel*, trans. Anthony Bower (New York: Vintage, 1956), p. 285, Albert Camus writes, "If rebellion exists, it is because falsehood, injustice, and violence are part of the rebel's condition. He cannot, therefore, absolutely claim not to kill or lie, without renouncing his rebellion and accepting, once and for all, evil and murder. But no more can he agree to kill and lie, since the inverse reasoning which would justify murder and violence would also destroy the reason for his insurrection. Thus the rebel can never find peace. He knows what is good and, despite himself, does evil."

25 Jean-Francois Steiner, *Treblinka*, translated by Helen Weaver, preface by Simone de Beauvoir (New York: Simon & Schuster, 1967), pp. 7–12; Claude Lanzmann, *Shoah; An Oral History of the Holocaust: The Complete Text of the Film*, preface by Simone de Beauvoir (New York: Pantheon, 1985), pp. iii–vi; Simone de Beauvoir and Gisele Halimi, *Djamila Boupacha*, translated by Peter Green (New York: Macmillan, 1962), pp. 9–21, 194–97.

26 I will return to this reference in relation to Beauvoir's concept of ambivalence.
27 The references to women and death are drawn from Beauvoir's chapter, "Dreams, Fears, Idols."
28 Note that this is related to Freud's notion of ambivalence, which refers to the simultaneity of hate and love towards the same object.
29 Penelope Deutscher argues in *Yielding Gender* (London and New York: Routledge, 1997) that it is precisely because of its contradictions that a patriarchal discourse maintains itself.
30 Claudia Card, *The Atrocity Paradigm; A Theory of Evil* (Oxford: Oxford University Press, 2002), p. 9.
31 ibid., p. 16.
32 This is also Nel Noddings' starting point in *Women and Evil* (Berkeley and Los Angeles: University of California Press, 1989). See Card, *Atrocity Paradigm*, p. 11.

12 Simone de Beauvoir: (Re)counting the sexual difference

EXISTENTIAL CERTAINTIES

"One is not born, but rather becomes a woman." These most quoted words of *The Second Sex* became the centerpiece of first-wave feminism and the signature of their author, Simone de Beauvoir. Their meaning, fleshed out in *The Second Sex*'s descriptions of women's daily lives, once seemed obvious. They seemed to point to the difference between sex and gender. They seemed to indicate the ways in which human beings born with vaginas were habituated and initiated into the roles of adults called women. Today things seem less clear. Do these words mean that sex and gender are radically distinct – that any sexed body can become whatever gender it chooses? Could any body become a woman? Should Beauvoir's critique of the "biology is destiny" argument be taken as an argument for the complete malleability of the body? Or should her words alert us to the fact that the different materialities of human bodies constitute us as sexually distinct but that the sex/gender differences mandated by patriarchy are epistemologically untenable, ethically intolerable, and politically unjust (*SS* 267)?[1]

"One is not born, but rather becomes a woman." When originally written, these words produced shocking effects. They soon became central to the feminist critique of patriarchy. Eventually they became familiar, obvious. Contemporary theorists and advanced technologies have returned these words to their radical origin. Without allowing for a return to the position that there is no distinction between sex and gender, and far from assuring us that sex produces gender, today's thinkers and technologies have shown us that what seemed to be a clear divide between nature and culture is a rather blurred border. The experiences of transsexuals, of the transgendered, and of the intersexed réveal the ways in which sex and gender bleed into each other. They also suggest that to ask whether sex and gender are natural givens or cultural constructs is to ask the wrong question. Nothing human is naturally given. No cultural construct arises *ex nihilo*.

Beauvoir, whose legacy to us includes the concept of ambiguity, would, I think, have been pleased by this turn of events. For by pausing over these now famous words, instead of taking their meaning for granted, we learn more about the complexity of Beauvoir's thought and more about women's situation within patriarchy. Joining those who celebrate the words "One is not born, but rather becomes a woman" as an invitation to rethink the structures of patriarchy, I bring this familiar line of *The Second Sex* to some of the less well-known passages of Beauvoir's feminist manifesto to show that in arguing for women's equality Beauvoir was also arguing for women's sexual difference. What is unique about this argument is its appeal to the concept of ambiguity.

Beauvoir introduces *The Second Sex* with a question. "What," she asks, "is a woman?" (*SS* xix). Within the space of a page she determines that although it is certain that women exist, it is also clear that women's existence can only be admitted provisionally (*SS* xxi). Beauvoir is certain that women exist, because she cannot doubt that she exists. She must, if she wishes to affirm her existence, "*first* of all say: I am a woman; on this truth must be based all further discussion" (*SS* xxi, emphasis added). Her existential certainty, however, is riddled with problems. For once Beauvoir asks for a definition of woman (of herself insofar as she is first of all a woman) she discovers that so many accounts are provided (many contrary to each other) that she cannot say which, if any, are real or true. Caught in the Cartesian dilemma, she is certain that she is but doubts who she is, Beauvoir cannot follow Descartes' strategy, for she acknowledges a certainty that escaped Descartes. There are two distinguishable human types: men and women. It is impossible to identify oneself as a human being without first taking one's place in the sexual register. The certainty of being sexed is inseparable from the existential certainty of being human.[2]

Noticing what Descartes missed, Beauvoir understands his inattentiveness. As a man, Descartes' sex/gender is un(re)marked. He can dismiss it as irrelevant to his identity because as a man he is "the absolute human type" (SS xxi). The sexed/gendered term that identifies him, man, is also used to designate human beings in general. Thus, his existence as distinctly sexed/gendered goes unnoticed (SS xxi). The philosopher of the cogito, eager to evade the deceptions of the senses, is duped by language. Careful to avoid all prejudices, he fails to discern the patriarchal biases embedded in his meditative discourse.

Beauvoir cannot follow Descartes' path to certainty. She is a woman. Her sex/gender is the negative of the absolute human type. Her name, woman, is never used to designate human beings in general. Being a woman who is also a philosopher, Beauvoir cannot begin with the one, the neutral subject. She cannot escape the weight of the senses. She is a woman. For her, the two, the sexed/gendered existential certainty of having to be either a man or a woman, is the necessary point of departure.

Descartes is not the first philosopher to be taken in by language. Beauvoir is not the first philosopher to note the ways in which language (mis)informs epistemology and metaphysics. Nietzsche found all philosophers guilty of mistaking grammatical structures for philosophical categories. Even he, however, missed what Beauvoir saw. For he, too, was a patriarchal man. Attentive as he was to differences, he did not examine the meaning or structure of the sexual difference – the two that is the condition of the possibility of the many that are others, rather than repetitions of the same one.[3]

Descartes' epistemology of the one produces the lie of abstract consciousness. This consciousness becomes the autonomous subject of the Enlightenment. It grounds the politics of the social contract tradition that secured freedom for men (the sex/gender identified as the one) by removing women (the second sex/gender) from the political scene.[4] Plato's Republic anticipates this political strategy. It draws the line between this epistemology of the one and the politics of exclusion. By showing how the epistemology of the one is the necessary ground of a politics of the one, The Republic also shows why the sexual difference is politically intolerable. Women can participate in the governance of the ideal state only if their difference is erased. Plato is more forthcoming than most political thinkers. He acknowledges that to be members of the guardian class, women must be counted as men. He determines that this is possible because the sexual difference is an accidental rather than an essential human difference. He also recognizes the difficulty of sustaining this erasure of the sexual difference. Thus the political lie that compensates for refusing the sexual difference by instituting the necessary and natural reality of the class difference.[5]

According to *The Republic*'s noble lie, there is only one mother – mother earth. We are all her children. Women are not, therefore, essentially mothers. We are not really of women born. Rendering women and men equally peripheral to the birth of the child, the noble lie renders us different only insofar as we are made of either gold, silver, or bronze. Shorn of our sexed bodily differences, we are segregated according to our mental capacities. Enlightenment politics reverses Plato's account of the difference. The sexual difference is affirmed, the class difference (in theory at least) is denied. Its noble lie, that women are naturally mothers and are therefore unfit for public life, differs in content but not in intent from Plato's. For the myth of the Enlightenment, like the myth of *The Republic*, is aimed at convincing those denied access to power on the basis of their difference that their exclusion is just. They must be convinced that their exclusion is a matter of destiny and that their exclusion is actually a form of inclusion – it is necessary for the common good. It is in the name of this justice that woman consents to become the inessential Other: the one who exists only as the subordinated part of the one (man), and only insofar as she fulfills her role as part object (for example, the wife, the mother, the helpmate), contributing to the good of the whole object (man). Having become this part object, this inessential Other, this patriarchal woman, Simone de Beauvoir finds that it is impossible for her to experience herself for herself and impossible for her to know whether she really exists.

Unlike Descartes, whose doubts are self-generated, Beauvoir's existential certainties are challenged from without. The problem is not that she doubts *her* understandings of who she is but rather that she has no resources from which *she* might produce an understanding of herself to doubt. Everything that she knows about herself is "simply what man decrees" (*SS* xxii). Men have decreed that, being a woman, she cannot exist for herself. This decree is countered by her immediate experience of herself as a woman who exists for herself. She is faced with an impossible choice. She can either deny the certainty that she exists for herself or deny the certainty that she is a woman.

The patriarchal category of the inessential Other freezes her in this impossible position. She must sever herself from the certainties of her existence and split these certainties apart. She must refuse the experience of certainty that ties her being for herself to her being a woman and accept the idea that her existence as a woman precludes her existing for herself. Having not been born a (patriarchal) woman, she must become one. As a patriarchal woman, she finds that doubt lies at the core of her being. Not only is the self she identifies with given to her by man, and therefore a doubtful indicator of who she is, but the experience through which she might discover herself is rendered doubtful, put out of play, by the patriarchal decree.

If the politics of patriarchy relies on mystifications that have the power (derived from their epistemological, metaphysical, and linguistic alliances) to falsify the certainties of experience, then retrieving these lived certainties becomes a necessary political strategy. It becomes a matter of finding the gaps in this decertification–mystification grid and of finding ways to exploit it. It becomes a matter of finding the place where the experience of the "essential" otherness of woman contests her position as the inessential Other, of finding the site where the epistemology and politics of the one can be contested by the lived experience of the two. Following Beauvoir's lead, I find this site in the heterosexual couple. For it is here, in the intimacies of the caress, that the immediate experience of the two can find its voice and contest the patriarchal one.[6]

Within the modern western world this voice is beginning to get a public hearing. The ideology of the patriarchal heterosexual couple, although still alive and well in many religious communities and secular movements (for example, the US covenant marriage movement), is no longer universally accepted. The "I now pronounce you man and wife" is more often than not replaced with the "I now pronounce you husband and wife." As man and wife the married couple replicated the rule of the one subject (man). As husband and wife the married couple invokes the rule of the two. Neither claims the position of the only subject. Religious ceremonies that included the ritual reading of the Genesis rib story have, in many cases, adopted the custom of reading the Genesis account of the equal and simultaneous creation instead. The whole and the part object model gives ground to the biblically sanctioned image of two whole objects. The laws that defined a wife as her husband's property and that negated the married woman's status as a legal adult are all but forgotten in the West. No longer required to inscribe herself in a place that is part of him, or to identify herself with the obligation to serve, please, and complete him, a woman may now charge her husband with rape and abuse. Always vulnerable to being divorced, she may now file for divorce.

The patriarchal strategy of claiming that men (can) represent the whole of humanity is undermined by these changing facts on the ground. These intimate, social, and political changes would seem to indicate that the feminist critique has taken hold. It would seem to indicate that we acknowledge the injustice of invoking the idea of sexual difference to justify the subordination of women to men. It would seem to indicate that patriarchy is ready to wither away. For that would be the effect of allowing women to affirm the certainty of their experience of being women who exist for themselves. Whether, however, patriarchy is ready to see the two as prior to the one, that is, whether it is ready to see the subject as sexed or whether we remain where Plato left us (where sex is deemed accidental to one's status as a subject and where the *subject* is identified as the one) remains unclear. Until this becomes clear, women's existence will remain doubtful.

The issue may be put as a series of questions. Will justice be served when women's existence for themselves is recognized, that is, when they too are identified as the one? Does justice require the resolution of women's doubts regarding their existence as women, the recognition of the two? Is a woman's first experience of herself as sexed a product of a patriarchal mystification that should be falsified? Is it an existential certainty that requires certification? Asking Beauvoir for her answer to these questions before formulating ours, we find *The Second Sex* speaking in two voices. Its dominant and best-known voice seems to support the logic of the one. Its muted and less heard voice finds this logic problematic. This voice is first heard in the opening of *The Second Sex*, where Beauvoir asks whether she exists as a woman. It speaks in her objections to abstract philosophy, in her attention to embodiment, in her insistence on the importance of the situation. This voice is most clearly heard in Beauvoir's discussion of the heterosexual couple and the bond. For it is here that she finds resources for discovering something about women not decreed by men. It is here that she alerts us to the ways in which her idea of ambiguity allows us to think the two before the one and to think of the one as grounded in the two. Listening for this voice, we can take up Beauvoir's call to "get out of [the] ruts; [and] discard the vague notions of superiority, inferiority, and equality which have hitherto corrupted every discussion of the subject and start afresh" (SS xxxiii).

A NEW BEGINNING

For Beauvoir, starting afresh means adopting the perspective of an existential ethics where the justice of a political institution is judged not according to the criteria of the common good or individual happiness but in terms of liberty. She writes: "For our part, we hold that the only public good is that which assures the private good of the citizens; we shall pass judgment on institutions according to their effectiveness in giving concrete opportunities to individuals" (SS xxxiv).

Explaining what she means by opportunities, Beauvoir stipulates that to be human is to be possessed of an ontological need to transcend oneself; that human existence is justified through its expansion into an indefinitely open future, its engagement in freely chosen projects, and its reaching out toward other liberties (SS xxxiv–xxxv). When these possibilities are foreclosed, there is, Beauvoir says, a "degradation of existence into...the brutish life of subjection to given conditions...[that] is an absolute evil" (SS xxxv).

Having begun by alerting us to the difference between the sexes, Beauvoir now insists on their ontological identity. Patriarchy is now identified as evil, not because it refuses the sexual difference embedded in the existential certainty of our existence, but because it uses the sexual difference to reject the human ontological need to engage in freely chosen projects of transcendence. Has Beauvoir brought us back to the domain of the one? Perhaps, but perhaps not. There is the matter of the bond. There is the ambiguous discussion of marriage. There is the attention to the lived erotic experience of the heterosexual couple.

Knowing Beauvoir's position on the certainty of the two (her certainty that she is a woman not a man) and aware of her ethical affirmation of the project, transcendence, and liberty, we can anticipate and understand her critique of marriage. Attending to what is surprising rather than to what is predictable about this critique, however, gets us to the complexities of her thinking. The first surprise is that Beauvoir's critique of marriage is historical, not absolute. She finds marriage objectionable in its current form. She does not, however, equate its current form with its essential structure. We do not know, she tells us, what the possibilities of marriage are. The second surprise is that her critique of marriage is not a critique of the heterosexual couple (SS 425–83). Putting these surprises together, I find that Beauvoir sees the heterosexual couple as the site where the mystifications that position woman as the inessential Other can be challenged. In reserving judgment on the institution of marriage, Beauvoir is, I think, leaving the possibility open that this institution, lying at the heart of patriarchy, might be its undoing. For if the heterosexual couple's lived experience of the bond informed the structure of marriage, the paradigm of the heterosexual couple that now sustains patriarchal politics would lose its hold on the erotic and political imaginary.[7]

To get at what is going on we need to return to the question that troubles Beauvoir from the very beginning. Women, she notes, are not the only group that have been exploited. What makes them unique is their refusal to demand recognition as subjects, their refusal to rebel. Trying to understand this refusal, which is analogous to trying to understand why women consent to marry, Beauvoir proposes the following explanation: "woman may fail to lay claim to the status of subject because she lacks definite resources, because she feels the necessary bond that ties her to man regardless of reciprocity and because she is often very well pleased with her role as the [inessential] Other" (SS xxvii).

Two parts of this explanation are familiar. The idea that women lack definite resources refers to the need for economic opportunities and calls for a liberal or Marxist solution. The idea that women are pleased with their role as the inessential Other recalls us to the existential category of bad faith. It chides women for not accepting the responsibilities of freedom. The idea that women feel the necessary bond that ties them to men regardless of reciprocity, however, does not lead us down liberal, Marxist, or existential roads. Instead, it directs us to Beauvoir's ethics of ambiguity and to the possibilities this ethics holds for a liberatory politics grounded in the two.

In identifying women but not men as committed to the value of the bond, Beauvoir discovers a fundamental difference between women's and men's attitude toward the heterosexual couple. The difference is historical, not necessary. Given the ubiquitous presence of patriarchy, it appears essential. The difference is this: although both men and women need and desire the Other, they live their needs and desires differently. Men orient their desire around the requirements of reciprocity; women privilege the bond. Men will sacrifice the desire for the bond to the demands of reciprocity; women will forgo the requirements of reciprocity in the name of the bond.

To adequately understand this difference between men and women, we need to focus on the terms *necessary* and *reciprocity*. Read historically, women's feeling of their necessary bond to men refers to the fact that women lack definite resources for independence. Read from the point of view of patriarchy, this feeling of the bond is a sign of a natural dependency. Women's feeling of the necessity of the bond is translated: she needs a man; she cannot exist on her own. It is assumed that women would not privilege the bond, would not experience it as necessary, if they could demand reciprocity – if they were less dependent.

Patriarchy values reciprocity more than the bond. It sees men's demand for reciprocity as a demand for recognition and reads this demand as a sign of independence and autonomy. Men are said to subordinate the value of the bond to the values of recognition and reciprocity because they can, it is said, stand on their own. For patriarchal men the issue is clear: no recognition, no relationship. Better to break or refuse the bond. Better to be alone, on one's own, than to accept a relationship without recognition.

If we step back from the patriarchal understandings of these different attitudes toward the heterosexual couple, that is, if we pause before speaking of this difference in terms of men's independence and women's dependency, we discover certain phenomenological possibilities. To fully appreciate these possibilities we need to turn to *The Ethics of Ambiguity*. For it is there, in amending the traditional phenomenological understanding of the relationship between consciousness and being, that Beauvoir introduces us to the difference that grounds the concept of ambiguity. It is there that we find the resources for attending to the muted voices of *The Second Sex*.[8] Beauvoir writes:

Thanks to [man], being is disclosed and he desires this disclosure. There is an original type of attachment to being which is not the relationship "wanting to be" but rather the relationship "wanting to disclose being." Now, here there is not failure, but rather success...I take delight in this very effort toward an impossible possession...This means that man, in his vain attempt to *be* God, makes himself exist *as* man...It is not granted him to exist without tending toward this being which he will never be. But it is possible for him to want this tension even with the failure which it involves. [*EA* 12–13]

With this description of consciousness as comprised of two intentional moments and ways of relating to being, Beauvoir identifies two types of transcendence. Each is characterized by a unique desire. These desires contest each other. The desire for disclosure of the first intentional moment cannot take up the desire for possession of the second intentionality without negating itself. The desire for possession cannot accept the aimlessness of the desire for disclosure without denying itself. As contesting and negating each other, these different desires and their attendant modes of transcendence intersect each other. The desire to disclose being finds itself moving toward the world it discloses possessively. The desire to possess the world finds itself thwarted. In its failure it is driven back to the moment of disclosure; it seeks new worlds to possess. To mark us as this tension of divergent, contesting, negating, and intersecting desires, Beauvoir calls us ambiguous. Neither this desire nor that, we are the ambiguity of the two desires that run through each other. We are the one of the ambiguous flow that is also and necessarily a two.

To understand the full meaning of our ambiguity, we must remember that the play of desire it identifies is never the isolated play of the desires of an autonomous subject. In *The Ethics of Ambiguity* these desires are identified as the desires of a singular subject always engaged in a world and always engaged with others. In *The Second Sex* these desires are identified as the desires of sexed subjects whose engagement in the world and with others is always and necessarily a matter of their embodied social, political, and economic situations. In alerting us to the patriarchal demands of recognition that structure relationships among men and that circumscribe relationships between men and women, and in attending to the ways in which women forfeit claims to recognition for the value of the bond, Beauvoir directs us to the ways in which patriarchy perverts our engagement with each other by sexing and severing the ambiguous desires of consciousness.[9] She shows us that in transforming the ambiguity of our twofold consciousness into the clarity of the either/or of single-sexed subjects (subjects who must embody only one desire of consciousness), patriarchy has inverted the relationship between disclosure and possession. It sexes as male the secondary mode of transcendence associated with the desire to possess the world and privileges it as the original mark of the subject. It sexes as female the inaugural mode of transcendence associated with the desires of disclosure. It marks these desires as weak and passive and identifies them as the signature of the secondary, inessential Other.

What does it mean to say that woman feels the necessity of the bond? What are the implications of the fact that she disregards the requirements of reciprocity for the sake of the bond? How might this disregard and feeling of necessity provide clues to escaping the ruts of patriarchy? What sort of sexual difference would emerge if the sexed difference of the inessential Other (the ploy of the logic of the one) were rejected and if in its place we forged a logic of sexual difference scripted through the concept of ambiguity? What if we tried an experiment? What if we read *The Ethics of Ambiguity's* description of consciousness into *The Second Sex's* discussions of the heterosexual couple, generosity, the gift, and the erotic?

THE EXPERIMENT

Putting on my philosophical lab coat, I begin by reading women's commitment to the bond (cited in *The Second Sex* as a partial explanation of women's refusal to rebel) as a concrete expression of the original relationship of consciousness to being, identified in *The Ethics of Ambiguity* as the desire of disclosure. This original relationship is best described as an active passivity. As a desire, it is active. As a mode of consciousness that is receptive to the unfolding that we call world, it is passive. As an intentionality, it is an active passivity. It may also be understood as an aimless generosity. Aimless, because it refuses to impose the lens of its purpose on being. Generous, because in becoming the site of the disclosure of being, it asks for nothing in return. This active passive generosity can best be captured in the concept of the gift. Gifts, situated outside the fields of exchange, debt, and accountability, also lie outside the fields of reciprocity and recognition. There is no debt, there is no demand for recognition, there is no law of exchange. As generous, the gift enacts the desire that takes delight in the disclosed otherness of the world. Living this delight and forgoing the transcendence of purposefulness, I go toward the world by situating myself within it. Instead of fleeing the spontaneity of being revealed in this moment of disclosure, I allow myself to meet the otherness of the world and to value it for itself rather than for the use that may be made of it. I celebrate the bond between us that makes our meeting possible. I allow myself to become vulnerable to the surprise of the event.

Once *The Ethics of Ambiguity*'s question of intentionality and relatedness is transformed into *The Second Sex*'s and *Must We Burn Sade?*'s question of relationships, the experience of vulnerability becomes crucial. Phenomenologically, our relatedness to the world marks us as ambiguous. Existentially our relationships with each other mark us as vulnerable. To live our ambiguity we must risk becoming vulnerable. *The Ethics of Ambiguity* reveals our tendency to refuse the tensions of lived consciousness. *The Second Sex* and *Must We Burn Sade?* point to the ways in which we flee the vulnerabilities of lived relationships. Patriarchy codes this flight. Teaching women that they must become woman and subordinate their desire for reciprocity and recognition to the demands of the bond, it teaches women that they must be generous and must not take up the risks of recognition associated with the desires of the second intentional moment. Teaching men that they must be man and subordinate their desire for the bond to the demands of recognition and reciprocity, patriarchy teaches men that they must demand recognition and refuse the risks of vulnerability. Phenomenological and existential ambiguities are bifurcated in patriarchal sexed/gendered identities. These identities and their associated values and risks are not, however, equally esteemed. Patriarchy privileges the risks of recognition. Further, it associates the risks of recognition with violence. One receives recognition by demanding it. The only recognition worth having is the recognition won in combat or competition – the recognition that comes from having stood up for yourself like a man. In barring women from the sphere of actively initiated violence (it being clearly unfeminine for a woman to stand up for herself like a man), patriarchy bars women from the contests necessary for recognition. Thus patriarchy makes it impossible for women or men to live the ambiguity of their desire. Women coded as woman must live the desires of generosity; men coded as man must not. Men coded as man must live the desire to be God; women coded as woman must not.

As Beauvoir's analysis of the doubled desires of intentionality in *The Ethics of Ambiguity* provides the phenomenological ground for exposing the perversions of patriarchy, so her analyses of the erotically fleshed body in *The Second Sex* and *Must We Burn Sade?* show us how to challenge these perversions. For it is here, at the erotically fleshed body, that the disaster of patriarchal perversion is clearest. It is here that the phenomenon of ambiguity is concretely lived. The spontaneities of erotic desire disrupt the patriarchal codes of subjectivity and risk – now the moment of disclosure's generosity takes precedence. Here the desires of reciprocity are coupled with the experience of mutual vulnerability and decoupled from the spheres of violence, competition, and exchange.

The ways in which erotic myths of romance and love sustain patriarchal power are well documented. The ways in which the erotic is corrupted by sadistic, masochistic, and abusive practices is also well known. Turning to the erotic to counter patriarchal mystifications is a dangerous business. Asking it to show us a path out of patriarchy treads treacherous ground. This experiment is a risky business. It appeals to the techniques of bracketing as a way of guarding against the seductions of the patriarchal erotic. Knowing the limitations of these techniques, I do not claim to be able to return to the erotic experience itself. Knowing the possibilities of these techniques, I allow that in using them we can strip the erotic of many of its current covers and that we can, in this way, retrieve the concept of ambiguity for an ethics of sexual difference.

The following passages from *The Second Sex* set my path: "In both sexes is played out the same drama of the flesh and the spirit, of finitude and transcendence; both are gnawed away by time and laid in wait for by death, they have the same essential need for one another" (SS 728); "The erotic experience is one that most poignantly discloses to human beings the ambiguity of their condition; in it they are aware of themselves as flesh and as spirit, as the other and as the subject" (SS 402); and "in the midst of carnal fever [men and women are] a consenting, a voluntary gift, an activity; they live out in their several fashions the strange ambiguity of existence made body" (SS 728).

These passages make certain things clear. First, we are returned to the questions of need and the bond. Where patriarchy equates valuing the bond with woman's neediness, in the "drama of the flesh" lovers experience and affirm their fleshed and sexed otherness to and mutual need for each other. Rather than place the value of the bond and the demands of recognition at odds with each other, lovers live the carnal bond as a fleshed supplication. Each risks being violated in their otherness. Each asks to be received by the other in their vulnerability. Each offers themselves to the other as a fleshed gift. Each lives its excess with the other. Each turns to the other in the generosity of disclosure where the aimlessness of desire immerses itself in the flows of the flesh. Here the mood of our original intentionality prevails.

Like the first intentional moment, however, the erotic is neither stable nor self-sustaining. It is soon taken up by the second moment of intentionality's desire to be God. Judgments move in to capture and stabilize the flow of the gift. A distinction is made between foreplay and "the act." The erotic is identified with the projects of intercourse, orgasm, and reproduction. Given our ambiguity, these moves are inevitable. What is not inevitable, however, are the particular interventions of patriarchy. We are not destined to forget the excessive generosities of the erotic, to forgo the gift of the flesh, or to equate risk with violence. It is not necessary to choose between the bond and recognition. No necessity drives us to value the commitment to recognition more than the commitment to the bond. Nothing requires the stabilization of sexed/gendered otherness into the patriarchal categories man and woman.

To see the erotic as the concretely lived original intentionality and to experiment with the argument that our critique of patriarchy ought to be guided by the event of erotic generosity allows us to critique established sexual differences on two fronts. First, we are able to trace the current coding of the sexual difference to the patriarchal perverse (mis)reading of the vulnerability-risk-subjectivity relationship. From the perspective of the erotic, we see that this misreading is not innocent. It is directed by the desire to evade the necessary failure of the desire to be God. By equating risk with subjectivity,

subjectivity with recognition, and recognition with violence, patriarchy pacifies those whose bodies are designated as strong. It allows them to believe that their strength will save them from their failure. It allows for the fantasy of invulnerability: the James Bond fantasy.

In patriarchy the lived reality of the sexed vulnerable subject who is always at risk before the Other and who must fail in the attempt to possess the world is exchanged for the myth of man and woman. According to this myth a man is a real subject because he takes up the risks associated with violence. Woman is defined as the weaker sex. As weaker she is deemed unfit for the risks associated with violence. Barred from engaging these risks, she is positioned as the inessential Other, the inadequate subject. It is impossible for her, insofar as she is a woman, to challenge man's position as the subject. He may be vulnerable before other men; he may lose his bid to possess the world in the world of men, but among women he is always assured of success. She will not challenge his status as the subject. It is said that she is a stranger to the world of risk. The risks of valuing the bond are rendered invisible. The risks associated with her body, the risks of childbirth for example, are said to be imposed on her by nature. The lived erotic explodes this myth of woman's passive body. It renders the risks of the bond visible. It unravels the patriarchal equation of risk, violence, and subjectivity. It shows us that the vulnerabilities of the flesh are embedded in our sexuality, that these vulnerabilities are entwined in the immediate and certain existential experience of existence, that they lie coiled within our sexually embodied human condition.

More than providing the principles of a critique, however, the erotic of the two offers positive ethical and political guidance. It leads us to formulate an ethic grounded in the principle of generosity where openness to otherness is accorded moral value. It directs us to a politics where projects of liberation and judgments of good, bad, and evil affirm our responsibility for each other in ways that remember our vulnerability to each other. The paradigm of the one subject (the whole [man] object and the part [woman] object) created by patriarchal marriage is replaced by the paradigm of the couple, where the generosity of the gift, rather than the demands of recognition, constitute the ways in which ambiguously sexed whole objects return themselves to each other.

This paradigm also challenges the assumption that only hetero-sexual couples are legitimate. On the patriarchal model, the couple merges the sexual difference of part objects into a complete whole object. As a patriarchal heterosexual couple, we are one. In Beauvoir's model the sexual difference must be refigured. Both women and men are whole ambiguous objects who bring to the couple their difference of otherness. It is difficult for us to imagine otherness along these lines. It seems to bring us back to the one. Beauvoir, however, directs us to think ambiguity where the two never coalesces into a one.

As I try to imagine the sexual difference after Beauvoir, I find it helpful to think of it as a fleshed erotic difference, which is not equiv-alent to the embodied sexual difference. Vagina and penis are but one way of encountering the erotic Other. Although Beauvoir's discus-sions of the couple in *The Second Sex* speak of erotic otherness in heterosexual terms, I find these discussions leading beyond the het-erosexual erotic. Once I bring Beauvoir's portrayal of intentionality to her descriptions of the erotic's challenge to the patriarchal het-erosexual couple, I find that the erotic difference that draws us to the drama of the flesh cannot be equated with the difference be-tween men and women. The heterosexual sexual difference is but one instance of otherness. As the receptive generosity of the original intentional moment, we engage the Other in its exuberant prolifer-ations. The erotic event registers this exuberance. Allowed to speak in its own register, it neither validates the patriarchal script of het-erosexual otherness nor legitimates the patriarchal demand that the couple be heterosexual. It explodes the patriarchal meanings of the erotic and transforms the meanings and lived experiences of other-ness. This explosion rebounds to the ways in which we figure the differences of sex/gender and to the ways in which we understand the erotic otherness of the two.

An ethic and politics guided by the principles of this lived erotic of the otherness of the two carries two injunctions. First, I am enjoined to assume the tensions of my ambiguity. Second, I am enjoined not to violate the Other's vulnerability. Together, these injunctions cre-ate the opening for a meeting between us – an opening that we might call the space of generous intersubjectivity. Within patriarchy this space is a feminine place. Taking up Beauvoir's legacy, I experiment with the possibility of transforming it from a place reserved for those who have become woman to the space of the sexual difference. As

the place of the sexual difference, this space of generous intersubjectivity affirms the value that women as woman have represented
throughout the patriarchal era – the value of the bond. It transforms
this feminine value into a value of sexual, erotic difference. It refuses
to allow the value of the bond to be perverted by the demands of a
subject committed to the intersubjectivity of violence and violation.
It refuses to allow the value of the bond to become a sacrificial value.
It rejects the idea that those who value the bond are obliged to submit
to the demands of those who claim to be God. It refuses to subordinate those who value the risks of the transcendence of disclosure
to those who value the risks of the transcendence of the project. It
refuses to sex these different modes of transcendence as either male
or female and refuses to erase the sexual differences through which
we live the ambiguity of our desire.

In entering the opening of generous intersubjectivity, men and
women allow themselves to be guided by the generosities of the
erotic event. They embrace their capacities for active passivity and
take up the risks of the flesh, the gift, and the bond. They bear witness against the myths and politics of the one that renders the existence of women doubtful by bearing witness to the experience of
the lived certainty of the two. They challenge the injustices of the
myths of femininity by practicing the justice of ambiguity and sexual
difference.[10]

NOTES

1   SS (New York: Vintage Books, 1989). For a sense of the ways in which
    "One is not born but rather becomes a woman" has become the subject
    of readings that raise these questions, see Judith Butler, "Sex and Gender
    in Simone de Beauvoir's Second Sex," Yale French Studies, 72 (1986):
    35–49 and Monique Wittig, "One is not Born a Woman," in The Straight
    Mind (Boston: Beacon, 1992), pp. 21–32. For a sense of the ways in which
    medicine and technology have also rendered these words ambiguous and
    controversial, see Ricki Anne Wilchins, Read My Lips: Sexual Subversion
    and the End of Gender (Ithaca, NY: Firebrand Books, 1997), and Suzanne
    J. Kessler, Lessons From the Intersexed (New Brunswick, NJ: Rutgers
    University Press, 1998).

2   For a discussion of the relationship between Descartes and Beauvoir, see
    Peg Simons, "Beauvoir's Early Philosophy," in Beauvoir and The Sec-
    ond Sex: Feminism, Race and The Origins of Existentialism (New York:

Roman & Littlefield, 1999), p. 202, and Nancy Bauer, *Simone de Beauvoir: Philosophy and Feminism* (New York: Columbia University Press, 2001), chapter 2.

3 See Luce Irigaray, "The Blind Spot of an Old Dream of Symmetry," in *Speculum of the Other Woman*, trans. Gillian C. Gill (Ithaca, NY: Cornell University Press, 1985), pp. 11–132.

4 See Carole Pateman, *The Disorder of Women: Democracy, Feminism and Political Theory* (Stanford, CA: Stanford University Press, 1989).

5 For a provocative discussion of the relationship between the ways in which social structures must compensate for minimizing sex differences by creating other fundamental differences, see Julia Kristeva's discussion of the Indian caste system, *Powers of Horror: An Essay on Abjection*, trans. Leon S. Rioudiez (New York: Columbia University Press, 1982), pp. 79–81.

6 Adrienne Rich finds this opening in the experience of motherhood in *Of Woman Born: Motherhood as Experience and Institution* (New York: Norton, 1996).

7 For reflections on this relationship, see Marquis de Sade, *Justine, Philosophy in the Bedroom and Other Writings*, trans. Austryn Wainhouse (New York: Grove, 1966).

8 For an extended discussion of intentionality, Beauvoir's muted voice, and the heterosexual couple see, Debra Bergoffen, *The Philosophy of Simone de Beauvoir: Gendered Phenomenologies, Erotic Generosities* (Albany, NY: State University of New York Press, 1997).

9 For a detailed discussion of this phenomenon, see Debra Bergoffen, "Disrupting the Metonymy of Gender," in *Resistance, Flight, Creation: Feminist Enactments of French Philosophy*, ed. Dorothea Olkowski (Ithaca, NY: Cornell University Press, 2000), pp. 97–112.

10 For a powerful account of the way in which a traditional feminine place can become the site of a transvaluation that challenges injustice, see Jean Bethke Elshtain, "Mothers of the Disappeared: An Encounter with Antigone's Daughters," in *Representations of Motherhood*, ed. Donna Bassin, Margaret Honey, and Meryle Mahrer (New Haven: Yale University Press, 1994).

13 Beauvoir and biology: a second look

Among the many eminently quotable lines from the corpus of Sigmund Freud are those concerning his supposition about the response of the young girl when she first sees the penis of a sibling or playmate: "She makes her judgement and her decision in a flash. She has seen it and knows that she is without it and wants to have it."[1] Even if a generous reader were to grant Freud his contentious supposition, a question remains: what does the girl see, and judge, on a second, or a third, or even a fourth look? According to Simone de Beauvoir, Freud's judgment about the role anatomy plays in the formation of the psychic life of women is based on "a masculine model" and envy "could not arise from a simple anatomical comparison." "[T]his outgrowth," Beauvoir continues, "this weak little rod of flesh can in itself inspire [young girls] only with indifference, or even disgust. The little girl's covetousness, when it exists, results from a previous evaluation of virility. Freud takes this for granted, when it should be accounted for."[2]

Taking little for granted, Beauvoir argues that whether girls will judge the penis to be enviable, "insignificant, or even laughable" (SS 300) will depend on its importance, its symbolic and social value "within the totality of their lives." In any event, whatever attitude a girl may adopt, "it is wrong to assert that a biological datum is concerned" (SS 307). Unlike Freud, Beauvoir endeavors to offer a comprehensive account of girls' and women's desires, attitudes, and judgments as these are formed within the totality of their always situated existences. Keeping faith with the existentialist assertion that "existence precedes essence," Beauvoir offers the following caution to readers of The Second Sex: "When I use the words woman or feminine I obviously refer to no archetype, no changeless essence whatever; the reader must understand the phrase 'in the present state of education and custom' after most of my statements" (SS 31, emphasis original). Apparently forgetting this caution, or perhaps understandably being perplexed by the qualifying phrase "after *most* of my statements" (but which?), many contributors to the critical appraisal of *The Second Sex* have judged Beauvoir's comments on biology, the female body, and femininity to be both essentialist and derogatory.[3]

This chapter argues that despite the ever-increasing amount of commentary on Beauvoir and biology, many critics continue to over-look vital elements in her account of the role played by biology in being, or, as she insists, "becoming," a woman. Such critics mis-interpret Beauvoir's view of womanhood and thus fail to note the continuing relevance of her philosophy for present-day readers. This chapter is in four sections. First, I consider the broad aims of *The Second Sex*, including Beauvoir's central question: why has woman occupied the place of "the Other" in human culture and history? Second, I offer an account of Beauvoir's views on the importance of the cultural meanings of biology, along with a critical appraisal of some exemplary feminist commentary that interprets these views as favoring a radical social constructionism. The third section ques-tions the widely held assumption that Beauvoir was the mother of the sex–gender distinction. Moreover, I suggest that her actual views about sexual difference are more complex than this binary distinc-tion allows. Finally, I argue that Beauvoir's views on biology – on a "second look" – may yield a more radical view of the human subject than feminists have hitherto supposed her to have held.

WOMAN AS "OTHER"

One wonders if women still exist, if they will always exist, whether or not it is desirable that they should ... [SS 13]

Commentators on *The Second Sex* often fail to note the degree to which its concerns are ethically driven. The aim of the study is to determine what is a woman, or what is her present "situation," and to explore what she may become, or her "possibilities." How-ever, this aim is not undertaken in a vacuum; it is not a disinter-ested search for knowledge. Rather, *The Second Sex* is animated by values, particularly freedom, its highest value, but also by the desire for solidarity, particularly between men and women, and finally, by a call for liberation. The ethical dimension that structures the text is made clear in its introduction. Echoing the sentiments of John Stuart Mill, Beauvoir writes: "I am interested in the fortunes of the individual as defined not in terms of happiness but in terms of liberty" (SS 29). Rejecting happiness as an adequate indicator of the worth of a life because "[i]t is not too clear just what the word *happy* really means and still less what true values it may mask," Beauvoir favors instead the perspective of an existentialist ethics. From this perspective, "[e]very subject plays his part as such specifically through exploits or projects that serve as a mode of transcendence; he achieves liberty only through a continual reaching out towards other liberties. There is no justification for present existence other than its expansion into an indefinitely open future" (SS 28–29).

From this existentialist perspective, human being has no fixed nature, no essence, no determined way of being. As will become apparent, this does not mean that biology, history, and culture are irrelevant to what a human being may become, but such constitutive elements of one's overall situation cannot dictate *which* meanings, significances, and values will be chosen. One's biological sex may be experienced as a boon or a burden, one's skin color may be lived in pride or in shame, and one's social status may be lived in acquiescence or revolt. If woman's being is to be understood, then an account must be offered of both "what humanity has made of the human female" (SS 69) *and* how any individual woman has become what she currently is through the exercise of her freedom to form attitudes and commit herself to projects in the face of her total situation. For some individuals it may be that the total situation in which they "become women" is so constrained by social, economic, and historical factors that they are prevented from exercising their freedom. This is a case of oppression. However, in other circumstances an individual may consent to the weight of free choice being carried by another, in which case the individual is morally culpable. Beauvoir judges both cases to be "an absolute evil" (SS 29). One of the dominant threads in *The Second Sex* is the exploration of which kind of absolute evil (oppression or moral culpability) marks the case of woman. Predictably, this question does not have a straightforward answer. Beauvoir's analysis of "woman as the Other" and woman's responsibility, or not, for this status, cannot be understood without some account of her philosophy of intersubjective relations.

Adapting the philosophy of Hegel and Sartre, Beauvoir holds that "[t]he category of the *Other* is as primordial as consciousness itself" (*SS* 16, emphasis original). Furthermore, "the subject can be posed only in being opposed – he sets himself up as the essential, as opposed to the other, the inessential, the object" (*SS* 17). In the case of sexual difference, the self–other opposition is intensified because "the duality of the sexes, like any duality, gives rise to conflict" (*SS* 21). However, the hostility of each subject toward every other subject does not preclude the possibility of "being with" (*Mitsein*) others. There is nothing in human ontology to preclude reciprocal relations, although such relations will be held "sometimes in enmity, sometimes in amity, always in a state of tension" (*SS* 93).

The puzzle, for Beauvoir, is to understand why the relations between women and men have reified in the oppositional stance and why woman has been locked into the subordinate pole of the Other, the inessential, the object. This brief account of Beauvoir's views on intersubjective relations should serve to demonstrate the extent to which *The Second Sex* is, first and foremost, a book of ethics, that is, a book that is concerned to investigate, first, the moral responsibilities of free human subjects, second, the joint evils of oppression and complicity with one's oppression, third, the scope for solidarity between subjects whose primordial stance is to oppose each other and attempt to reduce the Other to a thing, and, finally, the means through which those who have been objectified and subordinated may liberate themselves (and, *ipso facto*, also their oppressors).

Given this interpretation of *The Second Sex* as an ethical project, the structure of the book may be understood as an attempt to account for the various elements that constitute the situation of women as the "Other" and to explain how this situation figures in women's capacities to exercise freedom and so transform the sociohistorical status they have inherited from their foremothers. The upshot of Beauvoir's analysis is her claim that the outline of an individual woman's life will be structured, although not determined, by her biological, economic, historical, and cultural situation, by the attitudes of others, and by the affective characteristics and creative intelligence she brings to her situation. In the final analysis, none of these factors may meaningfully be separated from the others, and taken together they form the contours that constitute the overall shape of a life.

BIOLOGY, THE "BODY," AND SOCIAL CONSTRUCTIONISM

Woman, like man, *is* her body; but her body is something other than herself. [*SS* 61, emphasis original]

The existential and phenomenological framework that Beauvoir brings to her analysis of woman forecloses the possibility of any suggestion that woman's nature, character, or situation can be reduced to her biological make-up. Human freedom is inescapable, and one's biology can offer no certain indication of what one should choose or which projects one should adopt. The capacity to bear a child, even being a mother, dictates neither how to "live" such capacities or roles nor what one may decide to do with one's life in the future. This is because, for Beauvoir, an "existent *is* nothing other than what he does; the possible does not extend beyond the real, essence does not precede existence; in pure subjectivity, the human being *is not anything*" (*SS* 287, emphasis original). Although biology will play a crucial role in deciding one's health, one's sex, one's strength, even one's life span, it does not, and according to Beauvoir cannot, determine how one interprets these factors or how they are lived by the free subject. This is why Beauvoir can state that biological facts "are one of the keys to the understanding of woman" and "constitute an essential element in her situation," on the one hand, and "deny that they establish for her a fixed and inevitable destiny," on the other (*SS* 65).

The section in book 1 entitled "The Data of Biology" has been the focus of decades of strident criticism of Beauvoir's alleged essentialism. At the same time, it has provided material for those who have interpreted Beauvoir as a social constructionist. It is not difficult to see why. Consider the following statements as support for the first, essentialist, view.

the individuality of the female is opposed by the interests of the species... [*SS* 57]

From birth, the species seems to have taken possession of woman and tends to tighten its grasp. [SS 58]

From puberty to menopause woman is the theatre of a play that unfolds within her and in which she is not personally concerned. [SS 60]

here we find *the most striking conclusion of this survey*: namely, that woman is of all mammalian females at once the one who is most profoundly alienated (her individuality the prey to outside forces), and the one who most violently resists this alienation; in no other is enslavement of the organism to reproduction more imperious or more unwillingly accepted. [SS 64, emphasis added]

These statements appear to endorse a view of women's biological disadvantage and to tell a story of an intrinsically alienated relation between the female body and womanhood: "her body is something other than herself" (SS 61). Considered in isolation, they also pose a very serious problem for the philosophical framework favored by Beauvoir: existentialist phenomenology. Beauvoir quotes Merleau-Ponty's view that "I am my body" and that my body may be likened to "a preliminary sketch for my total being" (SS 61, n. 10). The body, she adds, should be understood as the "instrument of our grasp upon the world" (SS 65). Where does this leave woman's grasp on the world or the identity between her body and her subjectivity? In order to respond adequately to this question it is necessary to recall that brute fact alone cannot determine human action. It is the human subject's own choice how to read and use the cards she has been dealt in life. In some ways the card game is a good metaphor for the situation of the human subject. She cannot determine the conventions that govern the game, the value of the cards, or the hand she is dealt, but she is nevertheless free to choose how she plays the game. Will she be defeated in advance if she feels she has been dealt a bad hand, or will she interpret it as a challenge? Will she play a "safe" game or a reckless one? It is through the attitudes she forms, and the manner of exercising her freedom, that woman will decide how her body is lived.

Now consider the following statements, which support the second, social constructionist view.

facts cannot be denied – but in themselves they have no significance. Once we adopt the human perspective, interpreting the body on the basis of

existence, biology becomes an abstract science; whenever the physiological fact (for instance, muscular inferiority) takes on meaning, this meaning
is at once seen as dependent on a whole context. [*SS* 66–67]

it is not upon physiology that values can be based; rather, the facts of biology
take on the values that the existent bestows upon them. [*SS* 68–69]

Thus we must view the facts of biology in the light of an ontological, economic, social, and psychological context. [*SS* 69]

It is not nature that defines woman; it is she who defines herself by dealing
with nature on her own account in her emotional life. [*SS* 69]

It is not easy to know how to balance the two kinds of statement.
The temptation, of course, is to remove the ambiguity by being se-
lective in one's reading and to thereby stress one set of statements
at the expense of the other. This has often been the tendency in
feminist scholarship on Beauvoir and biology, a tendency that I treat
below.

The unclarity of Beauvoir's thought invites these kinds of unsat-
isfactory "either/or" feminist readings. Such interpretations *either*
insist on Beauvoir's social constructionism, because the ambiguity
appears to be removed if one argues for value "all the way down"
(where human life is concerned, there are no "facts" of the matter), *or*
they interpret Beauvoir's negative comments on female embodiment
as embarrassing evidence of her "essentialism" and her inability to
escape misogynist evaluations of the female body.[4]

In a pathbreaking essay, originally published in 1986, Judith Butler
offered an interpretation of *The Second Sex* that has greatly influenced an entire generation's attempt to theorize "woman" and "the
body."[5] The processes through which we become women, according
to Butler, have not to do with the facts of female biology but rather
with interpretation and social values. Butler's contentious claim is
that "If being a woman is one cultural interpretation of being female, and if that interpretation is in no way necessitated by being
female, then it appears that the female body is the *arbitrary* locus
of the *gender* 'woman'" ("Sex and Gender," 30, emphasis added).
Taking the account of the "body as situation" as the definitive word
in Beauvoir's account of human subjectivity, Butler argues that "the
body is a *field of interpretive possibilities* ... a peculiar nexus of culture and choice" ("Sex and Gender," 38, emphasis original). She

understands this interpretative field to involve two aspects: first, the body is "a locus of cultural interpretations," and second, it is also "the situation of having to take up and interpret that set of received interpretations" ("Sex and Gender," 38). Given that Butler has interpreted Beauvoir as saying "woman" should be understood as a (culturally variable) gender, arguably it follows that "it is our genders we become, and not our bodies" ("Sex and Gender," 32).

Something has gone awry in this account of the "body as situation," at least insofar as it purports to be a reading of Beauvoir. There are two points that require further analysis. First, does Beauvoir hold that the female body is the arbitrary locus of the "gender" woman? Second, is it viable to maintain that the embodied situation of woman amounts to a series of ongoing (re)interpretations (or, "culture and choice")? In each case Butler's views tell only part of the story. First, the idea that the relation between the lived experience of women and the female body is an arbitrary one is directly contradicted by Beauvoir. She holds that in spite of cultural or historical variability in interpretations of sexual difference, a certain relation between the female body and womanhood will always remain. For example, woman's eroticism, and therefore her sexual world, have a special form of their own and therefore cannot fail to engender a sensuality, a sensitivity, of a special nature. This means that her relations to her own body, to that of the male, to the child, will never be identical with those the male bears to his own body, to that of the female, and to the child (SS 740).

Although it would be a mistake to read too much into this passage, Beauvoir is certainly claiming a link between the specificity of the female body, and its capacities, and the way womanhood will be lived in *any* and *every* sociohistorical situation. To maintain, as Beauvoir does, that the capacities of the body – understood in naturalistic or biological terms – always require interpretation, is not equivalent to maintaining that the body is itself an interpretation or pure social construction. Butler is right to argue that "'being' female and 'being' a woman are two very different sorts of being" ("Sex and Gender," 31). However, the leap to the claim that there is only an arbitrary relation between the female body and the "gender" woman cannot easily be justified as a reading of Beauvoir. Moreover, as I will argue, Beauvoir does not understand "woman" to be a *gender* category at all.[6]

Second, to interpret Beauvoir's account of the body as situation in terms of "a field of interpretive possibilities" (or as a nexus of culture and choice) fails to attend sufficiently to the seriousness with which Beauvoir treats historical materialism and economics. The economic conditions of any given society – the means through which it reproduces its material conditions of existence – are a crucial element in the situation of its members. In the case of the "primitive horde" or "nomads," whom Beauvoir treats in book 1, it is the *fact* of women's reproductive capacities and the *fact* of man's superior strength that cannot help but become socially significant. Situated sexual differences constitute the conditions that require interpretation. In some conditions the physical costs for women of their reproductive capacities may render them incapable of adequately providing for themselves or their offspring. Beauvoir refers to such conditions as ones in which "we have a first fact heavily freighted with consequences" (SS 94). The less mastery a society has over its environment, the more limited will be the range of possible interpretations of the biological differences between the sexes. Furthermore, the body will bear the consequences of the values that are bestowed on it, thus forming an interactive loop between bodies and values. It is surely not a matter of mere interpretation when a society prefers to feed boys rather than girls in times of famine, with the result that men's health and longevity outstrips that of women. The power of social values to influence the material well-being of individuals, and thus their life chances, is undoubtedly one of the reasons why Beauvoir states that oppression is "an absolute evil."

Beauvoir's broad historical account of human civilization is intended to show that in some circumstances the different biologies of men and women will inevitably take on social significances of enormous import. Her point in *The Second Sex* is not that the natural body has no hold on social values or that it is "value all the way down." Rather, her argument concerns women in the West in the mid-twentieth century and the possibilities open to them to create a new future beyond what she takes to be the "historical facts" of their past conditions of existence. A historical fact cannot, she insists, establish "an eternal truth; it can only indicate a situation that is historical in nature precisely because it is undergoing change" (SS 723).

Like Butler, Julie K. Ward makes a significant contribution to Beauvoir scholarship by carefully articulating the two senses of the "body" she finds in *The Second Sex*. Ward is concerned to address critics who read Beauvoir's account of the female body as essentialist. She advises that when reading *The Second Sex* she will follow the heuristic principle of looking for a deeper meaning capable of reconciling apparently contradictory claims. The two senses of the body she finds in *The Second Sex* are, first, "the body conceived of as inert matter or stuff, 'a thing,'" and second, the body as "situation," that is, the way in which "the physical body is experienced, given the social and economic conditions."[7] This distinction is certainly present in Beauvoir's analysis, and it serves to challenge any view that would claim to derive a woman's role or status from her biological capacities. At the same time, the distinction is used to articulate how some of those capacities may be highlighted or constrained by economic and social conditions.[8] However, the distinction does not warrant the claim that, along with gender, "the body itself is socially constructed" ("Two Senses of 'Body,'" 226). Nor does it support the view "that there is no 'natural' body" ("Two Senses of 'Body,'" 238). When confronted with the either/or problem – either social constructionism or essentialism – Ward, like Butler, opts for one side (social constructionism) over the other.

Social constructionist interpretations of Beauvoir rely on statements such as "the body is not a *thing*, it is a situation" (*SS* 66, emphasis original). This statement occurs in the context of Beauvoir's reflections on woman's possibilities and capabilities by contrast with what she currently is or has been. In the context of existentialism, this may seem disingenuous given that a subject is and should be judged by what she does, not by what she could do. Then again, insofar as existentialism is concerned with the free subject, "a being whose nature is transcendent action, we can never close the books" (*SS* 66). It is in this context that Beauvoir goes on to add:

Nevertheless it will be said that *if* the body is not a thing, it is a situation, as viewed in the perspective I am adopting – that of Heidegger, Sartre and Merleau-Ponty: it is the instrument of our grasp upon the world, *a limiting factor for our projects*. Woman is weaker than man, she has less muscular strength, fewer red blood corpuscles, less lung capacity, she runs more slowly, can lift less heavy weights, can compete with man in hardly any sport; she cannot stand up to him in a fight. To all this weakness must be added the instability, the lack of control, and the fragility already discussed: *these are facts.* [*SS* 69, emphasis added]

Of course, Beauvoir then goes on to argue that such facts do not carry fixed meanings – it is the free acts of individuals, the choices made in society, and the material contexts of life that will determine their significance. Moreover, the facts themselves are not stable: in contemporary life we are beginning to see what an enormous difference may be made to women's sporting achievements when they are allowed to enjoy nutrition, training, and opportunities similar to those of men. Beauvoir's argument is that from the point of view of the free existent, conscious of herself and her situation, facts lack any force to determine her to do or become this rather than that kind of subject, because, as she maintains, "the human being *is not anything*" (*SS* 287, emphasis original). We could add, "apart from what she freely makes of herself, given the facts of her existence." Even in the context of discussing biology, femininity, and womanhood, Beauvoir has the ethical dimension of existentialism firmly in place.

For her, "becoming woman" does involve elements of choice and interpretation, because the human existent always exists within a particular culture, with specific economic, historical, and social features, which must be negotiated. Understanding sexual difference in terms of gender, performativity, interpretation, and choice is only part of Beauvoir's ambiguous story, because, for her, the whole story would involve understanding "becoming (a) woman" as an *ethical* project – a project that is necessarily an ethics of *ambiguity*.[9]

THE SEX–GENDER DISTINCTION AND THE CONCEPT OF WOMAN

The division of the sexes is a biological fact, not an event in human history. [*SS* 19]

Beauvoir is widely thought to be the mother of the sex–gender distinction, that is, the distinction that allows one to separate nature from nurture by way of positing women's biological nature, or their sex, on one hand, and women's socially constructed identity, or their gender, on the other. For example, Butler argued that Beauvoir's famous phrase, "One is not born but rather becomes a woman," "distinguishes sex from gender and suggests that gender is an aspect of identity gradually acquired" ("Sex and Gender," 30). However, despite the readings offered by Butler and others, it is doubtful whether Beauvoir understood "woman" in terms of *gender*.[10] If Beauvoir were to have made a sex–gender distinction, there is much evidence in *The Second Sex* to suggest that she would have made it along lines other than those drawn by contemporary feminism. It is not woman or women that Beauvoir identifies with gender categories throughout *The Second Sex*, but, rather, femininity, that is, those ways of behaving, those typical traits and values, that conventionally mark women off from men. The typical qualities that Beauvoir notes throughout her study include dependence, passivity, weakness, docility, "neatness," narcissism, inferiority, timidity, coquetry, and impotence. It is not woman, *simpliciter*, or the female body, *simpliciter*, that she wishes to criticize, but, rather, those (gendered) ways of being that attach to woman (understood both as "symbol" and as the individual concrete existent) and the female body (the material "ground" of the existent) and that are operative in depriving women of the opportunity to become authentic, ethical subjects. Such deprivation functions through the forcible confinement of woman to the negative pole of man's positive self-conception and by symbolically and actually denying them access to the (supposedly neutral) conception of what it is to be a free human subject. Another name for this deprivation is oppression. If women have the means to free themselves from this social and historical confinement but do not act, then they become complicit in their own oppression and are morally culpable. Hence "becoming a woman," for Beauvoir – at least, for women who live in the West in the mid-twentieth century, and after – is an inescapably ethical process.

On Beauvoir's account, it is femininity itself – or, at least, femininity as constituted under oppressive conditions – that should be abandoned. She makes her view clear in the conclusion to *The Second Sex*, where she remarks that the quarrel between the sexes "will go on as long as men and women fail to recognize each other as equals; that is to say, *as long as femininity is perpetuated as such*" (*SS* 727–28, emphasis added). It is femininity, not woman, that is the proper locus of gender and the target of Beauvoir's barbs, because she understands socially sanctioned femininity in terms of "mutilation" (*SS* 429). Femininity is "mutilating" because it denies women the opportunity to exercise their *human* capacities for choice. Psychoanalysis, for example, displays a bias of this sort against women when it uncritically accepts "the masculine–feminine categories as society currently defines them." Beauvoir continues:

Whenever she behaves as a human being, she is declared to be identifying herself with the male. Her activities in sports, politics, and intellectual matters, her sexual desire for other women, are all interpreted as a "masculine protest"; the common refusal to take account of the values towards which she aims, or transcends herself, evidently leads to the conclusion that she is, as subject, making an inauthentic choice. [SS 428]

"The chief misunderstanding underlying this line of interpretation," Beauvoir retorts, "is that it is *natural* for the female human being to make herself a *feminine* woman" (SS 428, emphasis original). Presumably, it is her views on femininity that explain her otherwise perplexing approval of the "'modern' woman [who] accepts masculine values" (SS 727). This is to say that where men have audaciously occupied both the masculine pole and the neutral, human, middle ground, it is right that women should wrest back those values that express activity and transcendence as values that are appropriate to them also.

There are, then, at least three terms at work in *The Second Sex*: the "female human being," "femininity," and "woman," and Beauvoir says some surprising things about the connections between these terms – things that challenge a neat sex–gender divide. For example, in her discussion of the post-menopausal woman, she writes: "she is no longer the prey of overwhelming forces; she is herself, she and her body are one. It is sometimes said that women of a certain age constitute 'a third sex'; and, in truth, while they are not males, *they are no longer females*" (SS 63, emphasis added). There is clearly a good deal more ambiguity in Beauvoir's account of "the second sex" than some commentators have allowed. Table 1 attempts to capture at least five different ways in which Beauvoir describes existing as a female, as feminine, and as a woman. There may, of course, be other permutations that the table fails to reflect (or that she does not note). The value in the rows registers the presence or absence for each individual (1–5) of the three characteristics that head each column. Row 1 describes a biological human female who is feminine and who meets the normative criteria for womanhood current in her cultural, historical situation. Row 2 describes a biological human female who is not feminine but who nevertheless identifies herself, and is identified by others, as a woman. Row 3

Table 1 *States of existence*

Female	Feminine	Woman
1. Yes	Yes	Yes
2. Yes	No	Yes
3. Yes	No	No
4. No	Yes	Yes
5. No	No	Yes

describes a biological human female who is not feminine and does not identify, and is not identified by others, as a woman. Row 4 describes a post-menopausal woman who is feminine and who identifies herself, and is identified by others, as a woman, that is, those who occupy row 1, and who live long enough, will in time inevitably occupy row 4. (Some may want to argue that certain transgender individuals also belong in this row.) Row 5 describes a post-menopausal woman who is not feminine but who nevertheless identifies herself and is identified by others as a woman, that is, those who occupy row 2, and who live long enough, will in time inevitably occupy row 5.

It is difficult to see how the notion of "woman" in table 1 may be understood in terms of the sex–gender distinction; at the same time it seems to be the case, as mentioned above, that the female body does have a crucial role to play in what it means to become a woman. If the sex–gender distinction is an inappropriate grid to impose on *The Second Sex*, what would constitute a felicitous reading of "becoming woman"? Clearly, such a reading must pay due respect to: the importance of biology; the meanings, interpretations and values – both cultural and personal – that attach to biology; the psychological, phenomenological, and comportmental elements of being "feminine"; and, finally, the situated free human existent, who is designated "woman."

In a recent paper that addresses the notorious problem of "essentialism" in contemporary feminist theory, Natalie Stoljar offers an ingenious and very promising account of woman as a "cluster concept."[11] Stoljar is not directly concerned with Beauvoir or with *The Second Sex*, but the problems she addresses in large part grow out of the ways in which that text has been problematically interpreted.

Furthermore, Stoljar's theory of woman as a "cluster concept" does pay due respect to the *desiderata* listed above.

Stoljar derives the idea of a cluster concept from Wittgenstein's notion of family resemblances, that is, the idea that some things in the world, although not identical, resemble each other closely enough to bear a common designation. The favored example of family resemblance is that of the concept "game," which may include a diversity of activities (jumping, running) and objects (tennis rackets, footballs, chess pieces) but nevertheless constitute a recognizably common practice. Stoljar's account of "woman" as a cluster concept is composed by four general elements:

First, womaness is attributed on the basis of female sex. Female sex includes having the characteristics of a human female (XX chromosome, sex characteristics, and general morphology) and having other bodily characteristics such as gait or voice quality. Secondly, a range of phenomenological features, or aspects of what it *feels* like to be a woman, or are typically associated with women: for example, physical feelings, like having menstrual cramps ... The phenomenology also includes feelings which are the product of social factors, like ... fear of rape. Thirdly, there are roles such as wearing typical female dress, or being oppressed on the basis of one's sex ... Finally, there are self-attributions and the attributions of others ... calling oneself a woman and being called a woman. [Stoljar, "Essence, Identity," 283–84, emphasis original]

Just as any given game need not satisfy all the elements that fall under the concept "game," so any given individual woman need not satisfy every element of the concept "woman." Stoljar lists five advantages of the model she puts forward. First, although her concept "woman" crucially involves female biology, it is not necessary for every individual woman to satisfy that conditon, provided she does satisfy enough of the other elements. As Stoljar explains, to treat woman "as a cluster concept explains both why female sex is centrally important to the notion of woman and how individuals can be women without being of the female sex" ("Essence, Identity," 285). Second, being a woman becomes a matter of degree in this model. Third, being a woman is not understood as wholly a matter of social relations – or "values all the way down" – since it allows a role for the "natural body" and biological sex difference. Fourth, the cluster concept may explain how women from very different contexts may nevertheless identify with each other on the basis of "felt similarities" without denying the real differences (such as class, race, age, sexuality, ethnicity) that divide women. Finally, although the class or type "woman" really is a resemblance class, it nevertheless includes many constructed elements and so is a revisable concept. In the context of *The Second Sex*, it may be said that "woman" is a concept that entails a "becoming."

Stoljar's innovative treatment of "woman" as a cluster concept is a more productive way of interpreting Beauvoir's views on "woman" in *The Second Sex*. It pays full due to the notion of "situation" and so lends coherence to the concept "woman" without denying the variety of situations within which individual women assert their freedoms. Her treatment of "woman" includes biological facts, but does so not in a reductive fashion.[12] However, Stoljar is not directly concerned with the issues that dominate *The Second Sex*, and her notion of woman as a "cluster concept" has only indirect implications for "becoming woman" as an ethical project. The final section of this chapter returns to this issue.

BIOLOGY, AMBIGUITY, AND ETHICS

Science regards any characteristic as a reaction dependent in part upon *situation*. [SS 14, emphasis original]

I have suggested that important aspects of Beauvoir's "philosophy of woman," which are relevant to women today, have been overlooked in contemporary interpretations of *The Second Sex*. In particular, I have argued that the essentialism–social constructionism debate that tracks the sex–gender distinction has overshadowed the ethical dimensions of Beauvoir's account of "becoming woman." Part of the explanation for why these debates have been so dominant in contemporary feminism is because naturalist or biological accounts of human nature often are understood to cancel human freedom and social agency. It is clear that Beauvoir did not share this view of nature or biology. For her, the situation of the existent is composed of both facts and values, both nature and culture, both biology and consciousness.

The epigraph to this section would suggest that Beauvoir was not unaware of the interdependent ways in which the two terms of each pair (namely, facts/values, nature/culture) may be understood. More-over, her philosophical perspective was avowedly antidualist. More importantly, perhaps, the incessant play between the two terms of a pair, say, nature and culture, is what constitutes our situation as always ambiguous, always involving a free "becoming," rather than mere "being." Restoring this essential ambiguity to *The Second Sex* opens it to contemporary research in biology that supports the essentially indeterminate character of the nature–culture complex. Susan Oyama, for example, has introduced the term *constructivist interactionism* to describe her view that organisms and their environments develop codependently and are codefining. She views nature "as a result, not an initial condition; multiple, not unitary; and inseparable from particular developmental circumstances."[13] For Oyama, "organisms organize their surroundings even as they are organized by them."[14] This idea challenges the view that where human life is concerned, nature is always already culture, or the view that there is no natural body, precisely because to say these things continues a dualistic view of life that (some) contemporary science rejects.[15]

Charlene Seigfried has suggested that Beauvoir's notion of "the body not as a thing but as situation, [provides] a better model not only for cultural explanations, but for biological explanations as well," and she cites some promising feminist work in contemporary evolutionary biology as heading in the right direction.[16] Although Seigfried is doubtful that Beauvoir's own researches into the biological sciences are of much value today, there remains much to be commended in Beauvoir's characterizations of all the domains of human knowledge. For one thing, she always took up a stance of epistemic modesty – there are facts, of course, but these facts are constantly undergoing change; there are truths, but these truths are not static. Restoring this essential ambiguity to the human condition also returns the ethical concerns of *The Second Sex* to center stage.

Beauvoir shows how the situation of woman – her biology, her history, her economic, social, and symbolic context, *and* man's desire to be sovereign subject[17] – have combined to make her "the Other." The questions she puts to her readers in the introduction – "How can a human being in woman's situation attain fulfillment? What roads are open to her? Which are blocked? How can independence be recovered in a state of dependency? What circumstances limit woman's liberty and how can they be overcome?" (*SS* 29) – act as incitements to break free from the role of "Other" and reach beyond the present "into an indefinitely open future" (SS 29). What women's future possibilities are cannot be known in advance because there is no (fixed) truth of the matter. And who knows this better than a woman.

Woman does not entertain the positive belief that the truth is something *other* than men claim; she recognizes, rather, that there *is not* fixed truth. It is not only the changing nature of life that makes her suspicious of the principle of constant identity, nor is it the magic phenomena with which she is surrounded that destroy the notion of causality. It is at the heart of the masculine world itself, it is in herself as belonging to this world that she comes upon the ambiguity of all principle, of all value, of everything that exists. [SS 624, emphasis original]

Perhaps the meaning, not to mention the truth, of *The Second Sex* will always involve a necessary incompleteness. The meaning of "woman," after all, is a meaning-becoming, and Beauvoir herself argued that it is women who collectively shall decide their own future. It was a similar thought, no doubt, that prompted her to write, just ten years after the publication of *The Second Sex*: "If my book has helped women, it is because it expressed them, *and they in turn gave it its truth.*"[18]

NOTES

I would like to thank the following people for their valuable comments and for help with references: Paul Patton, Linnell Secomb, Natalie Stoljar, and Elisabeth Thomas. My thanks to Claudia Card for her patience and generosity.

1 Sigmund Freud, "Some Psychical Consequences of the Anatomical Distinction Between the Sexes," in *The Standard Edition of the Complete Psychological Works of Sigmund Freud*, trans. and ed. James Strachey (London: Hogarth, 1978 [1925]), xix: 252.
2 Simone de Beauvoir, *The Second Sex*, trans. H. M. Parshley (Harmondsworth: Penguin, 1975), p. 73 (emphasis added).
3 See, for example, Judith Okely, *Simone de Beauvoir: A Re-reading* (London: Virago, 1986), pp. 89–99.
4 For a comprehensive account of the reception of *The Second Sex* by 'second-wave' feminists, see Jo-Ann Pilardi, "Feminists Read *The Second Sex*," in *Feminist Interpretations of Simone de Beauvoir*, ed. Margaret A. Simons (University Park, PA: Pennsylvania State University Press, 1995), pp. 29–43.

5 Judith Butler, "Sex and Gender in Simone de Beauvior's *Second Sex*," reprinted in *Simone de Beauvoir. A Critical Reader*, ed. Elizabeth Fallaize (London and New York: Routledge, 1998), pp. 29-42. Further references to this article will appear in parentheses in the text.

6 Other theorists have made this point. Most strikingly, Stella Sandford, who asks, "Is there a sex/gender distinction in *The Second Sex*?" and responds that "the notion of 'woman' in *The Second Sex* is not simply translatable into the category of 'gender', indeed...it cuts across or problematizes the traditional sex/gender distinction." Stella Sandford, "Contingent Ontologies: Sex, Gender and 'Woman' in Simone de Beauvoir and Judith Butler," *Radical Philosophy*, 97 (Sept./Oct. 1999): 21. Many thanks to Elisabeth Thomas for bringing this article to my attention.

7 Julie K. Ward, "Beauvoir's Two Senses of 'Body' in *The Second Sex*," in Simons, *Feminist Interpretations*, p. 231. Further references to this article will appear in parentheses in the text.

8 Seigfried puts this well, arguing that for Beauvoir, "Even though values and meaning take up and transform biological facts, such facts in turn exercise a limiting function on the range of options available. For humans, choice is decisive, but does not work in a vacuum, but out of actual situations." Charlene Haddock Seigfried, "Second Sex: Second Thoughts," in *Hypatia Reborn: Essays in Feminist Philosophy*, ed. Azizah Y. al-Hibri and Margaret A. Simons (Bloomington, IN: Indiana University Press, 1990), p. 318.

9 Claudia Card argues along similar lines when she suggests thinking about sexual orientation in terms of authenticity and responsibility in the context of Beauvoir's comments on "lesbian attitudes" in *The Second Sex*. See Card, "Lesbian Attitudes and *The Second Sex*," in al-Hibri and Simons, *Hypatia Reborn*, pp. 290-99. See also Toril Moi, *Simone de Beauvoir: The Making of an Intellectual Woman* (Oxford: Blackwell, 1994), chapter 6, in which Moi argues for the important role of ambiguity in *The Second Sex*.

10 To complicate the issue, there is a translation problem at stake here. Several theorists have pointed to the fact that in French there are no straightforward terms to translate sex and gender. Sandford ("Contingent Ontologies"), for example, writes: "In *The Second Sex* one finds the words *sexe* (obviously), *la femme* or *les femmes* (woman, or women), *la féminité* (femininity, a noun), *féminin/féminine* (an adjective) and *le femelle*, or *les femelles* (the female or females), also *femelle* as an adjective, often with the word *humaine* – that is, in phrases such as 'the human female.'" See also Toril Moi, *Sexual/Textual Politics* (London: Methuen, 1985) p. 97, who understands this translation problem to have

important political consequences for the reception of "French feminisms" in Anglophone contexts.

11 Natalie Stoljar, "Essence, Identity, and the Concept of Woman," *Philosophical Topics*, 23, 2 (fall 1995): 261–94. Further references to this article will appear in parentheses in the text.

12 Indeed, Stoljar is happy to admit the transgender character Dil, from
the film *The Crying Game*, into the type "woman" (even though Dil
satisfies the conditions somewhat marginally).

13 Susan Oyama, *The Ontogeny of Information: Developmental Systems
and Evolution* (Durham, NC: Duke University Press, 2000), p. 125.

14 ibid., p. 169.

15 Susan Oyama, *Evolution's Eye: A Systems View of the Biology–Culture
Divide* (Durham, NC: Duke University Press, 2000), pp. 180–81.

16 See Seigfried, "Second Sex: Second Thoughts," p. 311. Nancy Tuana has
offered a similar view about the need for contemporary feminism to
move beyond the "either/or" stance of essentialism vs. constructionism. She writes: "We must develop frameworks which will enable us
to see biological and cultural adaptation as interdependent processes.
Cultural innovations may have biological consequences which in turn
may have cultural consequences, and so on." Nancy Tuana, "Re-fusing
Nature/Nurture," reprinted in al-Hibri and Simons, *Hypatia Reborn*,
pp. 84–85.

17 This chapter has not considered the ethical responsibilities of men
in relation to the situation of women. Beauvoir is very clear on this
question – men are complicit in perpetuating the situation of woman-
as-Other. For a sample of some of her more damning criticisms of men's
roles in women's situations, see *SS* 728–37.

18 Simone de Beauvoir, *The Force of Circumstance* (Harmondsworth:
Penguin, 1963), p. 203 (emphasis added).

14   Beauvoir's *Old Age*

Surely one of the more off-putting aspects of Simone de Beauvoir's work is her negative depiction of old age in *The Second Sex* and elsewhere. In the 1940s Beauvoir argued that it was both a woman's "erotic attractiveness and...fertility which, in the view of society and in her own, provide the justification of her existence."[1] For this reason she depicts aging as the deprivation of femininity and value for a woman. She repeatedly describes the experience as *une mutilation*. Beauvoir suggests that the experience of most women is similar: "Long before the eventual mutilation [la définitive mutilation], woman is haunted by the horror of growing old" (*SS* 587; *DS* 11 400), she writes confidently, not distinguishing at this point in her work among the experiences of old age in women of different cultural backgrounds, eras, or life-history.[2]

As is so often the case in her writing, Beauvoir's rhetoric plays two hands at once. On the one hand, throughout *The Second Sex* she depicts societal views about femininity and aging that she does not herself support. On the other hand, her writing seems on occasion to abet these views. Her use of the brutal word *mutilation* is a case in point. Beauvoir uses the term to forcefully remind us that the rejection of older women from the public sphere and the domains of value should be regarded as a violent form of social exclusion. Yet the reader remains unconvinced that Beauvoir resists adequately the devaluation of older women. One reason is the absence of a countering rhetoric in *The Second Sex*. The reader expects but is not provided with reminders about the many women who have written, worked, loved, and been valued late in their lives. Does the word *mutilation* bear witness to Beauvoir's disturbing belief that an older woman is indeed mutilated? Perhaps the term works rhetorically in both of these ways in her writing, both depicting societal views and abetting them.

Beauvoir's writing on old age partly answers one of the questions she famously asks in *The Second Sex*: what is a woman? Her response eventually connects femininity to age constraints. Beauvoir is already a woman, and yet she remarks on the first page of *The Second Sex* that one finds oneself exhorted to be a woman or to be more of a woman. She pursues the question by reconstructing what this exhortation assumes women to be. According to "From Maturity to Old Age," older women are no longer considered women. Not yet women, children and adolescents might look to this future with anticipation, as the people around them also anticipate their future femininity on their behalf. But an older woman has no such future to look forward to, and her peers do not usually anticipate that her destiny still includes the greater incarnation of a valued femininity. For this reason, Beauvoir proposes, "when the first hints come of that fated and irreversible process which is to destroy the whole edifice built up during puberty, she feels the fatal touch of death itself" (*SS* 588; *DS* II 400). In this passage we see that Beauvoir does not consider aging to be some kind of intrinsic mutilation. Rather, a woman experiences it in the context of a socially lived puberty in which her value has been strongly associated with her fertility, her appearance, and her youth. In the context of such an edifice, aging may well signify to many women a kind of death before death. In the context of this edifice built up throughout puberty, so profoundly formative of female subjectivity, Beauvoir considers that it must at some level represent a form of death before death to all women.

Her argument in this regard is clear, but the countering voice is missing. Beauvoir often affirms in opposition to restrictive stereotypes about women the possibility of alternative experiences. Karen Vintges has argued that Beauvoir autobiographically depicted her own life so as to remind readers that women could live independent, active, intelligent, and erotically expressive lives in the face of prejudices to the contrary.[3] By contrast, throughout most of her writing (up until *La Vieillesse* [Old Age]) Beauvoir fails to counter stereotypes about aged subjectivity with alternative possibilities. She does not, as she had done in relation to adult femininity, positively revalue aged subjectivity, offering it strong and alternative meanings.

There is a further reason readers wonder if Beauvoir merely compounded the view that one suffers a mutilation of embodiment and subjectivity late in life. Beauvoir lived very badly the onset – as she saw it – of her own old age.[4] In her autobiographical writing this onset is depicted as tragic and frightening. This attitude seems to be anticipated by sections in "From Maturity to Old Age" (in *The Second Sex*) that depict how a woman "helplessly looks on at the degeneration of this fleshly object which she confuses with herself [avec lequel elle se confond]" (*SS* 588, translation modified; *DS* 11 400). Such descriptions are later echoed by passages in *Force of Circumstance* in which Beauvoir depicts herself as helplessly looking on at her own aging in just this way.[5] Readers familiar with this later autobiographical material may be all the more likely to interpret "From Maturity to Old Age" as an indication of how thoroughly Beauvoir believed old age to be a mutilation for women.

Although they are not the most common thematic in Beauvoirian commentary, Beauvoir's writings on aging deserve attention. Moving from an adolescent relationship to time that (in *Memoirs of a Dutiful Daughter*) is primarily anticipatory, through to the Beauvoir of *All Said and Done*, who in her sixties renegotiates the status of her shorter future, the four volumes of her autobiographical work reflect on embodied temporality. In particular, the third volume, *Force of Circumstance*, stages a crisis that occurs as Beauvoir finds an aging woman in her mirror. Her response seems to break faith with the philosophical account according to which biological facts are not intrinsically obstacles.

During a considerable period in her writing Beauvoir associates aging with the inevitable loss of sex, mountain climbing, and new desires. Much of her fiction that discusses aging returns to the moral problems Beauvoir had addressed earlier in her work. How is an existential philosophy that emphasizes freedom to negotiate the physical and subjective changes associated with aging? Is it bad faith to understand aging as the loss of energy, innovation, desire, originality, and alacrity? Disturbing as the question is, Beauvoir gave it serious consideration at a certain point in her career. In *The Woman Destroyed*, the novella "The Age of Discretion" presents a female narrator's passage from an initial impatience with her aging partner to reconciliation with their situation. Beauvoir seems to suggest that the narrator is wrong in her skepticism about her partner's belief that he is too old for new ideas. Her skepticism lasts only until, climbing a slope, she, too, is exhausted in a way that is new to her. The novel depicts consent to the idea that one can be "too old" for some of the passions and activities about which we care most. This conclusion concurs with the autobiographical voice that writes in *Force of Circumstance* of being too old. The material represents a fundamental philosophical shift from Beauvoir's earlier emphasis on existential choice. In her fiction, Beauvoir distances herself from the glibness of a voice that affirms freedom easily and that gives little credit to one's embodied context. That voice would reprove us for preferring to interpret our lives in terms of those passions and activities that have become impossible for us. Beauvoir draws back from that glibness. She depicts with sympathy the shock of the woman who loves to climb and who experiences the loss of sufficient energy to do so, particularly in a social context that values energy and youth.

Toril Moi has argued that much of this material stages Beauvoir's recurrent depression. According to Moi, "the massive and explicit discussions of old age and death block a closer investigation of the fear of emptiness and loss of love."[6] Certainly that fear is suffused through much of her writing on the subject and might cause readers to consider it one of the more unfortunate aspects of her literary career. But Beauvoir's intermittent reflections on aging should not be easily dismissed. As Moi points out, these reflections were eventually "turned into a source of activity: *Old Age* (1970) represents Beauvoir's triumphant settling of scores with her old enemy. Now she can face her age with equanimity."[7]

Old Age is a fascinating work for readers familiar with *The Second Sex*. Many of Beauvoir's themes from the earlier theoretical work return twenty years later. In both works she asks how we should understand the nexus of ontological freedom and social marginalization. What moral responsibilities ensue from that nexus? In *Old Age* Beauvoir argues that the aged are the Other, whereas she had argued in *The Second Sex* that women are the Other. She considered the marginalization of women and the aged identifiable in demeaning representations, economic inequality, and exclusion from employment. Beauvoir interrogates the relationship between one's social status as Other and one's lived embodiment. She uses both sex and age to argue that there are no biological facts. She means by this that biological facts are always already synthesized with historical, social, and psychological factors. In the experience of being too old to climb or of suffering overly from menstrual pain, for example, one cannot separate the physiological condition from its mediation by the othering of women and the aged. One's living of the negative connotations of one's own embodiment leads to a less positive embodiment, an experience of one's embodiment as that which "cannot." Our bodies, Beauvoir argues, are always social.

Confronted with the question of how ontological freedom intersects with social inequality, one is faced with a dilemma. An ontologically free subject is at the same time an embodied subject. If the social status of one's embodiment leads to one's experiences of the world in terms of the "cannot," the status of one's ontological freedom is altered. That freedom is an embodied locus of interpretation. The body is both this interpreting subject and that which is interpreted by us. Social inequality produces a body experienced as limiting and in this sense impinges on ontological freedom. This realization led to Beauvoir's concern with our moral responsibilities under these circumstances. Is it fair to criticize one's capitulation to being too old to climb hills? In *The Second Sex* Beauvoir was ambivalent about a similar issue as it confronted women. She did criticize women who accepted conventions about what was possible for a woman. This was taking the easy slope (*SS* 730; *DS* ii 564). But, in *Old Age*, Beauvoir shifted the focus of moral responsibility. However much her reasons might have been depression, anxiety, or fear of death, Beauvoir is notably more sympathetic with the various ways in which we negotiate the dilemma of a body that appears to us old. She continues to strongly criticize the social marginalization of old age, but she moves the focus of moral responsibility more squarely to the factors contributing to this marginalization. But how we negotiate our situation – whether we experience new desires or not, find new ways of climbing mountains, new sources of innovation, or look more to the past and our memories – Beauvoir spares her readers the language of easy and hard slopes. In the passage from *The Second Sex* to works such as *Old Age* and *All Said and Done* Beauvoir also moves away from her early neglect of a countering, innovative, and resistant rhetoric about the life of an older woman to the depiction of old age as a time in which one may be delighted by one's lover, one's travels, and continued studies and stimulated by one's political activism, one's friends, and one's literary work.

In *The Second Sex* Beauvoir had unfavorably compared the quality of life of those who are constantly stimulated by new and diverse projects to those who are confined to a repetitive existence. Later, she had likened women to the elderly as being so confined. But in her sixties Beauvoir refigures the potential meaning of repetition. Her days do resemble each other, she acknowledges. "Yet my life does not seem at all stagnant to me. Its repetitive side is no more than a background against which new things perpetually appear."[8] Beauvoir's final writings provide alternatives to her earlier anxieties. At the end of her career she modifies the position of *Force of Circumstance*, depicting autobiographically in *All Said and Done* the possibility for a highly innovative, physical, and satisfied life for an older woman. Such a life is possible, even in the context of the marginalization of women and the aged, she affirms. Yet she continues her belief that old age is also a limit. It turns one backwards, not forwards, and alters one's focus so as to find the novel at the heart of repetition, rather than in a life of external change. Living one's life with the sense of impending death is a reality, though one's response is open for negotiation. One's negotiations are mediated by the social, and that fact may take the diversity of possibilities out of one's negotiations. We may be more likely to feel that desire or new ideas are no longer possible. If they are no longer possible, Beauvoir will not conclude that we have chosen the easy slope. She will not imply that the harder slope should have been preferred. This might be considered an important development from her treatment of women in *The Second Sex* and *Ethics of Ambiguity*.[9] *Old Age* provides the theoretical analysis to accompany that transition.[10]

Perhaps we should conclude that in the middle period of her writing and in such works as *Force of Circumstance* the social attitudes so acutely depicted by Beauvoir got the better of her when she came to write of aging? Perhaps this phase of her autobiographical writing and some of her literature depicts in an exemplary, if naive and unreflective way, the very conventions and prejudices she analyzed acutely elsewhere in her work? Naive and unreflective may be a fair assessment of a considerable period in her writing on the subject. But one should not underestimate the extent to which she contributed to a philosophical reflection on aging, considering it to be a crucial existential problem not reducible to the finality of death. Beauvoir's analyses of our lived relationship to impending death are not just the anxious actings out of a writer who has succumbed to the social devaluation of aged femininity and fears her degradation. They also allow us the opportunity to reassess her relationship to the philosophies of death with which she was familiar, most directly that of Sartre.

One of the reasons that old age is rarely analyzed as a dominant theme in Beauvoir's work is that her frequent discussions of it are often subsumed by commentators under the general category of a preoccupation with death. In an early work on the subject, Elaine Marks considers Beauvoir's preoccupation with death to be partly explicable in terms of the sensibility of a certain epoque, which conventionally thematizes death in terms of the death of God, nihilism, absurdity, and the feared emptiness of existence.[11] Thus old age receives no index entry in Marks' *Encounters with Death*, even though it is frequently thematized in the work. Old age finds its place in that work only in terms of an overall argument that Beauvoir suffers from a particularly extreme version of the phenomenon of flight from death, which she also depicts and analyzes theoretically. Yet the fact that Beauvoir published a full work on old age[12] suggests that we should attend more to the specificity of her discussion of the topic. According to Marks, Beauvoir depicts her fictional and autobiographical characters in terms of a constant thinking of, waiting for, and arming oneself against death, irrespective of her theoretical conviction that this is in principle an impossibility. All of Beauvoir's interest in and anxiety about old age would then become part of this larger project of thinking of, waiting for, and staving off death.

True, some of Beauvoir's comments do understand old age in terms of the approaching limit point of death. But her interest in age is not reducible to this understanding. There is much – indeed, a 604-page work dedicated to the topic – to suggest that aging is a more distinct object of reflection for her. For Beauvoir, death was not philosophically interesting when considered as a finite point in our future, nor as the prospect of our own nonexistence. Certainly her autobiographical writing bears witness to the fear, trauma, and depression that death and old age can represent. But death did interest her philosophically insofar as mortality intertwines with a changing, aging embodiment. Our trajectory from birth to death represents an embodiment which is both socially and temporally located, the site of perpetual alteration, and as such the site of a changing corporeal relation to futurity.

Commentators have long debated Beauvoir's relationship to Sartre. For those interested in the question, *Old Age* is a key text. "Time, History, Activity" is one of the most important chapters in *Old Age*. It contains a more sustained and critical engagement with Sartre's writing than is seen in other works, particularly *The Second Sex*. Beauvoir dialogues with Sartre's discussion of death in *Being and Nothingness*, and her position unfolds through her remarks about his analysis, to which she provides an alternative. This chapter is another factor among the many that allow a reevaluation of the Sartre–Beauvoir relationship, in which Beauvoir has been commonly regarded as simultaneously overly faithful and philosophically inferior to Sartre.

Given that he is her most constant theoretical reference on the subject, how does Beauvoir's approach to death compare with that of Sartre? On Sartre's analysis, death is not an ontological structure of my being: "There is no place for death in being-for-itself; it can neither wait for death nor realize it, nor project itself toward it...What then is death? Nothing but a certain aspect of facticity and of being-for-others...an external and factual limit of my subjectivity!"[13] We are then ontologically free in relation to death. Beauvoir comments favorably on this section from *Being and Nothingness*. Death is, she agrees, unrealizable, the external limit.[14] For Sartre, she notes, my freedom remains "total and infinite" in relation to death and "death is not an obstacle to my projects" (*BN* 547; *EN* 632). Thus we see Beauvoir agreeing with Sartre's conclusion:

Since death escapes my projects because it is unrealizable, I myself escape death in my very project. Since death is always beyond my subjectivity, there is no place for it in my subjectivity. This subjectivity does not affirm itself against death, but independently of it... Therefore we can neither think of death nor wait for it nor arm ourselves against it [and] our projects as projects are independent of death – not because of our blindness... but on principle. [*BN* 548; *EN* 632–33]

Beauvoir reiterates this formulation and its terminology:

Death belongs to that category in which we have placed old age and which Sartre calls the "unrealizables"; the for-itself can neither reach death nor project itself towards it; death is the external limit of my possibilities and not a possibility of my own. I shall be dead for others, not for myself: it is the other who is mortal in my being. I know myself as mortal, just as I know myself as old, by adopting the outsider's view of me. This knowledge is therefore abstract, general and assumed from without. My "mortality" is in no way the object of any close, inward experience. [OA 491, translation modified; V 465]

Perhaps the very proliferation of references to Sartre should make us suspicious of Beauvoir's stance here. She assiduously, and apparently faithfully, references Sartre on death. As she does so, however, she also revises Sartre's discussion when she incorporates old age into the discussion of death.[15] Beauvoir does not draw the reader's attention to the fact, but adopts the tone of respectful citation of a revered colleague. Yet Old Age can be read as questioning the contribution of Being and Nothingness on the topic, insofar as Sartre's discussion of death interconnects with his treatment elsewhere in the work of embodiment.

In considering the problem of embodiment Sartre argues that "being-for-itself must be wholly body and it must be wholly consciousness: it cannot be united with a body" (BN 305; EN 368). Similarly, he writes that "the body is nothing other than the for-itself; it is not an in-itself in the for-itself... the body is not distinct from the situation of the for-itself since for the for-itself, to exist and be situated are one and the same" (BN 309; EN 371–72). What ramifications might there be for the argument we have seen that "there is no place for death in being-for-itself; it can neither wait for death nor realize it, nor project itself toward it"?

Beauvoir seems to respond as follows. What of the fact that this body which I am ages? Could one say more about this aging body in contexts where it does more literally or physically seem to anticipate death? More generally, how might it be important to depict the qualitatively different relationship to affect, physiology, will, practical freedom, and being for others, depending on what kind of body one is, youthful or older, and depending on how one's embodiment is perceived by others? To pursue the question it is first necessary to follow the distinction Beauvoir established in her work between ontological and practical freedom.

As Sonia Kruks emphasizes, Beauvoir should be understood as deploying two distinct concepts of freedom from her earliest work, radical (or ontological) freedom and "effective freedom" (or power).[16]

Kruks' interpretation dates the distinction to Beauvoir's early book *Pyrrhus et Cinéas*, particularly in the light of comments about that early work in the second volume of Beauvoir's autobiography, *The Prime of Life*.[17] Reflecting on *Pyrrhus et Cinéas* in 1960, Beauvoir described the work as one in which she "attempted to reconcile Sartre's ideas with the views I had upheld against him in various lengthy discussions: I was reinstating a hierarchy between situations" (*PL* 549, translation modified; *FA* 627). As Kruks interprets this passage, her attempt involved adopting a distinction between indestructible freedom (*liberté*) and that which can be restricted: power (*puissance*). Here is Beauvoir on power, in the early work: "Power is finite, and one can augment or limit it from without; one can throw a man in prison, take him out of it, cut off an arm, lend him wings; but in all cases his freedom remains infinite" (*PC* 86, trans. Kruks).[18]

In Kruks' argument, Beauvoir was not able to consistently sustain this distinction, but Kruks reminds us that these distinct concepts of freedom ("effective freedom" and "nihilating" or ontological freedom) are to be found throughout Beauvoir's work.

Beauvoir continues to draw on the terminology of the subject conceived as for-itself, as "nothingness which is at the heart of man," "negativity" that is revealed as "anguish, desire, appeal, laceration" (*EA* 44; *PMA* 63), and to associate this terminology with a concept of freedom on which she will later continue to draw all through her work until *Old Age*. According to this terminology, to deny that a subject is free is to argue that this subject is a self-coinciding, essential, brute object. It is to claim that there is no rupture at the heart of a subject's being and that the subject confers no meaning on the world, itself, or others. Insofar as we never entirely coincide with ourselves, the world, or others, and insofar as our world is imbued with meaning, we are, in this sense of freedom, always and constantly free. It is incoherent to talk about a child or an older person as "more" or "less" free, according to this terminology.

So, in *The Ethics of Ambiguity* Beauvoir asks, rhetorically (for the answer will be no), "Does not this presence of a so to speak natural freedom contradict the notion of ethical freedom?" (*EA* 24; *PMA* 35).

Beauvoir emphasizes the difference between the way in which we are originally (and always) free and what she differentiates from this: the capacity for what she calls ethical freedom. Ethical freedom has gradations. We can be more or less free in the ethical sense of freedom.

What are the implications for a comparison between a Sartrean and a Beauvoirian discussion of aging? Sartre would hardly deny that we age, but he would account for this corporeality via the route of his explanation that the body is what I nihilate (*BN* 309; *EN* 372). To have a body is "to be the foundation of one's own nothingness and not to be the foundation of one's being; I *am* my body to the extent that I *am*, I *am not* my body to the extent that I am not what I am" (*BN* 326; *EN* 391).

Sartre, like Beauvoir, emphasizes that we are bodily. He does not deny the point that Beauvoir says concerned her in *Pyrrhus and Cinéas*: that situations are graded. He will not deny that as the years go by it is factually true that we have more years behind us. But he will deny that the relationship between ontological freedom and such facts is other than nihilating. Although Sartre acknowledges that the body is indissociable from being-for-itself, he gives the focus of his discussion to the body as the in-itself that is nihilated. The for-itself is not (just) that aging body, for example, which it (also) is. Although the bodies in question certainly are qualitatively different, that "not" (that negating gap whereby the for-itself does not entirely coincide with itself as a body) cannot be qualitatively different for the young student and the elderly woman. I am, in this sense, no more or less (ontologically) free for Sartre at 20, 40, or 90.

Although Sartre does not discuss older bodies, he does discuss physically fatigued bodies, and this case allows the best illustration of the point. It is the gap at the heart of being that opens up the myriad of possibilities for how we suffer that fatigue. We might suffer it "flexibly" or "sternly," or with a feeling of "inferiority" or else "difficulties can appear 'not worth the trouble of being tolerated'"(*BN* 457, 464; *EN* 534, 542). As Sartre writes, "there are as many ways of existing one's body as there are For-itselfs" (*BN* 456; *EN* 533). The range of these possible modes demonstrates the ontological freedom on which they are based. Sartre's point is that we do not give up in fatigue because our body is exhausted, nor do we persevere because it is not. I could have done otherwise. This is not to say that one might arbitrarily select any of these possibilities: "I have yielded to fatigue, we said, and doubtless I *could have* done otherwise but *at what price?* ... it becomes evident that we can not suppose that the act could have been modified without at the same time supposing a fundamental modification of my original choice of myself" (*BN* 464; *EN* 542).

It is striking that Beauvoir agrees with much of this language. Nevertheless her concern is as much with practical freedom, ethical freedom, as with ontological freedom. Living in time, we have a different relationship to practical, ethical freedom relative to our qualitative relationship to our age. What, she asks, are the implications of the embodiment of old age for ethical freedom? She points out that the physical effects of aging can result in a restriction of the possibilities and world in which one lives. The distances one moves may be circumscribed, the speed at which one moves may slow. One may move one's body with less ease, see or hear with less acuity, one may breath less deeply, with greater effort. But, she considers that these apparent physical facts cannot be understood in abstraction from their embeddedness in a complex range of factors, which include how respectfully one is seen as aged, what social identities are attached to us as the aged Other, what opportunities are available to us for employment and for economic independence, and so on. Physical change may be experienced as an impediment of activity, as it might not in other circumstances in which physical change is differently understood and differently valued.

Beauvoir does offer an analysis that is in some ways pessimistic about the freedom possible in one's older age. That pessimism is disconcerting. But it is also connected to the analysis she offers in *Old Age*, that old age is in western culture the Other, held in disregard, in economic and social impoverishment. For Beauvoir, since physical facts do not exist in abstraction from social, historical, subjective, and economic factors, it is the combination of all of these that produced the state she analyzed somewhat pessimistically. Only in the context of this analysis does Beauvoir ask whether an older person in western society is equally free to live repetition of the same or openness to the new, to cling to habit or break habits, to turn to the past, or turning to the future, to live in restricted or open space, bitterness, or *joie de vivre*.

Beauvoir offers a critical alternative (particularly an alternative of emphasis) to the Sartrean approach she discusses. Sartre may argue that "being-for-itself must be wholly body and it must be wholly consciousness: it cannot be *united* with a body" (*BN* 305; *EN* 368), and again that "the body is nothing other than the for-itself; it is not an in-itself *in* the for-itself... the body is not distinct from the *situation* of the for-itself since for the for-itself, to exist and to be situated are one and the same" (*BN* 309; *EN* 371–72). But it is surely the absence of a reflection on different kinds of bodies that allows him to evade an account of freedom adequate to those differences, a philosophical interest in reflecting on practical or ethical freedom as much as on ontological freedom. Beauvoir's concern was with the social change that could increase the possibilities for ethical freedom of all subjects and allow a qualitatively improved relationship to the anticipation of one's future.

In this respect, commentators are in disagreement about whether Beauvoir does or does not maintain a coherent distinction between ontological and practical freedom. Kruks' interpretation of the status of ontological freedom in Beauvoir's work has been summarized as follows: "It is this lack of an 'open' future which begins ... to imply that there is a qualitative modification of transcendence itself. This is to say also that the lack of an open future implies a modification of transcendence itself ... of the for-itself, of ontological freedom."[19]

Gail Linsenbard disagrees with this interpretation. Beauvoir could not be arguing that the lack of an open future impinges on transcendence, for this is not how Beauvoir and Sartre understand ontological freedom.[20] The implication seems to be that only a reader who did not understand the proper use of the term *transcendence* could see in Beauvoir's work a depiction of the impoverishment of transcendence in women or the aged. But one of the more innovative moments in Beauvoir's thought may arise from her blurring of the concepts of practical and ontological freedom.

Beauvoir's greater interest in and focus on issues of practical or ethical freedom is clear, although concepts of both ontological and ethical freedom are simultaneously at work in her writing. Instead of asking whether she confuses the two terms, we could ask what opens up in her work through her apparently confused tendency to locate a potential impingement on ontological freedom through an impingement on ethical freedom. Beauvoir's work on old age depicts this impingement. As this work and this tendency develop, perhaps Beauvoir's use of the concept of transcendence interestingly exceeds the limits of its own possibilities? Must we see Beauvoir as merely unable to grasp and master its proper usage?

The issue is not the brute fact of having so many or few years left to live. Beauvoir agrees with Sartre on the following point: "If I were to have a short expectation of life and if at the same time I had the physical and mental potentialities that I had when I was twenty, then my end, faintly seen through the crowding projects, would still seem to me remote" (*OA* 420; *V* 400). But she tries to articulate a philosophical apparatus adequate to the fact that, owing to the complex interconnection of economic, social, physiological, historical, cultural, and subjective factors, I do not have the same physical and mental potentialities at different stages of my life. At times it seems as if Beauvoir is claiming that it is the very difference in quantity of years to live that generates the difference to which she refers: "There was once a time when we could not make out a boundary-mark upon the horizon: now we do see one" (*OA* 421, translation modified; *V* 400). However she also suggests that the issue is not the exact number of remaining years but the energy of the subject who looks forward to those years. According to my weakness or strength, my end may be vividly anticipated or sensed faintly through crowding projects. That energy is not a simple matter of physiology, nor of a concerted faculty of will. Above all one cannot, she underlines, ascribe that energy only to the given facticity of a nihilating subject who lives in and as that context but forever transcends that facticity, as in Sartre's discussion of physical fatigue. Instead, she suggests that we need to emphasize a concept of freedom as crucially grounded in our interest in the world and in our energy for imagining it otherwise. Although Beauvoir describes old age as unrealizable, a crucial issue in this regard is whether her health is good: "Seeing that my health is good, my body gives me no token of age. I am sixty-three: and this truth remains foreign to me" (*AS* 30; *TC* 40). This truth is less likely to be foreign when her aged body's health is poor.

Beauvoir would not deny that for Sartre this subjective-physical capacity remains that in relation to which we are always ontologically free. This bodily conscious event of fatigue or loss of interest would take on the status of the nihilated in-itself in his work in relation to ontological freedom. But why? Surely it is to derive metonymic profit from the fact that, being always ontologically free, we might provocatively say to others that they "choose" their lack of interest in the future. When challenged about the meaning of this freedom, a Sartrean analysis explains that this freedom is ontological, the nihilating gap at the heart of being. But as deployed, it is used to depict agents in terms of choice in a more provocative sense. (In this sense, it might be said that it is Sartre, as much as Beauvoir, who blurs ontological and practical freedom.) Perhaps it is this deployment or blurring that is targeted by Beauvoir when she emphasizes circumstances in which ontological freedom may not allow for practical freedom in a useful sense, as when she depicts times in a life when "the future is no longer big with promise: it contracts to accord with the finite being who must live it [il se contracte à la mesure de l'être fini qui a à le vivre]" (OA 420, translation modified; V 399). When Beauvoir suggests that biological decay *can* be the impossibility of surpassing oneself, of being passionately concerned with anything, of all projects dying, she counters the way Sartre's framework gives ontological freedom the metaphorical connotations of practical freedom.

Beauvoir reaches for a philosophical framework according to which one could say that an impingement of ethical or practical freedom on to ontological freedom is possible. This is seen in her approach to gender, but much more clearly in her approach to aging. The same Beauvoir who energetically reminds us that shortness of breath need in no way amount to shortness of freedom also wants to allow for the possibility that the subject who is short of breath can importantly feel shortness of life and live shortness of freedom. She seems to ask readers to respect this as a subjective possibility. Such a respect would not amount to a mere tolerance of the delusions of bad faith. Instead, perhaps even literary novellas, such as Beauvoir's "The Age of Discretion," call for a reformulated philosophical respect for the phenomena – in other words, a philosophical account adequate to it.[21] In Beauvoir's own work such a respect amounts to the view that ethical freedom could impinge on ontological freedom. The subject who slows from failing lungs may live a slowing of the future. One whose horizons limit the future to the road that must be crossed is a subject who may live this limit as a physical compression of the future. Beauvoir's point is that we need a stronger philosophical account of our relation to this shortness of breath and of our being this shortness of breath. At the heart of that nihilating ontological freedom we also need interest in the world, interest in and will for the future, a sense of a physical future. To emphasize the equivalence of ontological freedom for all subjects without regard for bodily difference is not rhetorically useful, but, rather, is deceptive.

As a result, according to the most extreme version of this position, Beauvoir holds that there are embodied contexts in which we are conscious but do not transcend extreme shortness of breath. One might breathe in, with shallowness of breath, with the very effort to breathe, impingement of ontological freedom. Transcendence would become for her, as it is not for Sartre, qualitative. Nihilation is retheorized in its interconnection with the quality of one's interest in the world, an interest that can be impaired by the complex interconnection of forces to which Beauvoir wants us to attend.

Beauvoir analyzed death insofar as it is often mediated by the slow process of aging. Sudden death held little philosophical interest for her. Nor did our living with the existential certainty of eventual death. Instead, Beauvoir was interested in a human's embodied relationship to time, in embodied futurity: the differences involved in anticipating the future as an adolescent girl, a mature woman, and an octogenarian. She did not theorize human existence from the position of a neutral body looking towards its future. Her bodies are, for example, specifically sexed. Her work has been well recognized, in this regard, for its amendment and contribution to philosophies of embodiment of the period, most particularly those of Jean-Paul Sartre and Maurice Merleau-Ponty, both of whose work (for all their other differences) was rife with references to the subject's relation to "the body," as if this relation could be neutrally depicted. Beauvoir's simultaneous amendment with regard to differentially aged bodies has been less well recognized. But in her literary, autobiographical, and theoretical writing she also avoids the depiction of neutral embodiment insofar as the bodies she depicts are always of specified age: young bodies, adolescent, mature, ill, or dying. Her depiction of aged bodies interconnects with her depiction of sexed bodies. Just as her work tends to avoid theorizing embodiment that is not specified as male or female, the sexed bodies she depicts are also of determinate age: pubescent or sexagenerian. Although many critics have highlighted the inadequacy of feminisms that assume an implicitly white body, Beauvoir gave little consideration to this point. But she made a different contribution: emphasizing the socially mediated age specificity of human embodiment that proves to be critical to the subjectivity, freedom, futurity, and morality that preoccupied her.

Beauvoir's writing on old age does require considerable care in approach. *Old Age* offers a vast array of differing experiences of and approaches to aging. One must be critical of her most negative depictions. She walked a fine line. To claim that everyone is always equally free to choose an interest in climbing mountains seemed to her insensitive. But her alternative attempt to depict the loss of will and desire to climb mountains runs its own risk. It seems to rigidify old age and deny the experiences of those whose desire and capacity to climb mountains continues unabated.

Beauvoir's desire to give equal importance to questions of practical and ontological freedom leads to her attempt to better reconcile these problems. She gave more serious consideration to the importance of practical freedom than did Sartre, and her attention to differences of gender and age allowed her to do so. Although some of her later work does depict very aged subjects who retain extreme interest in the world and energy for attacking its possibilities, the more significant shift in Beauvoir's thinking probably occurred with her renewed and sympathetic attention to subjects who lack interest in the world and do not feel like living. This shift cannot be reduced to Beauvoir's anxiety about aging, although her autobiographically depicted feelings about her own old age may be so reducible.

As a dialogue with Sartre on the weighting attributed to ontological freedom, Beauvoir's material on the subject acts as an important intervention. Sartre's subject is embodied, sometimes sick and fatigued, but patently a young adult body. Beauvoir's response is that an excessive weighting of ontological freedom generalizes and neutralizes those lived and embodied differences that should also hold our theoretical attention. Depicting the approach of death as irrelevant to ontological freedom maintains consistency in Sartre's work. However, Beauvoir could be regarded as suggesting to her readers that this approach to freedom is also the least interesting or least relevant. Despite the difficulties it causes her negotiation of depicting both ontological and practical freedom, the experience some have of old age seems to have prompted her to rethink the adequacy of an account according to which practical freedom may be limited, but ontological freedom is not.

NOTES

1 SS (London: Picador, 1988) 587; DS II 399.
2 Later, in La Vieillesse (Old Age), Beauvoir would attend more to such differences, discussing variations in the treatment of the aged in different historical periods. Although she clarifies that she "confine[s] herself to a study of Western societies," she does discuss what she takes to be

some exceptions, such as the privileged status of older men in China
(*OA* [Harmondsworth: Penguin, 1977] 102; *V* 99).

3   Karen Vintges, *Philosophy as Passion: The Thinking of Simone de Beau-voir* (Bloomington, IN: Indiana University Press, 1996), p. 107.

4   On how Beauvoir lived the onset (as she saw it) of her own old age, see
Toril Moi, *Simone de Beauvoir: The Making of an Intellectual Woman*
(Oxford: Blackwell, 1994) pp. 236–42.

5   *FC* (London: André Deutsch and Weidenfeld & Nicolson, 1965) 657;
FCh II 505.

6   Moi, *Simone de Beauvoir*, p. 242.

7   ibid., p. 243.

8   *AS* (London: André Deutsch and Weidenfeld & Nicolson, 1974) 35;
TC 45.

9   Beauvoir briefly comments on women in her early work, *The Ethics of
Ambiguity*. She considers that western women, since they are exposed
to the possibility of liberation, resign their freedom in not exploiting
the possibility. Insofar as this is the case, western women are described
as dishonest and at fault (*EA* 38; *PMA* 55).

10 One other important text in this regard is her narrative about her
mother's death, *A Very Easy Death*. Gail Weiss has argued that this
work depicts Beauvoir's acquiescence "in her mother's tacit, but none
the less forceful demand to pretend she is not in fact dying." Weiss concludes that in this regard Beauvoir "acts against her own, very Sartrian
'moral principles' and, in so doing, reveals the limits of [those] moral
principles themselves." See Gail Weiss, *Body Images: Embodiment as
Intercorporeality* (New York and London: Routledge, 1999), p. 150.

11 See Elaine Marks, *Simone de Beauvoir: Encounters with Death* (New
Brunswick, NJ: Rutgers University Press, 1973), p. 3.

12 *Old Age* was published shortly before Marks' study and so not included
in her analysis.

13 *BN* (London: Methuen, 1958) 547; *EN* (Paris: Gallimard, 1943) 613–32.

14 *OA* 491; *V* 465. The point is that unlike Sartre, Beauvoir likens the un-
realizability of death to that of old age, in her discussion of the Sartrean
material. In *All Said and Done* she writes, "Like everybody else, I am
incapable of an interior experience of [old age]: age is one of the things
that cannot be realized" (*AS* 30; *TC* 40).

15 In *The Ethics of Ambiguity* a tone of appreciative commentary about
Sartre's analysis of ontological freedom becomes the context for a shifting of emphasis towards the will, the will to will, power, and effective
and ethical freedom. If we assess this writing as an interpretation of
Sartre, we may consider, as does Peter Caws, that "Sartre proves too
subtle for Simone de Beauvoir, who simplifies things in her *Ethics of*

Ambiguity." He remonstrates, "Neither will, nor passion ... accounts for the original drive towards projected ends; they are merely its modalities." But what if we assess the writing insofar as it displaces Sartre's priorities? See Peter Caws, *Sartre* (London: Routledge & Kegan Paul, 1979), p. 115.

16 Sonia Kruks, *Situation and Human Existence: Freedom, Subjectivity and Society* (London: Unwin Hyman, 1990), p. 90.

17 *PL* (Harmondsworth: Penguin, 1965) 548–50; *FA* 626–29.

18 Kruks, *Situation and Human Existence*, p. 90.

19 Gail Linsenbard, "Beauvoir, Ontology and Human Rights," *Hypatia: A Journal of Feminist Philosophy*, 14, 4 (1999): 145–62, 157 citing Kruks, *Situation and Human Existence*, p. 51.

20 Opposing this view, Gail Linsenbard argues, "When Kruks imputes to Beauvoir the view that 'woman is locked in immanence by the situation that man inflicts on her' ... she [erroneously, according to Linsenbard] seems to suggest that woman is effectively cut off from the possibility of transcendence." Linsenbard, "Beauvoir, Ontology and Human Rights," p. 156.

21 This suggestion is further discussed in Penelope Deutscher, "Bodies, Lost and Found: Simone de Beauvoir from *The Second Sex* to *Old Age*," *Radical Philosophy*, 96 (1999): 6–16.

BIBLIOGRAPHY

WORKS BY SIMONE DE BEAUVOIR

French

L'Amérique au jour le jour (Paris: Editions Paul Marihien, 1948).
Les Belles images (Paris: Gallimard, 1966).
Les Bouches inutiles (Paris: Gallimard, 1945).
La Cérémonie des adieux, suivi de entretiens avec Jean-Paul Sartre, Aout-/Septembre 1974 (Paris: Gallimard, 1981).
Le Deuxième sexe, 2 vols. (Paris: Gallimard, 1949).
Les Ecrits de Simone de Beauvoir, ed. C. Francis and F. Gontier (Paris: Gallimard, 1979).
L'Existentialisme et la sagesse des nations (Paris: Nagel, 1948) (four essays that originally appeared in *Les Temps modernes*).
"Faut-il brûler Sade?," *Les Temps modernes*, 74 (Dec. 1951): 1002–33; 75 (Jan. 1952): 1197–230.
La Femme rompue (Paris: Gallimard, 1967).
La Force de l'âge (Paris: Gallimard, 1960).
La Force des choses (Paris: Gallimard, 1963).
L'Invitée (Paris: Gallimard, 1943).
Journal de guerre, Septembre 1939–Janvier 1941, edited by Sylvie Le Bon de Beauvoir (Paris: Gallimard, 1990).
Lettres à Nelson Algren: un amour transatlantique: 1947–1964, compiled, annotated, and translated from English and annotated by Sylvie Le Bon de Beauvoir (Paris: Gallimard, 1997).
Lettres à Sartre, I, *1930–1939* and II, *1940–1963*, ed. Sylvia Le Bon de Beauvoir (Paris: Gallimard, 1990).
"Littérature et métaphysique," *Les Temps modernes*, I, 7 (April 1946): 1153–63.
La Longue marche, essai sur la Chine (Paris: Gallimard, 1957).

Les Mandarins (Paris: Gallimard, 1954).

Mémoires d'une jeune fille rangée (Paris: Gallimard, 1958).

"Merleau-Ponty et pseudo-sartrisme," *Les Temps modernes*, 10, 114–15 (July 1955): 2072–122; reprinted in *Privilèges* (Paris: Gallimard, 1955).

Une Mort très douce (Paris: Gallimard, 1964).

"La Phénoménologie de la perception de Maurice Merleau-Ponty," *Les Temps modernes*, 1 (Oct. 1945): 363–67.

Pour une morale de l'ambiguïté (Paris: Gallimard, 1947).

Preface to *La Bâtarde* by Violette Leduc (Paris: Gallimard, 1964).

Preface to *Djamila Boupacha* (Paris: Gallimard, 1962) (listed as coauthor with Gisèle Halimi).

Preface to *Shoah* by Claude Lanzmann (Paris: Fayard, 1985).

Preface to *Tréblinka* by Jean-François Steiner (Paris: Arthème Fayard, 1966).

Privilèges (Paris: Gallimard, 1955).

Pyrrhus et Cinéas (Paris: Gallimard, 1944).

Quand prime le spirituel (Paris: Gallimard, 1979).

Le Sang des autres (Paris: Gallimard, 1945).

"Simone de Beauvoir," in *Que peut la littérature?*, ed. Yves Buin (France: L'herne), pp. 72–92 (contribution to a symposium).

Tous les hommes sont mortels (Paris: Gallimard, 1946).

Tout compte fait (Paris: Gallimard, 1972).

La Vieillesse (Paris: Gallimard, 1970).

English

Adieux: A Farewell to Sartre, trans. Patrick O'Brian (London: André Deutsch, 1984; New York: Pantheon, 1984).

All Men Are Mortal, trans. L. Friedman (Cleveland, OH: World Publishing, 1955).

All Said and Done, trans. Patrick O'Brian (London: André Deutsch and Weidenfeld & Nicolson, 1972; New York: Putnam, 1974).

America Day by Day, trans. Patrick Dudley (pseudonym) (London: Duckworth, 1952; New York: Grove, 1953); trans. Carel Cosman (Berkeley, CA: University of California Press, 1999).

Les Belles Images, trans. Patrick O'Brian (London: Collins, 1968; New York: Putnam, 1968).

The Blood of Others, trans. Y. Moyse and R. Senhouse (London: Secker & Warburg and Lindsay Drummond, 1948; New York: Knopf, 1948).

"Brigitte Bardot and the Lolita Syndrome," *Esquire* (August 1959), trans. Bernard Frechtman (London: André Deutsch and Weidenfeld & Nicolson, 1960; New York: Arno, 1972).

The Coming of Age, trans. Patrick O'Brian (New York: Putnam, 1972).

The Ethics of Ambiguity, trans. B. Frechtman (New York: Philosophical Library, 1948).

Force of Circumstance, trans. R. Howard (London: André Deutsch and Weidenfeld & Nicolson, 1965; New York: Putnam, 1965).

Letters to Sartre, ed. and trans. Quintin Hoare (New York: Little, Brown, 1992).

The Long March, trans. Austryn Wainhouse (Cleveland, OH: World Publishing, 1958).

The Mandarins, trans. L. Friedman (Cleveland, OH: World Publishing, 1956; London: Collins, 1957).

Memoirs of a Dutiful Daughter, trans. James Kirkup (London: André Deutsch and Weidenfeld & Nicolson, 1959; Cleveland, OH: World Publishing, 1959).

"Merleau-Ponty and Pseudo-Sartreanism," trans. Veronique Zaytzeff with the assistance of Frederick Morrison, *International Studies in Philosophy*, 21, 3 (1989): 3–48; reprinted in *The Debate between Sartre and Merleau-Ponty*, ed. Jon Stewart, (Evanston, IL: Northwestern University Press, 1998), pp. 448–91.

Must We Burn de Sade?, trans. Annette Michelson (London: Peter Neville, 1953; New York: Grove, 1955); reprinted in *The Marquis de Sade: The 120 Days of Sodom, and Other Writings*, trans. Austryn Weinhaus and Richard Seaver (New York: Grove, 1966).

Old Age, trans. Patrick O'Brian (London: André Deutsch, 1972).

Preface to *La Bâtarde: An Autobiography* by Derek Coltman (Manchester: C. Nicholls & Co., 1965; New York: Farrar, Straus & Giroux, 1965).

Preface to *Crimes Against Women: Proceedings of the International Tribunal*, edited by D. H. Russell and N. Van de Ven (Milbrae, CA: Les Femmes, 1976).

Preface to *Djamila Boupacha: The Story of the Torture of a Young Algerian Girl Which Shocked Liberal French Opinion* by Gisèle Halimi, trans. P. Green (London: Weidenfeld & Nicolson, 1962; London: Macmillan, 1962).

Preface to *Shoah: An Oral History of the Holocaust: The Complete Text of the Film* by Claude Lanzmann, subtitles of the film in English by A. Whitelaw and W. Byron (New York: Pantheon, 1985).

Preface to *Treblinka* by Jean-François Steiner, trans. Helen Weaver (Hemel Hempstead, UK: Simon & Schuster, 1967).

The Prime of Life, trans. P. Green (Cleveland, OH: World Publishing, 1962; London: André Deutsch and Weidenfeld & Nicolson, 1965).

The Second Sex, trans. H. M. Parshley (New York: Knopf, 1952; London: Jonathan Cape, 1953).

She Came to Stay, trans.Y. Moyse and R. Senhouser (London: Secker & Warburg and Lindsay Drummond, 1949; Cleveland, OH: World Publishing, 1954).

Transatlantic Love Affair: Letters to Nelson Algren, ed. Sylvie Le Bon de Beauvoir (New York: New Press, distributed by Norton, 1998).

A Very Easy Death, trans. P. O'Brian (London: André Deutsch and Weidenfeld & Nicolson, 1966; New York: Putnam, 1966).

When Things of the Spirit Come First: Five Early Tales, trans. Patrick O'Brian (London: André Deutsch, 1982; New York: Pantheon, 1982).

Who Shall Die?, trans. C. Francis and F. Gontier (Florissant, MO: River Press, 1983).

The Woman Destroyed, trans. Patrick O'Brian (London: Collins, 1969; New York: Putnam, 1969).

WORKS ABOUT BEAUVOIR

Treatises focusing on Beauvoir or containing significant discussions of Beauvoir

Appignanesi, Lisa, *Simone de Beauvoir* (Harmondsworth: Penguin, 1988).

Ascher, Carol, *Simone de Beauvoir: A Life of Freedom* (Boston: Beacon, 1981).

Bair, Deirdre, *Simone de Beauvoir: A Biography* (New York: Summit Books, 1990).

Bauer, Nancy, *Simone de Beauvoir: Philosophy and Feminism* (New York: Columbia University Press, 2001).

Bergoffen, Debra B., *The Philosophy of Simone de Beauvoir: Gendered Phenomenologies, Erotic Generosities* (Albany, NY: State University of New York Press, 1997).

Brosman, Catharine Savage, *Simone de Beauvoir Revisited* (Boston: Twayne, 1991).

Cottrell, Robert D., *Simone de Beauvoir* (New York: Unger, 1975).

Crosland, Margaret, *Simone de Beauvoir: The Woman and Her Work* (London: Heinemann, 1992).

Evans, Mary, *Simone de Beauvoir: Feminist Mandarin* (London: Tavistock, 1985).

Fallaize, Elizabeth, *The Novels of Simone de Beauvoir* (London: Routledge, 1988).

Fraser, Mariam, *Identity without Selfhood: Simone de Beauvoir and Bisexuality* (Cambridge: Cambridge University Press, 1999).

Fullbrook, Kate and Edward Fullbrook, *Simone de Beauvoir: A Critical Introduction* (Malden, MA: Polity Press and Oxford: Blackwell, 1998).

Simone de Beauvoir and Jean-Paul Sartre: The Remaking of a Twentieth-Century Legend (New York: Basic Books, 1994).

Francis, Claude and Fernande Gontier, *Simone de Beauvoir: A Life... A Love Story*, trans. L. Nesselson (New York: St. Martin's Press, 1987).

Hatcher, Donald, *Understanding The Second Sex* (New York: Peter Lang, 1984).

Heath, Jane, *Simone de Beauvoir* (Hemel Hempstead, UK: Harvester Wheatsheaf, 1989).

Keefe, Terry, *Simone de Beauvoir: A Study of Her Writings* (Totowa, NJ: Barnes & Noble, 1983).

Kruks, Sonia, *Retrieving Experience: Subjectivity and Recognition in Feminist Politics* (Ithaca, NY: Cornell University Press, 2001).

Situation and Human Existence: Freedom, Subjectivity and Society (London: Unwin Hyman, 1990).

Le Doeuff, Michèle, *Hipparchia's Choice: An Essay Concerning Women, Philosophy, etc.*, trans. Trista Selous (Oxford: Blackwell, 1989, 1991).

Leighton, Jean, *Simone de Beauvoir on Women* (Rutherford, NJ: Farleigh Dickinson University Press, 1975).

Lundgren-Gothlin, Eva, *Sex and Existence: Simone de Beauvoir's "The Second Sex,"* trans. Linda Schenck (London: Athlone, 1996; Hanover, NH: Wesleyan University Press, 1996).

Mahon, Joseph, *Existentialism, Feminism, and Simone de Beauvoir*, consultant ed. Jo Campling (New York: St. Martin's Press, 1997).

Marks, Elaine, *Simone de Beauvoir: Encounters with Death* (New Brunswick, NJ: Rutgers University Press, 1973).

Moi, Toril, *Feminist Theory and Simone de Beauvoir* (Oxford: Blackwell, 1990).

Simone de Beauvoir: The Making of an Intellectual Woman (Oxford: Blackwell, 1994).

Okely, Judith, *Simone de Beauvoir: A Re-reading* (New York: Random House, 1986; London: Virago, 1986).

Pilardi, Jo-Ann, *Simone de Beauvoir: Writing the Self – Philosophy Becomes Autobiography* (Westport, CN: Greenwood Press, 1999).

Sanday, Peggy Reeves and Ruth Gallegher Goodenough, *Beyond "The Second Sex": New Directions in the Anthropology of Gender* (Philadelphia: University of Pennsylvania Press, 1990).

Scholz, Sally J., *On de Beauvoir* (Belmont, CA: Wadsworth and Thomson Learning, 2000).

Schwarzer, Alice, *After the Second Sex: Conversations with Simone de Beauvoir* (New York: Pantheon, 1984).

Simons, Margaret A., *Beauvoir and The Second Sex: Feminism, Race, and the Origins of Existentialism* (Lanham, MD: Rowman & Littlefield, 1999).

Vintges, Karen, *Philosophy as Passion: The Thinking of Simone de Beauvoir* (Bloomington, IN: Indiana University Press, 1996).

Whitmarsh, Anne, *Simone de Beauvoir and the Limits of Commitment* (Cambridge: Cambridge University Press, 1981).

Winegarten, Renée, *Simone de Beauvoir: A Critical View* (Oxford: Berg, 1988).

Anthologies, special journal issues, and special clusters in journals

Du Plessis, Rachel Blau and Reyna Rapp (eds.), *Feminist Studies*, 6, 2 (summer 1980). Special cluster on Simone de Beauvoir. Essays by Mary Lowenthal Felstiner, Michèle Le Doeuff, Sandra Dijkstra, and Jo-Ann P. Fuchs.

Evans, Ruth (ed.), *Simone de Beauvoir's "The Second Sex": New Interdisciplinary Essays* (Manchester: Manchester University Press, 1998). Introduction by Ruth Evans and essays by Margaret Atack, Catherine Rodgers, Lorna Sage, Catriona Mackenzie, Stephen Horton, and Nicole Ward Jouve.

Fallaize, Elizabeth (ed.), *Simone de Beauvoir: A Critical Reader* (London and New York: Routledge, 1998). Selections from Judith Okely, Judith Butler, Sonia Kruks, Toril Moi, Eva Lundgren-Gothlin, Francis Jeanson, Alex Hughes, Elaine Marks, Hazel Barnes, Jane Heath, Anne Ophir, and Elizabeth Fallaize.

Forster, Penny and Imogen Sutton (eds.), *Daughters of de Beauvoir* (London: Women's Press, 1989). Reminiscences by Hélène de Beauvoir, Kate Millett, Jenny Turner, Margaret Walters, Angie Pegg, Ann Oakley, Marta Zabaleta Hinrichsen, Eva Figes, Joyce Goodfellow, Marge Piercy, and Sylvie Le Bon de Beauvoir.

Hawthorne, Melanie C. (ed.), *Contingent Loves: Simone de Beauvoir and Sexuality* (Charlottesville: University of Virginia Press, 2000). Essays by Luise von Flotow, Serge Julienne-Caffié, Melanie C. Hawthorne, Åsa Moberg, Barbara Klaw, Richard J. Golsan, and Liz Constable.

Joeres, Ruth-Ellen Boetcher and Barbara Laslett (eds.), *Signs: Journal of Women in Culture and Society*, 18, 1 (autumn, 1992): 74–161. Special cluster: Simone de Beauvoir. Essays by Mary G. Dietz, Sonia Kruks, Linda M. G. Zerilli, and Margaret A. Simons.

Kruks, Sonia (ed.), symposium on Simone de Beauvoir in *Women and Politics*, 11, 1 (1991). Introduction by Sonia Kruks and essays by Hester Eisenstein, Sondra Farganis, Linda Zerilli, and Mary Caputi.

Marks, Elaine (ed.), *Critical Essays on Simone de Beauvoir* (Boston: G. K. Hall, 1987). Interview of Sartre on Beauvoir by Madeleine Gobeil;

essays by Colette Audry, Alice Schwarzer, Maurice Merleau-Ponty, Mary McCarthy, Elizabeth Hardwick, René Etiemble, François Mauriac, Claude Roy, René Girard, Jacques Ehrmann, Mary Ellman, Francis Jeanson, T. H. Adamowcki, Elizabeth Janeway, Juliet Mitchell, Terry Keefe, Michèle Le Doeuff, Gerda Lerner, Catherine Clément, Mary Evans, Carol Ascher, Kate Millett, Alice Jardine, Béatrice Slama, Mary Lydon, and Virginia M. Fichera.

O'Brien, Wendy and Lester Embree (eds.), *The Existential Phenomenology of Simone de Beauvoir* (Dordrecht: Kluwer, 2001). Contributions by Wendy O'Brien, Margaret A. Simons, Edward Fullbrook and Kate Fullbrook, Elizabeth Fallaize, Eva Gothlin, Suzanne Laba Cataldi, Ursula Tidd, Gail Weiss, Sarah Clark Miller, Michael D. Barber, Kristana Arp, Debra B. Bergoffen, and Ted Toadvine.

Patterson, Yolanda Astarita (ed.), *Simone de Beauvoir Studies: The Golden Anniversary of "The Second Sex,"* 15 (1998–99) (Menlo Park, CA.: International Simone de Beauvoir Society). Essays by Ursula Fabijancic, Servanne Woodward, Dominique Van Hooff, Hazel E. Barns, Guillermine de Lacost, Christine Angelfors, Annie Jouan-Westlund, Meaghan Emery, Carolle Gagnon, Renée Fainas Wehrmann, Alison Holland, Simona Barello, Liliane Lazar, Bianca Lamblin, Betty Halpern-Guedj, Eugenia Zimmerman, and Yolanda Astarita Patterson.

Simons, Margaret A. (ed.), *Feminist Interpretations of Simone de Beauvoir* (University Park, PA: Pennsylvania State University Press, 1995). Essays by Jo-Ann Pilardi, Karen Vintges, Michèle Le Doeuff, Eleanore Holveck, Sonia Kruks, Kate Fullbrook and Edward Fullbrook, Jeffner Allen, Céline T. Léon, Kristana Arp, Debra B. Bergoffen, Barbara Klaw, Juli K. Ward, Margaret A. Simons, and Julien Murphy.

Hypatia Special Issue: The Philosophy of Simone de Beauvoir, 14, 4 (1999). Essays by Eleanore Holveck, Debra Bergoffen, Julie Ward, Edward Fullbrook, Suzanne Laba Cataldi, Eva Gothlin, Linnell Secomb, Sara Heinämaa, Karen Vintges, Gail E. Linsenbard, Ursula Tidd, and four book reviews.

Women's Studies International Forum, 8, 3 (1985). Essays by Iris Marion Young, Alison M. Jaggar and William L. McBride, Arleen B. Dallery, Ann Ferguson, Claudia Card, Marilyn Frye, Charlene Haddock Seigfried, and Linda Singer.

Sullivan, Shannon (ed.), *Journal of Speculative Philosophy.* n.s. 14, 2 (2000), "The Work of Simone de Beauvoir." Essays by Margaret A. Simons, Emily Zakin, Elain P. Miller, Tina Chanter; review of Margaret A. Simons, *Beauvoir and "The Second Sex,"* by Barbara Andrew.

Wenzel, Hélène (ed.), *Yale French Studies: Simone de Beauvoir: Witness to a Century,* 72 (1986). Wenzel interview with Simone de Beauvoir;

essays by Judith Butler, Virginia M. Fichera, Martha N. Evans, Yolanda
A. Patterson, Catherine Portuges, Isabelle de Courtivron, Deirdre Bair,
Margaret A. Simons, and "In Memoriam" by Margaret A. Simons,
Yolanda A. Patterson, and Deirde Bair.

Essays

Algren, Nelson, "The Question of Simone de Beauvoir: Review of *Force of
Circumstance*," *Harper's Magazine*, 230, 1380 (May 1965): 135.
Andrew, Barbara, "Care, Freedom, and Reciprocity in the Ethics of Simone
de Beauvoir," *Philosophy Today*, 42, 3–4 (1998): 290–300.
Bair, Deirdre, "Introduction to the Vintage Edition," in Simone de Beau-
voir, *The Second Sex*, trans. H. M. Parshley (New York: Vintage, 1989),
pp. xiii–xxiii.
Barnes, Hazel, "Simone de Beauvoir's Journal and Letters: A Poisoned Gift?,"
in *Simone de Beauvoir Studies*, ed. Yolanda Patterson, 8 (1991) (Menlo
Park, CA: California State University Press).
Brison, Susan, "Simone de Beauvoir," in *The Encyclopedia of Philosophy.
Supplement*, ed.-in-chief Donald M. Borchert (New York: Simon &
Schuster Macmillan, 1996), pp. 53–54.
Butler, Judith, "Gendering the Body: Beauvoir's Philosophical Contribu-
tion," in *Women, Knowledge, and Reality: Explorations in Philoso-
phy*, ed. Ann Garry and Marilyn Pearsall (Boston: Unwin Hyman, 1989),
pp. 253–62.
Deutscher, Penelope, "Bodies, Lost and Found: Simone de Beauvoir from
The Second Sex to *Old Age*," *Radical Philosophy* 96 (July–Aug. 1999):
6–16.
"The Notorious Contradictions of Simone de Beauvoir," in Penelope
Deutscher, *Yielding Gender: Feminism, Deconstruction and the History of Philosophy* (London: Routledge, 1997), pp. 169–93.
Fallaize, Elizabeth, "Narrative Structure in *Les Mandarins*," in *Literature
and Society: Studies in Nineteenth- and Twentieth-Century French Lit-
erature*, ed. C. Burns (Birmingham, AL: University of Birmingham Press,
1980), pp. 221–32.
Gothlin, Eva, "Ethics, Feminism and Postmodernism: Seyla Benhabib and
Simone de Beauvoir," *The Postmodernist Critique of the Project of
Enlightenment*, ed. Sven-Eric Liedman, Poznan Studies in the Philoso-
phy of the Sciences and the Humanities, 58 (Amsterdam: Rodopi, 1997):
79–88.
"Gender and Ethics in the Philosophy of Simone de Beauvoir," *NORA,
Nordic Journal for Women's Studies*, 1 (1995): 3–13.

"Simone de Beauvoir," in *Routledge Encyclopedia of Philosophy* (10 vols.), ed. Edward Craig (London and New York: Routledge, 1998), 1: 685–87.

"Simone de Beauvoir and Ethics," *History of European Ideas*, 19, 4–6 (1994): 899–903.

"Simone de Beauvoir's Ethics and its Relation to Current Moral Philosophy," *Simone de Beauvoir Studies*, 14 (1998): 39–46.

Greene, Naomi, "Sartre, Sexuality, and 'The Second Sex,'" *Philosophy and Literature*, 4, 2 (1980): 199–211.

Hansen, Linda, "Pain and Joy in Human Relationships: Jean-Paul Sartre and Simone de Beauvoir," *Philosophy Today*, 79 (winter 1979): 338–46.

Heinämaa, Sara, "What is a Woman? Butler and Beauvoir on the Foundations of the Sexual Difference," *Hypatia*, 12, 1 (winter 1997): 20–39.

"Woman – Nature, Product, Style? Rethinking the Foundations of the Feminist Philosophy of Science," in *A Dialogue Concerning Feminism, Science, and Philosophy of Science*, ed. Lynn Hankinson Nelson and Jack Nelson (Dordrecht: Kluwer, 1996), pp. 289–308.

Jardine, Alice, "Death Sentences: Writing Couples and Ideology," in *The Female Body in Western Culture*, ed. S. Suleiman (Cambridge, MA: Harvard University Press, 1986), pp. 84–96.

"Interview with Simone de Beauvoir," *Signs: Journal of Women in Culture and Society*, 5 (1979): 224–35.

Kaufmann McCall, Dorothy, "Simone de Beauvoir, *The Second Sex*, and Jean-Paul Sartre," *Signs: Journal of Women in Culture and Society*, 5, 2 (1979): 209–23.

Keefe, Terry, "Psychiatry in the Postwar Fiction of Simone de Beauvoir," *Literature and Psychology*, 29, 3 (1979): 123–33.

Kruks, Sonia, "Simone de Beauvoir and the Limits to Freedom," *Social Text: Theory/Culture/Ideology*, 17 (fall 1987): 111–22.

Langer, Monika, "A Philosophical Retrieval of Simone de Beauvoir's *Pour une morale de l'ambiguïté*," *Philosophy Today*, 38, 2 (summer 1994): 181–90.

"Sartre and Merleau-Ponty: A Reappraisal," in *The Philosophy of Jean-Paul Sartre*, ed. Paul Arthur Schilpp (La Salle: Open Court, 1981), pp. 300–25; reprinted in *The Debate Between Sartre and Merleau-Ponty*, ed. Jon Stewart (Evanston, IL: Northwestern University Press, 1998), pp. 93–117.

Le Doeuff, Michèle, "Simone de Beauvoir and Existentialism," *Ideology and Consciousness*, 6 (autumn 1979): 47–57.

Lundgren-Gothlin, Eva see Eva Gothlin.

Morgan, Kathryn Pauly, "Romantic Love, Altruism, and Self-Respect: An Analysis of Simone de Beauvoir," *Hypatia*, 1, 1 (spring 1986): 117–48.

Pilardi, Jo-Ann, "The Changing Critical Fortunes of 'The Second Sex,'" *History and Theory: Studies in the Philosophy of History*, 32, 1 (1993): 51–73.

"Female Eroticism in *The Second Sex*," in *The Thinking Muse: Feminism and Modern French Philosophy*, ed. Jeffner Allen and Iris M. Young (Bloomington, IN: Indiana University Press, 1980), pp. 18–34.

"Philosophy Becomes Autobiography: The Development of the Self in the Writings of Simone de Beauvoir," in *Writing the Politics of Difference: Selected Studies in Phenomenology and Existential Philosophy*, ed. Hugh J. Silverman (Albany, NY: State University of New York Press, 1991), pp. 145–62.

Seigfried, Charlene Haddock, "Gender-Specific Values," *Philosophical Forum*, 15, 4 (summer 1984): 425–42.

Suleiman, Susan Rubin, "Life-Story, History, Fiction: Reflections on Simone de Beauvoir's Wartime Writings," *Contention: Debates in Society, Culture and Science*, 1, 2 (winter 1992): 1–21.

Walters, Margaret, "The Rights and Wrongs of Women: Mary Wollstonecraft, Harriet Martineau, Simone de Beauvoir," in *The Rights and Wrongs of Women*, ed. Juliet Mitchell and Ann Oakley (Harmondsworth: Penguin, 1977), pp. 304–78.

Willis, Ellen, "Rebel Girl," *Village Voice*, 27 May 1986. Obituary for Beauvoir.

Background

General works

Barnes, Hazel, *The Literature of Possibility: A Study in Humanistic Existentialism* (Lincoln, NE: University of Nebraska Press, 1959).

Barrett, William, *Irrational Man: A Study in Existential Philosophy* (Garden City, NY: Doubleday, 1958).

Bernet, Rudolf, Iso Kern, and Eduard Marbach (eds.), *An Introduction to Husserlian Phenomenology* (Evanston, IL: Northwestern University Press, 1993.

Butler, Judith, *Gender Trouble: Feminism and the Subversion of Identity* (New York: Routledge, 1990).

Collins, James, *The Existentialists: A Critical Study* (Chicago: H. Regnery, 1952).

Cooper, David E., "Existentialist Ethics," in *Routledge Encyclopedia of Philosophy* (10 vols.), ed. Edward Craig (London and New York: Routledge, 1998), III: 502–05.

Debray, Regis, *Teachers, Writers, Celebrities: The Intellectuals of Modern France* (London: Verso, 1981).

Embree, Lester, "Phenomenological Movement," in *Routledge Encyclopedia of Philosophy* (10 vols.), ed. Edward Craig (London and New York: Routledge, 1998), VII: 333–43.

Fink, Eugen, "The Phenomenological Philosophy of Edmund Husserl and Contemporary Criticism" (1933), in *The Phenomenological Philosophy of Husserl: Selected Critical Readings*, ed. R. O. Elveton (Chicago: Quadrangle Books, 1970), pp. 73–147.

"The Problem of the Phenomenology of Edmund Husserl" (1939), in William R. McKenna, Robert M. Harlan, and Laurence E. Winters, trans. and eds., *Apriori and World: European Contributions to Husserlian Phenomenology* (The Hague: Martinus Nijhoff, 1981), pp. 21–55.

Gatens, Moira, *Feminism and Philosophy* (Bloomington, IN: Indiana University Press, 1991).

Guignon, Charles (ed.), *The Cambridge Companion to Heidegger* (Cambridge: Cambridge University Press, 1993).

"Existentialism," in *Routledge Encyclopedia of Philosophy* (10 vols.), ed. Edward Craig (London and New York: Routledge, 1998), III: 493–502.

Howells, Christina (ed.), *The Cambridge Companion to Sartre* (Cambridge: Cambridge University Press, 1992).

Kaufman, Walter (ed.), *Existentialism from Dostoevsky to Sartre* (Cleveland, OH: World Publishing, 1956).

Langer, Monika M., *Merleau-Ponty's Phenomenology of Perception: A Guide and Commentary* (Gainesville, FL: Florida State University Press, 1989).

Lloyd, Genevieve, *The Man of Reason* (Minneapolis: University of Minnesota Press, 1984).

Olafson, Frederick, *Principles and Persons: An Ethical Interpretation of Existentialism* (Baltimore, MD: Johns Hopkins University Press, 1967).

Sapontzis, S. F., "A Note on Merleau-Ponty's 'Ambiguity,'" *Philosophy and Phenomenological Research*, 38, 4 (June 1978): 538–43.

Silverman, Hugh, "Merleau-Ponty's Human Ambiguity," *Journal of the British Society for Phenomenology*, 10, 1 (1979): 23–38.

Smith, Barry and David Woodruff Smith (eds.), *The Cambridge Companion to Husserl* (Cambridge: Cambridge University Press, 1995).

Sokolowski, Robert, *Introduction to Phenomenology* (Cambridge: Cambridge University Press, 2000).

Solomon, Robert, *From Rationalism to Existentialism: The Existentialists and their Nineteenth-Century Backgrounds* (New York: Humanities Press, 1972).

Spiegelberg, Herbert, *The Phenomenological Movement: A Historical Introduction* (3rd edn) (The Hague: Martinus Nijhoff, 1982).

Stewart, Jon (ed.), *The Debate Between Sartre and Merleau-Ponty*, (Evanston, IL: Northwestern University Press, 1998).

Warnock, Mary, *Existentialism* (Oxford: Oxford University Press, 1970, 1979).

Weiss, Gail, "Ambiguity, Absurdity, and Reversibility: Responses to Indeterminacy," *Journal of the British Society for Phenomenology*, 26, 1 (1995): 43–51.

Zahavi, Dan, "Husserl's Phenomenology of the Body," *Etudes phénoménologiques*, 19 (1994): 63–84.

Significant contemporaries

Algren, Nelson, *The Man with the Golden Arm* (Garden City, NY: Doubleday, 1949).

Colette, *Chéri and The Last of Chéri* (1920, 1926), trans. Roger Senhouse (London: Secker and Warburg, 1951).

The Complete Claudine (1900–03), trans. Antonia White (New York: Farrar, Straus & Giroux, 1976).

My Mother's House and Sido (1922, 1929) (New York: Farrar, Straus & Giroux, 1966).

The Pure and the Impure (1932), trans. Herma Briffault (New York: Farrar, Straus & Giroux, 1967).

Fanon, Frantz, *Black Skin, White Masks* (1952), trans. Charles Lam Markman (New York: Grove, 1967).

Faulkner, William, *Light in August* (New York: Smith & Haas, 1932).

Heidegger, Martin, *Being and Time* (1927) trans. John Macquarrie and Edward Robinson (New York: Harper, 1962).

Introduction to Metaphysics (1953), trans. Ralph Manheim (New Haven, CN: Yale University Press, 1959).

Hemingway, Ernest, *A Farewell to Arms* (London: Cape, 1929).

Kafka, Franz, *The Castle* (1926) introduction by Thomas Mann, trans. Edwin and Willa Muir (New York: Knopf, 1947).

The Trial (1925) introduction by George Steiner, trans. Edwin and Willa Muir, revised and with additional material trans. E. M. Butler, drawings by Franz Kafka (New York: Schocken, 1995).

Koestler, Arthur, *Darkness at Noon*, trans. Daphne Hardy (New York: Modern Library, 1941).

Kojève, Alexandre, *Introduction to the Reading of Hegel: Lectures on the Phenomenology of Spirit* (1947), trans. James H. Nichols, Jr. (New York: Basic Books, 1969).

Lévinas, Emmanuel, *The Theory of Intuition in Husserl's Phenomenology* (1930), trans. André Orianne (Evanston, IL: Northwestern University Press, 1973).

Time and the Other (1947), trans. Richard A. Cohen (Pittsburgh, PA: Duquesne University Press, 1987).

Merleau-Ponty, Maurice, *Humanism and Terror: An Essay on the Communist Problem* (1947), trans. John O'Neill (Boston: Beacon, 1969).

The Phenomenology of Perception (1945), trans. Colin Smith (Atlantic Highlands, NJ: Humanities Press, 1981; London: Routledge & Kegan Paul, 1981).

Sense and Non-Sense (1948), trans. Hubert L. Dreyfus and Patricia Allen Dreyfus (Evanston, IL: Northwestern University Press, 1964).

Millett, Kate, *Flying* (New York: Knopf, 1974).

Sexual Politics (Garden City, NY: Avon Books, 1969).

Myrdal, Gunnar, Richard Sterner, and Arnold Rose, *An American Dilemma: The Negro Problem and Modern Democracy* (New York: Harper, 1944).

Rich, Adrienne, *Of Woman Born: Motherhood as Experience and as Institution* (New York: Norton, 1977).

Sartre, Jean-Paul, *Anti-Semite and Jew* (1946), trans. George J. Becker (New York: Schocken, 1948).

Being and Nothingness: A Phenomenological Essay on Ontology (1943), trans. Hazel Barnes (New York: Washington Square Press, 1966).

Existentialism and Humanism (1946), trans. Philip Mairet (London: Methuen, 1948).

No Exit (1945), trans. Stuart Gilbert (New York: Vintage, 1947).

Quiet Moments in a War: The Letters of Jean-Paul Sartre to Simone de Beauvoir, 1940–1963 (1983), ed. Simone de Beauvoir, trans. Lee Fahnestock and Norman MacAfee (New York: Scribner's, 1993).

The Transcendence of the Ego: An Existentialist Theory of Consciousness (1936–37), trans. Forrest Williams and Robert Kirkpatrick (New York: Hill & Wang, Noonday Press, 1957).

What Is Literature? (1948), trans. Bernard Frechtman (New York: Philosophical Library, 1949).

Witness to My Life: The Letters of Jean-Paul Sartre to Simone de Beauvoir, 1926–1939 (1983), ed. Simone de Beauvoir, trans. Lee Fahnestock and Norman MacAfee (New York: Scribner's, 1992).

Weil, Simone, *Formative Writings, 1929–1941*, ed. and trans. Dorothy Tuck McFarland and Wilhelmina Van Ness (Amherst, MA: University of Massachusetts Press, 1987).

Weil, Simone, *The Simone Weil Reader*, ed. George A. Panichas (New York: McKay, 1977).

Woolf, Virginia, *A Room of One's Own* (New York: Harcourt Brace & Co., 1929).

  Three Guineas (New York: Harcourt Brace, 1938).

  To the Lighthouse (New York: Harcourt Brace & Co., 1927).

Wright, Richard, *Native Son and How Bigger Was Born* (1940) (New York: HarperCollins, 1993).

Historical sources of influence

Bergson, Henri, *Creative Evolution* (1907), trans. Arthur Mitchell (New York: Modern Library, 1944).

  Matter and Memory (1896), trans. Nancy Margaret Paul and W. Scott Palmer (London: George Allen & Unwin, 1911).

  Time and Free Will: An Essay on the Immediate Data of Consciousness (1889), trans. F. L. Pogson (London: G. Allen; New York: Harper, 1959, 1960).

Dubois, W. E. B., *The Souls of Black Folk* (1903) (New York: New American Library, 1969).

Engels, Frederick, *Origin of the Family, Private Property, and the State, in the Light of the Researches of Lewis H. Morgan* (1884), trans. Alec West (New York: International Publishers, 1972).

Hegel, G. W. F., *Phenomenology of Spirit* (1807), trans. A. V. Miller (Oxford: Oxford University Press, 1977).

Husserl, Edmund, *Cartesian Meditations* (1950), trans. Dorian Cairns (Dordrecht: Martinus Nijhoff, 1954).

  The Crisis of European Sciences and Transcendental Phenomenology: An Introduction to Phenomenological Philosophy (1936), trans. David Carr (Evanston, IL: Northwestern University Press, 1970).

  Ideas Pertaining to a Pure Phenomenology and to Phenomenological Philosophy, First Book: General Introduction to Pure Phenomenology (1913), trans. F. Kersten (The Hague: Martinus Nijhoff, 1982).

  Ideas Pertaining to a Pure Phenomenology and to Phenomenological Philosophy, Second Book: Studies in the Phenomenology of Constitution (1952), trans. Richard Rojcewicz and André Schuwer (Dordrech: Kluwer, 1989).

  On the Phenomenology of the Consciousness of Internal Time (1928), trans. J. B. Brough (Dordrecht: Kluwer, 1990).

  Thing and Space: Lectures of 1907, ed. and trans. Richard Rojcewicz (Dordrecht: Kluwer, 1991, 1997).

Kierkegaard, Søren, *Either/Or* (1843), trans. H. V. Kong and E. H. Kong (Princeton, NJ: Princeton University Press, 1987).

Fear and Trembling and The Sickness unto Death (1843), trans. W. Lowrie (Garden City, NY: Doubleday, 1954).

The Present Age (1846), trans. A. Dru (London: Fontana, 1912).

Malebranche, Nicolas, *The Search After Truth* (1674), trans. and ed. Thomas M. Lemmon and Paul J. Olscamp; *Elucidation of The Search after Truth*, trans. Thomas M. Lemmon/Nicolas Malebranche (Cambridge: Cambridge University Press, 1997).

Marx, Karl, *Capital: A Critique of Political Economy* (3 vols.), ed. Friedrich Engels (1867–94), trans. Samuel Moore and Edward Aveling (New York: International Publishers, 1967).

Writings of the Young Marx on Philosophy and Society, ed. and trans. Lloyd D. Easton and Kurt H. Guddat (Garden City, NY: Doubleday, 1967).

Marx, Karl and Friedrich Engels, *Basic Writings on Politics and Philosophy*, ed. Lewis S. Feuer (Garden City, NY: Doubleday, 1959).

Nietzsche, Friedrich, *Basic Writings of Nietzsche*, trans. and ed. Walter Kaufmann (New York: Random House, 1966).

INDEX

abortion, 196, 199
abstractions, 70, 77, 175, 209
action
  Beauvoir's view of, 175, 182,
    184
  freedom of, 124, 126, 145, 271
  literary, 196, 203
  passions and, 154
  possibility of ethical, 28, 276
  and relationality, 183
activism, 203, 205, 206
admiration See esteem
adolescence, 26, 98, 288
affects, classification of the, 154
African-American influence, 6, 37
"Age of Discretion, The," 288, 300
agency, 14, 21
agent perspective in ethics, 11, 241, 243,
  244
aging See old age
Algerian war, 228
Algren, Nelson, 10, 201–202
alienation, 194
  bodily, 30, 224, 271
All Men are Mortal, 36
All Said and Done, 2, 210, 211, 224, 288,
  290, 291
altruism, 191
ambiguity, 25, 26, 87–105, 219, 241, 243,
  283
  and ambivalence, 240
  biology and ethics, 281–283
  comparison of Sartre's and Beauvoir's
    ideas, 89–93, 95, 219
  derivation of word, 89
  and eroticism, 41, 43

  in ethics, 1–21, 87–88, 255, 276
  and evil, 10, 228–244
  and existentialism, 229
  "gray zone" (Levi), 15
  and immortality, 36
  limits of Beauvoir's concept, 244
  Merleau-Ponty's influence on
    Beauvoir's concept of, 5, 87–105
  as paradox, 90
  and sexual difference, 249, 254, 263,
    264
  in *She Came to Stay*, 145–147
  and situation, 96
  of violence, 238
ambivalence, 240, 241
America Day by Day, 2, 233, 238
analytic philosophy, 14
Andrew, Barbara S., xii, 4, 24–43
androcentrism, 82
anthropology, philosophical, 235, 236
antirape movement, 196
anxiety, 26, 27
  in adolescence, 26
  male, 82
aphasia, 104
Aquinas, Saint Thomas, 24
Arc, L', 192, 200
"Arcueil affair," 171, 181
Arendt, Hannah, 16
  Eichmann in Jerusalem, 236
Arnauld, Antoine, 153
Aron, Raymond, 46, 217
Arp, Kristana, 29
atrocities, 238, 243
atrocity paradigm, 243
Ausdruck See expression

321

master–slave dialectic (Hegel), 7, 58,
150, 151, 155
meaning, freedom to create, 26, 283
Medici Fountain, Luxembourg Gardens,
Sartre and Beauvoir, 9, 216
memoirs, 208–226
compared with autobiography, 221
Memoirs of a Dutiful Daughter, 2, 9,
121, 194, 211, 213, 221, 223,
288
attitude to philosophy, 110, 216
feminist reading of, 9
irony in, 214
persona in, 221
reference to Bergson, 107
memory
subject and, 221, 222
utilitarian vs. pure, 118
men
anxiety, 82
experience of domination, 150
experiences of embodiment, 82
married, 20
projection onto women, 240
representation of the world by, 239
women's situation in relation to,
39
men and women
and cultural representations of
women as evil, 239
different needs and desires, 256
explaining relations between, 149,
155, 269
and *Mitsein*, 57
paradigms for relations between, 75
similarities and differences, 82
Merleau-Ponty, Maurice, 4, 5, 24, 134,
212
on ambiguity, 87–105
and the body-subject, 74, 76, 78, 103,
271, 301
Humanism and Terror, 88, 101
influence on Beauvoir, 33, 54, 73,
152
influence of Husserl on, 77
on perceptual experience, 79, 88
phenomenology, 5, 29, 72
Phenomenology of Perception;
Beauvoir's review, 29, 66, 73, 87–88,
94, 102

Mill, John Stuart, 268
Millett, Kate, 38
Flying, 193
misogyny, 198, 272
Mitchell, Juliet, 38
Mitsein See also Being-with
MLF *See* Mouvement de Libération des
Femmes
Moi, Toril, 38, 289
Montaigne, Michel Eyquem de, 88, 90,
228, 230
Montherlant, Henri, 157
Montreuil, Renée-Pélagie de, 171
moral emotions, 3
moral pseudo-propositions, 3
moral psychology, 17th century, 153
morality, 100, 216
bourgeois, 174, 175, 180
continuum of, 236
self-preservation in, 173
mortality, 54, 213, 230, 292
Moscow Trials (1937), 100, 102
mother–child bond, 76
Mouvement de Libération des Femmes
(MLF), 199
murder
constitutional, 175, 179, 186
in *She Came to Stay*, 134
"Must We Burn Sade?," 2, 7, 168–170,
259
mutilation
femininity in terms of, 277, 286
of old age, 286, 288
Myrdal, Gunnar, 37
An American Dilemma, 233
myths, 242, 251, 260, 262

narrative
and the constructed reader, 215
metaphysical, 137, 138–145, 146
of past selves, 224
presence of underlying "monologue,"
146
shaping of life-story, 209, 211
See also self-narrative
naturalism, against, 73–76
nature
man and woman, 239
psychic, 68
as a result, 282